Folklore of the Great West

with line drawings by
Glen Rounds

Folklore
of the
Great West

Selections from Eighty-three Years of the
JOURNAL OF AMERICAN FOLKLORE
Edited with extensive commentary by

John Greenway

AMERICAN WEST PUBLISHING COMPANY

PALO ALTO / CALIFORNIA

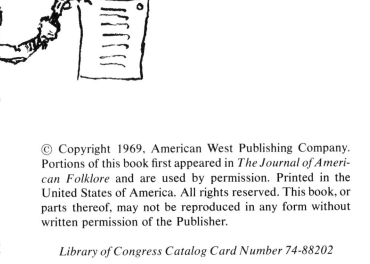

Library of Congress Catalog Card Number 74-88202

For Carolyn, who helped . . .

And Matthew, who hindered

Contents

I

Following the Lore of the Folk

II

The Good Old Days

III

The Indian at Home   89

IV

The Indian and the White Man   131

V

Cowboy Songs 179

A Montana Cowboy Poet *by John I. White*
The Bee County Iliad *by W. Prescott Webb*
El Cancion del Rancho de Los Olmos *by J. Frank Dobie*
The Decline and Fall of the Cowboy Ballad *by John A. Lomax*

VI

Songs of the Old Country, Songs of the New 229

A Missouri Dance Call *by Ruth Ann Musick*
The Singing Kentucks Move West *by Asher E. Treat*
Mormon Songs *by Levette J. Davidson*
Jimmie Rodgers, a Folksong Catalyst *by John Greenway*
Woodrow Wilson Guthrie *by John Greenway*

VII

The Days of Gold and the Days of Dross 283

Folklore from Utah's Silver Mining Camps *by Wayland D. Hand*
John Neuhaus: Wobbly Folklorist *by Archie Green*

VIII

Bad Men and Big 331

Robin Hood and the American Outlaw *by Kent L. Steckmesser*
Paul Bunyan in 1910 *by W. W. Charters*
W. B. Laughead's Great Advertisement *by Max Gartenberg*
More Light on Paul Bunyan *by Rodney C. Loehr*

IX

Whippers and Witches and Heavenly Helpers   *361*

X

Having Fun   *409*

Index   *449*

I

Following the
Lore of the Folk

THE FOLK LIVE on islands in a sea of land.

A suitcase farmer, gazing hopelessly from his sod house at feeble wheat rippling on to an unbroken horizon, wheat that didn't care if it did, didn't care if it didn't.

A little Mormon girl, sad for the loss of a pony, glad for the finding that her hair was naturally curly, overwhelmed by the coming to her desert community of a visitor from the Outside, and determined one day to see that Outside.

A miner, living in a shack when it would have been better for him to live in the adjoining mine shaft but for the shame of reverting to life in a cave after millennia of civilization, knowing that there was gold in his mountain, knowing too that it was not worth taking out for thirty-five dollars an ounce, and knowing finally that this would always be life for him, regardless of the price of gold.

An Indian youth, living in a mud pueblo in the degenerate fifth phase of his people's culture, knowing nothing of the third phase a thousand years before when his ancestors built the greatest civilization on the continent, thinking only of how he could overcome his enemy's witchcraft before the baseball game that afternoon.

An ancient Wobbly, making pretense of guarding a warehouse in San Pedro against juvenile trespassers, letting his thoughts drift back to when he took fifty sticks of dynamite and blew a shackful of strikebreakers all over the side of a mountain.

An old sheepshearer, fingers crippled with arthritis and a crook stomach from years of bending at the waist while taking off the fleece, content with life and singing to himself,

> *I'm one of the has-beens, a shearer, I mean,*
> *I once was a ringer, I used to shear clean;*
> *I could make the wool roll off like the soil from the plow,*
> *But you may not believe me, because I can't do it now.*

And the sailors of the dry sea, the nomads, the hoboes, the tramps, the cowboys, each with his bit of American culture and each cut off from that culture by whatever in his case makes him a member of the folk.

A private organization in these United States in this year of 1969 is pouring uncalculated millions of dollars into the tunneling of a vault out of solid granite under a mountain — an impregnable vault a quarter of the size of the NORAD underground complex. In this vault will be stored microrecords equivalent to half a billion pages, computers to complete a job now requiring one hundred and twenty million man-hours of calculation, and other valuables of an incredible nature. The organization? U.N.C.L.E.? T.H.R.U.S.H.? No, the Church of Jesus Christ of the Latter-Day Saints. The work, so heavily protected against atomic holocaust? Tracing and recording the genealogies of nearly three million souls a year. Having cut themselves away from a culture felt to be inferior and known to be inimical, the Mormons, for all their computers, are inescapably members of an American folk.

This country has more of these islands of separated enclaves than any other nation in the history of mankind. Each has taken a piece of the mother culture and overdeveloped it to make up for the part discarded. But since advance lies with numbers in the evolution of culture, such dissident groups are condemned to fall backward, the faster for their coherence.

It is the responsibility and pleasure of folklorists to study these people — recording their customs, attitudes, beliefs, artifacts, and arts — preserving their memories for the sake of preserving knowledge; studying the processes of their thinking and behavior, the better to understand themselves. Most folklorists are professors of English literature — not because training in literature has any special relevance, but because tradition obtains in scholarship as it does among the folk whom scholars study. The early founding fathers of the science of folklore were scholars in the processes of literature, and so their posterity continue in the same paths. The second largest group of folklorists are anthropologists, for the logical reason that the province of social scientists is man and his works. Some folklorists are amateurs, by definition lovers of what they do; these few work at a disadvantage in a world where it is fondly believed that no one can do competent mental work without the certification of a doctorate in something or other. Let us hear one of these unsung scholars — for scholars they are, in spite of their anomalous position — tell what it is to be a true professional in a work in which he is regarded as an amateur. This is Vance Randolph, whose contributions are sprinkled throughout the book that follows this chapter; a man who has collected the lore of his Ozark Mountains and written about it successfully for more than half a century. The quotation is taken from a vignette written about him by Dr. Richard M. Dorson, my predecessor as Editor of the *Journal of American Folklore* and one of the world's most honored folklorists.

All my work is with the Ozark country and people [said Randolph]; I don't attempt to do anything with outside folklore. I've lived and collected here most of my life, but I could have collected a lot more, if I could have gotten any help. Just a dollar a day would have kept me going, in the Ozarks. But the foundations turned me down twenty-eight years in a row. Mencken, Frank Dobie, Louise Pound, wrote letters for me, but I didn't have a Ph.D. [Randolph has a Master's degree in psychology from Clark University.] So I've had to make what money I could writing. What the magazines won't take, I send to the folklore journals. Now there's a funny thing; the folklore journals get what the paying magazines reject. I once told my friend Otto Rayburn [author of *Ozark Folkways* and present president of the Arkansas Folklore Society to write an article for the *Journal of American Folklore*. He's written a great deal about Ozark folklore, in different newspapers and magazines, that the folklorists never see. Well, he asked me how much they paid, and when I told him nothing, he took the paper out of his typewriter and tossed it in the wastebasket.

Professor Dorson, whose own eminence in the academic community has given him the knowledge and the courage to write of *its* folklore, does not share the prejudice of his lesser fellows in the profession against the amateurs. His tribute to Randolph is worth a paragraph of our space:

Everyone I met in northern Arkansas who knew Randolph—folksingers, fellow collectors, faculty people—spoke of him with great regard. One soon understands why, after meeting him, and I left this perceptive and dedicated collector and skillful writer with a sad heart, thinking that he had never been able to afford a recording machine, and that a life of honorable achievement had left him with illness, worry, and the constant problem of paying rent and food bills. The outstanding collector of our time, who perhaps alone knows how to avoid commercial shoddiness and scholarly dullness, without sacrificing readability or integrity, deserves the best tribute American folklorists can tender.*

The layman in the professional study of man has a respect for the archaeologist that has been transmuted into dozens of best-sellers drawn from the often dry tale of digging up the past. Those of us who have worked in both areas of anthropology and who have gravitated toward other corners of the pasture tend to see archaeology as less rewarding and interesting than cultural archaeology, which includes the pursuit of folklore. We understand the tangibility of a golden mask, a fragile pot from a lost civilization, a skull of one of man's ancestors, or an undisturbed tomb—the tangibility that appeals to the beginner in any profession. These are all good things—the mask, the pot, the skull, the tomb—but they are Morphy's Game in the Opera Box against

*"A Visit with Vance Randolph." JAF Volume 57, 1954. ("JAF" in the documentation of this book will mean *Journal of American Folklore*.)

the Evergreen Zugswang Game, Edgar Guest against Gerard Manley Hopkins, Roger Maris against Don Drysdale — flashy but shallow. It is far more satisfying to deal with the intangibles, the spirit of diffusion that turns an Irish broadside about a young man dying of venereal disease into "Streets of Laredo," "St. James Infirmary," or "The Bad Girl's Lament," depending on which folk group takes it up.

When the anthropologist talks about folklore, he extends its meaning to include primitive peoples as well as folk groups (which we will define as homogeneous, unsophisticated enclaves living within, but isolated from, a surrounding sophisticated society by such factors as geography, race, topography, educational or economic deprivation, religion, or simply choice). It has always been the policy of the *Journal of American Folklore* to accept articles on the lore of primitive peoples as well as better recognized folk peoples, even though some of its editors, like myself, frown on the unjustified extension of the definition. However, when it suits my purpose, I can think like an anthropologist and include my own work among the primitives as being in the province of the folklorist.

With this apologia, I can make here the first extensive selection from material published during the last eighty-one years in the *Journal of American Folklore*. It is a preface I wrote for a special issue entitled *The Anthropologist Looks at Myth* (and published in book form under that title by the University of Texas Press in 1966). I used the passage in that book to illustrate the fascinating things one finds in studying the lesser-known peoples of the world. Here it demonstrates how rewarding a profession one has in following the lore of the folk, for these things are much the same, regardless of the complexities of the cultures involved.*

Twenty-seven years ago, while working in the white dunes of the Southern Ocean near the two long-abandoned and sand-filled telegraph stations that constitute the present "town" of Eucla, Western Australia, the eminent Australian anthropologist Norman B. Tindale found a hoard of knapped flint once hidden and never recovered by an aboriginal flint trader. The war intervened before Tindale was able to locate precisely the source of this flint, the best in all Australia. Later, his

*JAF Volume 79, v-ix.

work took him to other parts of the island continent and into other problems, and the location of the flint mine fell into that accumulation of work one day to be done that all of us save for our retirement.

Two years ago, while conducting ethnographic research among the Pitjandjara people on the edge of the western desert, seven hundred miles, as the bare foot walks, from Eucla, Tindale recorded a mythic song cycle named "Keibara Tjukurpa," one of those typical Australian myths that sing of how, in the Dreaming, totemic animals made things as they are today. In this story Keibara, the turkey bustard, owner of fire-flints, came out of the northwest to feed on arungoli among the Waljuna Pitjandjara. Like all owners of fire in world mythology, Keibara believed that the keeping of the secret of fire was more important than the keeping of the fire itself, so that when the fireless spirits of the desert approached him, he fled south and west across the treeless plain of the Nullarbor to the sea, where he dived to drown the fire he carried on his head. But just as he reached the great water, two Promethean hawks pounced upon him, stole the fire flints, and implanted them in a great rock at the ocean's edge, where they would forever be available to mankind. Remembering his flint discovery of a quarter century earlier, Tindale knew that he had in the Keibara myth the religious distillation of fact, stone transmuted into song; but there remained still the small but vexing problem of the mine itself.

Several weeks ago, while the galley proofs of this issue were coming to me over another ocean, Tindale and I set out across the 770 miles of waterless plateau along the southern Australian coast to tie up this last loose end. From the desolation of Eucla we worked back in a Land Cruiser along the cliff edge to where we could descend to the beach. The entire area was strewn with ancient campsites where natives had shaped the raw material of their flint into forms suitable to be carried in trade to the stoneless people of the North. Eventually we found a traversable slope and made our way to the narrow beach, along which we walked, our glasses sweeping the limestone cliffs. We passed around a small promontory, and suddenly, looming two hundred and fifty feet straight out of the sea, the mine joined the myth, its flint reefs unmistakably sparkling in the afternoon sun. Birds swooped around the bluff, as if they were re-enacting in ritual their ancestors' salvation of fire, just as the Pitjandjara old men, the custodians of religion, re-enact the great event symbolically in the dry dust of their desert home. At the mine itself the work of centuries of primitive merchant manufacturers was everywhere evident: every part of the reefs that a human hand unhelped by technology could reach had been mined; every place on the bluff flat enough for a man to perch on was littered with flakes struck off from the flint boulders embedded in the sterile limestone.

What we had found, beyond the pleasure of the experience, was more evidence, if any more was needed, that myth is sublimated reality. Before the white man came to this southern coast a century and a half ago to gather sandalwood, the Mirning tribe worked this mine and traded its product east and north to the Wirangu, Pangkala, Kokata, Arabana, Tirari, Jangkundjara, and Pitjandjara—all people who were tied to their myths, attendant spirits, and ecology of their several homelands. No Pitjandjara in the mythopoeic days ever saw the sea or appreciated the concept of great waters. Over much of this coastal land the only potable water must be drained from the roots of the mallee tree. The stone came up from the South, and a reasonable account of its origin was invented; in the Australian mythic dimension—the Dreaming—it is not only more romantic but more believable to have flint implanted in a cliff by hawks than to have it made slowly by impersonal and inanimate geological processes.

Some months later, after the preceding paragraphs were published, Dr. Tindale and I made another, much longer trip up the west and northwest coasts of Australia, filling in the remaining indistinct lines in the tribal map that was his lifework in Australian anthropology. We asked every old man who knew anything about his dying culture whether he knew the "Keibara Tjukurpa." None could sing any of its mythic songs (which was only to be expected, since a myth is restricted to the tribes that own it and for which it is a charter of existence), but all had heard of a song about a turkey bustard that carried fire to the southern sea and had it taken away by brown hawks.

Nor was that all we found relevant to folklore among these people, some of whom came in out of the Old Stone Age in their own generation. One eight-year-old boy, a part aborigine, sang for me a song about the Australian state of Queensland. One stanza of this Australian song went:

*Oh, they chew tobacco thin
    in Queensland,
They chew tobacco thin
    in Queensland;
They chew tobacco thin
And they spit it on their chin
And they lap it up agin
    in Queensland.*

I was delighted to find this stray bit of the old sodbusting Kansas song so far from its native home, and I wished there were some way to tell the little boy about the song "In Kansas"; but I couldn't, for he had no idea what a "Kansas" was.

THE *JOURNAL OF AMERICAN FOLKLORE*

For the last eighty-one years the medium for communicating to the interested layman and the scholar what is found by professionals who follow the lore of the folk has been the *Journal of American Folklore.* For most of that time the *Journal* has been the outstanding organ of folklore anywhere in the world. (Foreign-language journals of folklore have to serve political interests too slavishly to compete with a periodical that observes no tabus except those of its Editor, and its English counterpart is oriented too closely to the interests of elderly clergymen.) It is the second oldest journal of anthropology in the United States, and its Editor, in consequence of his charge's seniority, sits immediately below the Editor of the *American Anthropologist* and far above the salt.

The *Journal* has had thirteen editors in its long lifetime:

William Wells Newell (1888–1900)
Alexander Francis Chamberlain (1901–1907)
Franz Boas (1908–1923)
Ruth Benedict (1924–1939)
Gladys Reichard (1940)
Archer Taylor (1941)
Erminie Voegelin (1942-1946)

Wayland D. Hand (1947–1951)
Katharine Luomala (1951–1953)
Thomas A. Sebeok (1954–1958)
Richard M. Dorson (1959–1963)
John Greenway (1964–1968)
Américo Paredes (1968-   )

All except the author have been or are internationally eminent scholars. Several were the greatest folklorists of their day. Franz Boas, for example, is the father of American anthropology. He is also the father of abominable editing of a scholarly journal, the father of interminable Indian myths, and the father of several particularly mischievous ideas in anthropology. During his fifteen years and the fifteen years of his protegée, student, and fellow indiscriminate lover of Indians, Ruth Benedict, the *Journal* was the refuge for the dispossessed redskin. Some think it was the Depression that cut the list of sub-scribers in 1935 to 191; I think it was those incessant Coyote Trickster stories.

Subscribers during the Boas-Benedict years were a staunch and indomitable band. We shall not see their like again. They supported with their hard-to-come-by dollars a journal that gave them in return page after page like the following:

(117) Cʻąwaʻkʻą kį el iʻpi śni tkʻa watʻoʻg.laohʻapi kį ų kaʻna inaʻ-żipiʼⁱ. (118) Ną ecʼiʼyatąhą yuoʻwecʼįhą kuʻpiʼⁱ. (119) Hehaʼn kʻo-śkaʻlaka kį henaʼ aoʻkawįh awiʻcʻakupi ną kʻohąʼ hʻokʻaʼ naʼżipi kį eʼtkiya buʻhįg.leʼᵉ. Cʻokaʻp wahpeʼ ptaʻyela paslaʼl eʼg.lepiʼⁱ. (120) Tu-waʼ tʻokáheya cʻą tʻoʻka wążiʼ heʻcʼel kteʼkta keyaʼpiʼⁱ. (121) Cʻąkeʼ heų́ tʻokeʼya el iʻpiktehciʼⁱ.

(117) Sacred tree / the / at that place / they arrive / not / but / they act like wild animals / the / on that account / there / they stop. / (118) And / from there / single file / they return. / (119) Then / youths / the / those / circling around them / they bring them homeward / and / mean-time / accompanists / they stand / the / towards them / a rushing takes place. / In the midst / leaves / in a cluster / planted into the ground / they place. / (120) What one / first in order / then / enemy / a / that way / he will kill / they say. / (121) Therefore / for that reason / first / to that place / they arrive / would very. /

Through thick and thin they stuck it out, through Coyote Trick-ster tales, through articles printed in Neo-Melanesian (pidgin), whole issues in Canadian French, Coyote Trickster tales, arti-cles in specialized variants of the International Phonetic Alpha-bet, pieces in Latin, German, and similar outlandish languages, Coyote Trickster tales.

Things have improved since World War II, which was a terrible conflict bringing much suffering upon the world, but worth it in that it put an end to Coyote Trickster tales in the *Journal of American Folklore*. The editors have grown better, but the contributors have improved, too, at least in their own esti-mation of their worth. Four years ago my Book Review Editor (or myself) inserted the wrong initial in the name of a book re-viewer. Immediately upon publication of the issue containing this regrettable error, I received two letters of an intemperate kind, calling me all manner of evil things. One came from the man who had written the review; his bitter complaint was that one of the best reviews of the century had been printed over an impostor's name. The other came from the man whose name inadvertently had been cited as the author; his bitter complaint was that his good name had forever been sullied by being associated with one of the worst reviews in the entire Christian era. Both demanded retraction, apology, and reparation. Both got it in the following notice:

CONFESSION OF EDITORIAL ERROR

The Editor of the *Journal of American Folklore* reluctantly and under duress acknowledges having erred in attributing authorship of the review of Greig's *Folk-Song in Buchan and Folk-Songs of the North-East* in the January-March issue to the wrong George Simpson. The real George Simpson, who stood up to claim authorship, also protests that he is presently in Bethesda, Maryland, and not in Nigeria, though the Editor wishes he were, along with the other George Simpson, who has returned from Ibadan to Oberlin, Ohio, to protest that responsibility for the review was imposed on him while he was helplessly out of the country. Both George Simpsons speciously claim differentiation on the basis of their middle initials. The Editor begs all owners of issue number 307 to help him placate the several Georges Simpson (and the Book Review Editor) by changing the initial "E" to "A" on page 82 (readers who consult the *Journal* in libraries are also asked to make this correction, surreptitiously). Meanwhile the Editor advises both the Messrs. Simpson that so long as they insist on calling themselves "George Simpson" this sort of error can occur. He also warns Claude M. Simpson (Junior), who between submission of manuscript copy and return of galley proofs changed his academic address from Columbus, Ohio, to Stanford, California, that he and his movements are being carefully watched.

Such is life among the folklorists. Share some of their pleasures and accomplishments in the following pages. If you see in these things the gratification and enjoyment that their authors found in collecting and publishing them, you are invited to make that delight continuous by joining the American Folklore Society, which for ten dollars a year will supply you with four issues of the *Journal, Abstracts of Folklore Studies*, and occasional *Memoirs* of the Society's scholars.

II

The Good Old Days

ANTHROPOLOGISTS, whose job is not just to find out what man is and how he got that way but also to discover why he behaves as he does, recognize a universal phenomenon they call "metataxis." Like other anthropological terms describing the behavior of man and his culture, "metataxis" hides in its Greek etymology the terrible truth of reality from the generality of human beings whose lives are sustained by illusions. Even its formal definition is esoteric to the man in the street: " . . . obsolescent traits and artifacts that once had survival value often pass out of a society's culture slowly rather than suddenly by taking on recreational function." To put the matter most simply, things on the way out become toys.

The bow and arrow was one of man's greatest inventions; it may have enabled the more modern forms of *Homo sapiens* to destroy the spear-bearing Neanderthals. Today it is a toy, used not only by small surrogate Indians to kill small surrogate cowboys, but by adults who have persuaded themselves that hunting is a subsistence action—though hunting, like running, jumping, wrestling, boxing, throwing weights, throwing javelins, even walking, is a metatactic activity. The Olympic Games are a quadrennial debauch of useless skills governed by amateurism, which itself is metatactic in an acquisitive world. A passenger liner costing fifty million dollars can transport fewer people across an ocean than a five-million-dollar jet plane. Why, then, build steamships? Because "half the fun is getting there." The *Queen Mary* was as much a toy when it was sailing as it is now— tied ignominiously to a Long Beach pier. Even automobiles are largely metatactic. Unimaginative critics have condemned the automobile as wasteful, inefficient, dangerous to life, limb, and lung, and altogether the product of mass insanity. In San Francisco the city fathers took such criticism seriously and plunged into the building of a public transportation system that looks now like a failure of "megabuck" proportions. Any anthropologist could have told the San Franciscans that what they really needed was more cable cars, since the principal *raison d'etre* of San Francisco, so far as the rest of the nation is concerned, is to provide "charm" (by which is meant antique unreality); to be an adult Disneyland for visitors who want two weeks of the past; to be, in short, metatactic. Sears Roebuck sells a variety of modern electric kitchen ranges. One of them costs twice as much as a stove of comparable efficiency—because the working parts are concealed in the shell of an old-fashioned wood stove. When the owners of such a monstrosity are not cooking food on this working antique, they are out on the patio gathered around the barbecue grill, trying to relive their Paleolithic past. Gold-backed currency, the stock market, antiques, swords at the Air Force Academy, home cooking, a thousand other moribund activities hang around for people submerged in an automatic world to play with.

Time is a toy, too. Everything a person does, even making anonymous contributions to charity, is in some way pleasurable, since it is a gratification of the organism. And all of pleasure is either anticipation or remembrance. Anthropologists have found some few societies on earth who seem to live in the present, but it is not just a philosophical quibble to say that except in an arbitrary sense the present does not exist. For the young, anticipation of the pleasures of a future that certainly will not come to pass is the overwhelming non-sensory pleasure. For the old, the remembrance of things thought to have been is the last pleasure before the grave.

Wordsworth defined poetry as powerful emotions recollected in tranquility. So are the Good Old Days. Life is made bearable by the willing suspension of reality, by forcing unpalatable facts into the shape of delectable truth. John Paul Jones, the founder of the American Navy, ended his career as an admiral in the Russian Navy. Captain James Lawrence surrendered less than fifteen minutes after he said, "Don't give up the ship." The Alamo held out for only a few minutes longer than Captain Lawrence after Santa Anna's attack began. Paul Revere saw no lanterns in the belfry, he never completed his ride, his horse was captured by the British, and he was court-martialed by the United States Army. General Ulysses S. Grant was cashiered out of the Army by Secretary Jefferson Davis. General Thomas Jackson acquired his famous nickname when General Bernard Bee accused him of standing there like a damned stone wall when Bee begged him for assistance at First Manassas. Abraham Lincoln said explicitly and unequivocally that he did not believe the Negro to be the physical or social equal of the white man, that he should not have citizenship, and that he should be shipped back to Africa. Henry Ford did not invent or devise the automobile, the first Ford car, the Ford Motor Company, the theory of line production, mass production methods or management, sales driving, the planetary transmission, the standardization or interchangeability of parts, the "Five Dollar Day," the Model T, the Model A, the Ford V-8, the Lincoln, or even his own "signature." These are all matters subject to the easy verification of written history. What, then, can one expect of matters whose only source is in the wishful mind? chaos — in which the trained and diligent folklorist can sometimes distill the actuality from the illusion.

Since illusion is nearly the only resource man has to make actuality bearable, it is a powerful force, as the play *Death of a Salesman* made clear. There is even a nationally distributed magazine called *Good Old Days*, which stirs up the memory of vanished things for readers whose own imaginations are inadequate. And John Kenneth Galbraith showed how "social nostalgia" stimulates not only individual pleasure but unrealistic and very dangerous beliefs in society, economics, and politics.

Still, in these latter days of rampant enlightenment, when even professors of English literature contend for computer time, it is good now and then to remind ourselves that there is still a small place in folk scholarship for the not only accurate but articulate human observer — not only the illiterate informant whose reminiscences never leave our archives except in the form of statistics, but those eminently literate persons whose memories of lives begun in folk societies can give us not only understanding of such cultures but sheer gladness in the telling. There are few Hamlin Garlands left, and ere the days of their pilgrimage vanish, we must encourage them to tell us in their eloquence just how it was in those days and those places, gone forever.

Juanita Brooks began writing her Mormon memories when Hamlin Garland was still alive. In recent years she has interested herself in the history of the Church of Jesus Christ of Latter-Day Saints, and particularly in John D. Lee, the murderer and martyr who was not spoken about publicly in Mormon country until Mrs. Brooks published *The Mountain Meadows Massacre* in 1950. In 1955, descendants of the Gentile pioneers massacred by Mormons and Indians under Lee erected a monument in Arkansas at the place where, a century earlier, their forefathers departed for their grisly fate in southwestern Utah, not far from where the following stories take place. It was fitting that they should have asked Mrs. Brooks, herself a Mormon, to speak at the memorial. The short address she gave there is movingly reminiscent of the exhortations to charity, understanding, and forgiveness made by the Reverend Joseph Green in Salem Village after the witch trials and hangings of 1692 had torn apart that tragic community.

"The dark happenings," Mrs. Brooks told the Fancher descendants, "were made possible only by what had gone before." From one community to another the followers of Joseph Smith were driven by their Gentile neighbors until at Nauvoo, Illinois, the Prophet himself was killed, and they were forced in midwinter to embark across the wilderness to their Deseret. "We will not run again!" their leaders vowed; "this time we will defend our homes." But Brigham Young preferred avoidance; he settled his people far from those who lived in darkness. When he brought the Saints into the valley of the Great Salt Lake, he thought he was upon Mexican soil. Later, after the discovery of gold in California set his followers squarely in the stream of Gentile emigrants, he decided to colonize wherever there was enough water and arable land to support a settlement. The most marginal of the desert Southwest was settled at the outbreak of the Civil War, when the supply of cotton cloth was cut off. The cotton plantations, then begun by "the Dixie Mission," seeded tiny communities all along the streams that now fill Lake Mead above Boulder Dam. Such a village was Bunkerville, which I will let Mrs. Brooks describe:

The village of Bunkerville, Nevada, scene of these stories, is on the lower Virgin River across from Mesquite, which present road maps list on U.S. 91 as seventy-seven miles north of Las Vegas.

It was founded in 1876 by a group of Mormons, sent by their leaders to raise cotton and other semitropical crops. According to the pattern, as many families as the land and water would support were "called" to a location and moved there together. They selected their townsite, surveyed it, and marked it off into uniform square blocks with wide, straight streets. The heads of families drew numbers from a hat to correspond with the numbered lots.

All had to cooperate to build a dam and canal to bring water to the land; all had to work together to clear and fence and cultivate a common field during the first years and individual tracts as more land was brought under cultivation.

By the time I was born, the town was well established. The trees along the sidewalks were large and shady; figs, pomegranates, and grapes were plentiful, and orchards of other fruit producing. Some substantial brick homes with decorated porches and cornices stood among the smaller adobe ones; yards bloomed with hollyhocks all summer, and chrysanthemums lasted almost until Christmas.

While none in town could be classed as affluent—unless it might be the Bishop—neither were there any in actual want. Among them they raised cuttings of alfalfa hay, and melons and squash were of especially good quality. The people even hauled their own salt in large crystalline rocks from a salt cave some forty miles away.

The one problem was the river. First, last, and all the time, they struggled to keep the water in the Big Ditch—that magic line which held the desert at bay. Most of the time it was a small, sluggish stream meandering among its own sandbars, but during the spring runoff it became a major river, and in flood, a raging, rampaging torrent.

The two towns, on opposite sides of the stream, had dealings with

one another, but trips farther away were rare. St. George, Utah, was
the religious and cultural center; it was two days away by team. In the
opposite direction, Las Vegas, still little more than a ranch, was three
days away, two of them over a waterless waste. As Las Vegas grew, it
was considered to be "the Devil's land," because it fostered gambling
and drinking, and people were warned not to go there.

Juanita Brooks still lives in St. George, "the religious and
cultural center," now a town of five thousand people, improved
somewhat over its condition as described by one of its founders,
Charles Walker:

Oh, what a dreary place this was when first the Mormons found it;
They said no white men here could live, and Indians prowled around
      it;
They said the land it was no good, and the water was no gooder,
And the bare idea of living here was enough to make men shudder.

Refrain: Mesquite, soap root, prickly pears and briars;
            St. George ere long will be a place that everyone admires.

Now green lucerne in verdant spots redeems our thriving city,
Whilst vines and fruit trees grace our lots with flowers sweet and
      pretty
Where once the grass in single blades grew a mile apart in distance
And it kept the crickets on the hop to pick up their subsistence.

The sun it is so scorching hot it makes the water sizz, sir,
And the reason that it is so hot is just because it is, sir.
The wind with fury here doth blow, that when we plant or sow, sir,
We place one foot upon the seeds and hold them till they grow, sir.

Bunkerville did not prosper; like the colony of the other Pilgrims, Plymouth, she was "left like an ancient mother grown
old and forsaken of her children . . . and she like a widow left
to trust only in God." Today, only two hundred people remain.

I first heard these stories at a party one evening during the
1963 regional meeting of the American Folklore Society in
Logan, Utah. At the home of J. Golden Taylor, himself named
for the famous — or infamous — Mormon divine, we had been
convulsed for hours by Hector Lee's tales of that most outrageous preacher in the history of Christendom, J. Golden Kimball;
and later Mrs. Brooks made the warmth suffusing by telling us

the memories you will read on the following pages. I contended with Professor Taylor for the privilege of getting these reminiscences into print first; but, though he prevailed by succeeding in persuading Juanita Brooks to write them down, he most graciously relinquished his claim to our greater need in the humanization of folklore.

We hope that our readers will share the delight of that evening in these reminiscences of Juanita Brooks's childhood—of the cow that obstinately insisted on fulfilling her watery fate in the stream that was both the life and terror of the village of Bunkerville; of the Outsider that came in from the darkness to lead Juanita to "that untravell'd world whose margin fades for ever and for ever"; of Selah, whose theft by an escaping convict made the child Juanita into the woman and caused her to "put away childish things."

MEMORIES OF A MORMON GIRLHOOD*

OLD TUBUCKS

This morning did not seem different from any other. I had done the chores, had my breakfast, and started the cows out toward the pasture. The water was in the ditch after the washout in August, so I really didn't need to take them around the river road. They had made it a habit while the water was out, so I just let them go.

I trailed along, scuffing my bare feet through the dust and remembering that I had forgotten my bonnet again. It was not that I didn't want to wear it; I just didn't think of it. It didn't seem the same to be alone on this road after all the herds that had traveled it twice a day for the last three weeks. The cows went down the dugway to the stream from

*By Juanita Brooks. JAF Volume 77, 1964, 195-219.

habit; I splashed through it without even holding up my dress—it was that shallow on this side.

I was looking at some houses we had started building on the sandbar when just a whiff of a breeze from the other side carried a faint, different sound. I stopped dead-still to listen. It was not an owl—this wasn't the season or the time of day for owls. It was not a bullfrog, either—for the same reason. Just a low, guttural, half-moaning sound, and then a long silence. As I turned to go on and forget it, there it was again. Just once. Silence again. The sound repeated. Well, it was something alive; it must be. It had to be. I turned sharply and walked toward it, every sense alert.

Just around a bend on the other side of the island, near where the largest part of the water ran, I saw her—a cow buried almost to the ridge of her hips; and her head, with high, proud horns, stretched out upon the sand which had hardened around her like cement.

"Oh, you poor, poor thing!" I cried, running to her. "How could you be here so close and so long, and nobody find you?"

Again the moaning sound from her throat, not so strong a sound as she had made when she first was caught here three weeks ago. I myself had come this way twice every day during that time, but sometimes there were others to talk to and sometimes, riding Selah, I had not heard or paid attention. Had I been guided here today?

I wanted to cry for her—she looked so pitiful, so skinny and dry and hopeless, and the water only a few yards away. What could I do? Why had I left my sunbonnet home? I tried to carry a little water in my two cupped hands, but it leaked out. Then I had an idea. Taking my skirt by the hem, I scooped up a lapful of water and ran to her. Though some leaked through, she got three good, big swallows. Back I went for more, but alas! I filled it too full. When I stood up, my dress ripped from the belt to the hem, and the water fell around my feet in one big plop. The pity of it!

Then it occurred to me that maybe this was the Hand of the Lord, too, just like my finding her in the first place. I remembered how Grandpa had told of crossing the desert from Las Vegas during June, long ago before there was a road, and how he was nearly dead of thirst and starvation when some friendly Indians found him. They wrapped his belly round and round with a buckskin strap so he would not feel hunger so much, and two of them supported him to their camp not far away. Here the squaws measured out only a half a gourd of water and a few kernels of parched corn which he had to chew for a long time. Then they loosened the strap and gave him a few sips of water again, repeating this every hour or so until he could take a full meal. Too much food too soon would kill him ("Heap yakeway, purty dam quick," they said).

So maybe I should give her just a little food at first. I ran back across the river and climbed into the nearest field, where I found a clump of alfalfa that the mower had missed, tall stalks with flowers and leaves, as much as I could put my two hands around. As I approached with it, I decided that I would name her Star, because she had a white spot right in the middle of her forehead, and Star seemed a romantic name. I knew that she did not belong to us, but I thought she was mine if I saved her life.

As I hurried on to turn the cows into the field, I made plans. This was Friday morning; Pa left with the mail long before daylight and would not be home until about four o'clock tomorrow afternoon. If he couldn't get her out then, I'd use the Scripture about the ox in the mire on Sunday, and in the meantime I would bring down the little brass bucket to carry water in and the sickle to cut the lucerne with. I'd not tell a soul until I talked with Pa. I'd have to disobey him too, for he told me to leave Selah in the pasture. With all the trips I'd have to make, I'd simply have to ride.

I cut across the pasture and the hayfield to where the mail ponies were. At the fence I whistled for Selah. She came trotting up, her flaxen mane and tail still shiny from the grooming we gave them when she was in the parade. A piece of rope for the ring in her halter, my toe against her knee, and I was off for home, eager to carry out my plans.

As soon as Pa had delivered the mail the next day, I was there to meet him. I couldn't wait to tell him about Star.

"Pa, I found a cow in the sand on the river bottom. She's in an awful shape, in almost over her back."

"Take care of the team," he answered shortly, as though he hadn't heard a word. The team was always his first consideration after that long, strenuous run.

I waited until the ponies had rolled in the sand, shaken themselves, and had a drink at the trough, and then I measured out their grain and put on the nose sacks. While the horses ate, I would go in and tell Pa.

He was all washed and fresh and on his second cup of tea when I came in.

"Now what about the cow you found in the mud?" he asked.

I almost fell over myself trying to explain how I happened to hear her, and how far gone she was, and how solid the sand was around her. I even told why I didn't give her much at first, but she had really perked up even in two days.

"Any idea who she belongs to?"

"No."

"Don't you know any marks and brands?"

"Well, I know our own—a peak on the left ear and a swallow fork in the right. She's got the tip cut off square on one and a slit in the bottom of the other."

"A crop on the left and an undercut on the right—the Adams marks. You go on down to where she is, and I'll see if I can locate Thomas or one of the boys."

When I saw Pa and Thomas ride down into the river, I stood up on the sandbank and waved and called. Pa was riding Flax; he always looked heroic on Flax—a fine man on a fine mount. Thomas rode at an easy canter while Flax did a nervous little step dance on the side; Pa was reining him in and touching him lightly with his spur. They rode up and looked at Star awhile and then got off and walked around her. She might be doing an act herself, for she just stretched out quietly as if she thought her time had come.

"The little gal there got the wind of her Friday morning, she says. Heard her a-moanin' or tryin' to beller. She been carryin' water 'n' hay fer a coupla days now."

Thomas studied her a while, still not saying anything.

"Might be better to put her outta her misery," Pa suggested.

"You can't do that!" I cried out. "You just can't! Look how long she's been here, and how hard she has tried to get out. And then I heard her call, and I come, and I've brought her back to life when she was just a-breathing her last."

The men didn't have either gun or ax to kill her with, but I knew about Pa's pocketknife with the long, wicked blade that could cut her jugular in one quick stroke and let her blood out onto the ground.

Thomas looked at me as if he had seen me for the first time.

"Well," he said with some hesitation, "the hide is worth a coupla bucks."

Pa was not one to cut a man down on his price. "You name it; I take it or leave it," was his motto. Without another word he pulled two silver dollars out of his pocket and handed them over. Two dollars was the standard price for a hide after it was skinned and dried.

"You go on down and get the cows and leave Selah where you got her from. One more night won't make much difference to this one here. Better come back this way." Pa was back on Flax and headed for town, riding along and visiting with Thomas.

By the time I got back, Pa was already there again, digging the sand away from one side of the cow, talking to her as he worked.

"Quite a time you've had here, Old Two-Bucks. We'll have to get at you to see if you're worth the price." Old Two-Bucks! the name Star just faded out of my mind.

I had already wondered how it was that Pa had two silver dollars so handy, loose in his pockets, without untying a pouch or counting out coins. Money was scarce in our town; paper money was not known. Most of our dealings were carried on with "Bishop's Chips," octagonal lead coins stamped in denominations of 5¢, 10¢, 25¢, 50¢, and one dollar, and were good only in trade at the store which the Bishop ran. He took our butter and eggs, and our gleanings of wheat or barley and gave us these coins in return. Then his teams would haul the accumulated produce to the mining camps at Pioche or Bullfrog and sell it for money. We counted our silver as two-bits, four-bits, six-bits, and a buck. *Two-Bucks* gave meaning to her name; besides, it was individual and different.

Before Pa had finished his digging, I heard a wagon; and here came the two Hancock boys driving our outfit, with our own little boys along. The Hancocks were new in town and were not to stay long, but for now they were anxious to get work of any kind and were big, strong, and willing. They brought another shovel, and the way they made the sand fly would do your heart good.

In no time they had the hole finished, and one at the horns and the other at the tail, had loosened Two-Bucks and laid her over on her side, leaving the imprint of her body opposite. Now to get her out and on the level. I thought they'd pull off both head and tail before they put a strap around her middle and all three pulled and lifted. Pa directed the handling of the wagon, backing it up to within a few feet of her head. Now some more shoveling to lower the hind wheels to the X in the sand. Next a wide plank from the wagon bed to her shoulders and a rope around her horns to help with the pulling. Heaving and grunting and resting, pulling at her head with the rope snubbed around the upright on front, they finally got her in—just so much dead weight.

I rode with her and the little boys in the back and sat near her head, talking to her and trying to reassure her, while the boys rubbed at her front legs to see if they would bend.

"Tubucks, Tubucks," they kept saying, slurring over the last syllable as though the word were a twin to the Indian *Tobuck*, which meant "very, very angry." She would give her own meaning to the name.

It was dark by the time we got home. Pa had the boys drive right into the stackyard, where they unloaded Old Tubucks, sliding her down the plank easily and then driving the wagon away.

"Don't bother with her any more tonight," Pa said. "She's had all the company she needs for now. We'll see how she is in the morning."

I was there bright and early to put a flake of hay within her reach and to try to bring life back into her legs. I brought a big pan of hot water with epsom salts and tore a towel in half to use for hot packs on her knee joints and scrubbed them all down with the currycomb to help the blood to circulate.

When I got home from Sunday school, Pa had her suspended in the tarpaulin, with a rope through the end holes and fastened to the hay-fork crane. Her feet touched the ground, but she didn't have to hold her own weight up, and her knees did bend a little now. She soon got tired, though, so tired that her head just drooped like a wilted flower, and I had to run for Pa to come and let her down.

School started the next day, and I was so excited with all the new books that I almost forgot Tubucks, but Pa seemed to think she was too important to trust to me, anyway. He hired Herb to ride the mail buckboard this trip.

The stronger she became, the more Old Tubucks seemed to resent us all. Even when she was still straddle-legged with weakness, she would face us with a head-on threat of her horns. Griz she hated especially, though none of the other cows took him seriously yet; he was too young. At first Pa wouldn't put her in with the other cows for fear they would hook her, and then his concern was that she might gore one of them. So all winter she had full run of the stackyard, eating direct from the haystacks and drinking from the end of the trough on that side of the fence. By spring when she shed her old hair, she was a beautiful young animal—a cow that had borne not more than two calves, maybe only one. Large and light-colored—if she had been a horse, we'd have labeled her a buckskin—wild and proud, she was the typical range animal.

Pa must have guessed when he paid for her that she would be with calf. Range animals have a way of caring for those details themselves. As soon as she began making bag, she got restless, always walking the fence, looking for a place to go over or break out; so Pa, sensing her need for privacy during her ordeal, drove her down to the salt grass pasture where there were a few other animals—cows and yearlings—and space and mesquite tree shelter. All the way down she darted this way and that, her head with the regal horns held high and her long legs now very active, her whole bearing that of a frightened wild thing running away.

I didn't see her often now, but at last I knew that she had had her calf. When I reported to Pa, he just said, "Leave her alone. Don't try to find her calf; it will be out in time. You keep your distance, even on a horse."

Within a week the calf, a fine little heifer, was following her around. She did not relax her vigilance and faced every intruder with a head-on threat.

"We'll keep her in the pasture until fall and then beef her," Pa said. "A cow like that is no good to us. Some animals just don't tame, and Old Tubucks is one."

A banging of the screen door in the darkness and an urgent voice calling out, "Telephone from Littlefield! A flood a-comin'! The biggest in history! If you've got any cattle on the river bottoms, better get 'em off P.D.Q.!" Running steps out and along the sidewalk to warn the neighbors below.

The scratch of a match and Ma in her shimmy, her bob all awry on top of her head, was replacing the lamp chimney. Cherri and I were already on our feet and pulling our dresses over our heads. Pa was in Moapa with the mail.

"Hurry now. Be careful!" Ma said, as we darted out.

Down the middle of the street, our bare feet silent in the dust but keeping perfect time, we ran. A light at Adamses'. Their stock would be by the upper fields, but they had big boys and horses to get to them. Across the log bridge that spanned the Field Ditch, we plunged into the dark tunnel of the lane, trotting a while and then walking a stent to get our breath. We could not talk; we could only wonder how come a flood? We had seen no rain in months. Somewhere far away and high in mountains there had been a cloudburst or a warm rain on the winter's snow, and we on the lower reaches of the stream got the disastrous results.

The darkness had dissolved into the gray of coming daylight as we emerged from between the trees to the pasture and hurried down the bank to the barbed wire gate. It took us both to open it and drag the wires their length against the fence so that they would not be in the way as the cattle went through. Nothing was changed. The cattle were still lying down, the blackbirds in the slough just beginning to stir and chirp. But there was the smell of the flood, and the river was running its full width, covering our island completely.

Each with a long stick, we started in different directions to rouse the cattle by yelling and striking at them. Fifteen head. All here and accounted for, and not too far away.

We had them all moving toward the opening in the fence when a sudden wave covered all the pasture, and we splashed through water up to our ankles. Perhaps they sensed our panic; perhaps we crowded them too fast. All but five went through and up the rolling bank to higher ground and safety. These five were our dry cows and feeders for the sale next fall; they meant much in our family economy, so much that we must get them in.

Cherri ran to turn them back, and I stationed myself to head them in. "Easy now; take it easy now," I was yelling in the manner of the cowboys, while she was singing out for them to "get along there, you 'onery old basties."

Success. Old Brin turned in, and the others followed, even the calves

—that is, they all followed but Old Tubucks. Right at the post she panicked and tore off in the opposite direction, head and tail both high. And at the same instant another wave brought the water to our knees.

What to do now? I felt that I must go get her, but with the water at this depth I dare not go out toward the stream for fear of stepping off the bank. Maybe I could go to the high land and run down to where she stood at the end of the fence and the beginning of the jump-off place. If I could succeed, it would be worth it.

"Let'r go. It's her own fault." Cherri was saying aloud what I thought. "It just serves her right. She's got it comin' to her."

"It's dangerous. Pa wouldn't want us to take the risk just for one crazy old cow," she went on. "Besides, it looks like everyone in town is there at the Place waiting to see the flood."

For a minute I hesitated, and then I turned resolutely and followed her across the Con Neagle field to the high point where all the wagons were in line, parents high on the spring seats keeping the younger ones together, teen-agers out running around.

"It's a-comin'!" someone called, and everyone looked. A wall of black debris advanced like a rolling wall some three feet high, behind it trees, cottonwood and cedar, the ridge of a barn bobbing along, a churn, a limp little calf, some squash swinging near the bank.

People higher on the stream had lost everything—homes, corrals, crops. Our dam would be gone, but not much of the ditch damaged (it was the local cloudbursts that wrecked the ditches). The breakers built out into the stream at such great labor and with such high hopes, the wooden ricks filled with rocks, the piles driven into the sand, the barbed wire entangled to catch and hold trees and limbs—all these were scooped out and tossed about as a man would destroy the play cities we children made on the island. Fields before the cutting edge, where the flood whipped into the bank on our side, would melt away in chunks as big as houses, and where it swung away to cut into the opposite bank there would be a large extension of new sand deposited which could be farmed for years, or until the river changed its course again.

So we would accept this. We would put the dam in again and adjust as best we could. And Pa would praise us for our promptness in getting out the fourteen head and say that we did exactly right not to risk our lives for Old Tubucks.

For me, this fell on deaf ears. I could still see her, proud and defiant, facing the sunrise and her certain death. I loved her for the service I had done her earlier; I admired even her suspicion and hostility. The thought that I could have saved her—but she would not—always gave me a pang, both for her misunderstanding and for my own inadequacy and lack of courage. I really should have saved her in spite of herself.

THE OUTSIDER

He came in on the mail rig from Moapa. Pa stopped at the house just long enough to set his suitcase on the porch and tell Ma that he might be here for two nights, depending on whether he got done the things he had come to do. He was an Outsider, Pa said, but he seemed very nice, and she needn't worry; he'd make some contacts up town and likely be back in an hour or so.

An Outsider! I had never seen one before in all my life. Most of our visitors were relatives, who came in wagons from Mesquite, five miles away and across the river. Those who came representing the Church leaders in St. George always stayed at the Bishop's home and spoke to the people in meeting, reminding us of our part in the Great Plan of establishing the Kingdom of God upon the earth and making the desert blossom. They always praised our efforts. Even the drummers who came to sell things at the store were from ZCMI in Salt Lake City, and church men also. And the trustees wouldn't think of hiring a teacher who wasn't a member of the church or who didn't keep the Word of Wisdom.

What would an Outsider want in our town? What was he here for, anyway? At our family prayers each morning both Pa and Ma (when it was their turn—the older children shared in this, too) always asked God to remember the missionaries who were abroad preaching the Gospel to those who sat in darkness. While this might be only figurative, I had somehow the idea that all Outsiders would be under-privileged.

Ma was a little troubled at having to entertain him. We weren't set up to run a hotel; we had enough children to fill our house. But she marshaled all hands to help, one to clean the washdish outside the kitchen door on the back porch, wipe off the splashings from the oilcloth behind it, and put a fresh towel in the roller; another to carry fresh ashes and a new catalogue to the outhouse and clean it out. She herself would change the sheets on our bed upstairs, pick up our things, and arrange there. I swept the front porch and dusted the living room.

I had hardly finished when the Outsider came. Instantly I sensed that there was something different about him, even more than that he was wearing a suit and tie on a weekday. Sitting in darkness, indeed! He seemed so vibrant and alive that his just standing there made things seem different. Could he have a drink of water, please? I ran to get it.

We were very proud of our water, for we had one of the few cisterns in town, and, in fact, the very first one. At any rate, we had clear, cool water, put in during the spring run-off and so not so heavy with alkali as that dipped up each day from the ditch into barrels. Even so, the first drink of our water was always an experience for the stranger, and initiating the schoolteachers each fall was a town joke.

As I handed it to him, I noticed how soft and white his hands were, with the half-moon showing clearly on his fingernails and no dirt under the nails. He sipped at the glass gingerly. This was clearly not his first taste of the Virgin River water. Noticing my interest, he asked, "Is it all like this?"

"Yes," I said. "Only that out of barrels is worse. We don't mind it, but strangers always say that it tastes like a dose of epsom salts."

"A good comparison," he admitted, then added generously, "but this really *is* better." And he drank it quickly as an ordeal to get through with.

It was still not sundown. If I would direct him to the home of some of my Grandfather's descendants by his Indian wife, he would appreciate it very much. He was representing an eastern university where people of Indian extraction could get a free education, he explained. So I pointed out the house where Aunt Annie lived, just one block south, and Aunt Jane in the other direction about three blocks away.

So that was why he was here! I told Ma, and together we wondered how much he had learned from Pa on the trip over, but he evidently did know about Grandpa's five wives, and that one of them was an Indian girl. Pa likely wouldn't go into any detail of how Grandpa had come to marry this girl, or what it had meant to the rest of the family to have Grandpa referred to by some of the uppity-ups as a "squaw man." We had all been trained to call all of the wives "grandma": Grandma Mary, Grandma Mariah, Grandma Thirza, Grandma Janet, and Grandma Martha.

Grandpa had married Grandma Mary when they lived at Tooele, and he was twenty years old and she eighteen. Two years later, when he was called to the Dixie Indian mission and had to bring his young wife with a baby girl (Aunt Hannah) and with another child to be born in a few months, he brought along also Mary's younger sister Mariah, who became his second wife two years later. The next year Grandma Thirza's family arrived from England, and the general legend was that she, only seventeen years old, fell in love with twenty-six-year-old Grandpa Dudley—or at least selected him from among the other possibilities. Since she was my very own grandma, and my father her youngest son, we had heard just a little of this: how she had long braids of hair which came well below her waist; how she had loved to dance and considered the trip across the plains a lark, walking all day and then dancing at the campfire at night; how one and another single man had tried to court her, but she could see only Dudley Leavitt.

She had not been married a year when Dudley went north to trade their dried fruit, molasses, and wine for supplies and dry goods. On his way up he stopped overnight as usual at the home of his cousin, Sister Smith, of Parowan, who had raised the Indian girl, Janet. Janet had been stolen from her home in the North and was being carried by Chief Walker to Mexico to be traded off for horses. At the camp in Parowan Mrs. Smith saw the child tied to a bush, chewing at grass and a cast-off rabbit head which had been thrown out. Kindhearted Mrs. Smith persuaded her husband to buy the child, took her to her heart and loved her as her own, dressed her well, and trained her in all the household arts. Now at sixteen, she had an offer of marriage from a white man in Parowan, but refused it, telling her mother privately that the only man she had seen that she wanted to marry was Dudley Leavitt.

Wholly unsuspecting, Dudley came into Parowan on his way back, but this time did not stop at the home of Sister Smith. He made camp on the edge of town with two other men returning to the Santa Clara. The next morning, after he was an hour on his way, he was overtaken by a horseman who told him that he was wanted back at Parowan by Apostle Amasa M. Lyman. Such an order could not be refused or ignored.

Dudley went back to the home of Sister Smith, where the Apostle was staying. They were alone in the parlor. Had Dudley ever thought of taking an Indian girl for a wife? the authority wanted to know. He had not. Had he ever made any advances to, or show of interest in, the Indian girl, Janet? He had not.

Brother Lyman explained the situation and then solemnly promised the young man that if he would take this girl to wife and honor the marriage by giving her a home and children, from among her seed should come some of the finest and best of all his posterity.

What else could he do?

He said jokingly later that he suspected Sister Smith of listening behind the door, she brought Janet in so promptly, dressed in her finest clothes and with a scarlet flower in her hair. The ceremony was said at once, the trunk of clothing and linen loaded, along with a box of excellent food including little decorated cakes of Janet's making, and three fine new quilts. Side by side on the high spring seat, after their first and only kiss, they set out on a three-day honeymoon.

Dudley drove up to his home just at dusk. None of the first three wives was happy at the sight of the girl in the wagon, but when Thirza found that it was an Indian girl, she flounced back into the house, bundled up her clothes, and cut cross-lots through the field to the home of her parents. She would be the wife of no squaw man!

Her parents gave her little sympathy, reminding her that the other wives had made some adjustments to take her in. For two days she sulked at home, waiting for Dudley to come and coax her back.

In the meantime, the other wives were in a serious predicament. They could not find the mush kettle! Utensils of all kinds were scarce, and though they had a large wash kettle, a skillet, a dutch oven, and assorted other items, they had only one mush kettle of the right size for the morning cereal. They hunted high and low without success.

On the third evening after dark, Thirza opened the front door and put her head in.

"I just remembered about the mush kettle," she said. "I know you must have had a time to cook without it. But I was out at the back scraping it into the swill barrel when Dud drove up, and when I saw a woman in the wagon with him, I just dropped it and forgot about it until just now. Here it is."

She held out the brass kettle, now shining from the action of the sour milk. Now there was a general rejoicing and reconciliation of all the wives; now Dudley would unload the wagon and divide what he had brought equally among them in the presence of all the others, so there would be no favoritism shown.

That was many, many years ago, but the family all knew of the prom- ise made by the Apostle, and Grandma Janet was accepted, and all of her children. The expression "to find the mush kettle" came to mean to us all any good way to save face.

Now here was this Outsider come to offer these children a very special opportunity not open to any of the rest of us. Some of the older grandchildren were already married, but others just might be interested. In any event, the fact that we knew what the Outsider was in town for cleared the air for us all.

Before long he was back. Ma showed him where he would sleep, and the toilet facilities, and told him to make himself at home. He seemed to sense that we would be more comfortable if he stayed in the front room, so that is what he did, moving about it easily and casually as if he appreciated our efforts to have it attractive. He looked at the organ with its lattice work and its display of knicknacks, with my one "boughten" valentine in the center, and then sat down to it briefly and sounded out a few chords and ran a bit of melody with his right hand— not much, to be sure, but enough to show that he could play if he wanted to. I was so proud of that organ. There was only one other in the whole town, so when the Outsider said that it had a fine tone, I felt that he had paid a very special compliment. With him in it, the room now looked not so grand as when our Mesquite relatives visited, though the organ did help to redeem it.

At supper he met all the children, repeated our names, and remembered them. He ate our homemade bread and new milk, with the extras of molasses and preserves and butter and cheese, as though he enjoyed it, except that he paused a little on the milk at first. Ma always apologized if she had to serve morning's milk, even though the cellar kept it quite cool. She thought that fresh milk was much more healthful and palatable; it was the way everyone else did, besides.

The Outsider made talk for us all, asking what grades we were in at school and what we liked to do. He mentioned that on the way over the mesa today he had seen his first mirage and told how real the lake and trees and buildings looked, which led to the story of the Davidsons who had died of thirst about there and of the dangers of mirages in general. He mentioned that he had traveled in Mexico and South America but had never before ridden over a desert stretch such as this. This gave the little boys a chance to tell him about Old Griz and how Pa had found him out there, just about dead, and everyone got into the conversation until it seemed almost like a party.

When Ma thought the younger ones should go to bed, he suggested that maybe we could have a little picture show first. So with just a bit of adjusting of the lamp and some clever use of his hands, he made shadow pictures on the whitewashed wall. With a running commentary, he gave such an interesting program that no one wanted him to stop, not even Pa.

After the younger ones had gone to bed and things were cleared away a bit, Ma said she thought she would go to the dance. The Outsider said he would like to look in on it too, if there were no objection. I usually went along, though I was too young to dance, because Ma wanted company going and coming.

While we got ready, the Outsider sat in the front room reading. Ma had hopefully set the Bible and the Book of Mormon out on the stand and two or three tracts explaining about our faith. Whether he looked at them was not so important to her as whether she did her duty by making them available. In the meantime, Pa had gone out to the corral to check on the animals and to see that things were in order generally before he went to bed.

On this night I took special pains with my shoes, blacking even the heels, and using two stove-lids of soot in the process—the back lids near the stovepipe, which were always best. I touched up my hair with a bit of butter and rubbed some talcum on my face with a flannel cloth. I would pinch my cheeks a little just before we got there to make them red.

The Saturday night dance was a weekly event, enjoyed by young and old. In fact, it seemed a prelude to the Sabbath, for it meant that men would be bathed and shaved and hence almost ready for church. The

Bishop often called for the quadrilles, and some of those who danced and stamped the hardest would be first to bear their testimonies the next day.

The crowd was all gathered and the dance ready to begin when we got there. The benches had been pushed back around the walls, with surplus ones stacked on the back of the stage. The lamps were all cleaned and filled, the tin reflectors behind them polished. The girls sat demurely on one side of the room and the boys on the other, while a few couples who were going steady stood together near the door. The Outsider did not know the rules of our dances, for he came along with us and sat on the women's side of the hall — our men would have dropped dead before one of them would have done that! But the doorkeeper had accepted his fifty cents without giving him a ticket, so that he could sit where he pleased.

Ma certainly did enjoy the dances. Besides the music and the activity, there was the chance to visit with other women, to note the new dresses, and decide whether they were homemade or had come from Montgomery Ward or Bellas Hess. She noticed who danced with whom and how, and sometimes discovered a budding romance before the people were conscious of it themselves. She often held a baby while its young mother shook off her cares in the wide whirlings of a quadrille, or she exchanged experiences with one in a shapeless mother hubbard who couldn't dance herself but came along while her husband did. There was an unwritten rule that so long as he sat out the first and last dance beside his wife, a young man might dance as much as he cared to.

So on this night I sat between Ma and the Outsider, who was on the end of the bench near the stage. The musician, his hat pulled low over his eyes to protect them from the glare, was absentmindedly pulling his accordion in and out in long, windy chords, as though he were tuning it up.

The floor manager stepped to the center front.

"Give us your attention, please, and we will begin this dance. Brother Bunker, will you offer the opening prayer?"

"Friends, Romans, Countrymen, lend me your ears!" the Outsider said *sotto voce* to me as Brother Bunker came forward. He offered the stock petition for such occasions, asking God to help us all to enjoy ourselves in wholesome recreation and praying that no accident or evil might mar the activities.

"Fill up the floor for a waltz," the floor manager next called out.

The boys all hurried across the hall for their partners, and all promenaded arm in arm in a grand march until the floor manager gave the signal. This first waltz was precious and prolonged. Watching the musician, the Outsider imitated the jerky movement of the accordion and said, "Link-ed sweetness l-o-n-g drawn out."

It was as if he had shared with me a delicious tidbit. I knew that he did not make these up; he had found them in books.

As the dance went on, the men had to dance in turns and by numbers, either odds and evens or numbers 1 to 24 and 24 to 48. Each dance was repeated so that no one was cheated. Ambitious young men who wished to dance every time must either buy two tickets or perhaps borrow one from an older man who would sit his out.

The calling of the dance was important in the selection of a partner, for one who could waltz well might become confused in a quadrille, and another who could do the one-two-three-kick of the schottische would be like a cow in tow on the polka. At the end of each dance the young man accompanied his lady to her seat and then returned to his own side of the hall.

Through it all the floor manager moved among the crowd, not dancing himself but seeing that none of the boys should wring on or get too rowdy and keeping his eye on conditions in general. Meanwhile the Outsider seemed mildly amused at the gusto with which the young men stamped and whirled and swung their partners.

During the intermission the floor was swept—two boys pushing the dirt ahead of them in a long windrow. A few couples walked out during this process, but most of the people remained in their places. The floor manager walked back and forth behind the sweepers, whittling off a candle and scattering the shavings. Someone called from the sidelines for a step dance by Uncle Tom and Aunt Lene.

"Uncle Tom and Aunt Lene will do a double shuffle," the manager called out without stopping his knife.

Uncle Tom was tall and angular; Aunt Lene was short and plump. Both had great-grandchildren, so should have given up dancing long ago, yet they came promptly to the center of the hall and faced each other. The accordion started, lively, staccato. They waited for the exact note, bowed deeply to each other and began. Holding her skirt up slightly with one hand, Aunt Lene swayed gently as her feet did little shuttle steps in and out under the hem. Uncle Tom gyrated in a circle around her, one foot shuffling forward, the other kicking outward, one arm close at his side, the other flapping loosely in time with the kicking foot—the whole not unlike the preenings of an amorous turkey cock. There was a double figure eight, where they passed back to back in the middle of it; there were intricate cuttings in and out, until at the end, when they faced each other again and bowed.

The Outsider clapped and clapped, and even stamped his feet in approval too, as some of the others were doing. "Come and trip it as you go, on the light, fantastic toe," he said. "Truly a fant*a*stic toe!" Then when the floor manager shouted for everyone to fill up the floor again, he said right out loud, "On with the dance! Let joy be unconfined!"

I was so thrilled to see how he entered into the spirit of the party. I knew that he was saying things out of books again, but such appropriate things! Such unusual things! Surely he was not one who had been sitting in darkness, and whatever Light he had, I wanted some of.

At last it was time for the "Home Sweet Home waltz." Some of the married folks just waltzed as far as the door and went right on out so they'd not have to wait through the closing prayer. Others danced around once or twice before they escaped, so that by the time it was half done there was plenty of room on the floor.

The Outsider turned to me. "Would you like to try this one?"

Would I! I who had not danced at a grown-up dance in my life, would I like to dance with him, the best-dressed and handsomest man there! I stood up, but my heartbeat nearly deafened me. As we started, I looked down, because I didn't know where else to look.

"Don't watch your feet," he said softly. "Hold your head up. Listen to the music. Get the feel of it, and your feet will take care of themselves."

I did, and it worked. We went all the way around the hall twice without breaking step once, as though just by his skill he carried me along. I could not talk; I had nothing to say. He hummed the tune and kept his head up too, above mine.

As we started back to where Ma was still standing and visiting, I said, a little breathlessly, "Thank you. That was a new experience for me."

For a second he saw me. Then he quoted again: "All experience is an arch wherethro' Gleams that untravell'd world whose margin fades for ever and for ever when I move." He stopped as if at a loss to go on, then added, "You know. That *untravell'd* world."

We had stopped. His hand was on my arm just above the elbow, and I leaned against him just the least bit, hardly conscious that the doorkeeper had closed the door and was standing in front of it, that the floor manager had called on Brother Jones to say the closing prayer, and that Brother Jones had asked the crowd to "Please arise, and we will be dismissed." (In all our meetings the audience was asked to arise and stand during the benediction.) I stood with bowed head not heeding the prayer but with "that untravell'd world whose margin fades for ever and for ever when I move" saying itself through my mind.

With the "Amen," the door was opened and the general leave-taking made any further talk impossible. Outside I walked on one side of Ma and the Outsider on the other down the road. He asked about the musician and about Uncle Tom and Aunt Lene, so that Ma had a good time expla ning how things were in our town, even the using of the meetinghouse for the dance. Ma invited him to go to Sunday school, but he excused himself, saying that he had an early morning appointment that would prevent it.

Ma served breakfast to him and Pa by themselves the next morning while we were doing the chores. I guessed that he had met with no success in Aunt Annie's family, or any of the others. They did not want to be classed as Indians. They were not Indians; they were descendants of Dudley Leavitt, born under the Covenant and with special blessings already promised.

When I came in from Sunday school, he was gone. He had found a way back to Moapa with someone who was going, and he would get there in time to catch the night train, which would save a full day. My heart was like lead. I had thought that I would see him at dinner, at least, when we would have an ironed tablecloth on, and Ma was serving chicken and noodles, her very best dish.

That afternoon I took the mail ponies down to the pasture and rode Selah back, coming by the hill road. It was just past sundown, so I rode to the top of my favorite knoll, where I could see far in every direction. At the west the mesa stretched endlessly, pink in the reflection of the evening light.

Out into the vivid sunset the Outsider had gone to Moapa. Where would he go from there? I realized that while he knew a great deal about me, I knew almost nothing about him, not even his name. I looked over my world here on the edge of the desert, its sunblistered miles of rock and clay–a barren world, full of emptiness. I knew that there were places where grass and trees and flowers grew just for the fun of it, without having to be nursed along by irrigation. "That untravell'd world whose margin fades for ever and for ever when I move," I said to myself. Did that mean like chasing the end of the rainbow? Or like going off the road to find the greenery and water of a mirage? Or was it not the physical world at all to which the Outsider referred – but the world of thought, of knowledge?

So sitting astride my dappled pony, my bonnet on my shoulders, my braids undone, I studied this out and determined that I would see some of the world beyond the desert, that I would go to a college or a university or whatever it was that one went to in order to learn of books and how to talk like books. I would not wait for life to come to me; I would go out to meet it.

As I watched the glory in the west bloom to such brilliance that it almost hurt to see it, and then begin to fade, it seemed almost like the bright spot which he had made in my life. Maybe when I was all grown up and out in the great world, just *maybe* I would meet the Outsider there, and I would be so changed that he would not know me. But I would tell him, and then he would remember. Just like a storybook.

SELAH

"There's a man hiding in the salt grass pasture. He puts his horse into our field every night and takes it out every morning," I told Pa, as he sipped at his tea. "He's been there two or three days now."

"What makes you think so?"

"Well, there are tracks around the gate, tracks of a big man and of a horse with no shoes on its front feet. He takes the horse in after I leave with the cows at night and out again before I get there in the morning. I noticed it first several days ago, but forgot to mention it when you were in last time. This morning the water had run the place, and they were real clear in the damp sand. He wears a big shoe, lots bigger than yours, and the right one has a hole in the sole and the left one is cracked across. The horse is big, too, bigger than the mail ponies, almost bigger than Old Maje."

I could see that Pa was pleased with me. Part of it was because he had washed off the dust of the mail run and had downed one cup of tea. This always made him feel better. Then he was proud that I had been so observant. He himself had a reputation for reading tracks. Other cowboys said that he could follow miles behind a herd and tell how many were in it and what age and color they were and whose brand they carried. Cowboy exaggeration, to be sure, but with some truth in it.

He studied a minute and then looked at me sharply.

"You ain't scairt of him, are you?" Pa had a scorn of fear.

"Well, no. Not exactly. But it makes me feel kinda funny, knowing that he is somewhere around and likely watching me all the time. I hurry right on for fear I will see him. I think that he knows that I know he is there."

"You don't have no call to be afraid. No man is going to harm a little girl like you. No man will molest a girl who don't invite it. If you know where you're going and set out to go there, no one is going to stop you. It's the girl who dwaddles along and giggles or accidently drops her handkerchief that gets picked up. The girl who gets taken advantage of usually gives a little come-on herself."

I knew Pa wasn't talking about me. He was thinking of another girl, older than I, who was not married but had come home to have a baby and said that she was forced. Then Pa thought I just looked too young. Although I was past thirteen going on fourteen, I was still skinny and flat-chested and wore my hair in braids while some girls my age were "well rounded out in their curves," as Aunt Ellie often said.

Pa sipped at his tea in silence for a minute before he came back to the question at hand.

"We have plenty of good pasture," he said at last. "I don't think we will miss what one horse will eat during the night." Pa would be as glad to feed a hungry horse as a hungry man. Still he might have thought it important to know who was lurking in the brush at the bottom of the field and putting his horse in every night for a week.

True, it was a good pasture. I must even leave Selah there because we must husband the stacked hay for the winter. Selah was my very own pony. Pa had given her to me more than two years ago, when I was still eleven, not as any special birthday present, but just because he got her in a trade.

"She's yours," he had said. "You have so much running back and forth from the field that you need a horse of your own. Pinkie named her 'Selah'."

I had often wondered why a man so dark-complexioned as he was ever got the name of Pinkie. He was a good-natured fellow, a teller of tall tales, not a Jack Mormon exactly, but with a sacrilegious streak in him. He named his team Satan and Midnight because they were black and always traveled together. Everyone knew that Satan was turned loose at midnight and had free run of the earth until the first rooster-crow in the morning. A third horse was Beelzebub, because he was mean as hell. Gabriel, his favorite, was such an animal as could well bring glad tidings.

Knowing the names of these horses, I was not surprised that he should call the pony "Selah." Pa wasn't sure of the meaning, but thought it meant the equivalent of our "Amen" or the Indian "So let it be"; in some churches it might be the approval shown by the exclamation "Hallelujah" or "Praise the Lord." Our Bible study book said that the meaning is not definite, but since it appears seventy-one times in thirty-nine Psalms and three times in the Book of Habakkuk, always in places of strong emotion, it would seem to indicate a pause in the song during which a musical instrument might play an interlude or the chorus might echo a line. Whatever it might mean to others, it meant to me a beautiful little dappled mare, all my own, to ride whenever I wanted. Even when she must stay in the pasture, we managed a gallop around the field a few times just for fun, especially now, when the weather was so fine.

It wasn't the horse eating our feed that troubled me; it was the idea of a strange man hiding near. At this time of year — early November — such a person would not suffer. The days were still sunny and warm, the nights only cool. The last of the fall corn was at its best, and roasting ears a-plenty in the older rows. The casaba melons were not yet ripe, but other mushmelons were, and there were whole fields of squash and pumpkins just ready for harvest. There were several trees of late cling peaches along the fence between Wittwer's and Hardy's land, just below ours, and the brush was full of quail for anyone who knew how to trap them. So perhaps that was good reason why a traveler should choose to stay in the neighborhood for a while.

Two mornings later my intuition was proved right. He was near and watching me every time I came down. I dragged the heavy pole gate open just enough to let the cows through, going ahead of them as usual to keep them along the fence to go through a second gate — this one of wire — into their pasture. It was an awkward setup, typical of Pa's slipshod farming; but he had fenced off a part of the field for the cows, where there was some fodder left from the summer crop, some clover and browse, but to get them there, I had to herd them off the lucerne, which was now ready for its last cutting. Usually this was easy to do, for the cows were slow, plodding things, and the distance only a few rods. This morning they must have sensed the stranger in the brush, for they came through on a trot and headed straight for the lucerne. Like one possessed, Old Brin ran past me right into it. The field was swampy with irrigation water, and to chase her I must tromp into mud at every step. Then when I hit a gopher hole and one leg went in to my knee, I fell and came up with both hands muddy. I had been calling out and hollering at her; now I was crying with anger and frustration.

Suddenly he was there, standing at just the right place and waving his arms at the cows. He made no sound, but the animals now were docile and went obediently down and through the opening into the pasture. Pretending not to see, I hunted for water enough to wash my hands and the upper part of my leg where the mud would dirty my dress. I found enough for my hands only.

By this time the stranger had vanished — just disappeared entirely as though he had never been there. It took all the courage I could muster to go back and close the two gates — the wire one with the wooden arm around the upright and the large outside pole gate — but the rule of the shut gate could not be broken for any reason whatsoever. Again I saw the tracks, familiar now, of the man who had come out to head the cows back.

I was too shaken up to go to the horse pasture for my morning check on the mail ponies and my visit with Selah. Instead, I headed for the big irrigation ditch where I could wash myself decently, my mind full of conjectures about the stranger, and how quiet and obedient the cows became as soon as he appeared. Could he, by any chance, be one of the Three Nephites? What a wonderful story to tell during the testimony period in Sunday school tomorrow! Only, to be honest, this man did not answer the description at all. The Three Nephites were venerable old men with white beards, now immortal, resurrected beings, able to appear and disappear at will, and coming to the aid of faithful folks who were in trouble. Though there were three who had been translated and permitted to walk the earth until the Second Coming of the Savior, they always traveled singly, and had been seen at various times in far distant places. I had heard several stories of them:

Uncle Hube showed us the seam of a long, white scar that ran around the whole joint of his thumb inside his hand.

"Do you know how I got that scar?" he asked. "I was about ten years old, and Ma sent me to take Pa's lunch to him at the old flour mill. I was a curious kid and got to poking around the machinery when I caught my hand here in the cog wheel. I screamed to high heaven and somehow pulled it out all torn and bleeding like a stuck hog. Pa came running, flustered at the sight of all the blood and without a thing to do with. All of a sudden, here was this man, just standing there, a small, old, white-bearded man. He took hold of my wrist with one hand and held it tight, his thumb on the vein, and with the other hand he opened the flour bin behind him and took up big handfuls of flour which he clapped over the wound to soak up the blood and check the flow. He told Pa to tear up the sack I had brought the lunch in and give him the strips. You know how heavy and strong those old sacks were: just try to tear one without a scissors to start the place. Well, Pa did, and in quite even strips, too. The stranger bound them around the hand, neat and tight, round and round. 'There,' he said at last. 'Now don't you touch that or open it for three weeks.'

"Something attracted our attention, I've forgot what it was, but in an instant the man was gone You know how the road passes the flour mill clear for miles in both directions, and not brush enough anywhere to harbor a bull-lizard. We walked around the mill, but there wasn't a track to be seen. Then we knew: he was one of the Three Nephites, and

he had saved my life. I didn't unwrap my hand for three weeks, and when I did, it looked just like it looks today. Completely healed."

Another incident was told by Brother Rencher. He was on his way home to Grass Valley with a skittish team, and along the road he came upon this old man with a white beard. He thought it was a little strange that the horses didn't even shy at him. Brother Rencher invited the stranger to ride, and as they sat together on the high spring seat, they got to talking about the Book of Mormon. Brother Rencher was a good church member – not a preaching, praying one – but he didn't have a testimony of the Book of Mormon. Now he had everything made clear and all his questions answered. They rode past some settlements and saw people out at work, but Brother Rencher was so interested that he didn't stop to pass the time of day and exchange news, as he ordinarily would, traveling in general uphill all the way. He just waved his hand and went right on. At the Pine Valley junction the stranger said he must get off here; Brother Rencher offered to take him up into town and also urged him to come on and stay overnight at his home at Grass Valley.

The stranger insisted that he must go. Brother Rencher stopped to let him off, and as he did, the team, being skittish, as I said before, shied and reared back and kept his full attention for a few seconds. When he turned to tell the stranger good-bye, no one was there. In all the open country, nothing moved. And no tracks. Later Brother Rencher took pains to talk to the people he had passed and waved at, but not one had seen anyone with him on the spring seat. A few wondered why Brother Rencher had been so offish as not to stop long enough to wind his horses, though the animals seemed to be making it along all right without much sweat.

Another case was told by Sister Mortensen about her mother down in Old Mexico. There was an epidemic among the Mormon colonists there, in which two or three had died and others were critically ill. Though she was only a midwife, there was no doctor available, so people sent for her in all their sickness. One evening, as she passed through a wooded area on her way to attend one who was not expected to live, she met a white-bearded stranger who told her of a certain herb which grew near and which, properly prepared, would cure this disease. He showed her the plant and gave explicit instructions, with the result that there were no other deaths from this disease there at that time. The stranger was not seen again.

There were other stories of the Three Nephites, many of them, all with the same general ingredients. This stranger did not fit any of them, for he was not old. He was not even middle-aged. And his beard was dark — not as black as Pinkie's, but dark. And his hair, uncombed, was thick and dark, too. (Both beard and hair were those of a man for three weeks unshaven and unshorn.) And he definitely left tracks. As I walked home, I thought of him and decided that he must be a kind man at heart to come out and help me in my trouble. But I would tell Pa all about him as soon as the mail came in.

So I hoarded my secret all day, and then didn't get to tell Pa after all. He sent a boy home from the post office to bring the team, while he went down to the big public corral where the cowboys had put cattle from the late fall roundup. I grained the horses and watered them before I went to get the cows, hoping all the time Pa would come first so that I could report. But he didn't come.

Maybe it was just as well, I told myself, when I found no sign around the gate at the field. The stranger had probably gone on now that he had been seen and his horse had had a week in which to recuperate. I started the cows home, then went to check on the mail ponies. Since tomorrow was Sunday, they could stay here overnight and be taken up tomorrow to be ready for their run on Monday. Selah heard my whistle and came trotting to me as usual, as though wondering a little why I had neglected her this morning. I rubbed her neck and patted her shoulder and finally swung myself up onto her back for a little gallop around the field. Suddenly I had a great wish to just stay on and ride her home. The cows, started on their way, would go along without any driving and get there almost as soon as I did. And it would be fun to ride Selah and to detour a little to the top of the hill or to slow up for a bit of a visit with Rettie at Uncle Dud's place and see if she would be going to the dance and what she was going to wear.

I decided that I would do it, but at the gate I got off. The habit of obedience was strong in me, and there was no reason now to disobey, especially tonight when Pa was home from his mail run. Even on his nights off I would not take Selah home without a good reason, and then I would tell Pa myself before someone else did. Pa would not tolerate deceit of any kind. So now I got the currycomb I kept on a cottonwood stump near the gate, went over her with it, rubbed her down, patted her neck, and sent her back.

That night I went to the dance with Ma and had an exciting time. Charles's older brother was going steady, so he left the dance with his girl early and gave his ticket to Charles, who came for me first. Neither of us knew how to dance well, but we held to each other and managed to keep out of the way of the older dancers. After dancing with two or three others, Charles came back to me again, almost as if I were his girl. Actually, it was because we had herded the cows — his and ours —

together for a few weeks and had robbed mud hens' nests in the slough, boiled quail eggs when there were not more than four in the nest, and stolen watermelons from Con Neagle's patch.

Maybe it was more, because at the end of this dance he asked me if I would like some ice cream. The Sisters of the Relief Society were selling their delicious homemade vanilla–lemon custard ice cream, frozen with snow hauled in big gunny sacks from the mountain.

"A nickel dish and two spoons," Charles said proudly.

So we sat side by side on the bench at the back of the stage, the dish on a small table before us, and ate slowly and happily, spoonful for spoonful. I was careful not to take extra and not to take large dips, for I knew that this sharing represented a real sacrifice for Charles. When we were through I thanked him, and we went back to dance together the third time. I thought he wanted to ask if he could walk me home, but he knew that I had come with Ma, and so he didn't.

Then I had hardly got settled in bed before there was a banging on the front screen door and Uncle Nephi's voice calling, "Hen! Henry! Come on down, I've got to talk to you!" Pa was sleeping in the north upstairs room, and both his front door and mine opened on the same side. Our big two-story house had been designed for an upper porch or veranda which had never been finished. The screen doors of both were nailed securely in place, and the wooden doors usually kept open for ventilation, so the conversation came in to me as clearly as though it had been meant for my ears.

"What's the matter?" Pa asked, pulling on his pants as he came.

"Come on down. I want you to go with me as a witness. You remember when my cow was on the range for a while, and we brought her in without finding her calf? Well, it was brought in with the herd today and Rahlston recognized it, but it had Thomas's brand on it and earmark. We talked it over and got three of the men of the neighborhood and drove the cow down to the big corral. She owned the calf all right, ran to it bellering and stood licking it. They've all said that no longear is safe on the range, even with its mother, and now they want a case made of this."

Pa dressed and went down and they talked in lower tones about the case, the heavy fine and possible imprisonment of any man convicted of branding a calf which did not belong to him, with Uncle Nephi insisting that this kind of thing had gone on long enough, and it was time those fellows were caught up with and punished, and Pa cautioning against undue haste. Clearly this was the work of one of the boys rather than the father, but since it was the family brand, he must be held responsible. How about putting into effect the law of the Church that any man caught stealing should return what he had taken and pay the owner fourfold? Might not that be the better way to handle this? Or would it be better to go right now and face the family with the facts and bargain with them privately, without even bringing them into a Bishop's Court? Somewhere in this discussion I fell asleep.

I did not dare ask anything the next morning, for I must not betray the fact that I had overheard the conversation. All through my chores and on my way down with the cows, I mulled this over in my mind and tried to figure the outcome.

At the pole gate I stopped in horrified amazement. There was the story, as clearly as though I had watched it enacted—large tracks leading a large horse through the gate into the pasture; the same tracks leading Selah out. I could hardly collect myself enough to pull the heavy gate open, to follow the cows down and lock them in; but these were my chores, and I did them automatically. In the middle of the pasture was a large, raw-boned brown horse with a saddlesore on his shoulder. I sat on the ground against the gate utterly empty, utterly bereft. For a while I couldn't even cry. I was too full of self-blame.

Why hadn't I told Pa that I *was* afraid of this stranger, that he must be an evil, wicked man hiding there in the brush? Why hadn't I reported him to Uncle Jesse, the sheriff, myself? He would surely have come down to investigate, and put the man in jail. At least, after I had seen him, I should have reported. Why hadn't I ridden Selah home last night, as I was prompted to do? I looked again at the strange horse in the pasture and burst into tears, sobbing myself out on the ground.

What to do now? Get to Pa with this word as soon as I could; he would know what to do. So I started for home on a run, crying as I went, and I ran until a sharp pain in my side forced me to slow to a walk. In the back of my mind I knew that I was being foolish, for the man had evidently taken Selah out by dusk the night before. If she had survived the first twelve hours of travel from dark to daylight, she might be right now hiding in some brush along the river. But he was a big man, and she was a little pony hardly able to carry him. And if he should whip her or force her beyond her strength until she should actually fall dead—the thought was pure pain for me. I had seen men take out their anger and frustration on helpless horses; I knew of one pony ridden to death in just crazy kid races along the river bottom.

I knew just what had happened. Now that I had seen him, he knew that he must be off, and his own horse wasn't ready to travel. He had tried first to catch Flax, our beautiful sorrel so full of nerve and spirit that Pa would allow no one else to ride him. But Flax would not be caught by a stranger. The mail ponies were tough, but they were also wily and hard to catch. Only Selah, gentle little Selah, who had known only kindness and affection, would allow the stranger to approach.

When Ma saw my swollen eyes and mottled face, she was frightened.

"You silly girl," she said. "You'll kill yourself running like that for so far. Running and crying won't get Selah back. Now you lie down there and behave and compose yourself."

She sent one of the boys to the meeting house to tell Pa he was wanted at home, but he was not to break into the meeting, he should wait until it was dismissed and then talk quietly so that the others would not be disturbed or have their minds taken from the Sabbath worship. In the meantime, she tried to call to Littlefield to alert the folks there to be on the lookout for this man. He could about make it that far during the night. The operator reported that the line was down, evidently cut.

As soon as Pa came in, I started telling him and blaming myself.

"I knew I should have brought her home last night," I said. "I got on her and rode right up to the gate expecting to do it, wanting to do it. But you had said not to, and so I didn't. I wish now that I could do what I want to do once in a while. If I had brought Selah home, he'd have taken Jeff or Laid or Stoney."

Pa heard me out, and then said kindly, "My girl, I think that you should play your hunches—that is, when you have a strong presentiment like that, you should follow it, even when it goes against counsel, either mine or anyone else's. But be careful. In general, it is best to do your assigned duty. That is what you did last night—you knew why it was better to leave Selah in the field, but this warning was for a special danger that you didn't know.

"You did the best you could. That is all any of us can do. But you must learn too that life is full of sorrow and disappointment, and we must learn to accept it. We must take what comes with patience, especially when we can't change it. This may help you to know when to follow your own inner guide in the future."

Since nothing more could be done, the family all went on to Sunday school, leaving me to bathe my red, swollen eyes and to be alone with my grief. I thought of the many happy times I had shared with Selah, especially of the evening rides in the spring, when "between hay and grass" we turned our cows out into the hills to pick their food. Just before sundown I would set out to find them, riding to the top of the hill, where I could see over the valley and could hear Old Brin's cowbell. The air was fragrant with wild flowers—sugar flowers and desert poppies and sand verbenas—the sunsets were nightly miracles to sit through. The darkness did not "fall from the wings of night" but rose as though breathed from the ground, filling the washes first and coming up the sidehills, with the evening star low and luminous to meet it. Selah would listen to me repeat the poems I knew as if she enjoyed them. Then there was the time when we decorated her up and entered her in the parade on the Fourth of July, carrying four little children with another leading her.

Alone in the house, I prayed silently for her, that she would be spared alive and not be made to suffer more than she could endure. I tried to think of her rider as a kindly man, since he had come to my aid, a man who would realize that his own interest would depend upon his treating his horse with consideration. By the time the family came home at noon, I was composed and told them the whole story of the tracks and the man and how I had felt so strongly that I should ride Selah home, without mentioning that it was my own selfish desires to check with friends about the dance more than concern for her welfare that impelled me. I made a good story which brought me out in perhaps a better light than I deserved.

The days wore into weeks, and the hurt for the loss of my pony had softened somewhat when Uncle Herb, our relief mail driver, came in with word of her. She had been left at the Truman ranch away off the highway and up the Mogotsu branch of the Santa Clara Creek. The rider had left her a week after he had taken her, so that he had traveled in short stents with long stops between, which I felt was a direct answer to my prayers. The Trumans felt good about the exchange, thinking that Selah was worth more than the animal that had been taken.

Alive and safe! What a joy! Now we would only have to write some letters and arrange for her return. The letter was mailed. Weeks passed, and no reply. Then Uncle Herb stopped in again to have breakfast with us before he started the up-the-river run to Littlefield. The blessing had just been asked on the food and we were beginning to eat when he said, "Amm Truman is in town. He had been drinking some again last night and was saying that as sure as God lives, Hen Leavitt will never get that little mare back."

"Well, then we'll not get her," Pa remarked quietly, "for God sure does live."

"Talk of the Devil, and you'll smell the brimstone," Uncle Herb said, looking out the window. "Here comes Amm now."

Pa seldom waited for a friend to knock if he had seen him coming, so now he opened the door just as Amm reached the steps.

"How are you, Amm?" he said in his friendliest voice, holding out his hand. "Come on in. Will you join us at table?"

"I just et," Amm answered. "I'll wait out here. I'd like to talk to you alone."

Pa didn't come back to finish, but went right on out; I jumped up and went to the window to watch. I thought this was a conversation in which I should have a say, but Ma insisted that I come back and finish my breakfast or I'd be late for school. I waited to see the two men cross the street and settle themselves on the top pole of the horse corral, side by side. They were both big men—over six feet tall—but Amm was broader through the shoulders than Pa. If there should be a fight, I'd bet on Pa, though, as being quicker and more agile. But this didn't appear to be an argument; it looked more like a visit.

They were both there when I left for school, and Pa wasn't home at noon, so I had to wait till evening to learn about Selah. I found Pa out to the stackyard and hurried to talk to him.

"When are we going to get Selah back?" I asked eagerly.

"We are not going to get her back."

"But she is mine. You have no right to trade off my horse without even talking to me. You gave her to me, you know you did. And she is mine. You have no right—"

"You sit down here and listen to me." Pa's voice was almost stern. "You're getting a big girl now. Don't act like a baby. Selah was yours as long as she was here, but she was stolen and taken away and that has changed everything. It was not my fault, nor yours, either, I guess. But it happened. That's how life is with everybody. We have something today and tomorrow it is gone, like the river taking the grain field, and Aunt Dora's baby dying so sudden. We have to face up to these things and take them the best we can.

"You fretted and grieved for fear the man would mistreat Selah. You always made that more important than getting her back. Well, it seems that your prayers were answered. The man took ten days to make it— evidently stopped at Johnson's fields at least one day, then on to Big Bend, then to Littlefield, then to the Beaver Dams, all only a few miles apart. The only long, hard ride was the night he made it over the summit to the Santa Clara Creek, and then took a day or two more before he got to the Truman ranch. He seemed to know the territory well.

"Amm said that Selah was in right good shape when she was left, but the next ride out toward Modena and the railroad was a real hard one, so he changed her for a bigger horse, more like Old Bonyparts here.

"Amm thought she was really a gift of the Lord. You see, his daughter died a month or so ago and left two orphaned children, a girl and a boy. Little children hardly old enough for school. You know how gentle Selah is with children—well, she was really a godsend.

"We could go to Las Vegas and take out replevin papers and hire a lawyer and take the matter to court, but it's just not worth it. We would get the pony back at too high a cost—besides the money and the time, I would lose a lifelong friend, and two little children would cry more for her loss than you did.

"You are getting a big girl now. It's time you put away childish things. In a few weeks you'll be fourteen, and you'll start in high school next fall, and we'll have to let Melvin start to look after the horses. When you want to just go for a ride, you can ride Flax, and with some of the money on the trade, Ma can buy you a riding skirt, so you won't look like a tomboy."

Pa was right, as always. I did love Selah, and I had enjoyed many happy trips on her, but she was a child's pony. Flax, now, was different! To ride Flax would really give me a chance to show off my horsemanship. Especially if I had a new riding skirt.

And I really was getting to be a big girl now. I knew that in more ways than Pa did. Only last Sunday afternoon as I came following the cows home, I met two young couples who had started for a walk down the lane after meeting and were now taking shelter under a big cottonwood tree from a sudden shower. It was really only a sprinkle, and I had hardly noticed it.

"Here you! Come here a minute!" one of the girls called out as I came alongside.

"Just look at this," she exclaimed, taking hold of my shoulder and pulling me around to face her. "Look! See what the rain has done to this kid's hair! Curled it all up around the edges and under the back. Here I spent an hour this morning with the curling irons and lamp to put the curls in mine, and the least bit of rain has straightened it out till it looks like strings, and she doesn't even know that hers is curly." She began to push at my hair, loosening it up and pressing in waves near the front.

"There," she said at last. "Now don't you ever pull your hair into tight braids again. Loosen it up and try something else with it. You just don't know how lucky you are!"

I walked on air the rest of the way home. I, with my skinny legs and narrow face and sallow complexion and big teeth, suddenly had curly hair to compensate a little.

I studied all this out at night. Pa had argued with Uncle Nephi and persuaded him not to go to court over the calf, but to settle quietly and without publicity, so that he might keep the friendship of his neighbor. When Thomas bore his testimony in meeting and cried a little and asked the congregation to forgive his weakness as he had already asked God to do, and promised in the future to do better, only a few in the room knew the specific offense to which he referred. In this case Pa was only following his own counsel, to agree with thine adversary quickly, not because he was afraid, not because he couldn't win, but because he preferred to keep a friend rather than make an enemy.

As for me, Selah would always be a warm glow in my heart and the central figure of many pleasant memories. But life was ahead; life was wonderful and exciting. Some few cars had come through, one marking out the new "Arrowhead Trail." Right down from where we sat there was posted a white, painted four-by-four with two boards near the top and arrows pointing in opposite directions: SALT LAKE CITY 385 MI. — LOS ANGELES 385 MI. Here I was, exactly midway between those two big cities! Maybe I would get to visit one of them sometime!

Pa was right again. I must put away childish things.

America was never a "melting pot" — it was a Mulligan stew, in which incompatible ingredients were raised to the boiling point in the social pressure cooker of undesired contiguity. This nation was founded by a band of malcontents who wanted religious freedom — for themselves. Their attitude toward other refugees from social order was expressed succinctly by a cobbler spokesman, one Nathaniel Ward, who declared that all such "shall have free liberty — to keep away from us."

The American legend studiously ignores the reasons for settlement of many western communities that by any economic, ecological, or reasonable judgment should never have been established. While I was writing this book, I had to interrupt my work to lecture at the University of Oklahoma and to give the commencement address at a high school in Akron, Colorado. At Oklahoma one of my anthropological hosts was unable to meet me because he had to attend, as a matter of his research, a nearby Czech enclave's annual remembrance of the old country's Groundhog Day, or some comparable festival. At Akron a school official whom I expected to welcome me was off some miles to the south attending a meeting of the Mennonite fathers of some semidesert town. Just a bit into the mountains from my own residence in Boulder, Colorado, there is a community of Cornish miners. A few miles to the east is a nest of Italians, where one can get fine spaghetti for little and a black eye for less. To the south are the remains of a Greek mining town, destroyed during the infamous Ludlow Massacre of 1914. There are Koryaks, of all the odd people on earth, in Freehold, New Jersey. There are Sephardic Jews in Los Angeles, who still in times of crisis perform the rites of *Indulco* and *Mumia*. Around Lancaster, Pennsylvania, the outsider must pick his way through German syntax to understand what, if anything, is said to him by the Amish — but in the nearby fundamentalist town of Intercourse, he is not likely to be engaged in any at all by the natives.

Anthropologists speak of the isolating phenomenon of *campanilismo*, which distinguishes — if that is the proper word — members of strongly self-oriented peoples, like Italians and Greeks. They are said, by people who will say such things, to make "bad immigrants," since they encapsulate themselves in the imported culture. But there are "good immigrants" as well — people who give up the old ways immediately on their arrival and integrate with the earlier comers. Everyone knows that the best immigrants are the Scandinavians. They may say "yumping yiminy" for a few years, but after that they are indistinguishable from the sons and daughters of the American Revolution.

So we think, being outsiders ourselves. What really went on in the minds and hearts of the squareheaded people who made those square-streeted towns on the northern plains is hinted at in the following "Norwegian Dialogue on the New World."

A NORWEGIAN DIALOGUE ON THE NEW WORLD*

That a people's songs have a very real relationship to their history is one of the fruitful theses developed and exemplified in the recent volume by Professors Blegen and Ruud, entitled *Norwegian Emigrant Songs and Ballads.* This book is an outstanding contribution to the internal history of immigration, and demonstrates anew the value of cooperative enterprise in the various fields of humanistic study. In a recent review of this book the present writer expressed his desire to expatiate on some of the fruitful vistas and bypaths opened by its contents. Fortunately, not all of these have been exhausted by the conscientious and distinguished labors of the editors. Some gleanings remain, and the writer believes that certain literary and folkloristic comments might be

*From Einar Haugen, "Norwegian Emigrant Songs and Ballads."
 JAF Volume 51, 1938, 69-75.

worth contributing. He also wishes to present a Norwegian-American emigrant ballad not included in the Blegen-Ruud collection, a ballad which is in the true spirit of Norwegian folksong, as well as a lively example of the unceasing debate over the merits of America versus Europe.

One significant strain in the poems presented by Blegen and Ruud is the contrast they reveal in social attitudes. The common man sings the praises of America and extols the blessings of emigration, while the bureaucratic official frowns on the emigrant, and paints a dark picture of American life. No prose account could bring out so clearly the smug and pious self-satisfaction of the ruling class in nineteenth century Norway — bewildered and hostile at this unexpectedly rebellious movement among its inferiors. In passionately rhetorical questions leading clergymen and venerable poets demand of the emigrants: "Are not Norway's skies still blue, her meadows flower-bedecked, her fields golden?" Here are distinguished names, such as M. B. Landstad, P. A. Jensen, C. N. Schwach, and Andreas Munch. Coming from older men and representatives of the bureaucratic class, their writings became a link in the conservative political campaign of their day. On the other hand stood the representatives of rebellious youth, sympathetic to all movements directed at a better future for the common man, and significantly joining hands over the labor movement and emigration. All around them they saw evidence which gave the lie to Christian Olsen's lines, "The foundations of society are sound, and every citizen lives his life in peace." If it were not that Christian Olsen was an unimportant poet, and that sixteen years intervened between this poem and Ibsen's *Samfundets Stotter* (Pillars of Society), one might actually suspect Ibsen of ironically plagiarizing his title from this verse — "*dets Samfundsliv dog hviler paa trygge Stotter*" ("Its society, after all, rests on secure foundations"). In any event the verbal similarity is deeply significant, because it points to the revolution in outlook between 1861 and 1877 among the literary leaders of Norway. The new realism of Ibsen, Bjørnson, and Alexander Kielland reflected an upward surge of the common people, which was coincident with the rise of emigration. Who shall say that the agitation of the America letters and the America books did not help prepare the way for democratic government in Norway, and that conversely the democratic movement in Norway did not help to inspire emigration?

It might seem a contradiction that Henrik Wergeland, champion of the masses, should be on the side of the anti-emigration agitators. Wergeland, however, was against emigration because of his tremendous faith in the possibilities of Norway. His extreme national optimism led him to overlook the more immediate attractions offered by America.

Furthermore, his death (1845) came too early for a full realization of those attractions, even in the minds of the common people. Nowhere does he gloss over conditions in Norway, and his anti-emigration attacks are primarily attacks on the agents who no doubt were thoroughly unscrupulous in promoting their business. Wergeland did not live long enough to realize the connection between his own sympathies and the emigration movement. Another great poet, A. O. Vinje, who came to maturity a decade or two after Wergeland, did realize it and was so deeply sympathetic to emigration that he wrote the most moving poem of Professor Blegen's entire collection: *"Eg vandrar ut, ver med meg du!"* ("Wander out—come with me, you!"). But in spite of this declaration, he stayed in Norway, and thereby showed that in practice he had preferred the alternative advocated by Wergeland.

Few of the poems of emigration are marked by strikingly original forms and images. They fall into rather definite categories and frequently reveal the models that their authors followed. There is a good deal of the rather bombastic nationalism, which was initiated by such poems as Johan Nordal Brun's *"For Norge, kjaempers fødeland,"* ("For Norway, birthplace of giants") and continued into the years just after the separation from Denmark. In Ole Rynning's interesting seventeenth of May poem written in mid-Atlantic, 1837, such a phrase is the verse about "the day when the Lion wakened from his slumber, and drew from his broad and shaggy breast the keen battle-ax." The labor union song of 1850 is written to the tune of Brun's song and is verbally reminiscent of it. The reference to Norway's *"Klippeborge"* ("our castled crags") is a similar allusion. In the years from 1825 to 1850, however, a more elegiac note crept into Norwegian poetry, coincident with the general European victory of Romanticism. This, too, is reflected in these poems, as when Christian Monsen writes about the sea's throwing its soft, gentle arms around the great bosom of Norway with the passion of a beloved (p. 102), or when G. Verner writes of midsummer in Norway, when "the elves dance on the green in the reddening glow of the sun at midnight." The great poet of this movement was Welhaven, and it is natural that imitations of his and his contemporary Andreas Munch's poetry should be found among these poems. Characteristic is the stanza from Christian Olsen's poem:

Det var somom i denne Stund
Naturen dyssedes i Blund
og stille Suk udaanded;—
somom en dyb, tungsindig Ve—
for Tanken hemmelig at se—
bag Kvaeldens Slør sig vaanded.

It was as though Nature were being lulled to sleep and sighed softly, as though one heard the moan of some dark secret anguish from behind the veil of night.

I call attention to these two strains in the poems, not merely because of their interest for literary or linguistic history, but also because they represent two of the enduring strains in Norwegian-American poetry down to the present day. Incredible reams of verse in the old language have been written by the emigrants in their new homeland, and a rather considerable portion of it boils down to one or both of these strains — the bombastic patriotism of 1814 and the elegiac Romanticism of 1849.

Another strain, though a minor one, that is clearly detected in these poems, is the implied or expressed comparison of the emigrants to the Norse Vikings of old. The Vikings had just been exhumed by Norwegian scholars and poets of the Romantic and pre-Romantic period, and it is no wonder that they quickly entered the thoughts of the emigrants. This bond with the past is alluded to in nearly a dozen poems, first of all by Ole Rynning, who in 1837 hailed "once more the distant strand of Vinland the Good." Johannes Veseth in 1844 inquires, "Who can pledge that Famine may not some day find its way to Vinland the Good?" The relatively uneducated O. C. Mathiesen refers in 1849 to the dragon vessels of ancient days. That these similes have taken a deep root is evident in the Leif Ericsson movement, which in later years has given American Norwegians so much satisfaction.

In their linguistic form, also, these poems offer not a little of interest. Most of them are composed in the stilted Dano-Norwegian of their day, which only well-educated writers belonging to the bureaucratic class could master with any ease. The surprising thing is not that many of the poems are poorly composed, but that humble writers show even as good a command of the language as they do. The Norwegian linguistic anomaly of the nineteenth century, according to which all country and most city people spoke one language and wrote another, was of course carried over to the American settlements. It is therefore interesting to find in this collection from Norway six poems that break through the frame of official Norwegian into the more elastic medium of the native dialects. Besides these, there are two poems — one composed in Bergen, the other in Oslo ("Oleana") — which use certain dialect forms but apparently more for satire than for the sake of poetic expression. Of the six poems that use the native dialect as an instrument of serious feeling, it is striking that five are from one district, the perennially poetic Telemark. In this region have been most faithfully preserved the relics of Norway's poetic past, in the ballads and tales as well as in costumes and music. But the people of Telemark have gone on and made living use of the ancient forms, a fact amply confirmed by folklore investigators and modern poets alike.

One of these forms was the *stev*, a verse type consisting of four lines, with four beats each, rhymed in couplets, the first couplet having a feminine and the second a masculine rhyme. The ability to compose stanzas of this form was a social accomplishment in Telemark and Setesdal. In these valleys it frequently took the form of poetic debates in which two persons composed (or recited) alternate stanzas. Such a debate was called a *stevleik*, and samples may be found in any collection of Norwegian balladry, or in works, such as Aasen's *Ervingen*, that aim to imitate folk life. In Professor Blegen's collection two poems are composed in this verse form, though neither of them is in dialect and only one is in debate form. They were sung to a minor melody usually known as *A Ola, Ola, min eigen onge* ("Oh, Ola, Ola, my own child").

It is such a *stevleik* that I wish to present as a supplement to the excellent collection here discussed. Further research may possibly reveal the author's name and the publication date. It is signed H. F. (Hans Foss?), and was printed in a collection of songs published in Chicago in 1894. The poem presents a debate between one who has been in America a number of years and is accordingly well satisfied with his country, and one who has just arrived from Norway, still nostalgic for his home and antagonistic to the new conditions in America. The author gives the newcomer the last word and seems to sympathize with his pessimistic views. But both sides are well presented, and the whole ballad testifies to the skill and poetic talents of its author.

Ein Stevleik

Nykomargut

No er eg hugad, no vil eg kveda,
Med andre glade eg vil meg
  gleda.
Med ulveflokken eg er ilag,
Eg skal no tute den heile dag.

Norsk-Amerikaner

Ja glad, det kan du vel sagtens
  vera,
Som slap i Noreg paa posen
  bera.
No slepp du kravle i berg og ur
Og plage øyret med fossedur.

AN ARGUMENT IN VERSE

Newcomer Boy

Tonight I'm in good spirits, now I want to sing and make merry with others. All day long I have to run around and howl with the rest of the wolves.

Norwegian-American

Yes, you have reason to be merry, for now you'll never have to bear the poor man's lot in Norway. You'll never have to pick your way 'mid rock and precipice, or endure again the rumbling of the waterfalls.

Nykomargut

Javist, der rørde du ved dei
  strengjir,
Som drev or heimen so mange
  drengjir.
Den nye tid med si framskridts-
  and
Hev liten vyrdnad for heim
  og land.

Newcomer Boy

Yes, to be sure, there you
touched the strings that drove so
many lads from home. Our modern age with its spirit of progress
has so little respect for home and
native land.

Norsk-Amerikaner

Det høyrest snodigt, naar slike
  talar
Um vyrdnad, framskridt og
  heimsens dalar,
Som ikkje eigde en fod med
  jord
I draumelandi der langt mod
  nord.

Norwegian-American

It sounds odd to hear fellows
like you talk about respect, and
progress, and the valleys of
home, you who didn't own a foot
of ground in the dream land of
the North.

Nykomargut

Nei, brev og sjøte eg aldrig
  aatte
Paa gardelutar med skog og
  slotte,
Men heile landet laag frisk og
  frit,
Og alt tilsamman eg kallad mit.

Newcomer Boy

No, it's true I had no deeds or
documents to show my owner-
ship of farms and manors. But
the whole country lay fresh and
free before me, and I called all of
it mine.

Norsk-Amerikaner

Men skulde du deg som andre
  klare,
Du fik vist ikkje kring landi fare.
Taenk heile sumaren stande
  slaa
Framyver bøygd med en stutt-
  orvljaa.

Norwegian-American

But you didn't get much chance
to travel around and look at it, if
you were going to make a decent
living. Just think of having to
stand all summer bent forward
over a short-handled scythe!

Nykomargut

Du skulde vist, ho var rar, den
tidi,
Der uppaa saetrane under lidi;
Somangei løgje daa vinden bar,
Fraa ragstegjente til slaattekar.

Newcomer Boy

You should have known what rare experiences they were, those summer days on the mountain heights. So many a jest was bandied back and forth from boy to girl, while they worked at their haying.

Norsk-Amerikaner

Retso, no er du paa isen haale;
Jau, jentun dikkans, dei var nok
snaale;
Taenk, vadmaalsstakken av
spunnen traa,
Det var vel syn, som var vaerdt
at sjaa.

Norwegian-American

Indeed, now you're skating on thin ice, talking about those wonderful girls in Norway! What sights they must have been, in their coarse homespun skirts!

Nykomargut

Nei, gled deg du i dei fine
blanke.
Eg hever sannspurgt, der tidt
kan banke
Eit bedre hjarte, der armod
grin,
Held der, som gullet aa silkje
sjin.

Newcomer Boy

You are welcome to enjoy your pretty little dolls! I know it for a fact that often a better heart may beat amid the starkest poverty than in glittering gold and silks.

Norsk-Amerikaner

Aa stakkars gut, du bleiv hardt
bedregjen,
Som tok i skunndingen denne
vegen.
Her hev me bruk for din
spraeke arm,
Kon skjel det eit du er kold
held varm.

Norwegian-American

Poor boy, you were badly fooled when you all too hastily set out upon this course. Here we have use for your trusty arm, but care not a bit whether you are warm or cold.

Nykomargut	Newcomer Boy
Tak skal du hava for desse ordi!	I thank you for these words of
Ein laerer altid litt her paa jordi;	yours! One can always learn
Den laera hev eg no prentad	something everywhere in this
meg,	world; and the thing I have
I Noreg var eg mest lukkeleg.	learned for sure is that in Nor-
—H. F.	way I had the greater happiness.
	—H. F

Perhaps not exactly the heart of Texas, but some part of that state's viscera is the Texas Big Bend. Its boundaries are the Southern Pacific Railroad to the north and the Rio Grande sweeping in a great semicircle from Fabens on the west and Boquillas to the east. It is a country of big winds, arid sands, remains of camels and Indians, of gold and the memory of gold, and even of those flying witches peculiar to this part of the world. But its story is better told by Haldeen Braddy, one of the great team of folklorists who have made the Texas Folklore Society the strongest of all the regional groups preserving and propagating local lore.

IN THE TEXAS BIG BEND*

In all seasons and at all times in the Big Bend country of Texas there is the wind, and in the summers there are intermittent and widely-separated thundershowers. It is this wind, together with the occasional rain, which has created a territory of unsightly Badlands yet picturesque mountains and desert areas with oasislike springs. The Big Bend, too, is a land at once dead yet alive: here is a government-maintained highway and there, a vanished Apache trail. It is a country both forbidding and appealing—a mighty contradiction of mountains and arroyos. Nothing in this whole vast area of proverbial West Texas seems permanent or abiding or inevitable except the wind erosion and the progress of unpredictable old-time. Here, in the past, are the bleached bones of Confederate soldiers, the black stone image of an Indian god, the sandy trail of a camel caravan—all lost and gone and forgotten in dead time. Yet here too, in this moment that is today, is a busy mining

*From Haldeen Braddy, "Folklore of the Texas Big Bend."
JAF Volume 54, 1941, 60-70.

camp, a gasoline station with free air, and—wonder of wonders—a twentieth-century hermit on government relief! Only great distances and the long silence can explain this: the virile, unvocal people inhabiting the changing, soundless land.

Under the physical conditions here obtaining, man is often subjected to the most severe experiences. For one thing, there are seasons when he can expect no rainfall, when he must rely on his own strength and native ingenuity to hoard what water he possesses or to take advantage of occasional thundershowers occurring nearby. The existence of these drouths is, of course, a subject for lamentation, but the hardihood of the true westerner is not conquered by outrageous fortune. Moreover, since he is 100 percent American, he is able to extract humor from an altogether tragic situation. He tells no sad tales of the death of kings—but racy stories that invigorate the imagination.

Illustrating the length of one notorious drouth, natives tell the story of the father and his eighteen-year-old son who visited in New Orleans, where it rained almost every day. On the occasion of the first downpour, this father was heard to remark that he was "mighty glad it was a-raining; not for himself so much—because he had seen rain—but for the boy's sake!" Similarly, there is the account of the man who placed his children outside the door and threw pitchers of water through the screen in order to show them how rain looked and felt. To say the least, in the land "West of the Pecos," the rain it raineth differently. The precipitation in West Texas is at best a desperately local affair: sometimes it falls in the mountains but not in the valleys; sometimes at the ranch house but not in the corral; and sometimes, claims an old-timer, on one side of the road but not on the other!

In any event, once upon a time there was a "regular cloudburst" in the north-central, and no rain whatsoever in the south-central, Big Bend. On this special occasion it was very likely no other personage than Pecos Bill himself who had gone to sleep under a cactus bush with his double-barreled shotgun propped up beside him, for when he awoke, he discovered that the "north barrel of that double-barreled shotgun was plumb full of water and that the south barrel was as dry as a powder keg."

Rain in the Big Bend is indeed fabulous. But when it comes to telling when it is going to rain, then that, as a "Big Bender" might say, is "a pig of a different bristle." However, if you are really interested, take careful note of these phenomena: a cloudy sunset, an absence of whirlwinds, dead snakes that do not turn their stomachs up, rings about the moon, and prairie dogs that seek their holes. These signs clearly portend a change in the weather.

For another thing, in studying this wild, bewitching, and altogether incomprehensible country, one is always impressed with the remarkable vocabulary of the natives. Nothing so cultivates the acreage of one's imagination as to hear the lingo of the Big Bender. This cowboy entitles a gulley full of catclaw "Rattlesnake Draw"; a rough section near good terrain, "Hell's Half Acre." He calls hard liquor "Wild Mare's Milk"; an extended inebriation "a ring-tailed tooter"; and a skirmish with delirium tremens "a-seeing elephants and a-hearing owls." These are the men who tell the *cocinero* busy with a steak "to just cripple the steer and run him through." This westerner is the man who says when he is in a hurry that "I'm heading for water," who will be your friend "from now on," "give you the shirt off his back," and who will claim when you die that "your spur has rung its knell." These are indeed those Big Benders who at times are as reticent as claimed, who at others will "talk your arm off," who can tell "John D. golly-whoppers," who know the difference "between beef and bull's foot," and who finally and above all and "on all hands" and "forever and three days" are precisely, and nothing short of, nor more nor less than, just about exactly the "best doggone square shooters" anywhere at all.

It is not unnatural that the Big Bender should be inspired to recount stories to suit the Gargantuan geography of his habitat. However, it must be understood that it is not a love of lying, attractive as this may be, which impels the narrator. It is rather the love of romance and pride in the native soil. The typical tall tale of the Big Bend country may be easily illustrated.

Once upon a time — and it was when Pancho Villa raided Ojinaga — a group of Texans living in Presidio, just across the Rio Bravo from Ojinaga, were obliged to flee for their lives. Packing wives and children, and harnessing horses and mules, they set out at once for Marfa. Now it chanced en route that a matron — doubtless somewhat stimulated by the unusual excitement — gave premature birth to a bouncing baby boy. By the oddest coincidence or haphazard stroke of fate, a fine mare almost simultaneously delivered a fine male colt. Since Pancho was "whooping it up thereabouts," the party was in a pretty big hurry; so they decided to leave the baby and the colt on the road and to return for them later. But fortunately this proved entirely unnecessary. For "long" about sundown, when the Texans were preparing to return for the deserted child and colt, a swiftly-moving dust whirlwind was seen approaching. A few minutes later everybody was greatly relieved to see a young lad, with a rattlesnake for a quirt and the umbilical cord for a hackamore, come tearing down the big middle of Marfa's main street astride that fine young pony.

Now no one will be surprised to hear, next, that after this young man rejoined his parents, he shortly developed into a most excellent huntsman. For example, one day he sighted, at a great distance, a splendid buck standing almost entirely hidden between two large boulders. To say the least, it was a difficult angle for a shot. Taking dead aim at a certain special spot hardly visible, he let fire one volley. Immediately after the shot, the buck was seen to rock from side to side several times and then fall heavily. Upon reaching the boulders, this fancy shooter discerned that although he had fired only once, there were by actual count no less than seven bullet holes in the deer. He had aimed so that the bullet struck the far boulder, split up or ricocheted, and mortally wounded the animal in seven different places.

Meanwhile the colt had developed into a splendid but somewhat skittish stallion. It was high time to "break" the bronco. One time our hero was walking through a "draw" when he saw his stallion's luxuriant tail hanging directly down from the top of a cliff. Immediately he clambered up, grabbed this long tail, wrapped it three times about his right arm, braced his legs, and then pulled that great big stallion clean back down off that cliff. He did this in order to tie the tail to a sturdy juniper tree. Now this stallion also had a very long mane, mind you; so the cowboy just cut a portion of it off for a hackamore. After all this, he mounted the horse, cut the tail from the tree, and "lit a shuck outa there." It took him about three days and nights to "break" that bronco. But about three days later he rode him into the corral. Only then did he observe that six wild mares, three to the side, had become entangled in what remained of the stallion's incredibly long mane.

It is a distinct pleasure to report that this skittish stallion became an altogether satisfactory mount. Some people say he was the smartest horse ever to roam the ranges of the Texas Big Bend. Persons holding to this opinion point to the adventure involving a wild Brahma steer. It happened this way: Our hero and the celebrated stallion were one time chasing the steer. They went up, down, and across many a gulley; but finally the steer jumped a tremendous ravine. The stallion hardly knew what to do, but he made a gigantic effort. The jump, however, did not quite carry him to the opposite side; so when he was about half way across, that stallion simply showed his intelligence by turning right square-dab around and jumping back to safety.

The story of the fabulous cowboy of the Big Bend and his matchless steed goes on indefinitely, but it is sufficient to say that all ended happily and, furthermore, in prosperity. Why, even the year of the great drouth, when there was no end of cattle-rustling, every heifer on that cowboy's ranch had twin calves.

There is one disease fairly prevalent among the natives of the Big Bend country. Like Cortez and the Conquistadores, the Big Bend people "suffer of a disease in the heart that only gold can cure." Conditions being what they are, it is a wonder now that these prospectors survive their illness. But gold-hunting must certainly be a form of romanticism. The dyed-in-the-wool prospector lives for the most part in the undiscovered country along the borders of the mind, the land of the chimera. Yet one must add the phrase "for the most part," because there really are gold-producing mines in the Big Bend area. Today in Presidio County gold is being mined on a paying basis for shipment to Newark, New Jersey. This fact, however, by no means accounts for such remarkable stories as the famous "Nigger Mine" of the Big Bend. As most of the significant tales of this country have already been ably recounted elsewhere, only a few fresh episodes in these "floating" legends needs be told.

In the year 1916 or the year 1917, as a former banker will swear up and down, a certain *señor* was accustomed to bring various quantities of raw gold into Alpine. Sometimes the quantity was quite surprisingly large. These were always duly measured and subsequently sold at the local bank. For some twelve months this *señor* regularly traded in Alpine authentic gold for unequivocal greenback. But when someone began troubling this *señor* with questions, he decided never again to return.

It was only a year or two following this Alpinian episode that a Mexican of uncertain origin appeared in Marathon, a town about thirty miles from Alpine. This Mexican walked right into the middle of the leading drugstore of Marathon, as proud as you please. Moreover, he walked right up to the proprietor, and he clearly said: "What acid do you use for testing gold?" "Nitric," replied the proprietor, and sold this *señor* two or three bottles of this nitric acid. That is about all there was to the story for quite a time, because that Mexican just walked out of the drugstore and quietly, unobtrusively, vanished into the canyons and arroyos down Mexico way. The "boys" talked about the episode for quite a spell, but before long its proportions were growing.

Then one day, when least expected, that Mexican showed up in Marathon again. But he was certainly a changed man! He had on store-bought clothes for one thing. What is still more important, even his wife and children had on new clothes! Moreover, he was driving a "spanking new Chevvy." And, what seems most incredible of all, he went all around town and paid up his bills. Some people say that he even paid up the bills of some of his friends. In any case, he walked right over to the leading drugstore, stepped up to the proprietor, bought three more bottles of the acid, and was overheard to remark: "Well, that sure was gold, all right." The whole affair caused quite a stir. But the only drawback — the inevitable drawback — is that this happened quite a spell ago; that is, in the year so-and-so, or so-and-so, and that at exactly this same time this Mexican and his family and all his friends moved permanently away from Marathon. He has not since been heard from.

Of course there are people in the Big Bend who live a life highly civilized, but the important thing in the present connection is that in the Big Bend, not in the metropolis, there is also the primitive life of the Indian and the "wet" Mexican, a Mexican who has crossed the Rio Grande without passport. And these people have a story to tell that is worth the hearing, and a life to live very much worth the living. They know the wind and the rain, the canyons and the arroyos, and they know how to live under privation. Where there are no signs on trees, no moss to give directions, no rivers to follow, they yet know the precious secret of making a livelihood. They know, too, what various herbs and plants may be used for; and modern science confirms their ancient knowledge, which should satisfy the most materialistic modern.

For a long, long time the Indians have known that the strawberry cactus or pitaya (*Echinocereus stramineus*) is good to eat, and modern science employs the fruit in the treatment of diabetes. Tea may be boiled from the leaves of the Ephedra plant (*Ephedra antisyphylitica*) for treatment of venereal diseases. For hardening gums one may use the leather plant (*Jatropha spathulata*). Ocotilla (*Fouguieria splendens*) trunks are used to make fences. Roots of small mesquite (*Prosopis glandulosa*) trees whiten the teeth. Maguey (*Agave*) may be eaten when roasted. The berries of Silverleaf nightshade (*Solanum elaseagnifolium*) mixed with goat's milk are the ingredients of *Hasaderos* (white cheese). Bear grass (*Nolina texana* or *Nolian erumpens*) can be employed to make shoes. And it is generally known that the Mexican agave (*Agave wislezeni*) is responsible for such intoxicants as *aguamiel, pulque,* and *tequila.*

Outside the cities and towns there flourishes a land rich in story, breathing romance; a land strong in rugged flavor, inspiring in magnitude; and, unless, and even after, you have visited it, learned something about it, a land somehow awesome and incredible.

Winging after nightfall from the *Sierra Mojada* (wet mountain) in the interior of Mexico, the *brujas* (flying witches) are nocturnal visitants of the superstitious aborigines who live along the borders of the Rio Grande del Norte. These flying witches, who may assume the most tempting forms, are, perhaps, descendants of the ancient Aztec demons. Translated by the Indians into pseudo-Christian forms and variegated by their sex-obsessed imaginations, these flying, eternally feminine witches are of that stuff which in the faraway and long ago created *Quetzalcotl,* the flying serpent. Nonetheless, these *brujas* exercise over the superstitious mind the most terrifying and often pernicious influence. Goatherders dwelling all alone for long periods of time are most especially affected, the *brujas* not infrequently inducing them to suicide or madness.

Happily, there is one efficacious way to combat the flying witch. What you do is to take off your shirt, cross the sleeves, and then place in the opposite direction a pair of opened scissors. This cunningly designed charm guarantees the death of the bruja, for when she flies past this "crisscross" she finds her wings cut.

Plummet-like she hurdles to the moonlit, dead, cactus land, over which *Caro de Alicate*, the Apache God, looks down from the Chisos Mountains, inscrutably, upon the preposterous and yet — since it is the Big Bend country — the not impossible scene.

Folklore studies are too readily dissociated from their social setting, as Kenneth Wiggins Porter observed when he recovered the following reminiscence of Iowa a hundred years ago from Catharine Ann McCollum. In analyzing the materials of folklore — songs, stories, riddles, proverbs, customs — our profession does not often heed the warning of anthropology's functionalists, who tell us that these things are just parts of a working and integrated whole. Our reticence is understandable enough, when one considers that most contributions — unpublished and unpublishable — to journals of folklore are soppy poems of unquestioned originality from little old ladies in sneakers resident in many other places than Pasadena, dealing with Lo the Poor Indian and his friends Running Bear and Little White Dove, recently perished for love in a raging river. And factitious memoirs by retired clergymen about Abraham Lincoln. And interminable lists of profound sayings like "a rolling stone gathers no moss" from Woop Woop, Idaho. It does not take much of submissions like these to make an editor retreat to the safety of heartless and brainless computer analyses of Emerson's use of folklore.

In thus being human, the folklorist overlooks humanity. But once in a while there comes a Juanita Brooks who can integrate the scientific content of folklore with the personality of its bearers. Though she restricts herself to one evening in a stern United Presbyterian pioneer home, Catharine Ann McCollum, too, brings us close to understanding and vicariously experiencing life in a society surrounded by the United States, but hardly participating in it.

WINTER EVENINGS IN IOWA
A HUNDRED YEARS AGO*

We left the farm when I was only a small girl, but though nearly sixty years have passed, those winter evenings are still clear in my memory, and I often contrast them with the present.

We led the simple life; there was no other. We lived seven miles from a small town (Clarinda, in Page County, southwestern Iowa). A lumber wagon was our only conveyance; there was nothing to go to, and little money for any attractions there might have been. So we had to make our own entertainment.

Chores done, supper over, and dishes washed, we moved from the "lean-to" which was kitchen and dining room, to the "front room," which was also the bedroom for father and mother and the youngest member of the family, myself, who slept in the trundle bed. The room was about fourteen by sixteen feet, and the furniture, most of which had been brought from Pennsylvania, was old and of the plainest character. There was no plastering on the walls, just heavy building paper tacked to the studding. There was, however, always rag carpet on the floor, for mother kept herself well supplied in addition to weaving many yards for others. The bed, with the trundle bed under it, stood in one corner of the room and a lounge in another. A large wood heater was far enough away from the wall so that we could all find places around it (and what quantities of elm, hickory, oak, and ash it did consume!), and near the center of the room was a dropleaf table on which stood one or two coal oil lamps.

Iowa winters were very cold, and I well remember seeing the coal oil frozen in the lamps in the morning. I can't recall that we thought much about the cold, for we wore warm clothing: long woolen underwear, woolen stockings, and woolen mittens—all knit by mother— heavy shoes, and other garments in keeping with the weather. We certainly were comfortable while in bed, for we slept with a featherbed under us and another over us, with plenty of comforts, some of which were woolen throughout. One of three very large quilts covered the bed, piled high with the big feather ticks. There was the Queen's Fancy quilt, the Grape, and the Rose-in-the-Pattypan, all of which were very pretty and had been beautifully quilted by mother when she was a teacher in Pennsylvania and "boarded 'round" with the "scholars." At the head was a bolster, a long pillow reaching entirely

*From Catharine Ann McCollum, "Winter Evenings in Iowa."
JAF Volume 56, 1943, 97-112.

across the bed, and on this were set the two individual pillows. That bed was always perfectly "dressed."

Refreshments of some sort were always provided in the evening. Apples were plentiful and cheap. We raised our own popcorn, and we never seemed to tire of it. It was fun to scrape out turnips and apples and see who could do the neatest job and leave the thinnest shell. We had plenty of hazelnuts and walnuts. Then, mother's cooky jar never failed. The cookies were by no means rich confections, but they tasted good to us. Nothing but the leavening and salt had to be bought. Father raised wheat, took it to the mill, had it ground, and brought home flour and bran. He raised sugarcane, took it to the sorghum mill, and brought it home as molasses. Lard was provided by our hogs, eggs by our hens; Elrick, Reddy, and Whitey furnished the milk. These ingredients were combined in proper proportions and the result was plenty of cookies.

While eating apples, we sometimes told our fortunes from the seeds, using the rhyme:

> One, he loves,
> Two, she loves,
> Three, they both love,
> Four, he comes,
> Five, he tarries,
> Six, he courts,
> Seven, they marry.

Sewing carpet rags was the children's usual occupation. Mother paid five cents per pound, and occasionally a bit of a stone found its way into the carpet ball, but this was passed by with a smile and taken for the joke it was meant to be. I made a good many balls, but doubt that I ever had the patience to sew one which would weigh a pound. My two brothers earned many a nickel at this job. The woolen mittens and long woolen stockings for the entire family were knitted by mother largely during these winter evenings, and then, too, there was the never-ending patching of trousers and darning of hose. Indeed I can't remember her sitting down without some work in her hands. Father, before we were able to afford a corn-sheller, used to bring in tubs of corn, and then, by means of a scoop shovel placed well over the edge of a tub, he would shell corn for seed, using the sharp edge of the shovel to scrape the kernels from the cob. In doing this, father sat on the shovel, a seat made comfortable by putting a coat or two on it for a cushion. He often sewed carpet rags himself, more for a good influence on the boys than anything else. While carpet rags were being sewed, and other work went on, we might ask riddles, and no matter how old they were or how often we heard them, they never lost their interest for us.

We always began with: "What makes a cow look over the hill?" "Because she can't see through it."

Then would follow: "What walks in the water with its head down?" "The nails in a horse's shoe when he walks through the water."

High as a house,
Low as a mouse,
Bitter as gall,
Sweet after all? — — *A walnut—tree, nut, hull, meat.*

As I was going to St. Ives
I met a man with seven wives.
Each wife had seven sacks,
Each sack had seven cats,
Each cat had seven kits.
Kits, cats, sacks, and wives
How many were going to St. Ives? — — *One: I myself.*

Eye like a barn-door,
Ears like a cat—
Guess all night
And you can't guess that! — — *A big iron kettle—*
the "eye" being the bail.

Chip, chip, cherry,
All the men in Derry
Can't climb chip, chip cherry. — — *Smoke from the*
chimney.

"What goes 'round the house and 'round the house, and peeps in at every little hole?" "The sun."

"What goes 'round the house with a harrow after her?" "A hen with her chickens—all engaged in scratching up the ground."

"What's of no use to you and yet you can't go without it?" "Your shadow."

Father always asked this one:

Twelve pears hanging high;
Twelve men came riding by.
Each man took a pear—
And left eleven hanging there. — — *"Each man" was a*
man's name!

And this was mother's favorite:

>Within a fountain crystal clear
>A golden apple doth appear,
>No doors there are to this stronghold,
>Yet thieves break in and steal the gold. $--$ *An egg.*

Other favorites were:

There was a man who had no eyes,   *A man with one eye saw*
He saw a tree with apples on.   *two apples on a tree and*
He took no apples off   *helped himself to one,*
And he left no apples on.   *leaving one.*

A man rode over the London Bridge,   *He was accompanied by a*
And yet he walked.   *dog named Yettie!*

These riddles were asked over and over again, night after night, without ever becoming wearisome. Sometimes we tried to invent new ones, but they were very poor as compared to the old, and I can't remember even one of them.

We would usually spend part of the evening singing. Father was a fine singer and could read notes readily. He often sang the notes and beat time, much to our delight. My parents had a song book, *The Cithara,* out of which they had sung when they were young folk and attended singing schools in Pennsylvania. One of the numbers was an anthem, "Peace Be within Thy Walls." This father would sing, carrying all parts as nearly as was humanly possible. One of my brothers, when quite small, thinking that "peace" meant a piece of bread and butter, remarked confidently, "*My* peash [piece] is in the walls!"— meaning in the cupboard.

Another of father's songs was a ballad:

>Come all you good people
>Who've now come to view
>The sad unhappy fate
>I have now come to.
>
>'Twas in the County of Center
>Where first I drew breath
>And in that same county
>I meet my shameful death.

I shot Reuben Giles
Whom I'd never seen before
And left his body weltering
All in its purple gore.

His [?] and his saddlebags
I also took away....

Two familiar songs sung by my father were "Little Brown Jug" and "My Fither and Mither Were Irish."

My wife and I live all alone
In a little brown hut we call our own.
She loves gin and I love rum.
Tell you what it is, don't we have fun!

Ha, ha, ha! It's you and me!
Little brown jug, how I love thee!
(*Repeat last two lines*)

As I go travelling o'er my farm
I take my little brown jug in my arm.
My wife she did so sorely grieve
That I had my little brown jug for to leave.

If I had a cow that would give such milk
I'd dress her in the finest silk,
Feed her on the best of hay
And milk her fourteen times a day.

We children, in singing this song, used to say "*forty-five* times a day" for no reason that I know of.

My fither and mither were Irish (*thrice*)
And I was Irish too.
And I was Irish too (*twice*).
My fither and mither were Irish (*thrice*),
And I was Irish too.

They kept the cow in the kitchen (*thrice*),
And that was Irish too.
And that was Irish too (*twice*).
They kept the cow in the kitchen (*thrice*),
And that was Irish too.

They kept the pig in the parlor, *etc.*

Another song on an Irish theme, sung by my father, was:

> Go into old Ireland and soon you will know
> How many it takes to milk an old yowe;
> It takes two at the head and two at the hams,
> And two little boys to bring up the lambs.

Another song was sung by father and by my brothers:

> The old gray hoss he died in the wilderness,
> Died in the wilderness, died in the wilderness,
> The old gray hoss he died in the wilderness,
> Down in Alabama.

> Who stole the ham? Why Johnny stole the ham!
> He took it home to Mam and she hung it in the jam,
> And she hung it in the jam, and she hung it in the jam;
> He took it home to Mam and she hung it in the jam,
> Down in Alabama.

My father sang a number of "silly songs," in remembering one of which my brother Samuel has assisted:

> I bought my wife two cows and a steer,
> Nickeltin nickeltin new but new.

> They all went dry in the fall of the year,
> It is to be wallowed a bangoree.

> Halliday, walliday, bangor, noodelty,
> Hoffle come trosselmy, bangoree.

> She milks the milk in the slop-pail,
> She strains the milk through her shift-tail.

> She makes the butter both green and gray,
> The cheese takes leg and walks away.

> She takes her butter to Huckleberry town,
> The print of her foot in every pound.

Of another I remember only the refrain:

> Haram, skarum, stand a barum,
> Horam skoram skybo.
> Stim Stam a lababo,
> Rinktum bully mus a kybo.
> Then rarum skarum skimble arum
> Skitty wink skatty wink
> Clima cli clash to ma clingo.

Two other songs sung by my father were:

> Did you ever ever ever
> In your life did you ever
> See a whale catch a toad by the tail?
> No I never never never
> In my life no I never
> Saw a whale catch a toad by the tail.

> I am lame and cannot dance
> I am lame and cannot dance
> A water turtle bit me, bit me, bit me,
> A water turtle bit me and I can't dance!

Mother did not like the latter song for some reason, regarding it as not quite proper.

One of father's songs was a parody on the well-known hymn, "There is a happy land. / Far, faraway, / Where saints in glory stand, / Bright, bright as day." I can recall only one stanza:

> There is a happy land [boarding house?],
> Far, far [not far?] away,
> Where they have eggs and ham
> Three times a day.
> O how those boarders yell
> When they hear that dinner bell!
> O how those eggs do smell,
> Three times a day!

Of another song I recall only a single line:

> Madam, is your Johnny cake baking brown?

Father also sang:

> I dreamt a dream the other night
> When all around was still.
> I dreamt I saw my Susan Ann
> Acomin' down the hill.
> She had a wash bowl on her head,
> A tin pan in her hand. . . .

Another of my father's songs was:

> About half past four o'clock this morning
> The family was called
> Around the old man's dying bed,

And the old parson's groans did the heavens fairly rend
And I tell you now I felt mighty glad.

So it's hang up the shovel and the hoe
And take down the fiddle and the bow,
For old massa he is dead and he's gone to his grave
And he's gone where the slave-holders go.

To which father would add parenthetically, "And he's gone where they all ought to go." I don't know whether or not this last line belonged to the song. I rather think not, but father always tacked it on when he sang it. Another antislavery and Civil War song was "Jubilee," beginning "Say darkies, have you seen ol massa...?"

Another Civil War song contained the following lines, all I can remember:

Then up came Josy Hooker, with all his fighting train,
He whipped them on the third day and walloped them over again,
On the old Virginia lowlands low, on the old Virginia lowlands low.

One of my favorites was:

The old woman ran up to the top of the hill,
And blew her horn both loud and shrill.
"Good fathers and all, the gray goose is gone,
And the fox has gone out of the town oh!"
      Town oh, town oh!
      And the fox has gone out of the town oh!

My brother Sam remembers three lines of this song; the first two are similar to the first two above, but the third is "'Ho! Ho!', says the fox, 'there's music still'." I was particularly fond of this song, chiefly. I presume, because when it was sung, I was perched on my father's knee, and he used considerable facial expression and bodily action.

Another of father's songs seemed at the time to have no meaning:

It's raining and it's hailing
And it's cold stormy weather.
In comes the farmer drinking up his cider.
I'll go the reaper,
You go the binder
I've lost my true love
And where shall I find her?

Other songs also belonged to games which my parents had played in Pennsylvania:

> Green grow the rushes O!
> Tall grows the timber O!
> Kiss me quick and let me go
> And tell me how you love me O!
>
> All around the barbershop
> The monkey chased the weasel,
> The cobbler kissed the tailor's wife
> And pop goes the weasel!
>
> A penny for a ball of thread,
> A penny for a needle,
> And that's the way the money goes
> And pop goes the weasel!

Mother wasn't a very good singer, but that made little difference to us children, and we would tease her to sing "The Dying Californian," "John McAfee's Confession," "The Romish Lady," and "Miss Betsy." Never, never did we tire of "Miss Betsy":

> Miss Betsy being a maiden fair
> Just lately came from Lancaster.
> She hired maid for a merchant to be;
> This is which pleased Betsy to a high degree.
>
> This merchant had one only son
> Which Betsy's beauty favor done,
> And Betsy's beauty it shone so clear
> She drew his heart into a snare.
>
> One evening when the moon shone clear
> He said to Betsy, "I love you, dear.
> I love you as I love my life
> And I intend to make you my wife."
>
> His mother being in the next room
> And hearing this from her darling son,
> She resolved it was not all her mind,
> She'd disappoint him of his design.
>
> So early next morning she uprose
> And said to Betsy, "Get on your clothes,
> To go to some far counterie
> To wait on me for a day or two."

So she dressed herself in her finest 'tire
All for to go with a great desire,
To go to a ship way [weighed?] near the town—
Away to Virginia Miss Betsy was bound.

His mother made a quick return
And home she came to her darling son.
He said "Dear Mother, you're welcome home,
But where is Betsy, your waiting maid?"

"'Tis oh, my son, how plain I see
That your love is all for Miss Betsy;
But love no more, for it's all in vain;
Miss Betsy's sailing across the main."

In a few days her son took bad,
No kind of music could make him glad.
In troubled dreams he was heard cry
"Oh, Betsy, Betsy, for you I'll die!"

They sent for doctors both far and nigh.
They sent for doctors skill[ed?] to try.
But ah anee [ochonee?] 'twas all in vain.
There was none but Betsy could ease his pain.

And now her son, her son is dead;
She wrung her hands into her head.
If her son could only get breath once more
She'd send for Betsy to wait on him.

But Betsy's heart being like a dove
She'd sighed and mourned and died of love.

This song mother learned when she was but a young girl, from one of her schoolmates in Pennsylvania, now over ninety years ago.

Another of my mother's songs was connected with a game, played in Pennsylvania, something like "Skip to My Lou," of much more recent date:

Here comes two true-lovers
Joined heart and hand.
He wants a wife
And she wants a man.
Now if they are kind-hearted
And think they can agree
They'll march down together
In love and loyalty.

And now this couple's married
And since it is so
Away to the war, poor soul, he must go.
There's weeping and lamenting
And this shall be the cry
"Oh, if he does leave me
"I surely will die."

Another song, sometimes played as a game, was a dialogue between a suitor and his beloved:

HE: I'll give to you a paper of pins
And many other finer things
If you will marry me me me,
If you will marry me.
SHE: I'll not take your paper of pins
Or any other finer things
And I'll not marry you you you,
And I'll not marry you.

He keeps on offering a dress of silk, etc., until finally he offers gold, which she accepts, and then he

Will not marry you, you, you,
And *I'll* not marry *you.*

A counting-rhyme, repeated, not sung, by mother:

One, two, come buckle my shoe;
Three, four, shut the door;
Five, six, pick up sticks;
Seven, eight, lay them straight;
Nine, ten, a big fat hen;
Eleven, twelve, dig and delve;
Thirteen, fourteen, boys are courting;
Fifteen, sixteen, girls are fixin';
Seventeen, eighteen, girls are waiting;
Nineteen, twenty, girls aplenty.

There were other songs which did not "belong" so definitely to either father or mother. I recall just a few lines of one:

O-hi-o, O-hi-o, my true love and me will go
And we'll settle on the banks of the pleasant O-hi-o.

"O-hi-o" was sung by either father or mother or by both together sometimes.

Another song originated in Pennsylvania singing schools sometime
between 1860 and 1865 — in 1862 my father enlisted in the army, but
was mustered out in 1863, and in 1865 mother and he were married
and probably did not often attend singing schools thereafter. The verses
were probably impromptu, something like those now composed at student camps for such songs as "I Ain't Gonna Grieve My Lawd No
More." I can remember only two stanzas.

> I want a sled load of some poles
> To build my chimney higher,
> For when these fearful rains come on
> It drowns out all my fire.

> I want a sled load of some poles
> To fence my garden 'round,
> For all my neighbors' hogs break in
> And they "hoke" up the ground.

Mother and father sang this, verse about.

"Go tell Aunt Betsey" might be sung by either one, and was probably "strung out" like "A Sled Load of Some Poles."

> Go tell Aunt Betsey (*thrice*)
> That her gray goose is dead.

> The one that she's been saving (thrice)
> To make a featherbed.

> It died asquawking (*thrice*)
> With a brickbat on its head.

Mother and father used to laugh at a song which some wag in their
part of Pennsylvania had composed to make fun of the Lebanon town
band.

> The Lebanon band is very green,
>   And this you very well know, sir,
> For they sat up and sang their songs
>   About their bags of tow, sir.

> Ri-oot-the-toot, ri-oot-the-toot,
> Ri-oot-the-toot-the-daddy.
> Ri-oot-the-toot, ri-oot-the-toot
> Ri-oot-the-toot-the-daddy.

I do not know the writer's town nor the significance of his reference to
the "bags of tow." Mother and father seem to have thought it so funny
because they knew the author and his reputation as a wit.

My brothers contributed their share of the evening's entertainment by singing "The Yellow Rose of Texas," "Sweet Evelina," and "Darling Nellie Gray," and by playing on the Jew's harp and French harp while the rest of the family sang. "Nellie Gray" was usually a family affair, all singing with the exception of one who furnished a French harp accompaniment. Another minstrel song which we all sang was "The Little Old Log Cabin in the Lane," upon which were based the many western Kansas songs of fifty years and more ago, having to do with "The Little Old Sod Shanty on the Claim."

Our favorite songs by far were the ballads, with "Miss Betsy" in a strong lead.

Checkers was often played and was so interesting that it was hard to get the game put aside. The board was homemade, of real board, and the men were kernels of white and red corn. However, that five-cents-a-pound which mother paid for sewing carpet rags had its effect and many balls were made.

There were few books in the home, and all save one were theological, the exception being *Grant Around the World,* for which my brother Lincoln had canvassed, riding around the country on one of our plow horses, Sam or Fan, usually the latter because she was a safer mount and my brother was only twelve. Mother sometimes read to us from *Grant Around the World,* but we considered it dry and uninteresting. The theological books were saved for the Sabbath.

We were, however, subscribers to a weekly newspaper, the Chicago *Inter-Ocean.* One winter there was a continued story in it, a murder mystery, *Great Porter Square.* With this story mother, who was a good reader, entertained us, and not many carpet rags were sewed on the evening that paper came. We were all sitting on the edges of our chairs, far too excited to work, as the plots and counterplots were built up, and then slowly but surely the net closed about the murderer and he met his just desserts!

We never tired of hearing father and mother tell of their life in Pennsylvania, and so the "tell me when" stories were called for many times.

Family worship was the last event of the evening and was never neglected. The psalmbooks were passed—mine was bright red, my brothers' were tan—and father would announce the psalm number. Perhaps it would be the second:

> Why rage the heathen and vain things
> why do the people mind?
> Kings of the earth do set themselves
> and princes are combined
> To plot against the Lord and His
> Anointed saying thus,
> Let us asunder break their bands
> and cast their cords from us.

Then, from the Book, father would read a chapter. I can best remember him reading from Isaiah such passages as Chapter 53: "Who hath believed our report? and to whom is the arm of the Lord revealed . . . ?"

We knelt for prayer, and at its close we again sang a few verses. A familiar number was Psalm 92:

> To render thanks unto the Lord
> it is a comely thing,
> And to thy name, O thou most high,
> due praise aloud to sing.
> Thy loving kindness to show forth
> when shines the morning light,
> And to declare thy faithfulness
> with pleasure every night.

The brothers went to their room upstairs; mother pulled out the trundle bed and after my "Now I lay me," tucked me in for the night.

Father filled the stove with wood, closed the dampers, and wound the clock.

Lights out. Good night. Happy dreams.

In the West, the Good Old Days are not so far away. Helen Zunser's ethnographic study of a New Mexico village was written in 1935; elsewhere in the civilized world in that year people were still talking about the killing of John Dillinger, the death of Will Rogers, Adolf Hitler and his rejection of the Versailles Treaty, Clark Gable and Charles Laughton in *Mutiny on the Bounty,* Franklin Roosevelt's latest "fireside chat." But in Hot Springs, New Mexico, life — except for Mr. Jones and his icehouse — was much as it was when talk in New York was about the siege of the Alamo, the Black Hawk War, and the proclamation of Texan independence.

Hot Springs, like so many other rural towns of the West, is disintegrating now. Its population is down to forty-five families. Its icehouse is gone, and so is Mr. Jones. The Penitentes, who in Helen Zunser's time formed a moiety of the Catholic community, are gone, too—gone away or perhaps gone underground. The only industry now is a Catholic seminary, dedicated to maintaining the customs and morality of the dead past. The town has changed its name to Montezuma, perhaps as an expression of the new nativism that is beginning to catch fire in the Mexican Southwest under the fulmination of Reyes Tijerina and his prophets. Whether or not the Spanish-Americans get the three-trillion-dollars compensation Tijerina demands, one can be sure that women of the Lorenz family would rather have life as it was in the Good Old Days.

A NEW MEXICAN VILLAGE*

The town of Hot Springs is in the northeastern part of New Mexico, twelve miles from Las Vegas. The country is wild and mountainous, and Hot Springs itself is about six thousand feet above sea level. As its name suggests, Las Vegas lies on the mesa, a flat region of high elevation at the base of the Sangre de Cristo Mountains, of which Hermit's Peak is a part. The mesa is dry, dusty, and flat, poor even for herding. Cactus grows in profusion, and in the spring purple verbena and other small flowering plants cover the plains for a short time. Deep arroyos are cut into the soft earth by streams which disappear completely in winter and summer. Behind the mesa lie the hills, rugged and partly volcanic in origin. The colors of their rocks range from deep grey to reds and mottled blues. Some of the hills contain limestone in which sea fossils can be found, and among these are springs of the purest water. There are many varieties of coniferous trees, including fine blue pine. Aspens grow wherever there is natural water or an irrigation ditch, but the most common deciduous tree is the scrub oak which keeps its brown leaves all winter and gives a characteristic ruddy tint to the hills. Water is scarce, and though it is said that with proper irrigation the region might be fertile, there now seems to be little attempt at cultivation. Fruit trees are uncommon. Green corn, beans and chile are grown by the natives on their ranches, but not in the town of Hot Springs itself. In Las Vegas almost all fruit and vegetables are imported from

*From Helen Zunser, "A New Mexican Village." JAF Volume 48, 1935, 115-178.

Colorado. Climate has something to do with this, for the winter is long and rigorous, starting in November, and not really ending until May. Summers are very hot and start abruptly.

The city of Las Vegas was at one time the wool center of the region. It has huge railroad yards that are practically deserted now that a shorter route to the coast has been built. Its population of ten thousand has divided itself in two, socially and geographically, and one group has little to do with the other. The "natives" or New Mexicans live in the adobe house of "old town," the "Americanos" in the wood and brick houses of "new town." There is a movie house, a five-and-ten-cent-store, a normal school, and Catholic convent. Most of the food stores belong to chains, and the natives from the surrounding country-side come to town to buy and trade their beans and chile, while the Americans bring in eggs and poultry from their ranches. But business is slow. The great wool industry has left the district. There is a small tourist trade in silver and baskets brought in from the Indian reservations, but it is remarked by American and native alike that the town is dead and not at all as it used to be.

Twelve miles out of Las Vegas on a fairly good road is Hot Springs, a town centered around a large hotel built here for gambling purposes forty or fifty years ago. The hotel passed from hand to hand and in time became a Baptist college. Other college buildings were put up, but all are abandoned now except the big red hotel, which is now a hotel once more but contains in addition a post office and the general store for the community. Around it cluster a number of summer cottages, which are popular in season chiefly because of the warm mineral spring that lies at the bottom of the hill. This spring gives the name "Hot Springs" to the small native community which has sprung up near it. The Baptists at one time roofed over part of the spring and diverted it into a tank for their own religious purposes, but the tank is now used as a swimming pool and seems to be one of the few places where natives and Americans meet socially.

Hot Springs, like Las Vegas, knows depression. The large ice company, which at one time shipped its product all over the state, provides the few jobs obtainable. There are about twenty families in the town, and they are all dependent upon the company. The blacksmith grinds tools for it, the biggest job in town is caring for the company horses and mules. Watching the company dams, lumber-cutting, road-fixing are company jobs and eagerly sought after by every man of the town. The sole American inhabitant of Hot Springs is the company superintendent. His white frame house with its pretty garden is the pivot of the town's economic activity. If you want work, you must go to him, and Mr. Jones enjoys the position of local despot. He has little use for the natives and considers them dirty, lazy, and loose morally. Nevertheless, his life is bound up with theirs. When he rides on his slow, white horse to inspect the dams, or drives his Ford into town on a shopping tour, he is greeted respectfully by those he passes. But behind his back there are lush names for him. *Calbo* (baldy) and *Chipolete* (buzzard) are among the mildest.

Altogether, including children, there are about sixty residents in Hot Springs. Their houses of mud-colored adobe or wood are huddled together facing the main road. On the opposite side of the road are the company's buildings, Mr. Jones's white house, the river, and the dams. In front of each adobe house the earth is dry and packed tight. The houses are built directly on the earth, without cellars, but most have wooden planks laid for floors. Near each house are little buildings, an adobe or wire enclosure for goats or chickens, an outside toilet, and usually the hive-shaped 'dobe oven that is used for baking in the summer. Goats are valued for food, and in the spring you will see the kidskins tacked to the 'dobe walls to dry and making a fine decoration. Burros or horses are sometimes hobbled near the house to graze, but usually they are not kept in town. There are plenty of dogs and skinny cats, but no birds except the wild ones — the flocks of startling bluejays or gorgeous bluebirds. For water one goes down to the river across the road and fills a barrel or bucket. Sometimes one bathes there, too.

Physically the people of Hot Springs tend to conform loosely to one type. They all have black hair, dark eyes, and sallow complexions. All of them are thin, and the stout man or woman is laughed at and regarded as a clown. The children are beautiful, like Polynesian babies, with their transparent complexions and luminous eyes swimming in the blueish white. But the older people are not usually good-looking. After twenty it is hard to differentiate age in women, and they all look overworked. The men do not deteriorate so quickly, and sometimes a married couple who are both of the same age will look as if there were a great age difference. The only distinguishing parts of their costume are the black shawls the older women wear, like those you see in Venice, and the large *sombreros* of which the men are so proud. All the clothes are bought in Las Vegas or from the mail order houses. The men wear overalls at work, and the women dim cotton dresses; but every girl has something in which to dress up, and at dances the women have bright silk dresses or wear their bridal dress until that wears out.

Our most intimate friends in Hot Springs were the Lorenz family. Antonio Lorenz was the village blacksmith and the richest member of his community. He had built a fine home for himself and his mother and, in addition, owned the blacksmith's shop about twenty feet from his door and another building as well. Antonio was a mechanic of sorts as well as a blacksmith, and when my friend's car broke down, it was taken to Antonio's shop for repairs. It was a cold day, and Antonio invited the two Americans to "visit my home" and warm up. This was the first of a long series of visits.

The Lorenz family knew that it was "Old Spanish long ways back" but that was all they speculated about their origin. None of them had been born in Hot Springs, which was a new community, and the father of the family had set up his blacksmith's shop there because of the construction work on the dam. Mr. Lorenz was described by his children as having been a fine man, a hard drinker, a skilled rider and dancer. His son Fernán remembered that his father used to take him along to the saloons and to visit the city women when he was still a little fellow. When he was about forty, he became subject to epileptic seizures and was confined to the nearby hospital. (It should be remarked that a large proportion of the natives are said at some time or other to go "out of their minds." Whether this is a fact, or whether it is usual for diseases to have delirious aspects, or whether it is because the state institution for the insane is near and this diagnosis is suggested, I do not know. There seemed to be no diminution of social prestige because of confinement, and there was no fear of hereditary taint.) In any case Lorenz was sent there and allowed to come home only on weekend visits. On one such occasion he had an attack when crossing the railway bridge, fell, and was killed.

The family was left in the mother's care, and the responsibility of family head devolved upon Antonio, who was then about fourteen years old. It should be understood how serious a charge this is. Parents have absolute authority over their children, and in the absence of a father this absolutism is given to the oldest son. Antonio was in the position of father to three brothers and one sister, the oldest two years younger than himself, the youngest a baby of one. "A child has to obey its older brothers and sisters," we were told, "anything they say, until he's married. Then he has to listen still, but he don't have to do what they say." At the time that we knew the family, his two married brothers would not dare to contradict Antonio or answer him when he reprimanded them, which it was both his privilege and duty to do. He kept his sister from marrying, greatly against her will, and his mother was obedient to his desire as she would have been to her husband's, although she exercised a remarkable power over him and her other children.

When we met him, Antonio was about twenty-seven years old. He was not very tall, but thin, sallow, and with rounded shoulders. He had an extraordinarily small and delicate skull, covered with silky hair, and thin, refined features, much resembling his mother's. He spoke slowly and in a sweet voice, and both voice and features very quickly showed any feeling of happiness or pain. Antonio was wracked by real or imagined sickness, and his house was full of all sorts of patent medicines. He bought in good faith any drug whose name he saw printed and plied himself with it. The blacksmith's occupation seemed preposterous for one so delicate, and he chose it simply because it was his father's before him. He read anything he could get hold of, mostly religious tracts, and his English was rather quaint and literary. He had an elementary knowledge of machine-repairing, could shoe a horse, and sharpen tools. His brothers laughed at his lack of strength, his fear of women, and his poor horsemanship. There was something delicate about everything he did. When he picked up the guitar, it was to play very softly; and he sang in a sweet voice, while Fernán bellowed forth in a huge voice and strummed ardently, and Alex, the best musician in the family, played very quickly and merrily, but not sweetly.

Fernán was as different from his brother as it is humanly possible to be. He was about six feet tall, broad-shouldered, with brilliant flashing eyes and a swaggering, erect carriage. He was strikingly handsome and aware of this. Antonio, with the exception of one trip to Colorado, had never been far from home. Fernán had traveled in Texas, Wyoming, Colorado, and Arkansas, and all over his own state. He had worked as foreman of a railroad gang, in the coal mines, on a dude ranch, as a shepherd and as a horsebreaker. He had a flashing sense of humor, a hearty laugh, and a great appetite for women. He liked to drink, get drunk, to ride, and exert himself physically in any way. Antonio probably had not a friend in his own town. Fernán was greeted by smiles and friendly greetings wherever he went, and was in great demand at dances and social gatherings of people. He was married and had two children, but was restless, and had often wandered from home. He never read, and could not be considered to have an abstract interest in any question in the world.

Yet Fernán was very largely governed and dominated first by his mother, whom he hated, and by his brother Antonio, whom he despised. He told us of riding to a dance on a horse once, determined to break it up because he was not invited, quite drunk of course. He rode onto the floor on his horse, but when he unexpectedly saw his mother there, he turned and left; and he told this sheepishly but naturally. His mother refused him permission to marry the girl he liked, and he had to marry someone of whom she approved. He professed religious skepticism; "When I meet a stranger, I say I'm same religion as him, so we should get on good," and he had not been to mass for two years, but he was always sobered and upset by his mother's religious talks and promised her to attend mass and was preparing to do so. He was skeptical of the magical power of those friends of his whom his mother called "witches" simply because of their morals; he insisted on a real doctor when someone was sick, and was not content with a woman "physician," but he did believe in witches and in the power of witches to do harm.

There were three other members of the Lorenz family. Amalia, the only girl, looked thirty rather than eighteen. She was skeleton-thin, haggard, absolutely charmless. She lived with her mother and Antonio and because of their strictures was allowed little of the normal life a girl led in town. For a reason we never knew, her brother did not want her to marry. Alex, twenty-three or -four, had just married and lived in his mother's old house. He was thin, sickly, and extremely lively, with a fine musical sense and a fund of humor, but with no special talents. He admired Fernan and was led by Antonio and only rarely flared up to say that he was a married man and could do as he chose. Rubin, the youngest, was about fifteen. He was a tall, handsome boy and resembled Fernán. In school he was bright, and Antonio was anxious to have him go on to high school at Las Vegas, but Fernán lamented the fact that he was brought up to act like a child and not like a man.

There is no surer clue to your friend than to know what he thinks and does about love and marriage. If you have learned that, then you can be sure that there is a relation of fundamental character between you. We were told a good deal by the people of Hot Springs, but not everything.

To begin with, the natives are all Roman Catholics. Their public and formal lives are bound by the ideals of chastity and monogamy, and they are further restricted by custom requiring the parents' consent before marriage. No rebel would take the chance of marrying without his parents' blessing, even though it is legally possible. Formerly, we were told, the parents had still more to say about arranging a marriage, but now there is usually courting between the boy and girl. In any case, the boy makes a formal request of the girl's father. He is then told that he will get a reply, favorable or otherwise, in a week. At the end of this time he usually receives a letter in which the decision is made known. If he is accepted, there will be great preparations for the wedding feast and dance, for which the groom, with the help of his relatives, must pay. He must also buy his bride a trousseau; if he can afford it, the custom is to buy two sets of clothing, two dresses, two slips, two pairs of shoes, and two hats. But in Hot Springs the brides were satisfied with a single set.

Marriage is considered final. The divorce laws of New Mexico are among the most liberal in the United States, a simple statement of incompatibility being sufficient; but as far as we learned, no native New Mexican thought in terms of divorce. There were quarrels, of course, and separations, but divorce was unknown.

The marriage age is uniformly low, and an unmarried adult was rare. Poor Amalia at eighteen was considered an old maid and quite done for. Alex's wife was fifteen when he married her, but this was unusually early, and something in between is usual. The husband is often a few years older than his wife. Fernán was twenty-one to Romancita's eighteen, Alex twenty-three to Mary's tender fifteen.

Florippa was the "light woman" of Hot Springs. There were two "goats" living in Monkeytown, so-called because they "went everywhere they were not wanted"; Florippa was called Mosca, the fly, because she had her feet in everybody's business.

Florippa was about eighteen, slim, dark-haired, and pretty. She had not done the hard work of the other women and had kept her looks better. She lived with her grandmother, a tiny flat-faced wrinkled creature, who received a soldier's widow's pension. Florippa had a brother who lived in Monkeytown, a redheaded *tonto*, who went by the name of *Americano* since it seemed obvious that his father was not a New Mexican. Florippa's mother had pretty much the same reputation as her daughter, and so had her grandmother in her day.

At the time we knew her, Florippa was spending much time at the house of Mr. Jones, for whom she did housework, and so she was prettily dressed and was able to buy her baby fine clothes. For Florippa had a baby, and its father, she said, was Alex. Now Alex had been courting her for a long time. She was indeed the reason why he, of all the men in Hot Springs, was never given work of any nature at the ice company. Once Alex met Florippa in Mr. Jones's car; he stopped the car and made her get out, and since then had not been given an hour's work. Meanwhile, and for a long time, he said, Alex had been "waiting for" Mercedes. Mercedes' brother was his best friend. The two lived with their father on a ranch near Hermit's Peak, and Mercedes and her brother sawed logs which their father sold for three dollars a cord. The little girl was unusually thin, and her shoulders were twisted. One day she saw Alex as he passed on the road, and she called him and said, "If you want me, better take me now; after, too late." They were engaged, but her father argued that she was just beginning to be useful to him and that anyhow she was too young to marry. When he received a letter from Florippa saying that Alex was promised to her, he broke the engagement at once; the two were not allowed to see each other, and when Alex came up to the ranch, Mercedes was locked in her room. Fernán, as elder brother, then went with Alex to see Mercedes' *còmpadre* and argued, "If you don't let her marry, she steal away with Alex. She no child, you can't watch her every minute." At long last the father consented to allow the ceremony. Florippa then went to a lawyer, hoping that she could sue Alex for breach of promise (for he had undoubtedly promised her), but her way of living would not allow this claim, and as a last resort she went to the priest and told him that she was pregnant. When Alex and Mercedes came down to Las Vegas for the ceremony, the priest refused to marry them. They then went through a civil ceremony but had to return and tell the wedding party that they were not really married. However, when Florippa heard that they were civilly married, she went to the priest herself and gave her consent. "She good girl. They make her do this," says Fernán, and "they" refers to enemies of the family. But he does not believe that the child is Alex's.

All this happened six months before we knew them. Florippa was now in disrepute in Hot Springs. She was not invited into houses, and there were some who would not go to any place where she was present. Romancita was once terribly upset to find that a chicken she had cleaned for Mr. Jones had been given to *Mosca*. If she had known, she would have refused to clean it for fear of Mrs. Lorenz.

But Mercedes and Alex were said to be very happy. They were both thin and "poor" (ailing) but were high-spirited, always laughing and joking. Poor Alex had no regular work, and many times the two went without food. Sometimes he helped Antonio at the forge, or sold wood in town, or went to her father's ranch to help with the plowing in exchange for board. His only property consisted of three horses, his faithful dog Tulips, and his guitar. Since he lived in Antonio's house and got occasional work from him, he obeyed him; and when at last he went, against Antonio's wishes, to a dance where Florippa was, he had to leave the house. But Romancita told us that every morning when she wakes, Mercedes first of all thanks her husband for taking her away from her father's house.

All the young women to whom we spoke deplored the fact that they had married early, and all spoke against the early childbearing. Minna, a young and attractive woman of twenty-one, was especially bitter. As Catholics they are not supposed to practice contraception, but some primitive methods are used. Mint is eaten in large quantities as an abortive. One baby we knew was suckled till he was twenty-eight-months-old, and it was the nuns who made the mother stop. This is a usual practice. Drinking large quantities of water and vinegar is thought to prevent conception, as is urinating immediately after intercourse. Withdrawal is practiced.

Children are much loved and sometimes spoiled by our friends in Hot Springs. Families are not very large—three or four children seem to be the rule—but there are more miscarriages and deaths than we are used to. The little ones were charming to look at, with dark hair and pear-shaped faces, olive skins faintly touched with red. They ran about without shoes, except on the coldest days, and with a minimum of clothes. Even little toddlers, swaddled in skirts, wear no drawers. We heard talk of modesty only from Mrs. Lorenz, and nakedness among children was not remarked on.

Boys seemed to be preferred to girls, and little Eloy was favored in the way of food, while Cecilia was laughed at for eating too much. The little girl, though older, was expected to give way to her brother in most matters. Religion was the most important part of their education. Romancita was very proud that five-year-old Cecilia loved to pray, and she and Fernán used to say that they would like her to be a nun when she grew up, to "pull us all up to heaven." When three-year-old Eloy was severely punished, his father would take a religious picture from the wall, put it on the floor in a corner, and make the child kneel and pray to it, which he did between loud wails. Cecilia had to pray for an hour this way once when she climbed on a horse that ran away with her.

All the children, until they are fifteen, go to the little school that stands in the midst of town. The teacher is a young woman appointed in Las Vegas—when we were there, a well-educated, young native woman, interested in her pupils. We were told that former political appointments had included a man who could neither read nor write. The teacher lived in town, in Alex's house; she spoke English in school, but Mexican outside, and the children could read more English than they understood.

Children eat at the family table, listen to discussion, and go out with their parents. They are whipped sometimes and are always respectful, but the relation is on the whole a loving one. They are taken to weddings and dances from babyhood, and it is usual at a dance to see a baby complacently feeding till his mother is invited to dance. Then she shoves her breast into her dress, deposits the baby on someone's lap or under a bench, and whirls off.

Once at a party where we were all dancing, the children were as usual watching intently from the side or sleeping under the tables and benches. This time the violinist announced a special dance for the little ones. All the children, from four to about twelve, were persuaded to dance, and no adults went on the floor. One little boy of seven or eight danced for the first time publicly. He was picked up at the end of the dance and carried around the room while everyone followed in a procession and brought him to his parents. They proudly promised to hold a dance on the next Saturday in honor of the occasion.

One of the best-dressed children in town, and certainly the one with the most obvious love lavished upon her, belonged to an aunt of the Lorenz family, a gaunt, sickly woman who had had twelve miscarriages and who had in her house a photograph of the only baby that had lived at all, in its flower-decked basket coffin. The nuns in Las Vegas had given her a little abandoned *Americano* girl to adopt, and the child was the only fair-haired one in town. Fidel, her father, doted on Elida, and in the early evening after work he would be seen about town, in his ramshackle Ford, driving her and six other youngsters up and down the road. Elida would be perched proudly beside him in her pink party dress that she herself had put on backwards.

The houses in Hot Springs are built of adobe, that is, local mud mixed with straw and dried in the sun. The 'dobe house has thick walls and deep-set windows; its roof is not flat but pointed. In other parts we saw flat roofs and ladders leading to them, but not here. The windows are glass, and the doors and sashes bought ready made, but the building itself is done by the local men. Antonio's house, the most pretentious, is of wood, with a porch and a carved edging around the porch roof. There is an old house in town with timbered and 'dobe walls, but we were told no one can build that way anymore. With land, a house costs under fifty dollars to build complete.

The interiors are small and consist usually of one large room divided by a partition, which sometimes reaches the ceiling, or by cretonne curtains. When a new addition is wanted, a new 'dobe house is built right next to the old, so that there is some difference in floor levels. The biggest house of this sort that we saw was at Lojito, where there were ten rooms, all in single file like a railroad car.

All the houses in which we were had plank flooring laid directly over the earth, so that when one stamped or danced a cloud of dust rose. We were told that in one poor house there was only trampled earth and no wooden floor.

The houses are unexpectedly clean inside. There is an almost complete absence of furniture, except for the most necessary purposes — beds, benches or chairs, a table, and an iron stove, in which wood is burned for heating and cooking. The whitewashed walls are hung with family photographs, pictures clipped from magazines, and many religious pictures. These are mostly huge florid chromos, for "only the old women like old pictures," and old ones are traded for new ones, though many of the large gilt frames are kept. Some have frames made of tin cans. There are many holy images, given by the nuns to the children for special accomplishment. Usually there is a pictorial calendar, many years old.

Every house has a chest or trunk which contains the family's good clothes and treasures, and it is kept locked under the bed. In Antonio's house there were some plants, and he had built a reed flower stand exactly like one we later saw in Taos. Fernán's house was quite bare when we knew it; its only ornament was an Indian rug, given to Romancita as a wedding present. But Fernán at once got busy and started to make furniture modeled on ours—a desk which he ornamented with cow and deer horns nailed to it and the instruction "Hat" printed under the largest of these.

The day starts early in Hot Springs, at four or five o'clock for those who have work and not much later for others. If he has work, the father of the family has his breakfast and is off; if not, he may have wood to cut or someone to see about a trade; or he watches a horse being shod, or helps someone find a horse lost in the canyon. More likely, he lies in bed half the day and sleeps or dozes. But his wife has plenty to do. She hauls water, chops wood, cooks, washes clothes at the hot springs if the weather is pleasant. She may visit the *commadre* next door to return some kerosene she borrowed; but informal visiting is rare, and on the whole relations are not very friendly in town and are even formal in spite of intimate knowledge of the details of each other's lives. There are many antipathies and dislikes. Family ties are far more important than friendly ones. Minna would sometimes call over the fence to Romancita, who was within hailing distance; but if they called to see each other, they usually dressed for the occasion. Once Romancita changed her dress and put on a hat to visit her mother-in-law, three minutes away. They all dressed up if it was necessary to visit Mr. Jones across the road.

The major burden of work falls upon the mother of the family. But even for her, the days, though full, are not hurried. Each day eases into the next without difficulty. Dances, Sundays, holidays, break the smooth routine. Saturday is shopping day, if there is someone who will provide a lift into town. This is a greatly anticipated event, and when she has finished buying her flour and lard, the mother will look in the store windows, wander around Woolworth's, and maybe treat herself to a small bottle of perfume. For this is her greatest luxury, and there can never be too much of a good smell.

On some days the *tonto* will be around for a meal, and he cannot be refused. He is the "village idiot" of our own less gentle parlance. In Hot Springs the *tonto* was an old-looking man of about fifty, harmless and mild, who wandered around and was never refused food or lodging wherever he presented himself. He was sometimes employed to carry messages, and he joined any crowd of people and was accepted good-naturedly by them. He was well dressed in a suit of new overalls that Mrs. Lorenz had gotten for him. Many practical jokes were played on him, and one time Alex dressed as a bride and went through a mock ceremony with him, since which time the poor old creature asked always to be taken to his wife.

There are always dogs around the house, thin and faithful, but usually half starved and fed only occasionally. We never saw a cat given food; they are thin and miserable and have to live only by what they can catch, so that they seldom grow to be much larger than kittens. Perhaps you cannot speak of people being cruel to their animals who do not have enough to eat themselves; yet during his mother's illness Antonio completely neglected the animals, shutting them out of the house for two weeks. Alex's dog Tulips, who loved him devotedly, was an exception and always shared what Alex had and never left his heels for a minute. Paloma, a tiny white dog, was Romancita's favorite, and well taken care of. But Chongo, Watch, Kimo, were half starved, and we once saw Buster, a mastiff hunting dog, attack a burro and start eating it, until he was chased off.

The horses, of which most families own one or two, are also half starved. Burros are more useful and are better taken care of. They are usually not kept in town but at a relative's ranch, or turned out to winter in the hills. Even the hardiest hill pony will not get fat on a diet of withered oak leaves, and those not born in the hills are half dead in the spring when the dead leaves are gone and the new ones not yet unfolded. At this time they literally drop in their tracks with hunger, and dead horses and horse skeletons are terribly common along the roads or in the fields. Then the dogs wax fat on horsemeat. Yet the horses are the only real wealth the people have and are necessary for spring plowing and hauling. They are spoken of with affection, too, but the most that is done for them is to hobble them near the river when the spring advances, and they are wanted. Often a horse that has been let loose in the canyon will run wild on the hills and cannot be caught again without difficulty. They mate and foal in the hills, and there is no attempt to arrange a particular breeding. The young colts run after their mothers. Riding in the canyon you sometimes came upon a wild colt; its eyes peered at you a minute from behind its mane, and then it was off, its long slender legs unfailing on the shifting stones.

The one really characteristic craft in Hot Springs is that of cooking. Weaving, spinning, metal work, all of these either never existed or have completely disappeared, and even in cooking our friends were both too poor often to indulge their skill and too quick to learn American methods.

When Romancita went into town on a Saturday, she would invariably buy lard, flour, coffee, and sugar. Sometimes jam and bacon were added as a special treat. Her neighbors bought exactly the same when they could. Fowl, milk, eggs, and green vegetables were added to the diet in the summer, when they could be gotten from the ranches cheaply. Vegetables were sometimes prepared for the winter months by drying; pumpkin, spinach, apples, and chile being treated in this way. Butter was a luxury. Sometimes they would buy watery chopped meat at the butcher's and large quantities of beans and chile from passing wagons. You understood why the natives were so thin when you saw how little they ate. They were content in the morning with some weak coffee and a bit of cold *tortilla* left from the night before. For lunch they might have some potatoes fried in lard, and the evening meal was usually not much greater. Yet our friends all loved good food, and when an occasion arose, they made meals that were not to be forgotten.

The staple food was the *tortilla*, a flat, pancake-shaped bread, baked fresh almost every day — in winter in the wood stove, in summer in the outside 'dobe oven. It was made of flour, much baking powder and a little lard and water. After kneading, the dough was allowed to rise a little under a cloth, then was cut into pieces and skillfully rolled with a short, round stick on a board adjusted to slope upwards. A cake of about five inches diameter was rolled out and placed inside the hot oven, on the oven floor, for about two minutes, then quickly taken out when it started to rise and placed directly on top of the stove until each side browned. Hot, they were delicious, but were usually eaten cold. The same *tortillas* were sometimes fried in deep fat and sprinkled with sugar. These were called *manuellas*. The worst *tortillas* we had were Mrs. Lorenz's — thin, saltless, and doughy. The best were Minna's — warm, fluffy, and thoroughly baked. *Tortillas* were served on a central plate, and everyone broke off as much from one as he wanted and used it as a fork and to polish off his plate. Beans, chile, and potatoes were served in separate bowls in the center of the table. Underneath the table, meanwhile, lurked the hungry dogs, their eyes never leaving your face.

Chile was another staple, usually eaten with beans but sometimes with meat.

A rope of chile — the dried pods of a spicy pepper — lasted a family a few weeks. The string was a double one, each strand about three feet long. It was kept in a covered box, and a little before meal time the cook picked out a few handfuls, making sure that there were not too many seeds and stems and no black pieces. The chile was then "toasted" in the oven for a few minutes until it began to crisp, then it was broken into a fine powder and mixed with cold water, the whole being kneaded into a pulp. This made hot on the fire was chile sauce. Fried meat, potatoes or onions were sometimes added, or big red kidney beans, stewed with bacon. As you ate chile, fine little beads of perspiration rose to your forehead. You looked across at Eloy, the four-year-old, calmly shoveling spoonfuls of it down his throat. Even the cat, under the table, was lapping up her share. You might waver, but you could not give in.

A great delicacy was *pinocha*. Young corn grains are allowed to sprout, then ground into flour. The meal is cooked all day over a slow fire, with a little water and flour added. The taste is sweet and fermented.

The great treat of the year was kid meat. This should be commemorated as among the best foods in one's experience. You got a new appreciation for Homer when you had eaten your share of kid meat seethed over the coals.

A kid cost fifty cents to a dollar. They were bought in the next town or at the goat farm at Lojito and brought back bleating over the saddle-bow. The kid *baa*ed all the way and tried to suck your fingers. It was tied indoors, so that the dogs could not get it, and the next morning was taken into the yard, hung head downwards, and its throat cut. Every drop of blood was caught, and all the entrails saved to be stewed with chile seeds. The rest was cut up in small pieces, stewed, broiled, or fried. The whole was consumed not two hours after the last bleat. All that was left over was the skin, tacked on the wall to dry.

By all standards, our friends at Hot Springs were poor. In money some earned nothing at all, most of them a few dollars, and one of them seven dollars weekly. Most of them received federal relief baskets. Their clothes were secondhand. If a house had a kerosene lamp, it was not used every night because fuel was expensive. Lard tins were used for pots and jam bottles for glasses. Shoes were worn sparingly, and the "hide" of the foot was trained to be tough and not mind cinders and snow. Yet there was a dignity about native life which was partly associated with poverty. Clothes and homes had an absence of cheap trinkets and decoration, not because they were not admired, but because they were too expensive. Yet sometimes we thought that the people did not have that love for abstract property which we ourselves take so much for granted. No one, for instance, thought twice about spending what money he had for a quart of whiskey for his friends. Every house had a musical instrument.

Maybe the liberal use of whiskey might be thought of as a means of escaping from a life that was hard in many ways, and the men drank a great deal, and looked upon drunkenness with delight, and talked about past and future feats with relish. Yet in many ways their lives were richer than our own, and they themselves thought so. Only once did we hear anyone express the wish to go away for good. It should not be supposed that they were unconscious of the brilliant landscape around them, the wonderfully sweet air. "Fine in the morning to get up," said Fernán, "hear all the little birds, air so fresh three o'clock. Make me a little coffee, breathe fresh air, feel fine." And they spoke of low, flatland with derision and were only mildly curious about the sea which they had never seen.

III

The Indian at Home

WE ALL SEE what our culture wants us to see, what it has trained us to see. When the Japanese artists looked upon Commodore Perry's men in 1853, they saw the first Caucasians Japanese eyes of their time had ever rested upon. But sight is the interaction of the eyes and the object and the consciousness, so what they painted was a crew of Japanese in American sailor suits. Their Americans all had the epicanthic fold (which we still erroneously see as the "slant eye"). When an African sculptor was commissioned to mold a bust of Queen Elizabeth a few years ago, he portrayed her with ulotrichous hair and everted lips, just as Benin sculptors have always seen Europeans. And when the first English colonial artists painted the American Indians, they represented these Mongoloid natives as red-skinned Caucasoids. Even the red skin was a wilful illusion, exaggerated to make some distinction between themselves and the aborigines; the Eastern Indians had the fashion of rubbing themselves with hematite, and the artists thereby created a race out of red ochre. Anthropologists still can be heard talking about a "red race," though the only red Indians are those mortified with embarrassment, a condition not usual with our aborigines.

The Indian has been for the last four hundred years a self-fulfilling stereotype, shaping himself on the template given him by the first explorers. He even sees himself as red. In the early days he tried to retain his reality. When he was first questioned about his gods, he spoke of *manitou*. Since *manitou* is the Algonkin term for what anthropologists now know as *mana* — the impersonalized, immaterial spiritual power flowing from the other-world to this earth — the nearest the Indians could come to a translation was "the great spirit." Spirit it was in accuracy, but the colonists had long since lost the concept of *mana* (except in its attenuated form of "grace" and "luck"), so they translated "spirit" back again into God. It was not long before the Indians had themselves believing in a father God, a Great Spirit in a stratospheric heaven. Today, if you ask a Zuñi Indian why his *kiva* was shaped in plan like a keyhole, he will tell you that it is because the *kiva* was the key to heaven. The archaeologist knows that the pin of the key shape was an evolution from the circular body of the prehistoric Pueblo pithouse, and the web of the key a development of the ancient ventilator shaft, but there is no use telling that to a Zuñi. The Pueblos used to dig a little hole in the floor of the *kiva*, which was the entrance to the spirit world; they called it the *sipapu*. So when the bar was constructed in the visitors' area of Mesa Verde National Park, it naturally inherited the name *Sipapu*.

This is the stuff and the work of folklore — to examine the traditional irrationalities and unrealities of a folk enclave and find out how they got that way. In other countries than America, however, folklore studies have another function. They are the materials of a nativistic endeavor like the Sioux "Ghost Dance," the Celtic Renaissance, the nationalism of the emergent nations. With a sociopolitical purpose, folklore is the *Urgeist* of a people, the uncontaminated soul of the *Herrenvolk*, the adamant touchstone of all that is true and good and vital in a nation. This is a holy and wholesome attitude so far as one's own country is concerned, but it wrenches outsiders into unrecognizability, as the Japanese artists did with Perry's sailors. We have learned a lot about psychology and sight over the centuries, and it is possible to reconstruct what the Indian was probably like when the

first white men met him. But now we have another distorting
force at work, a force that takes away where it pretends to give.
Morality in its only universally valid definition is *whatever con-
duces to the preservation of the group.* In some circumstances
this means thou shalt worship other gods than one, thou shalt
make graven images, thou shalt not honor thy father and thy
mother, thou shalt commit adultery, thou shalt kill, thou shalt go
on raiding parties for scalps and coups and horses, thou shalt
eat thy neighbor, thou shalt develop an asymmetrical cross-
cousin kinship terminology. But this definition of proper behavior is valid and mentionable only when it is not appended to
an identifiable group. So even in anthropological writings the
American Indians are portrayed as palefaced caricatures of their
real selves, attaining to a way of life and a character that was
never of their own making.

In the selections from the *Journal of American Folklore* that
follow, observers in a more liberal time tell us what the Indian
was like before he decided to remold himself into a white Anglo-
Saxon Protestant Republican. If the image he presents is not to
our liking, the mote is in our own eye.

Now that we no longer engage in the practice of slavery, we
look upon the institution with all the sanctimonious intolerance
that teetotalers have for tipplers. As a matter of ethnographic
fact, however, slavery seems to be an unavoidable phase in the
evolution of culture. Whenever a society gains control of its food
supply, an accomplishment that usually means also the domestication of animals, it quickly notices that human beings are like
all other domesticable animals (except the troublesome cat) —
they are gregarious and they are leader-following. They are, in
short, ideally qualified to be domesticated, to be slaves. Slavery
continues until the owning society advances to the technological
level where human labor is not worth the keeping. Morality has
nothing to do with it.

Slavery was widespread in aboriginal America. Nearly every
tribe that could afford to keep slaves did so. Modern apologists,
imposing their own guilt upon the Indians, disguise the fact of
slavery. Edmund Wilson in his *Apologies to the Iroquois* speaks
of whites who were "adopted" by the Indians during raids on
settlements. Jack D. Forbes talks about the Quechans of the
Colorado as surviving the onslaughts of white encroachment,

but the fact of the situation is that the Quechans survived because the whites came in and saved them from the Maricopas and Gila Pimas and Halchidomas and Walapais and Havasupais and Cahuillas and Paipais and Kiliwas and Halyikwamais and Kohuanas, all of whom were fighting each other for slaves. Dale Van Every certifies in his book *Disinherited* that there was an "instinctive sympathy" between the Cherokee and the Negroes a century and a half ago, a sympathy based upon the "ingrained Indian abhorrence of slavery as an institution." But a census of the Cherokee Nation in 1825 lists 15,563 Indians and 1,277 Negro slaves — slaves, moreover, who were prohibited from owning stock, voting, or marrying Indians. The Cherokee, incidentally, were the victors in a bloody war to extermination or exile with other Indian tribes — the Yamasee, Creek, Choctaw, Shawnee, Catawba, Tuscarora, and Chickasaw — over which tribe should have the monopoly of selling slaves to the white South. The Seminoles took a different approach: they stole slaves and dashed over the international line into Spanish Florida, thereby establishing squatters' rights to Florida just recognized by the Indian Claims Commission. The Commission offered the Seminoles the usual cash settlement, but the Seminoles still take a different approach: they don't want the money; they want Florida.

The Haida (spelled "Haidah" in Deans's anecdote of the biter bit) were members of the Northwest Pacific Coast culture, in aboriginal and early contact times one of the earth's most frenetically Dionysiac people. Class and class contention, economic and social competition, and downright orneriness were developed to a level indistinguishable from mass insanity. One of the 658 titles among the Kwakiutl, neighbors of the Haida, was translatable as "He Who Creates Trouble All Around." The Haida were among the most enterprising of the slave-hunting Indians; they regularly made raids on places a full seven hundred miles away. Slaves in the Northwest Pacific Coast could hardly call their masters benevolent, for slaves were killed for potlatches, on the death of an owner, at the erection of a new house, or whenever their owner felt the need to demonstrate conspicuous consumption. The slaves in Deans's story were fortunate, for the Haida and their neighbors had other habits generally considered unpleasant in this age of nonviolence — they were headhunters and cannibals as well as slave traders.

WHAT BEFELL THE SLAVE SEEKERS*

A STORY OF THE HAIDAHS ON QUEEN CHARLOTTE'S ISLAND, B.C.

From time immemorial until the year 1875, or perhaps even later, every native tribe on the Northwest Coast of America not only used to keep slaves, but often made raids on other tribes, especially on those with whom they were not on friendly terms, and kidnapped all persons on whom they could lay their hands, in order to obtain slaves for domestic use and also for selling to others.

Early in the present century a large party of these Haidahs embarked in one of their large canoes, which hold from twenty-five to thirty warriors, for the purpose of making a raid on the Kittamats, a tribe living opposite the Queen Charlotte's Islands, on the mainland of British Columbia, upon the north arm of Gardner's Canal. Though their absence was prolonged, their wives and relatives, who expected them to be absent from five to six weeks, were not greatly disturbed. When weeks turned into months, their friends became alarmed, and strong search parties were sent forth in all directions. After visiting many islands and seeking far and wide, these tired of the fruitless search and gave up the wanderers as lost.

The slave raiders had intended to go to Kittamat. Had the search proceeded thither, such a course, under the existing conditions, would have been equivalent to a declaration of war. Pride and ignorance of the languages of their neighbors were the principal cause of the wars and ill feeling between the various nations; for example, some ill-timed joke would, through ignorance on the part of the members of another tribe, be construed into insult, which their pride would not allow to go unpunished. On other parts of this coast the traders found it necessary to create a trade language or jargon, the Chinook; I know nothing that has done so much to civilize our native races. It stimulated friendly intercourse between tribes, by enabling them to converse with each other, whence sworn foes became lasting friends; and when meeting at any of the Hudson Bay Company's trading posts, they would converse for hours of relatives who disappeared and never were heard of again. A few years ago the Haidahs and their ancient foes, the Kittamats, met and settled old feuds in a friendly manner. Among other topics, the conversation turned on the raid mentioned, when the following facts were elicited:

A long while ago, a large party of Kittamats were on a hunting and

*By James Deans. JAF Volume 1, 1888, 123-124.

fishing expedition, and having reached a little island, in which there was a good harbor, they hauled up their canoes. One of the party, during their stay, happening to go into the long grass and the bushes, found concealed a large canoe. This they hastily launched and departed, taking the canoe and everything in it away with them, well knowing it to be a Haidah canoe, and that its owners in all probability were not far off. When they reached home they told how they had taken the canoe and left the Haidahs to perish. Some time after, when they thought that the party on the island would be in a starving condition, and consequently glad to accept any terms, a large party of Kittamats went to look for them. Sailing cautiously around the island, they were seen by the Haidahs, who gladly hailed them. Going on shore, the latter presented a pitiable appearance and seemed ready to accept anything in preference to death from starvation. The Kittamats demanded what they were doing there. In answer they said they came to hunt, and that in their absence their canoe had been stolen, and they expressed their desire to get away. The visitors told them to come on board, and they would see what could be done.

These terms the sufferers disliked, but there was no choice. As soon as all were aboard, sail was made by their captors for the Kittamat village, where all the prisoners were made slaves. Some were kept for a time in the village, while others were sold to distant tribes; at the time of the interview, nothing was known, even to their captors, as to the whereabouts of any of them, if alive. So much is certain, that none of them ever returned to their native village. And thus it happened that the slave raiders were themselves made slaves.

Tastes in food are circumstantially determined. If Norwegian cows can be persuaded to eat fish, there is no metabolic reason why Haida should be required to defend their gustatory preference for people, who are, after all, made of meat. Washington Matthews, the eminent authority on Indians at the turn of the century, gives us in the following report of Navaho ichthyophobia a secondhand testament to the palatability of puppies. Having eaten dog while living with the aborigines of the Australian western desert, I can affirm firsthand that dogs are infinitely preferable to fish.

It is the tabu that requires explanation. The burden of accountability rests upon the abstainer in food as well as in drink. Yet curiously, every people has its cultivated dislikes. Even the Australian natives, who are reputed to eat anything digestible, cannot bear the thought of eating oatmeal porridge. Polynesians dote on the palolo worm, one of the earth's most repulsive organisms, but they find rice disgusting. Most of these food tabus defy rational explanation, for there is seldom any rationality in them. In this article Matthews suggests a reason for the Navahos' abhorrence of fish — an abhorrence, by the way, that was fairly common among the Great Basin and Oasis Indians and that has much to recommend it. In Australia once more, snakes are given the same respect as fish are among the Navaho, because in a land of almost unique aridity the presence of snakes usually means the presence of water. On the logical inference of *post hoc, ergo propter hoc*, the aborigines call waterholes "snake-possessing places" and propitiate the snake by keeping the premises clean, a courtesy they unfortunately do not accord other sources of water, such as drinking supplies brought in by anthropologists.

ICHTHYOPHOBIA*

In the year 1866, after I had spent about twelve months on the Upper Missouri among some of the most primitive tribes then within our borders, I came on to Chicago, and there made the acquaintance of a gentleman who had recently returned from New Mexico, having spent a year or more among the Navaho Indians. Oddly enough the gentleman's name was Fish, although this fact, like the vernal blossoms, had nothing to do with the case, since the Indians did not fear him.

In comparing notes of our experience among the Indians, he asked me, "Do the tribes of the Upper Missouri eat fish?"

"Of course, they do," I said.

"Is there anyone in the world who will not eat a good fish if he can get it?" I added.

"Yes," he replied; "the Navahoes will not eat fish; they will not even touch a fish, and I have known them to refuse candies that were shaped like fish."

At the time, although I had every reason to believe that my friend was a truthful person, I was half inclined to believe that his was a "fish story" in more senses than one, or that he had made some error in observation. But that was in the days of my youthful ignorance. I knew not then the extent and nature of the customs of tabu. I did not realize that I was myself the victim of tabu practices just as unreasonable as that of the Navaho fish-haters.

Fourteen years later I found myself a neighbor of these same Na-

*From Washington Matthews, "Ichthyophobia." JAF Volume 11, 1898, 105-112.

vaho Indians, and one of the first subjects I proceeded to investigate was the fish tabu, of which I had learned years before. I found that my friend, Mr. Fish, had told me the truth but had not expressed his case as strongly as he might have done. I found that the Navahoes not only tabued fish but all things connected with the water, including aquatic birds. Speaking of the Navaho repugnance to fish with the landlady of the Cornucopia Hotel (a slab shanty) at Fort Wingate, she related the following as a good joke on the Indian. She employed a young Navaho warrior to do chores around her kitchen. The Navaho warrior has no pride about the performance of menial labor. He will do almost anything at which he can earn money, and this one would do any work for her but clean fish. He would eat, too, almost anything in her kitchen except fish. Noticing his aversion to the finny tribe, she one day sportively emptied over his head a pan of water in which salt fish had been soaked. The Indian screamed in terror, and, running a short distance, tore in haste every shred of clothing from his body and threw it all away. She learned that he afterwards bathed and "made a lot of medicine" to purify himself of the pollution. He never returned to work for her, so this little trick cost her a good servant.

Our philanthropists wonder at the reluctance of Indians to send their children a distance to school and think it is but foolish stubbornness. They cannot realize that, in addition to many practical and sentimental reasons, there are long-cherished religious scruples to be overcome — reasons which are the most potent of all — and among these not the least is that they know their children will be obliged to violate tribal tabus. The Navahoes have heard from returning pilgrims that the boy who goes to the Indian school in the East may be obliged to eat geese, ducks, and fish, or go hungry; or that, if he eats not at first of these abominations, he may be ridiculed and chided till he changes his customs.

"What foolish scruples!" we say, and yet fail to realize that we all refuse certain edible and wholesome articles as food for no good reason that we can assign. What civilized father would send his child to a distant boarding school where he might be obliged to eat stewed puppy? Yet I have been informed by those who have tasted it that it is a very palatable dish. But we can find a better illustration of our case than this: there are many among the most cultured of our Christian communities who, for religious reasons, refrain on certain days and at certain seasons from articles of food which at other times are eaten. Such persons would not willingly send their children to places where they would be compelled to disregard these fasts. We may all understand and approve the sentiments which actuate them; yet we seem unable to extend an equal consideration to savages who are, perhaps, actuated by equally worthy motives. Often among the Navahoes children returning from eastern schools fall into feeble health. Their illness is almost always attributed to the violation of tabu while they were away from home, and costly healing ceremonies are performed in order to remove the evil effects of the transgression.

But these are not the principal lessons I desire to draw from the study of fish tabu. Ichthyophobia is not confined to the Navahoes; they suffer from it in common with many other tribes. We will endeavor to inquire into the real causes which lead to this particular form of tabu.

When I first obtained confirmation of the existence of this tabu in New Mexico, I asked for reasons, just as the author of the quoted article asked for them, not because I expected to get a true reason, but because I was anxious to get an insight into their modes of thought. Various trifling explanations were given and trifling tales were told, but the usual explanation was simply that fish made them sick; that they had heard of Navahoes who had eaten fish and become sick; that the thought of eating fish disgusted them. Such remarks were, no doubt, true; but while they accounted for the continuance of the tabu they did not account for its origin. There are few white men who would not be sickened if they unknowingly ate the flesh of a rat or a dog and were afterwards told what the food was, or if they ate it under constraint of hunger or from bravado. This is but natural; yet who among us could explain to some inquiring Indian why the flesh of these animals disgusts us? They are as healthy and as cleanly in their habits as the hog.

If you importune an Indian for an explanation, for a cause, you are very likely to get one, particularly if he finds, as was the case with the Apache just quoted, that there is a prospect of getting a piece of tobacco for his pains. The story here related, which is wisely discredited by Mr. Bicknell, may have been coined for the occasion; but it is more likely that it has been current for some time among the Indians. White men are not the only ones who are importunate to know the why and the wherefore. The inquisitive small boy whose business in life it is to ask questions exists among the savage as well as among the civilized; and there are boys of older growth who pester their seniors for explanations. To satisfy the mind of the inquirer with something in accord with his mode of thought, with the grade of philosophy which he has reached, is the aim of the man, in all ages of the world, who would gain and retain a reputation for wisdom. Milton's Adam explains everything to Milton's Eve according to the philosophy of Milton's time. Modern science has its myth-makers, no less than the wild Apache.

Mr. Bicknell considers the myth which he recounts of no value as an explanation. In this we agree with him, and regard the reasons which he offers in support of his opinion as cogent. But another reason which was given to him deserves more consideration. It is this: the fish is "all [the] same [as] water." This expression he supposes to mean, that the fish was to the Indian tasteless and useless for food; but a little reflection will, I think, show that this cannot be the meaning; for, if the Apaches never eat fish and have not eaten it for generations, they can know nothing of the taste or nutritive qualities from either personal experience or tribal tradition. If they should ask any of their fish-eating neighbors how the stuff tasted, they would get only favorable reports; or, if they should smell it broiling on their neighbors' fires, their noses would be regaled only by enticing odors. We may fairly say that Mr. Bicknell has not interpreted correctly the expression, "All same water." Let us see if it may have some other significance.

I questioned my friend Mr. Cushing, by letter, with regard to the existence of the fish tabu among the people of Zuñi (neighbors of the Navahoes), and of other pueblos with which he might be acquainted, and received the following reply, under date of October 5, 1897:

The Zuñis, like the Navahoes, will not, under any circumstances, eat fish or any other water animal. The reason is this: Abiding in a desert land, where water is scarce, they regard it as especially sacred; hence all things really or apparently belonging to it, and in particular all creatures living in it, are sacred or deified. But, in the case of the fishes, they eat water, chew it, and are therefore, since they also breathe water and the currents or breaths of water, especially tabued. The Zuñi name for the Isletas is Kyas-i-ta[w]-kwe, Fish Cannibals, because they ate fish formerly. I understand that the Keres share the Tinneh and Zuñi taboo, but do not know.

Amongst the Zuñis, a primary mode of classifying animals, with reference to their sacredness, is according to their relationship to water. Thus the animals of prey are, except in hunting and war, less sacred than game animals, and water animals are, in matters of peace, health, and life-making, the most sacred of all. Now these degrees of sacredness of the three classes of animals are strictly correlated to their observed ways of taking water. The animals of prey lap water; the game animals suck or sip it; the water animals gulp it; while fish not only drink water but, as their name implies, also breathe and even prepare and "eat" it, as we do sweet food.

There is a further reason why, with the Zuñis, fish are, in common with certain water snakes, sacred above all other creatures of the water: in that country fish live only in living springs, or in rivers perennially fed by springs. It is this which distinguishes them from such rainwater gods as tadpoles and frogs, and it is this which causes the Zuñis to believe that the water of springs (the water of life *par excellence*) belongs to the fish; they can pray it up from the depths of the underworld, as tadpoles and waterfowl can pray it down from the skies.

Under these circumstances, the eating of fish seems to the Zuñis no less than cannibalism, and is followed by the direst consequences, chief among which is madness—that kind of madness the first symptoms of which are incessant gasping and swallowing—or the giddiness which comes from gazing down into swift flowing waters, and is considered so fatal to reproduction that pregnant women must be guarded from the sight of moving water, fish, and water reptiles, no less than from fierce and fearful things.

This opinion of Mr. Cushing's agrees with one I had already formed with regard to the Navahoes, after long study of the traditions and customs of this tribe. Living in a desert land where water is so scarce and so obviously important to life, they come in time to worship water, either in itself or through water spirits and water gods. Regarding the water as sacred, it is an easy step for them to regard as sacred everything that belongs to the water — above all, fish, which cannot live away from the water. Hence it becomes a sacrilege to kill the fish or eat its flesh, and hence the significance of the Apache explanation of the tabu — that fish is "all same water."

But there are other interesting points connected with the study of this tabu among the Navahoes. From the evidence afforded by their physical appearance, tribal organization, traditions, and religious practices, we may confidently say that the Navahoes are a very mixed race. Their language is in the main of the Athapascan stock, and is related to tongues spoken in the far North, even within the Arctic circle; but there is some admixture of the languages of the South, and we know that their blood, perhaps even more than their language, is derived from the old pueblo and cliff-dwelling tribes of the arid region. In reading about the Athapascan tribes of the North and of the Pacific Coast, who dwell, be it remembered, in a land well watered, I never saw any mention of the fish tabu; yet, to learn with greater certainty of its existence or absence among these tribes, I communicated on the subject with Dr. Franz Boas, who, more than any other scholar, has investigated the various Athapascan tribes. The Doctor's reply, under date of October 7, is as follows: "The northern Athapascan tribes have no tabu against fish; on the contrary, they almost subsist on fish for a considerable part of the year."

If the Navahoes and the Apaches, as we have reason to believe, derived their Athapascan blood from the tribes of the North and of the Pacific, and if their Athapascan ancestors entered, as we have also reason to believe, New Mexico and Arizona within a comparatively recent period — say within five hundred years — it may fairly be inferred that they adopted this tabu since their migration from representatives of the sedentary tribes of this region, whom they met in friendly intercourse, or who became, in various ways, adopted into the Navaho nation. Of course, the desert environment would tend much to hasten or facilitate the adoption of the tabu if it were, as we suppose, the origin of it.

The example, as instanced by Mr. Cushing, of the people of the pueblo of Isleta, on the Rio Grande, who were once fish-eaters, but are no longer such, illustrates the readiness with which, under a new example and environment, a people may adopt a new tabu, and encour-

ages us to believe that similar causes may have operated to produce
similar effects among the Navahoes.

―――――――――――――

In ancient times a game was invented in India called *pachisi* or
parcheesi, the ancestor of Monopoly and all board games where
counters are moved by chance. But before Columbus or any
other white man found Mexico, the Aztecs were playing a game
called *patolli*, that had dozens of elements in common with the
classic game of India—a cross-shaped board, a separate scoring
board, rectangular stations, the idea of "killing" an opponent's
man, the idea of alternate moves, penalty stations, movable
symbols, flat dice, and others. The anthropological problem is
how the two games appeared in areas where there was no other
certain evidence of contact before the Age of Discovery. The
first solution that comes to mind is independent invention or
polygenesis. This has much to recommend it, since almost every
invention is polygenetic, regardless of how firmly people committed to simple solutions attribute inventions to Great Men. But
standing against this explanation is the complexity of the two
games, for the more complex a trait or artifact, the less likeli-
hood there is of independent invention. The great nineteenth-
century anthropologist Edward Tylor believed the game had
come to Mexico from India in precontact times; later anthropologists could not accept that explanation in the presence of the
fact that nothing else had diffused. Why import a game and reject more valuable contributions of the vastly superior Indian
civilization? We know the answer now—Tylor was right. Recent archaeological excavations in Mexico have turned up other
unquestionable borrowings from Asia.

The point here is that in primitive times—even in the Paleolithic—objects and ideas moved from region to region with almost the same inevitability, if not the same speed, as they do
now. And it is a mark of man's perversity that the things that
diffused most readily were the apparently useless things, like
songs, myths, and games. Even where neighboring peoples
looked upon each other as food, these things moved freely.

Folklorists recognize molecular elements of story which they
call "motifs"—components that cannot be further simplified
without destroying their nature. Thus we have the Three Wishes
motif, the Pardoner's Tale motif (found in India twenty-five
hundred years ago and in *The Treasure of the Sierra Madre*),

and thousands of others, all noted and numbered by folklorists. "How the Indians Taught Kindness" is an elaboration of the motif known as the Magic Flight or the Obstacle Flight, an escaping device whereby fugitives delay pursuit by throwing behind them three objects that magically transform themselves into great obstacles in the way of the pursuer. Most commonly in European versions, the three objects are a whetstone (which becomes a mountain range), a comb (which becomes a forest), and a mirror (which becomes a lake).

The fascinating thing about the Magic Flight is its universal distribution. It is found all over the world. An early, inchoate example is Medea's impeding the pursuers of Jason by throwing fragments of her brother's body into the sea. In its developed state, the motif appears in a Japanese Shinto myth written down as early as 712 A.D. The motif is known from oral literature in Asia, Siberia, Africa, Malaysia, North and South America. There is no question about its having been borrowed and lent wherever it is found. It is one of those ideas that do not particularly appeal to our sophisticated imagination but which other people liked as well as we like the Cinderella story.

HOW THE INDIANS TAUGHT KINDNESS*

White Loon lived with his mother at the edge of the forest. He was a handsome youth and much loved by the people of the tribe. He loved White Wing, a beautiful girl of a nearby village, and she returned his

*From Jessie E. Baker, "Piankishaw Tales." JAF Volume 44, 1931, 182-191.

love. Her parents, however, chose that she should marry Black Beaver because he was a great hunter, and both White Loon and White Wing knew that if she disobeyed her parents she would be taken off and killed by the old witch who punishes such disrespect. In their despair the two lovers left their homes and wandered about calling on the spirits. They did not care where they were going. So they met each other in the woods.

In the morning they came to a camp of Indians. On the edge of the camp lived an old woman. White Loon had nothing to give her, so he gathered a great pile of wood. When they were leaving she gave him a piece of rock and told him to drop it when he had need of anything. Soon the lovers saw that they were pursued by the girl's parents. White Loon dropped the rock, and a ridge of rock rose between them and their pursuers so that they escaped.

Again that night they came to a camp, and the youth gathered wood for an old woman, who in sign of gratitude gave him a thorn. She told him to drop it in need. That day White Wing's parents were almost upon them again when the youth dropped the thorn, and a great thorn hedge sprang up to protect them. The girl's parents had to find stones and make themselves stone axes before they could pursue them again.

A third time White Loon prepared wood for an old woman, and this time he received a cactus leaf. When their pursuers were almost upon them the youth dropped it and a forest of cactus sprang up.

The lovers came to a river. There was no boat. They asked for supernatural help, and the spirit took the dipper and made a path for them through the river. As soon as they had crossed, the waters rushed together, and the parents were left without any means of crossing. The girl's father turned back, but the mother was not so easily discouraged and pushed on.

The lovers found refuge with a village who killed a calf and scattered its blood about to deceive the girl's mother who was following them. When she came up to the village, another old woman to whom the lovers had been kind put into the boy's hand a feather and told him to drop it. As he did so, the lovers turned into ducks and flew away. They built their nest by a beautiful lake and lived happily.

This story is told to children to teach them kindness to old people.

The following "Sun and Moon" myth from the Blackfoot Indians is made up of three important motifs—the Magic Flight, the Pursuing Head, and the Rejected Gifts. All of these are found in places that the American Indians never visited, but the story idea passed to them from one people or another in a prehistoric bucket brigade. Curiously again, the motif of the Rejected Gifts has been used by disparate people to account for their own inferior culture when confronted by our modern technitronic civilization. Several of the Cargo Cults of the southwest Pacific — the oceanic equivalent of the American Indian Ghost Dance — incorporate into their associated myth the notion that in the distant past a god gave them the choice of such heavenly inventions as the gun or the bow and arrow, or motorboats/outrigger canoes, or sacked rice/*taro*. In each case the natives chose the "rubbish," and that is why they are in such poor condition today.

George Bird Grinnell was one of the great chroniclers of Plains Indian culture. His books *The Fighting Cheyenne* and *The Cheyenne Indians* are undisplaceable classics of ethnographic writing, but only slightly better known than his *Beyond the Old Frontier, The Story of the Indian, Blackfoot Indian Stories*, and *By Cheyenne Campfires*. He had the following myth about the Blackfoot creator, Napi, from an old blood chief, Menestokos, who in turn had it from his great-grandmother.

THE SUN AND THE MOON — A BLACKFOOT MYTH*

A long time ago, very far back, before any of these things had happened, or these stories had been told, there was a man who had a wife and two children. This man had no arrows nor bow, and no way to kill food for his family. They lived on roots and berries.

One night he had a dream, and the dream told him that if he would go out and get one of the large spider webs, such as hang in the brush, and would take it and hang it on the trail of the animals where they passed, he would be helped, and would get plenty of food. He did this, and used to go to the place in the morning and find that the animals had stepped in this web, and their legs were tangled in it, and they would make no effort to get out. He would kill the animals with his stone axe, and would haul the meat to camp with the dog *travois*.

One day, when he got to the lodge, he found that his wife was perfuming herself with sweet pine, burned over the fire, and he suspected at once that she had a lover, for he had never seen her do this before.

*From George Bird Grinnell, "A Blackfoot Sun and Moon Myth."
 JAF Volume 6, 1893, 44-47.

He said nothing. The next day he told his wife that he must set his spider web farther off. He did so and caught an animal and brought part of the meat back to camp. The next morning he told his wife to go and bring in the meat that he had left over in the hills.

Now the woman thought that her husband was watching her, so when she started she went over the hill out of sight, and then stopped and looked back at the camp. As she peered through the grass, she saw her husband still sitting in the same place where he had been when she left him. She drew back and waited for a time, and then went out and looked a second time and saw him still sitting there. A third time she came back and looked, but he was still there, so she went off to get the meat.

The man at length got up and went to the crest of the hill and saw that his wife was gone. He spoke to his children, saying: "Children, do you ever go with your mother to gather wood?"

They said: "No, we never go there."

He asked: "Where does your mother go to get her wood?"

They answered: "Over there in that large patch of dead timber is where she gets it."

The man went over to this big patch of timber and found there a den of large rattlesnakes. One of these snakes was his wife's lover. He gathered up wood and made great piles of it and set them on fire. Then he went back to the camp and said to the children: "I have set fire to that timber, and your mother is going to be very angry. She will try to kill us. I will give you three things, and you must run away. For myself, I will wait here for her." He gave the children a stick, a stone, and a bunch of moss, and said: "If your mother runs after you, and you see that she is coming up to you, throw this stick behind you on your trail; and if she comes up with you again, throw the stone back. If that does not check her coming on, wet this moss, and wring out the water on your back trail. If you do as I tell you, your mother will not kill you nor me." The children started off, as he had told them to. Then he went out into the brush and got another spider web and hung it over the door of the lodge.

When the woman, a long way off, looked back and saw that her timber patch was all on fire she felt very sorry, and she ran back as hard as she could toward the lodge, angry and feeling that she must do something. When she came to the lodge, she stooped to go in at the door, but got caught in the cobweb. She had one foot in the lodge, but the man was standing there ready, and he cut it off with his stone axe. She still struggled to get in, and at last put her head in, and he cut this off. When he had done this, the man ran out of the lodge and down the creek. His children had gone south. When the man ran down the creek, the woman's body followed him, while the head started after the children, rolling along the ground.

As they ran away, the children kept looking behind them to see whether their mother was following, but they did not see her coming until the head was close to them. The older of the two, when he saw it, said: "Why, here is our mother's head coming right after us!"

The head called out and said: "Yes, children, but there is no life for you." The boy quickly threw the stick behind him, as he had been told to do, and back from where the stick struck the ground it was all dense forest.

The children ran on, but soon they again saw behind them the head coming. The younger said: "Brother, our father said to throw the stone behind us if our mother was catching up. Throw it." The elder brother threw the stone, and when it struck the ground it made a high mountain from ocean to ocean—from the north waters to the south waters. The woman could see no way to pass this wall, so she rolled along it till she came to a big water. Then the head turned and rolled back in the other direction until it came to another big water.

There was no way to pass over this mountain. As she was rolling along, presently she came to two rams feeding, and she said to them: "Open a passage for me through this mountain, so that I can overtake my children. They have passed over it, and I want to overtake them. If you will open a passage for me, I will marry the chief of the sheep."

The rams took this word to the chief of the sheep, and he said: "Yes, butt a passage through the mountains for her." The sheep gathered and the rams began to butt the mountains. They knocked down rocks and peaks and cliffs and opened ravines, but it took a long time to butt a passage through the mountains. They butted, and butted, and butted till their horns were all worn down, but the pass was not yet open. All this time the head was rolling around very impatient, and at last it came to an anthill. It said to the ants: "Here, if you will finish the passage through those mountains, I will marry the chief ant." The chief of the ants called out all his people, and they went to work boring in the mountains. They bored a passage through the mountains south of the Dearborn River. This tunnel is still to be seen, and the rocks about it all bored and honeycombed by the ants. When they had finished the passage, the head rolled through and went rolling down the mountain on the other side.

The children were still running, and had now gone a long way, but after a long travel they could see the head rolling behind them. The younger one said to the older: "Brother, you must wet that moss"; and as they were running along they soaked it, and it was ready. When they saw that the head was catching up, they wrung out the bunch of moss on their trail behind them, and at once found that they were in a different land, and that behind them was a big water surrounding the country which they had just left. That is why this country is surrounded by water. The head rolled into this big water and was drowned.

When the children saw that the head was drowned, they gathered wood and made a large raft, binding the sticks together with willow bark, and at a place west of here, where the water is narrowest, they tried to sail back to the land that they had left. The wind was blowing from the west, and helped them, and they used sticks for paddles, and at last they reached the land.

When they had landed, they traveled east through countries occupied by many different tribes of Indians, to get back to the land that they had left, and when they reached this country, they found it occupied by a different people, the Snakes and the Crows. So the youngest boy said: "Let us separate. Here we are in a strange country and among a different people. You follow the foot of the mountains and go north, and I will follow the mountains south, and see what I can discover." So they separated, one going north and the other south.

One of these boys was very shrewd and the other very simple. The simple one went north to discover what he could and to make people. The smart boy is the one who made the white people in the South, and taught them how to make irons and many other things. This is why the whites are so smart. The simple boy who went north made the Black-feet. Being ignorant, he could not teach them anything. He was known across the mountains as Left Hand, and in later years by the Blackfeet as Old Man *(Nápi)*. The woman's body chased the father down the stream, and is still following him. The body of the woman is the moon, and the father is the sun. If she can catch him she will kill him, and it will be always night. If she does not catch him, it will be day and night as now.

At Cave Hill in the far northwest of South Australia, where white man intrudes only with a desert vehicle, water storage tanks, and transceiver radios, there is an unnaturally shaped natural formation that the natives say is the remains of a totemic hero who once pursued the Kungkarungkara — the "Seven Sis-ters" — across the antipodean skies. Farther west from Cave Hill the pursuer was Kidilli, the Moon, from whom the sisters were rescued by the greatest of Australia's totemic ancestors, the twin god Wati Kutjara.

This explanation of the cluster of stars known to astronomers as the Pleiades is similarly explained in the myths of people all over the world—the Lapps, the Finns, the Kaffirs of Africa, the Indians of South America, the Indians of North America. In the constellation Taurus, the Pleiades is accompanied by another group of stars known as the Hyades, which contains the bright star Aldebaran, called by the Arabs the "Follower," for its pursuit of the Seven Sisters. And in ancient Greek mythology the Sisters were the daughters of Atlas, transformed into stars to escape the pursuer Orion.

The teller of this Arapaho tale was Alfred L. Kroeber, the greatest of American anthropologists, who began and ended his life work with myths of the Indians.

THE ORIGIN OF THE PLEIADES*

A chief had a fine-looking daughter, who had a great many admirers. At night she was visited by a young man, but did not know who he was. She worried about this, and determined to discover him. She put red paint near her bed. At night he crawled on her bed, wearing a white robe. She put her hand into the paint and then on his back. The next day she told her father to call all the young men to a dance in front of his tent. They all came, and the whole village turned out to see them. She watched all that came, looking for the mark she had made. As she turned, she saw one of her father's dogs, with the mark on his back. This disheartened her, so that she went straight into her tent. This broke up the dance. The next day she went into the woods near the camp, with the dog on a string, and hit him. He finally broke loose. She was very unhappy. Several months later she bore seven pups. She told her mother to kill them, but her mother was kind toward them and made a little shelter for them. They began to grow, and at night the old dog sometimes came to them. After a time, the woman began to take interest in them and sometimes played with them. When they were big enough to run, the old dog came and took them away. When the woman went to see them in the morning, they were gone. She saw the large dog's tracks and several little ones, and followed them a distance. She was sad and cried. She came back to her mother, and said: "Mother, make me seven pairs of moccasins. I am going to follow the little ones, searching for them." Her mother made seven pairs of moccasins, and she started out, tracking them all the way. Finally, in the distance, she saw a tent. The youngest one came to her and said: "Mother, father wants you to go back. We are going home; you cannot come." She said:

*From Alfred L. Kroeber, "Cheyenne Tales." JAF Volume 13, 1900, 161-190.

"No. Wherever you go, I go." She took the little one and carried him to the tent. She entered and saw a young man, who, however, took no notice of her. He gave her a little meat and drink, which did not grow less however much she ate. She tied the little pup to her belt with a string. Next morning, she was left alone, and the tent was gone. She followed and again came to them. Four times this happened in the same way; but the fourth time the tracks stopped. She looked up, and there she saw seven pups (*Manootóxtcioo*); they were stars (the Pleiades).

Mythology is the narrative charter of a religion, and those people who truly believe in their religion see it not as literature (as our disbelieving age sees the Bible), but as a legal document that accounts for everything in their culture. Among some tribes if a thing is not in their mythology, it does not exist. The Yir Yoront of the Cape York Peninsula in northeastern Australia have no boats to traverse the several rivers in their tribal territory. Their neighbors have boats, and the Yir Yoront know about them, but since the Yir Yoront mythology does not mention canoes, the Yir Yoront must paddle across streams clinging to logs.

Where mythical explanations for a cultural phenomenon exist, the explanation is always as unreal as the world of the Yir Yoront. The explanations are never scientific, but religious. Since they do not depend upon logic, logic cannot refute them, and so mythic accounts of origins have an impregnable consistency that science cannot touch. They also very frequently have literary beauty, which science rarely attains to. Such a mythic fragment is the "Legend of Indian Corn," which originated in the East, but which is known to western Indians also.

THE LEGEND OF INDIAN CORN*

A long time ago, when Indians were first made, there lived one alone, far, far from any others. He knew not of fire and subsisted on roots, barks, and nuts. This Indian became very lonesome for company. He grew tired of digging roots, lost his appetite, and for several days lay dreaming in the sunshine; when he awoke he saw something standing near, at which, at first, he was very much frightened. But when it spoke, his heart was glad, for it was a beautiful woman with long *light* hair, very unlike any Indian. He asked her to come to him, but she would

*By Mrs. W. Wallace Brown. JAF Volume 3, 1890, 214.

not, and if he tried to approach her, she seemed to go farther away; he sang to her of his loneliness and besought her not to leave him; at last she told him, if he would do just as she should say, he would always have her with him. He promised that he would. She led him to where there was some very dry grass, told him to get two very dry sticks, rub them together quickly, holding them in the grass. Soon a spark flew out; the grass caught it, and quick as an arrow the ground was burned over. Then she said, "When the sun sets, take me by the hair and drag me over the burned ground." He did not like to do this, but she told him that wherever he dragged her something like grass would spring up, and he would see her hair coming from between the leaves; then the seeds would be ready for his use. He did as she said, and to this day, when they see the silk (hair) on the cornstalk, the Indians know she has not forgotten them.

———————————

The principal difference between gods and men, aside from such inconsequential things as immortality, is that the gods have unlimited supplies of *mana*, the supernatural energy resembling electricity that powers all things. To make things work in this terrestrial world, religious practitioners must somehow tap the powerhouse lines of *mana*. Advanced religions get the spiritual energy by propitiation of the gods (who by the time that level of religious evolution is reached, have become anthropomorphic) — that is, by sacrifice and prayer. On a more primitive level, the subtleties and the abasement are absent, and the spirit world is coerced into releasing the needful power — that is, by magic.

There are two classes of religious practitioners. One is the priest, the functionary in the higher religions who gets his power through membership in a duly organized and legitimatized cult. His efficiency does not depend on his own charisma; as the priest in Graham Greene's *The Power and the Glory* said, even a dissolute and abandoned wretch of a spoiled priest can put God in man's mouth.

The other class of religious practitioners is the shaman, who takes his name from the Tungus people of Siberia, where shamanism is most rampant. But shamans are found everywhere in the world; they even lurk in the darker places in highly developed religions. Wherever they are found, shamans have the same characteristics: they are not members of an organized cult or denomination (though some American shamanistic evangelists claim membership in the catch-all Baptist churches) — indeed, where higher religions exist, shamans are subversive to them; they are emotionally and often mentally unstable (to be an epileptic and an Eskimo, one is inescapably a shaman); they accompany their frenetic rituals of singing, dancing, and other manifestations of "possession" with peculiar costumes and customs; they heal by the laying on of hands, usually helping the credulity of their patients with prestidigitation; they "talk in tongues" when their frenzy addles the speech centers of their brains. And they tell lies and cause lies to be told by others. Thus Francis La Flesche, himself an Indian (and the native part of the outstanding ethnological team of Francis La Flesche and Alice C. Fletcher), makes implicit in the second of the two following articles on western Indian shamans his belief that gunshot wounds can be cured by magic.

SOME SHAMANS OF NORTHERN CALIFORNIA*

Perhaps the most striking feature of California from the standpoint of an ethnologist is the great diversity which is everywhere apparent. The following brief notes on the shamans of three of the stocks of the northern part of the state are offered merely as an outline of the beliefs of these tribes, with the intention of showing to what an extent the diversity so characteristic of the state appears in this single feature of their culture. The three stocks considered are the Shasta, the Hat Creek and Achomawi, and the Maidu.

Among the Shasta, the beginning of a shaman, the commencement of his career, is in a dream or dreams. It is said that a man suddenly begins to dream, frequently that he is on the edge of some high cliff, or on the top of a tall tree, and is about to fall when suddenly he awakes. Or the dream may be of being on the bank of a river, in which the man is about to drown, when he awakes with a sudden shock. Both men and women may have such dreams, and the dreams are a sign that the person is to become a doctor. As soon as dreams of this sort occur, the person at once begins to exercise care in eating, restricting the diet to vegetable foods, and being careful not to smell meat or fat cooking. They also paint their faces and bodies ceremonially. After the dreams have continued for some time, the person suddenly falls over in a swoon ("dies"), while engaged at some everyday duty. In this swoon, the person about to become a doctor sees what is known as an *Axeki* (Pain). The *Axeki* are small in stature, but otherwise like men, and carry

* By Roland B. Dixon. JAF Volume 17, 1904, 23-27.

a bow and arrow. The *Axeki* talks to the person, sings to him, and he or she must answer, repeating the song sung. Should any one fail to answer or repeat the song, the *Axeki* shoots and kills him. The song being repeated, however, the *Axeki* declares that he will be the friend of the person, and then tells him his name and where he lives. This dwelling place is usually in some large rock or mountain.

The novice, on recovering from the swoon, must dance for five nights. In the course of this dance, the novice performs several tricks to show his power, and is swung over the fire by those who are in attendance at the dance. During the whole period of the dance the *Axeki* is supposed to be present, visible only to the novice, however. Throughout the period the *Axeki* directs the novice in his actions. When he first appears to the novice, the *Axeki* gives him a "pain." This "pain" is a small needlelike object, about three inches long and appearing, it is said, like ice. Toward the end of the five nights' dance, the new doctor exhibits this object. He is supposed to keep it in his own body much of the time, but it can always be produced at will. When a shaman is angry with anyone, he throws a "pain" at them and thus causes sickness. A doctor may have many such "pains," as he may see a number of different *Axeki* at different times, and secure a "pain" from each one. Doctors generally begin their dreams and dancing early in the winter, as it is then that the *Axeki* are always about the camp.

There are a large number of these *Axeki*. Every rock and cliff, every mountain has one in it. Their nature is apparently evil, for they are always trying to injure people by shooting a "pain" into them. The doctors were the only persons who could extract "pain." It is not sucked out, but is seized in the hand and pulled out. Once having extracted it, the shaman places his hands in a basket of water. After a while the thing is placed in a mussel shell, pitch is put over it, and another shell put on as a cover. The whole is then put in the fire. Should it be supposed that the "pain" was sent by some other doctor in spite, then the "pain" is sent back to the sender and told to kill him. The "pains," after being extracted can talk and always call the shaman "father." He speaks to them as "son." They tell him who sent them. When a doctor dies, all the "pains" he has fly back to the *Axekis* who have given them to him.

Among the Achomawi and Hat Creek Indians, the method of acquiring doctorhood is somewhat different. Here it is connected with a period of fasting, bathing, and prayer, which is part of the life of every young man. Immediately after the ceremonial ear-piercing, the youth runs away into the mountains and lives for some days alone, bathing frequently in remote mountain lakes. He sleeps little, builds big fires, and piles up rocks in heaps, or places them on the tops of larger stones.

In the course of this period of fasting, he sees a vision or dreams a dream. He never tells this to anyone, and the spirit coming to him in his dream is his guide and helper through life. When he returns from his vigil, he has to observe many regulations in diet. Although all youths go thus to the mountains for their time of fasting, not all by any means see visions or dream dreams. Most of those people who do, become shamans, and no one may become a doctor without having had such dreams or visions.

Some time after his return he goes out into the woods and tries to find a *QaQu*. This is a bunch of feathers, described as like a small feather duster. They are found growing singly in remote spots. When the novice finds a *QaQu*, he endeavors to pick it but cannot pull it up, as when he pulls, the whole earth comes up with the *QaQu*. He leaves this and looks for another, which he succeeds in pulling up. When uprooted, the *QaQu* drips blood continually. In doctoring a patient, if the case be serious, the shaman goes out and finds a *QaQu*, and holds it while dancing near the patient, also using it as an aspergill to sprinkle the sufferer with water. The *QaQu* talk to the doctors and tell them in what part of the body the "pain" is. When he knows this, the doctor sucks out the "pain." The "pain" is a small black thing, like a bit of horse hair. When [it is] removed, the doctor shows the "pain" to the patient and to others, then he chews it up and swallows it, or else spits it out into a small hole dug in the ground, which is then filled up again, and stamped down hard. The "pains" were obtained from the *QaQu* by doctors who wished to injure anyone, and were then snapped toward the victim. The "pain" flew very fast toward the person, who, when the "pain" struck him, felt as if a wood tick had bitten him on the back of the neck. The "pain" always struck at that spot, it is said, and then crawled up under the hair to the crown of the head and there bided its time, till the period set by the doctor had elapsed. Then the "pain" entered the man's head and traveled to the portion of the body to which the doctor had sent it. The doctor who sends a "pain" knows when the victim dies. As soon as this takes place, he goes at once into the woods, finds an old stump, and places on this a skin and a cap and addresses it as a person. He then begins to talk to the "pain," now free from its victim, and returning to him who sent it. He soothes and pacifies the "pain," for, after killing a person, a "pain" is always very blood-thirsty. The "pain" returns flying rapidly through the air and strikes the stump which has been dressed up, thinking it is the doctor, for the "pain" always tries to kill the doctor who sent it, when it returns. Once the "pain" has struck the stump, the doctor catches it and quiets and soothes it. It is only by these means that the doctor escapes being killed by the returning "pain." Sometimes the doctor who extracts a "pain" from a patient gives it back to the one who sent it. The latter then thanks him and keeps the "pain" carefully in a hollow bone, stuffed with yellow-hammer feathers. If it was found out that a doctor had shot a "pain" into someone, then the doctor was sought out and killed by the family of the injured man or by the man himself if he recovered. If a doctor failed to cure a number of cases in succession, he was always killed. As a rule, doctors were more often men than women, but women doctors have in some cases acquired a great reputation.

Of the Maidu, only that port on living in the Sierra in the northern part of the Maidu territory are here referred to. These show again different customs. Here a doctor's position is almost always hereditary, and should a shaman have a number of children, all, men and women, become doctors after his death. Each doctor has a number of guardian spirits, and his children inherit these spirits, although they always acquire other new ones in addition. Soon after a shaman's death, his children begin to dream, seeing spirits and animals of different sorts. The person dreaming in this way becomes ill, and the dreams come more and more frequently. The man must answer these spirits, must talk to them, pay them beads and food and tobacco, or else they will turn on him and kill him. The guardian spirits of a person are always angry when the person dies, and some other person inherits them. As soon, therefore, as a person is in this state, his friends and family call a festival in his honor, to which several old doctors are asked. They come, sing and dance, try to aid him in pacifying the many spirits that trouble him, and make offerings for him of beads, food, and tobacco. The man himself must also sing and dance, not for a few nights only, but every other night, perhaps all winter. After one or two winters spent thus in dancing and singing, the man has pacified the spirits, and begins to doctor people.

Should a person, whose parents had not been shamans, desire to become a doctor, he can do so. To become one, he must go off by himself into the mountains, fast, build fires, swim in lonely lakes, and make frequent offerings of beads and food, and also of blood drawn from his ears. These offerings are made at spots known to be the dwelling place of spirits. After some time he begins to have dreams and visions, seeing the spirits to whom he has made offerings. He then returns to his village and begins to dream regularly, as do those who inherit their father's spirits. Subsequently he has to go through the whole series of ceremonies and dances that the hereditary doctors do.

Doctors throw "pains" at people. The "pains" are like bits of sharpened bone or ice. Sometimes, however, they are like little lizards, frogs, or mice. When a "pain" has been thrown at a person, the only way to recover health is to have a doctor suck out the "pain." When the doctor gets it out, it talks to him and calls him "father." It tells him who sent it. The doctor then either makes it disappear by rubbing it between his hands or else buries it. The doctors get these "pains" from the spirits they meet far away in the mountains or who come to them in dreams. The "pains" must be kept very carefully, and are usually secreted in some hollow log, far from the village. There were women doctors, but the men were more powerful and far more important.

These outlines of the beliefs held in regard to shamans and the cure and cause of disease, by the three tribes mentioned, will serve to show the considerable differences existing in a rather small area. Although each of these stocks is practically in contact with one of the others, there are many rather interesting differences. The strongly hereditary character of the shaman among this portion of the Maidu is noteworthy, together with the inheritance of the guardian spirits. On the other hand, the Hat Creek and Achomawi method of acquiring the position of doctor is suggestive of the usual method among tribes to the north and east of gaining a personal totem. Even within single stocks, as for example, the Maidu, the differences are almost as great as we find in this case between the three different stocks; and all the surrounding stocks again show equal or even greater differences than those noted here. The diversity which has been shown to be characteristic for the state in other features in thus seen to be present here as well, and offers a most fruitful field for study and comparison.

THE OMAHA BUFFALO MEDICINE MEN*

Among the bluffs of the Missouri River Valley, there stood an Indian village, the inhabitants of which were known as the Omahas. Although missionaries had been among these Indians, many were yet in their savage state. The traders, who were present long before the advent of the missionaries, taught the people nothing that would elevate them above their superstitions and strange beliefs; and the echoes of the Indians' religious and war songs still resounded through the hills, and in their ignorance they were happy.

*By Francis La Flesche. JAF Volume 3, 1890, 215-221.

In this village many of the days of my childhood were spent. By the lodge fire I have often sat, with other little boys, listening to the stories handed down by my forefathers, of their battles with the Sioux, the Cheyennes, and the Pawnees; to the strange tales told of the great "medicinemen," who were able to transform themselves into wild animals or birds, while attacking or fleeing from their enemies; of their power to take the lives of their foes by supernatural means; and of their ability to command even the thunder and lightning, and to bring down the rain from the sky. Like all other little savages of my age, I, too, loved to dream of the days when I should become a warrior, and be able to put to shame and to scalp the enemies of my people. But my story is to be about the buffalo medicinemen.

It was on a hot summer day that a group of boys were playing by the brook which ran by this Omaha village, a game for which I cannot find an English name. I was invited to join them; so I took part in the gambling for feathers, necklaces of elk-teeth, beads, and other valueless articles, which were the treasures of the Indian boy. In the village, preparations were going on for the annual summer hunt, and all the people were astir in various occupations. Here and there sat women in the shade of their tents or sod houses, chatting over their work. Warriors were busy making bows and arrows, shaping the arrowshafts and gluing the feathers to them; while in the open spaces or streets a number of young men were at play gambling as we were, but using a different game. Now and then a noisy dispute arose over the game of the young men, but by the interference of the older men peace would be restored.

Towards the afternoon our game grew to be quite interesting, there being but one more stake to win, and the fight over it became exciting, when suddenly we were startled by the loud report of a pistol. We dropped our sticks, scrambled up the bank of the brook, and in an instant were on the ridge, looking in the direction of the sound to see what it meant. It was only a few young men firing with a pistol at a mark on a tree and some noisy little boys watching them. One of our party suggested going up there to see the shooting, but he was cried down, as he was on the losing side of our game and accused of trying to find some excuse to break up the sport. We were soon busy again with our gambling, and points were made and won back again, when we heard three shots in succession; we were a little uneasy, although the shouts and laugh of the men as they joked quieted us, so that we went on with the game. Then came another single loud report, a piercing scream, and an awful cry of a man: "Hay-ee!" followed by the words, *"Ka-gae ha, wanunka ahthae ha!* (O friends! I have committed murder!)" We dropped our sticks and stared at one another. A cold chill went through me, and I shivered with fright. Before I could recover myself, men and women were running about with wild shouts, and the whole village seemed to be rushing to the spot, while above all the noise could be heard the heartrending wail of the man who had accidentally shot a boy through the head. The excitement was intense. The relatives of the wounded boy were preparing to avenge his death, while those of the unfortunate man who had made the fatal shot stood ready to defend him. I made my way through the crowd to see who it was that was killed. Peering over the shoulders of another boy, I saw on the ground a dirty-looking little form and recognized it as one of my playmates. Blood was oozing from a wound in the back of his head and from one just under the right eye, near the nose. The sight of blood sickened me, as it did the other boys, and I stepped back as quickly as I could.

A man just then ordered the women to stop wailing and the people to stand back. Soon there was an opening in the crowd, and I saw a tall man come up the hill, wrapped in a buffalo robe, and pass through the opening to where the boy lay; he stooped over the child, felt of his wrists, then of his breast. "He is alive," the man said; "set up a tent, and take him in there." The little body was lifted in a robe and carried by two men into a large tent which was hastily erected. A young man was sent in haste to call the buffalo medicine men of another village (the Omahas lived in three villages, a few miles apart). It was not long before the medicine men came galloping over the hills on their horses, one or two at a time, their long hair streaming over their naked backs. They dismounted before the tent and went in one by one, where they joined the buffalo doctors of our village, who had already been called. A short consultation was held, and soon the sides of the tent were thrown open to let in the fresh air, and also that the people might witness the operation. Then began a scene rarely if ever witnessed by a white man.

All the medicine men sat around the boy, their eyes gleaming out of their wrinkled faces. The man who was first to try his charms and medicines on the patient began by telling in a loud voice how he became possessed of them; how in a vision he had seen the buffalo which had revealed to him the mysterious secrets of the medicine and of the charm song he was taught to sing when using the medicine. At the end of every sentence of this narrative the boy's father thanked the doctor in terms of relationship. When he had recited his story from beginning to end and had compounded the roots he had taken from his skin pouch, he started his song at the top of his voice, which the other doctors, twenty or thirty in number, picked up and sang in unison, with such volume that one would imagine it could have been heard many miles. In the midst of the chorus of voices rose the shrill sound of the bone whistle accompaniment, imitating the call of an eagle. After the doctor had started the song, he put the bits of root into his mouth, grinding them with his teeth, and, taking a mouthful of water, he slowly approached the boy, bellowing and pawing the earth, after the manner of an angry buffalo at bay. All eyes were upon him with an admiring gaze. When within a few feet of the boy's head, he paused for a moment, drew a long breath, and with a whizzing noise forced the water from his mouth into the wound. The boy spread out his hands and winced as though he was again hit by a ball. The man uttered a series of short exclamations, "He! he! he!" to give an additional charm to the medicine. It was a successful operation, and the father and the man who had wounded the boy lifted their spread hands towards the doctor to signify their thanks. During this performance all of the medicine men sang with energy the song which had been started by the operator. There were two women who sang, as they belonged to the corps of doctors.

The next morning the United States Indian agent came into the village, driving a handsome horse and riding in his shining buggy. He first went to the chief and demanded that the wounded boy be turned over to him. He was told that none but the parents of the child could be consulted in the matter; and if he wanted the boy, he had better see the father. The agent was said to be a good man, and before he offered his services to the government as Indian agent he had studied medicine, so that he could be physician to the Indians as well as their agent. I had attended the mission school for a while and learned to speak a little of the white man's language; and as the government interpreter was not within reach, the agent took me to the parents of the boy, who were by the bedside of their sick one. On our way to the place we heard the singing and the noises of the medicine men, and the agent shook his head, sighed, and made some queer little noises with his tongue, which I thought to be expressive of his feelings. When our approach was noticed, everyone became silent; not a word was uttered as we entered the tent, where room had already been made for us to sit, and we were silently motioned to the place. We sat down on the ground by the side of the patient, and the agent began to feel of the pulse of the boy. The head medicine man, who sat folded up in his robe, scowled and said to me, "Tell him not to touch the boy." The agent respected the request and said that unless the boy was turned over to him and was properly treated, death was certain. He urged that a sick person must be kept very quiet and free from any kind of excitement, for that would weaken him and lessen the chances of recovery. All this I interpreted in my best Omaha, and the men listened with respectful silence. When I had finished, the leader said, "Tell him that he may ask the father of the boy if he would give up the youth to be cared for by the white medicine man." The question was asked, and a deliberate "No" was the answer. Then the medicine man said, "He may ask the boy if he would prefer to be doctored by the white man." While I was translating this to the agent, the boy's father whispered in his child's ear. I then interpreted the agent's question to the boy. He held out his hand to me, and said with an effort, "Who is this?" He was told that it was "Sassoo," one of his friends. I held his hand and repeated the question to him, and he said, "My friend, I do not wish to be doctored by the white man." The agent rose, got into his buggy, and drove off, declaring that the boy's death was certain, and indeed it seemed so. The boy's head was swollen to nearly twice its natural size, and looked like a great blue ball; the hollows of his eyes were covered up, so that he could not see, and it made me shudder to look at him.

Four days the boy was treated in this strange manner. On the evening of the third day the doctors said that he was out of danger and that in the morning he would be made to rise to meet the rising sun and to greet the return of life.

I went to bed early, so that I could be up in time to see the great ceremony. In the morning I was awakened by the singing and approached the tent, where already a great crowd had assembled, for the people had come from the other villages to witness the scene of recovery. There was a mist in the air, as the medicine men had foretold there would be; but as the dawn grew brighter and brighter, the fog slowly disappeared, as if to unveil the great red sun that was just visible over the horizon. Slowly it grew larger and larger, while the boy was gently lifted by two strong men, and when up on his feet, he was told to take four steps toward the east. The medicine men sang with a goodwill the mystery song appropriate to the occasion, as the boy attempted this feeble walk. The two men by his side began to count, as the lad moved eastward, *"Win* (one), *numba* (two), *thab'thin* (three)"; slower grew the steps; it did not seem as if he would be able to take the fourth; slowly the boy dragged his foot and made the last step; as he set his foot down, the men cried, *"duba* (four)," and it was done. Then was sung the song of triumph, and thus ended the first medicine incantation I witnessed among the Omahas.

Before the buffalo medicine men disbanded, they entered a sweat lodge and took a bath, after which the fees were distributed. These consisted of horses, robes, blankets, bears'-claw necklaces, eagle feathers, beaded leggings, and many other articles much valued by Indians. The friends of the unfortunate man who shot the boy had given nearly half of what they possessed, and the great medicine men went away rejoicing. One or two, however, remained for a time with the boy, and in about thirty days he was up again, shooting sticks, and ready to go and witness another pistol practice.

Back in the Good Old Days when the highlight of any rural summer was the arrival of the carnival, pitchmen who hawked Indian snake oil used to ask their innocent audiences, "Have you ever seen a sick Indian?" Of course the yokels had never seen a sick Indian (they had never seen many healthy Indians, either, but they never thought of that), and so they inferred that Indians were kept well by the pitchman's soothing syrup and its small content of alcohol.

To see sick Indians and Indians in the other ordinary conditions of life, one must spend some time with them when they are not on display. Anthropologists do (as one academic wag described Indian social organization, "A Navaho family consists of a father, a mother, four children, and an anthropologist"), but the rest of Caucasoid America assumes the whole of Indian life was a continuous galumphing over hills to attack wagon trains and platoons of cavalry, evolving ultimately to lying drunk in the gutters of Gallup, New Mexico. Who ever thinks of Indian children, except as amorphous victims of military atrocities? Do Indian children ever play, like children of our own society? How did they manage to get through childhood without a television set full of Spidermen, Birdmen, Supermen, Aquamen, Herculoids, Atom Ants, and Secret Squirrels? Alice C. Fletcher, who saw and described Plains Indian life as few men and no other women have done, gives us a day in the life of an Omaha child.

GLIMPSES OF CHILD LIFE AMONG THE OMAHA TRIBE OF INDIANS*

The Indian child is born in an atmosphere charged with the myths of his ancestors. The ceremonies connected with his infancy, his name, and later on, his dress and games, are more or less emblematic of the visible forms of the powers which lie around man and beyond his volition. This early training makes easy the beliefs and practices of the adult, even to the extravagances indulged in by the so-called medicine men.

The Omaha tribe is divided into ten gentes. Until within less than a score of years, the various ceremonies pertaining to the different gentes were performed. Even now, when the people have left their villages and are scattered upon their individual farms, many of the

*By Alice C. Fletcher. JAF Volume 1, 1888, 115-123.

customs which were purely social remain in force, and the distinctions of the gentes are still preserved.

The tribe used to camp in a circle, and each gens had its permanent place. When moving out on the annual hunt, the opening of the circle was always in the direction in which the tribe was going. The five gentes which formed the northern or Instasunda half of the tribal circle were always in the same relative position to the northern end of the opening. The same was true of the southern or Hungacheynu half. It was as though the circle, with its opening, was laid over either to the east or the west, without disturbing the divisions. Therefore, although the tribe might camp in different localities, the unchanged relative position of each gens gave a fixity to the home of the child and determined his playmates, as boys of one side of the circle played against those of the other side.

Each gens had its mythical ancestor or patron, to whom all the names given to its members referred. The name was bestowed by the father or grandfather on the fourth day after birth. Sometimes the occasion was marked by a feast or some ceremony, such as painting the child in a symbolic manner. These observances, however, were frequently omitted.

When the child can walk steadily, about the third year, it is taken by the parents to the tent of an old man of the Instasunda gens, to have its hair cut for the first time and moccasins put on its feet. Hitherto it had run about barefoot. When the child is presented, the old man gathers up the hair on the top of its head and binds it in a tuft, then severs it with a knife, and lays the bunch away in a pack. Then a new pair of moccasins are put on the child, and the old man lifts the little one by the arms and turns it round, following the sun, letting its feet touch the ground at the four points of the compass. When the east is reached, the child is urged forward and bade to "walk forth on the path of life." Upon reaching home, the father of the child cuts its hair after the manner which symbolizes the mythical patron of the gens in which the child is born. This cutting of the hair in a symbolic style is repeated every year, after the first thunder, when the grass has begun to be green, until the child is about seven or eight years old. The boy is taken to the old man only once. The father always cuts the hair symbolically, as among the Omahas the child belongs to the gens of its father.

The following are the different modes of cutting the hair of Omaha children. Beginning with the Waejinste gens, situated at the southern end of the opening, we will take up the gentes in their consecutive order in passing around the tribal circle, until we reach the Instasunda gens at the northern end of the opening.

I. Waejinste: Cut off all the child's hair from its head, leaving a tuft in front and a long lock behind—typical of the elk's head and tail.

II. Inkaesabbae: The head made bare, all but a front tuft, a short lock behind, and a lock on each side of the crown—symbolizing the head, tail, and horns of the buffalo.

III. Hunga: The head shorn, all but a ridge of hair, about two inches wide, from the forehead to the neck—representing the back of the buffalo.

IV. Thatada: This gens is peculiar, as its subdivisions have different mythical patrons, and the child's hair is cut according to the sub-gens in which he is born. *a.* The Wazhingaetaze (bird sub-gens) shear the head, leaving a fringe around the base of the skull, a short lock in front, and a broad lock behind. Sometimes, as among the Eagle people, broad locks are left on the sides. These represent the wings; the fringe, the body feathers; the other locks, the head and tail of the bird. *b.* The Kae-in (turtle sub-gens) make the head bare, leaving a short lock at the front and nape of the neck, and two short locks on each side of the head; symbolizing the shell of the turtle, with his head, tail, and four legs visible. *c.* The Wasabbae etaze (black bear sub-gens) have the head bare, with a broad lock over the forehead, to indicate the bear's head.

V. Kan-ze: In cutting the hair, leave a tuft over the forehead, one at the neck, one on each side, and from each of these four tufts, representing the four points of the compass, a narrow line of hair runs up to a round tuft on the top of the head. This cut is emblematic of the four winds.

VI. Ma-thin-ka-ga-hae: Cut off the hair from one side of the head, and leave that on the other side long. This style is sometimes used by men who have had certain dreams or visions, but this is distinct in its significance from the manner of cutting the child's hair. This cut, for the child, typifies the wolf.

VII. Tae-thin-dae: Make the head bare, with the exception of one long lock behind, and one short one on each side of the crown—indicating the buffalo horns and tail.

VIII. Ta-pa: All the hair is cut but a small bunch over the forehead and a long, thin lock behind—representing the head and tail of the deer.

IX. Ingrezhe-dae: Leave only a small lock in front, a similar one behind, and a tuft each side of the crown—representing the head and tail, and the knobs indicating the growing horns of the buffalo calf.

X. Instasunda: The head left entirely bare, or else a few thin and short locks around the bare head. The last symbolizes reptile teeth, the former the hairless body of snakes and creeping things. This is a thunder gens.

In seven of the gentes there is a Ne-ne-ba-tan sub-gens. These refer to the duties connected with the tribal pipes. The children born in these subdivisions have their hair cut in the manner peculiar to this sub-gens rather than in the style emblematic of the gens patron. The Ne-ne-ba-tan children have the head bare, except a lock on each side of the crown — indicating horns.

During the most impressionable years the children are accustomed to look upon the queerly symbolic heads of their playmates, and they never forget in afterlife the picture their comrades presented, nor its significance.

One of the favorite games of children from five to ten years of age is called *Ou-hae-ba-shun-shun,* the "crooked path." Fancy some ten or twenty youngsters: the boys under eight naked all but a string tied about their bulging little bodies, the girls in a short smock; the heads of the boys cropped after the manner of their birth gens, the breezes catching the odd locks, representing wings and tails, and waving them about. The leader, one of the older boys, sizes his crew, putting the smallest at the end of the Indian file. Each child grasps with his right hand the belt cord of the one in front. At the word of the leader all start off at a shuffling trot.

Under no circumstances must one break from the line unless so ordered, and all must follow the leader and do exactly as he does. Off they go, bent on mischief, winding around trees, bushes, tufts of grass, through puddles, and among the tents. If an old woman chances to be pounding corn, the line circles about her, and each little left hand will seize some corn, until at last, with exhausted patience, she rises to chastise the imps. But they are too quick for her, having, at the word, scattered like partridges to cover. Should anyone have hung his corn to dry on a frame low enough for this singing file of children to reach, each child will break off an ear, and the company make their way, sing-ing and trotting on their crooked path, to some sheltered nook, where they halt, kindle a fire, roast the captured ears, and merrily eat the same.

There is a similar game, played by older boys and even young men, called *Wa-tha-dae*—"to call upon one." The leader of the game orders one of the party to go and do some deed, generally mischievous in character. Witnesses are sent to see that the act is committed. If the youth fails to accomplish the commission, he is dipped in a stream or punished in some way. This game usually makes much sport for the youths and the elders of the tribe. . . .

There are many games played by children which mimic the occupa-tions of mature life: Going on the hunt, with all the stir of preparation; taking down and putting up tents, the tall stalks of the sunflower serving as poles; the attack of enemies; the meeting of friendly tribes and their entertainments—all these furnish incidents for days and days of play.

Deft-fingered children make toys out of clay, modeling men and animals and also any articles they may have seen white people use, even to the fashioning of houses after those seen at the agency or mission. . . .

There is much of the picturesque in the old circular earth lodge, with the fire burning brightly in the center; the inner circle is made smaller by hanging skins or blankets between the row of posts, to shut out the chilling draught. The children sit on the hard ground about the fire, or on the ends of the long logs that feed the flames, unwilling to go to bed and teasing for a story, a story, while the women clear away the remains of the evening meal, and the young mother dances her baby in her arms. Finally the grandfather yields to the children's importunities and tells the following:

"Long ago the muskrat had a long, broad tail. It was very useful and gave the muskrat much pleasure. The beavers, who had no tails at that time, used to watch the muskrat build dams and dwellings, and they were filled with envy. They saw how the muskrat enjoyed himself when he sat upon his tail and slid down the hills. So the beavers lay in wait for the muskrat. Suddenly they seized him. Some of the beavers took the muskrat by the head, while others caught hold of his tail and pulled. Finally the broad tail came out, and left the muskrat with only a thin little stem of a tail. The victorious beavers put on the broad tail and were able to do all that the muskrat had done. The muskrat was desolate. He wandered over the country wailing for the loss of his tail. The animals he met offered him such tails as they had, but he despised their offers and gave them hard words in return. It was the gopher that sang this song, and all the other animals repeated it to the muskrat as he went about crying:"

> *Ma-thin-ja thae, ma-thin-ja-thae,*
> *Ma-thin ka-ha thin-dae*
> *Kae al-i theh-snu-tha-thin-shae,*
> *Ma-thin-ja thae, ma-thin-ja thae!*

(The meaning of the words may be rendered: "Ground-tail, Ground-tail, you who dragged your tail over the ground; Ground-tail, Ground-tail!")

As the grandfather sings, slapping his thigh to keep the time, up jump the children and begin to dance, bending their knees and bringing down their brown feet with a thud on the ground. The baby crows and jumps, and the old man sings the song over and over again, until finally the dancers flag, and sleep comes easily to the tired children.

Among the stories told to children by their mother or one of the older members of the family, the following is a favorite. The writer has heard it told many times, with much dramatic action. It relates to one of the characters under which the rabbit appears in the myths.

"Wa-han-the-she-gae (the orphan) lived with his grandmother. They were both very poor. One day he went out to dig roots. A flock of turkeys were also out walking. He was about to pass them, when one called out, 'There goes Wa-han-the-she-gae; let us call to him and ask him to sing for us, that we may dance.' Whereupon one of the turkeys hailed Wa-han-the-she-gae, and he advanced toward them. Then the spokesman turkey said, 'We have no one to sing for us, and we want to dance.' Wa-han-the-she-gae told the turkeys to stand two by two in a circle. He sat down at one side, placing near him the bag he had brought to carry the roots in. The turkeys made themselves ready; they crooked their necks, made their wattles red, drooped their wings, spread their feathers and tails, and moved their feet uneasily, in anticipation of the dance. Then said Wa-han-the-she-gae, 'You must all shut your eyes as you dance; for whichever one of you looks will always have red eyes!' So he began to sing, and the turkeys to dance.

> *Hae! wa-dum-bae thin in-sta zhe-dae in-sta zhe-dae*
> *Im-bae-than the-an-jae im-bae-than the-an-jae.*

(The words may be rendered: "He who looks will have red eyes; will have red eyes. Spread your tails; spread your tails!")

"Soon he called out, '*Tun-gae gan machey agaha egaha; tungae-gan mashe agaha egaha!* (You who are larger dance outside; you who are larger dance outside!)' The turkeys obeyed the order. As a fine, plump turkey passed him in the dance, he would seize it and thrust it in the bag, singing all the while to keep the dance going. By and by one of the turkeys peeped a little bit, and saw Wa-han-the-she-gae in the act of bagging a turkey! He shouted, '*Wa-hoi! Na-thu-hakchee chey nu-ah-wa-the a-thae-ah-ka-ha! (Wahoi!* He has already nearly exterminated us!)' Then all the turkeys opened their eyes and saw it was true – but few were left! So they spread their wings and flew away over the trees, but their eyes became red as they flew. Wa-han-the-she-gae called out, as they rose in the air, 'You may go, but hereafter you shall be called "Zee-zee-ka!"' (the name for turkey). Then Wa-han-the-she-gae rose, shouldered his bag, and went home. Entering his tent, he tied the bag securely, laid it away, and called for his grandmother. Soon she came, and he said, 'Grandmother, you must not open this bag. I am going away for a little while, and you must let the bag alone.' He went out. While he was gone, the grandmother became curious about the bag. She looked at it, then felt of it; it was full of lumps that kept moving. 'This is very queer,' she said, feeling it all over. 'I will just peep in; there will be no harm in that.' So she untied the string and tried to hold it as she opened it a very, very little. All of a sudden the bag shook in her hands; there was a whirr, a dash of feathers over her face, and the tent was full of turkeys, flying through the opening and beating about, trying to get out. The old woman was frightened out of her wits. When she came to her senses, she slipped off her smock and began running after the sole remaining gobbler, whipping him as she ran. At last she caught him and put him back in the bag. Just then Wa-han-the-she-gae returned and, seeing what had happened, began to scold, telling his grandmother she 'had no ears,' for he had told her not to open the bag. More words passed between them, and then he bade her go outdoors and sit with her head covered, for he was going to make a feast for some Pawnees. She went out and did as she was bidden. Wa-han-the-she-gae cooked the turkey and dished it in a wooden bowl. When this was done, he went quietly out of the tent, made a great rattling of buffalo robes and, lifting the tent-door flap and letting it drop with a loud noise, would call out, *'Now-ah! See-thae-muc-ca thae-sha-thu!* (Hail! Rabbit-chief!)' He repeated these actions and greetings several times. And the old grandmother, sitting outside, said under her covers, 'Oh, my grandson! How well he is known by the great men of the Pawnees!' Then Wa-han-the-she-gae began to eat the turkey, keeping up the while a lively talk in Pawnee all by himself. He ate and ate, until nothing was left but the bones!'"

Many a group of children may be seen under the trees, in summer, playing *Imbae the-an-jae*. Putting their small robes or blankets about them, drawing the ends back with their arms, which they cross behind under the fall of the robe, spreading their hands and fingers beneath the robe, and flapping them in imitation of the turkeys' tails; then, hopping and jumping, they sing the song of Wa-han-the-she-gae and dance the dance of the turkeys.

Adult Indians played, too, whenever they grew weary (as any human being must do) of raping, looting, and killing. In fact, the literature describing adult Indian games, physical and intellectual, is so extensive that the wonder of it is how the redskins found time to accomplish all the depredations on which their reputation depends.

There was lacrosse of course, which has thoroughly infiltrated the sport of the white man, though some wonder what point there is in a game that requires a man to travel twenty miles to hit someone else over the head with a snowshoe. Some of the Oasis Indians marginal to classic Mexican Indian culture played a kind of basketball five hundred years before James Naismith invented the game; the Indians had a refinement that surely must have enlivened the sport for its spectators — whenever a goal was scored, the scoring team was allowed to invade the stands and relieve the audience of its wallets, watches, tiepins, and other valuables. And we must not forget that troublesome Aztec game of *patolli*.

J. R. Walker, Sioux ethnographer early in this century, listed the following games among the Dakota peoples: *wands and hoop, shinney, odd sticks, elk, foot bones, woman's shinney, dice, bowling, webbed hoops, winged bones, young cow, coat shooting, javelins, tops, boy's bow, bone whirler, wind whirler, popgun, horned javelin, dolls, little tipi*, and *scalping settlers*. In the accompanying excerpt, he describes the hoop game.

A SIOUX HOOP GAME*

Painyankapi is an ancient gambling game played by men. The Indians took great interest in this game, and so they became very skillful at it. Sometimes a band of Indians would go a long distance, taking with them their families and all their possessions, to gamble on a game between expert players. Such games were watched by interested crowds, and, as they offered many opportunities for trickery, fierce contests arose over disputed points, which sometimes ended in bloodshed and feuds.

The implements used in the game are: *cangleska*, the hoop; *cansakala*, the wands.

The *cangleska* is made from one piece, as long as the tallest man, taken from an ash sapling in the spring, while the sap is flowing. This is held in the fire, with the bark on, until it becomes pliable, when it is bent into the form of a hoop. It is then trimmed to a uniform diameter

*From J. R. Walker, "Sioux Games." JAF Volume 13, 1905, 277-290.

of about one inch, the ends lapped about three inches, and fastened together with thongs of rawhide.

Beginning near the lap, on each side of the hoop, four shallow spaces are cut so as to divide the hoop into quadrants. These spaces are about two inches long and half an inch wide, and those on one side are exactly opposite those on the other. Three transverse grooves are cut in each of the spaces nearest the lap, and these are called *canhuta*, or the stump. Two oblique grooves crossing each other at right angles are cut on each of the two spaces next to the lap, and these are called *okajaya*, or the fork. Six transverse grooves are cut on each of the two spaces opposite the stump, and these are called *wagopi*, or the stripes. The two remaining spaces are blackened and are called *sapa*, or black.

The *cansakala* are made of ash or chokecherry wood, about four feet in length and three-fourths of an inch in diameter. One end is flattened, or squared, for about ten inches. From the flattened portion to within about eight inches of the other end, they are wrapped with a rawhide or buckskin thong, applied in a spiral manner. They are held together in pairs by a buckskin thong about eight inches long, fastened to each about one-third of the length from their rounded ends. . . .

The rules governing the game are:

Before beginning the game, the players must choose an umpire, a hoop, and the wands, and agree upon the number of points in the count. The umpire must watch the game, decide all contested points, and call aloud all counts when made. One hoop must be used during the entire game. Each player must use his own pair of wands during the entire game. If the hoop or a wand becomes unfit for use during a game, the game is declared off, and a new game must be played. If a player persistently breaks the rules of the game, the game is declared off. The players roll the hoop alternately. To roll the hoop, the players stand side by side. One of them grasps the hoop between the thumb and the second, third, and fourth fingers, with his first finger extended along the circumference, with the hoop directed forward, and by swinging his hand below his hips he rolls the hoop on the ground in front of the players. If a player rolls the hoop improperly, or fails to roll it when he should, his opponent counts one, and rolls the hoop.

After the hoop leaves the hand of the player it must not be touched or interfered with in any manner until after the umpire has called the count. After the hoop is rolled the players follow it and attempt to throw their wands upon the ground so that the hoop will lie upon them when it falls. After the hoop has fallen the umpire must examine it and call the count aloud.

The count is as follows:

To count at all, one of the marked spaces on the hoop must lie directly over a wand. One marked space lying over one wand counts one. One space lying over two wands counts two. Two spaces lying over one wand counts two. Two spaces lying over two wands count two. Three spaces lying over two wands count three. Four spaces lying over two wands count the game. The first who counts the number agreed upon wins the game. If at the end of a play both players count the number agreed upon, the game is a draw, and a new game must be played.

Like so many other enterprises of the Indians, the hoop game had an associated myth to give it charter.

A band of Sioux Indians were traveling in the lake country of Minnesota. Game was very scarce, and they had little to eat for a long time. When they were nearly exhausted, their chief decided to camp. One of his young men requested that he be allowed to fast for four days. Permission being given, he went to the top of a high hill in full view of the camp. After two days and two nights the watchers from the camp saw a buffalo approach the man on the hill. The buffalo circled around him and then disappeared on the opposite side. At midday the young man returned to the camp. He stopped and sat down on the top of a small hill, and his younger brother went out to him. The young man told his brother to stand back and not approach him. He said, "I have a message for you to deliver to my father. Tell my father to place a tent in the middle of the camp circle. Tell him to scatter sage grass around the inside, and that he must select four good men to enter the tent and await me." Then the young brother returned to the camp and delivered this message to his father. Everyone knew that the young man had something important to tell the people.

The father did as requested. He believed the young man because the people of the camp had seen the buffalo on the hill with him. When the tent was ready, and the four good men had entered, the younger brother was sent to notify the young man. The young man approached, walking slowly. He stopped near the entrance of the tent, and after a few moments he moved still nearer and paused. He then approached the door, walked entirely around the tent, and entered. He produced a large pipe wrapped in sage grass. He sat down at the back of the lodge and asked the four good men to send for a good young man to act as his assistant. When the assistant came, the young man said to him, "Go out and cut a stick for me." When the assistant returned with the stick the young man ordered him to peel it. When this was done, the young man asked the four good men to make a sweathouse.

When this was ready, the young man and the four good men entered the sweathouse, while the assistant waited outside. When the ceremony in the sweathouse ended, the party returned to the tent. Then the young man told them that a buffalo had come to him on the hill, had given him a pipe, instructions, and a message to deliver to his people. He ordered his assistant to bring a coal of fire. With this he made incense with sage grass, held his hands in the smoke four times, took up the bundle containing the pipe, unwrapped it, and took out the pipe. The stem of the pipe was red, and the bowl was of black stone. "This pipe," said the young man, "was given me by the buffalo that you saw upon the hill, and he also instructed me as to its use."

The young man ordered his assistant to go out and cut an ash sapling and four cherry sticks. When these were brought, he gave a cherry stick to each of the four good men for them to peel. He, himself, took the ash stick and began to remove the bark. This done, he bent it into a hoop and tied the ends with sinew threads and buckskin strings. He held the hoop in the smoke from the sage grass, then took red paint in his hands, held his hands over the smoke as before, and painted the hoop. Then he placed his assistant at the door of the lodge, himself at the rear, and two of the good men on each side. He instructed the four good men to paint their cherry sticks red in the same way that he painted the hoop. The assistant then smoothed the floor of the tent, while the young man sang four songs. The words of the songs were as follows:

1. I have passed by the holy floor (earth, smooth and level like the floor of a tipi).
2. I have passed by the holy robe.
3. I have passed by the holy shell.
4. I have passed by an eagle feather, it is good.

Then the young man said, "Now I shall roll the hoop. It will circle the tent. You are to watch the tracks made by it. You will see that it leaves buffalo tracks, returns to me, and lies down." So the young man sang the four songs again and rolled the hoop. The hoop circled the tent and returned to the young man as he had said. The four good men saw in the trail left by the hoop the tracks of buffalo. The young man said that on the fourth day from this time there would be many buffalo. Then he took strips of rawhide and wrapped them around the cherry sticks. He tied red cloth around one and blue around the other. Then he put on a buffalo robe and asked the men to follow him. The young man passed out of the door, and the four good men took the hoop and the sticks and played the hoop game, as they walked behind the young man. The people of the camp watched them, and wherever the hoop rolled, buffalo tracks appeared.

The young man requested his assistant to call a good old man. The people of the camp were in a state of famine. When the assistant brought the old man to the tent, the young man requested him to ha-rangue the camp, as follows: "Ho, Ho, Ho, this young man wishes the people to make arrows, to sharpen them, and to sharpen their knives. He says that four buffalo will be here tomorrow morning. Let no one bother them, let no dogs chase them, let them go through the camp in peace. The four buffalo will come from the west."

Early the next morning the four buffalo came as predicted. They passed slowly through the north side of the camp and disappeared in the east. Then the chief of the camp sent a sentinel to stand upon the hill where the four buffalo were first seen. The sentinel looked down into the valley on the other side of the hill, where he saw vast herds of buffalo moving toward the camp. The chief had instructed the sentinel to run back and forth when buffalo were visible. The people of the camp who were watching, saw him run back and forth upon the hill, and began to prepare for the hunt. The young man, who was still in his tent, sent out his assistant to call the people to his door. He requested that they stand around and keep quiet. The sentinel who had returned now addressed the people, telling them of the buffalo he had seen and the direction in which they were moving. The young man then ad-dressed the people, giving them permission to chase the buffalo.

They had a great hunt. Buffalo were everywhere. They even ran through the camp, and were shot down at the doors of the tents. The people had meat in great abundance.

When the hunt was over, the young man requested the four good men to keep and care for the hoop and the sticks with which they had played. A tent was always kept in the middle of the camp circle, and the four good men spent most of their time in it. Whenever the people wished to hunt buffalo, the four men played the hoop game, and the buffalo appeared as before. In the course of time all these men died, except one. This last man made the four marks we now see upon the hoop. After his death, the game was played by all the people and be-came a great gambling game.

IV

The Indian
and the White Man

DOWN ON THE UTE RESERVATION in southern Colorado, on land their ancestors stole from the Pueblos, the Indians while away their time hunting with fiberglass bows and steel-tipped arrows. There is little else for them to do. They have farms, but they hire white laborers to plow, plant, and harvest for them. Their principal source of income is litigation. A battery of high-powered lawyers and expert witnesses settled with the Indian Claims Commission for $31,938,473.43 as token compensation for Pueblo land the whites took away from them back in the Good Old Days of rugged individualism. Nothing of what they make on their land is taxed. At the moment they are negotiating with the Department of the Interior to get fifty cents out of every admission charge to visitors at Mesa Verde National Park; since something like a half million tourists enter the park every season, that adds up to, let's see now, quite a bit of money. And yet, to get a drink, they have to go all the hell the way in to Durango or Cortez, because the Tribal Council won't let them drink on the reservation. The way they carry on, one would almost think they were palefaces instead of Indians.

The Indians have made out very well for a marginal subsistence culture occupying land coveted by a highly developed agricultural people. It is the nature of human ecology that hunting-gathering and Neolithic peoples cannot survive against the onslaughts of expanding agriculturalists. The fact that the Indians — and especially the Plains Indians, who upon their acquisition of the horse reverted to a hunting-gathering subsistence — managed to save not only their populating viability but also their pride and their culture, is a tribute to the psychic energy that made them and motivated them. All the tribes suffered hardships and psychological traumata in the process of surviving, and some were extinguished, but the survival rate has been unique for the culture clash they experienced. It is not, of course, a matter for us or our ancestors to be either proud or sorry for, since peoples replace peoples as generations replace generations. It is just a fact of nature.

For most commentators, however, it is a fact not admitted or admissible, so we cannot say why the Indian culture endured and the culture of the Negro vanished. One consideration, surely, was the surprising circumstance that the whites always feared the threat of the Negro slaves more than they feared the threat of the Indians. The languages of the immigrant slaves were taken away from them and extirpated, so that we have no more than a half dozen words of African origin in English. Africans communicated with drums, the slaveholders knew, so drumming was forbidden the slaves in fear of revolts like that of Nat Turner and some two hundred and fifty other nativistic Negro leaders. That prohibition led to another extirpation, and even today a Negro drummer is a rarity. Some social intercourse had to be permitted the slaves, so the church was developed almost especially for the black people. This, too, has left a legacy wherein most Negro leaders are clergymen.

For all the escalation of killings, retaliations, massacres, punitive expeditions, and reprisals that killed many thousands of people on both sides as the white settlers moved inexorably into Indian country, the whites never had the visceral fear of the Indians that they had of the Negroes. Thomas Jefferson never said of the Indian problem what he said of the Negro problem — "This momentous question, like a fire bell in the night, awakened and filled me with terror." Apprehension of such magnitude results in the most severe repression, not only of the people engendering it, but all that distinguishes them as well. On the other hand, the Indian, when he was not being killed, was being respected, and this land will forever keep many memorials to its aborigines — not in guilt-built statues and foundations, but in the small, natural things, the greater for their being small.

In an early issue of the *Journal of American Folklore,* J. W. Hudson made an incomplete and unsystematic list of such things — names on the land and on its biota — that establishes the point nevertheless.

MEMORIALS OF THE INDIAN*

The name "Indian," by which the aborigines of America are now generally known, had its origin in the fact that the Spanish discoverers of the New World, believing that they had landed upon some part of the coast of India, called the natives of the lands explored by them *Indios,* "Indians." And this term, passing into the various European languages, has clung to them in spite of the misleading connotation. Indeed, the substitute for "American Indian" adopted by certain eminent Americanists, "Amerind" (the word is due to the suggestion of Major J. W. Powell), would, etymologically, at least, perpetuate the mistake.

Things *Indian,* large and small, still dot over the American continent. In the United States we have an *Indian Territory*; a State of *Indiana* (also a place called *Indiana* in Pennsylvania) with its capital *Indianapolis* (another *Indianapolis* exists in Iowa); at least eight places called *Indianola* (one each in Florida, Illinois, Iowa, Kansas, Mississippi, Nebraska, Texas, Utah); several localities known as *Indio* (in California, Texas). There are also recognized in the gazetteers and kindred compilations the following local names:

Indian Bay (Ark.); —— *Bayou* (La.); —— *Bottom* (Ky.); —— *Branch* (Mass., N. J.); —— *Brook* (Mass., N. J.); —— *Camp* (O.,

*By J. W. Hudson. JAF Volume 15, 1902, 107-116.

W. Va.); —— *Castle* (N. Y.); —— *Creek* (13: one each in Ala., Ark., Ky., Miss., Mo., Neb., N. J., Va.; two each in Pa., Tenn.); —— *Crossing* (Tex.); —— *Diggings* (Cal.); —— *Draft* (Va.); —— *Falls* (N. Y.); —— *Field* (Mich.); —— *Fields* (Ky.); —— *Ford* (Wis.); —— Gap (Tex.); —— *Grove* (Mo.); —— *Gulch* (Cal.); —— *Harbor* (Conn.); —— *Head* (N. Y., Pa., Utah); —— *Hill* (Ala., Conn., 5 in Mass., O, S. C.); —— *Hills* (Mass.); —— *Lake* (Ill., Mich., N. Y.); —— *Mills* (N. J., W. Va.); —— *Mound* (La., Tenn.); —— *Neck* (Conn., Mass., Va.); —— *Orchard* (Mass., Penn.) —— *Pass* (2 in N. Y., Nev.); —— *Point* (Me.); —— *Pond* (Conn., Mass.); —— *Ridge* (Pa., Tenn.); —— *River* (Conn., Fla., Mass., Me., Mich., N. Y., R. I.); —— *Rock* (Me., Va.); —— *Run* (Ky., Pa.); —— *Spring* (Cal., Miss., Nev., N. Y., Utah); —— *Springs* (Cal., Fla., Ga., Ind., Md., Tenn.); —— *Swamp* (R. I.); —— *Town* (Mich., N. C., S. C.); —— *Trail* (N. C.); —— *Valley* (Cal., Idaho, Va.); —— *Village* (La., Minn., Okl.); —— *Wells* (Cal.).

The Topographical Dictionaries of the United States Geological Survey reveal a great many more names of this sort, and research into the minutiae of local nomenclature would doubtless add others to the list. Canada and Newfoundland likewise bring their quota. In Newfoundland we find: *Indian Brook, Bay, Arm, Lake,* etc., besides a number of things named *Red Indian* after the aborigines, now extinct. In Nova Scotia there are: *Indian Brook, Indian Harbor, Indian Point,* etc. In New Brunswick, according to Professor Genung: "The name *Indian River* occurs once, Indian Cove once, *Indian Falls* once, *Indiantown* twice, *Indian Beach* twice, *Indian Camp Point* once, *Indian Brook* twice, *Indian Bay* once, *Indian Lake* twice, *Indian Mountain* once, *Indian Island* eight times, *Indian Point* at least twelve times." Among the post offices in other parts of Canada are: *Indian Brook* (Ont.), *Indian Ford* (Man.), *Indian Head* (Assa.), *Indian Lorette* (Que.), *Indian River* (Ont.), and *Indian River* (P. E. I.).

Names of places are not the only things Indian. From time to time many other things have been called "Indian" because they were new or strange or had some real or fancied connection with the aborigines. Thus, wild species of plants have often been termed "Indian" to mark them off from the more familiar sorts, and children use "Indian" substitutes for well-known plants. Sometimes, again, actual use by the Indians in medicine, art, and industry has given rise to such names. Popular American names of plants abound in illustration of these points. Among things "Indian" of the kind in question are the following:

Indian arrow. Name applied in Salem, Ind., to the *Euonymus atropurpureus* or wahoo (Bergen).

Indian bean. Name given in Morristown, N. J., to the *Apios tuberosa,* "wild bean," or groundnut (Bergen).

Indian bed. A particular way of roasting clams: "The clams are simply placed close together on the ground, with the hinges uppermost, and over them is made a fire of brush" (Bartlett).

Indian boys and girls. Name applied in Madison, Wis., to the *Dicentra cucullaria,* or "Dutchman's breeches" (Bergen).

Indian bread. 1. Bread made from Indian corn and rye (other names are "rye and Indian," and "Boston bread"). 2. Cassava. 3. Tuckahoe *(Sclerotium giganteum).*

Indian chickweed. Name given to the *Mollugo verticillata* to distinguish it from the *Stellaria media* or common chickweed.

Indian chief. Name applied in Rockford, Ill., to the *Dodocatheon meadia* (Bergen).

Indian corn. Maize *(Zea mays).*

Indian cucumber. The *Mediola virginica* of the lily family.

Indian currant. The *Symphoricarpus communis* or Missouri coralberry.

Indian dab. "The name given in certain parts of Pennsylvania to a kind of battercake" (Bartlett).

Indian fig. 1. The fruit of a large species of cactus *(Cereus giganteus),* found in New Mexico and Arizona. 2. The *Opuntia rafinesquii* of the northeastern states.

Indian gift. A term "proverbially applied to anything reclaimed after having been given." The origin of the expression is as follows: "When an Indian gives anything, he expects to receive an equivalent, or to have his gift returned. This term is applied by children to a child, who, after having given away a thing, wishes to have it back again" (Bartlett).

Indian giver. The term "Indian giver" is also used in the sense of "repentant giver." According to Dr. H. C. Bolton: "If an American child, who has made a small gift to a playmate, is indiscreet enough to ask that the gift be returned, he (or she) is immediately accused of being an *Indian giver,* or as it is commonly pronounced, *Injun giver.* The child so unwise as to regret his gift is regarded with great disdain by his playmates, who always treat 'Injun givers' with scornful looks and sometimes with wordy derision as having committed a great offence to child-etiquette."

Indian gravel-root. A West Virginian name of the *Eupatorium purpureum,* Joe-Pye weed, or trumpetweed.

Indian hemp. 1. A name applied to plants used by the Indians for textile purposes—*Apocynum cannibinum,* A. *androsaemifolium.* 2. An Ohio name for the *Abutilon avicennae,* also known as "Indian mallow" (Bergen). 3. A West Virginian name for the *Linaria vulgaris.*

Indian Ladder. A tree ladder: "A ladder made of a small tree by trimming it so as to leave only a few inches of each branch as a support for the feet" (Bartlett).

Indian lemonade. A California name for the *Rhus canadensis.*

Indian lettuce. A California name for the *Montia fontana.*

Indian mallow. The *Abutilon avicennae*, also called "Indian hemp."

Indian meal. Maize or cornmeal. A mixture of the flour of maize and wheat was called "wheat and Indian," and a similar mixture with rye flour "rye and Indian" (Bartlett).

Indian melon. A name given in Colorado to a species of *Echino-cactus.*

Indian mozemize. A name given in Ferrisburg, Vermont, to the *Pyrus americana*, also known as mooze misse (Bergen).

Indian orchard. In certain parts of New England and New York, "an old orchard of ungrafted trees, the time of whose planting is not known" (Bartlett).

Indian paint. 1. A Missouri and Minnesota name for the *Litho-spermum canescens.* 2. A Wisconsin name for a species of *Trades-cantia.* 3. A name for the *Chenopodium capitatum.*

Indian paintbrush. A name given in Massachusetts to the *Cas-tilleia coccinea*, or "painted cup," of the figwort family (Bergen).

Indian peach. A term applied to "ungrafted peach trees, which are considered to be more thrifty and to bear larger fruit than others" (Bartlett).

Indian physic. A name given to the *Gillenia trifoliata*, a medicinal plant. In certain parts of North Carolina the *G. stipulatea* is called "Indian physic."

Indian pink. 1. An Illinois name of the *Castilleia coccinea*, called in Massachusetts "Indian paintbrush." 2. A name given in parts of Massachusetts to the *Silene pennsylvanica* and in California to the *S. californica.* 3. A name given in certain parts of Massachusetts to the *Polygala paucifolia* or fringed polygala (Bergen).

Indian pipe. The *Monotropa uniflora.* The bending of the young heads suggested the name.

Indian pipestone. A name for catlinite.

Indian pitcher. The pitcher plant *(Sarracenia purpurea).*

Indian plantain. The name given to a species of *Cacalia.*

Indian poke. The white (or false) hellebore, *Veratum viride.*

Indian posy. A name applied in Long Island and parts of Connecticut to the *Gnaphalium polycephalum* or fragrant life everlasting (Bergen).

Indian potato. 1. An Ohio name for the *Dicentra canadensis*, or "squirrel corn." 2. A California name for the *Brodiaea capitata.*

Indian pudding. A pudding made of cornmeal and molasses.

Indian rhubarb. A California name for the *Saxifraga peltata.*

Indian rice. A name sometimes applied to the "wild rice" (*Zizania aquatica*) of the region of the Great Lakes.

Indian root. A New Hampshire name for the *Aralia racemosa,* or spikenard, of the ginseng family (Bergen).

Indian slipper. A name given in certain parts of New England to the *Cypripedium acaule,* the pink "lady's slipper," or "moccasin flower."

Indian summer. The "second summer" or "short season of pleasant weather, usually occurring about the middle of November," corresponding to the European "St. Martha's summer," and "Summer of All Saints." The term is said to have originated "from the custom of the Indians to avail themselves of this delightful time for harvesting their corn; and the tradition is that they were accustomed to say they had always a second summer of nine days just before the winter set in" (Bartlett).

Indian tea. The name given to several plants, the leaves, and other parts of which were used by the Indians (and afterwards by some of the whites) to make "tea." In Newfoundland and Labrador the *Ledum latifolium* and *L. palustre,* better known as "Labrador tea," are called "Indian tea."

Indian tobacco. 1. A name applied to the *Lobelia inflata.* 2. A former name in New Jersey of the *Verbascum thapsus,* or common mullein (Bartlett). 3. A New York name of the *Nicotiana rustica.* 4. A name given to the *Antennaria plantaginifolia,* "chewed by children as a substitute for tobacco" (Bergen).

Indian turnip. 1. The New England "Wake Robin," or "Jack-in-the-Pulpit" (*Arum triphyllum*). 2. The *pomme blanche* or "prairie potato" (*Psoralea esculenta*) of the western plains.

Indian vervine. A Newfoundland name for the *Lycopodium lucidulum.*

Indian warrior. A California name for the *Pedicularis densiflora.*

Indian weed. An early name for tobacco.

Indian wheat. An early name of maize, or Indian corn.

Indian whort. A name given in Labrador and Newfoundland to the *Arotostaphyllos uva-ursi,* or "bearberry," of the heath family (Bergen).

Nor has the squaw, the Indian woman, been forgotten. *Squaw Mountain* in Colorado, *Squaw Creek* in Idaho, and a few other places scattered over the country, bear her name. A number of plants also have been called after her. Among them are these:

Squaw berry. 1. The partridgeberry (*Mitchella repens*). 2. The *Vaccinium stamineum* of the heath family, known also as "squaw huckleberry."

Squawbush. 1. A name for the *Cornus stolonifera* and *C. sericea* in Maine and the West respectively. 2. A California name for the *Canadensis.*

Squawflower. A Vermont name for the *Trillium erectum,* called also "birthroot," or "squawroot" (Bergen).

Squaw mint. The American pennyroyal, *Hedeoma pulegoides.*

Squaw root. 1. A New Hampshire name for the *Trillium erectum* (Bergen). 2. Cohosh, black and blue. 3. The *Caulophyllum thalictroides,* known also as papooseroot. 4. The *Conapholis americana.*

Squaw's carpet. A California name for the *Ceanothus prostratus.*

Squaw vine. A name given in parts of New England to the *Mitchella repens,* or "partridgeberry."

Squaw weed. 1. The *Erigeron philadelphicum,* a species of daisy. 2. The *Senecio aureus,* or golden ragwort.

After the squaw, too, are named the *old squaw,* or long-tailed duck *(Clangula hiemalis),* and the *squawfish.* Another interesting memorial of the squaw is the expression *squaw man* (=1. An Indian man doing woman's work; an effeminate. 2. A white man who has married an Indian and lives with her people). In questions of the disposition of Indian lands, the "squaw man" figures a good deal.

Even the *papoose* or Indian child is remembered in the term *papooseroot,* applied to the blue cohosh *(Caulophyllum thalictroides).*

Other languages besides English which have implanted themselves upon the American continent also have memorials of the "Indian." The French of Quebec possess, among others, the following interesting expressions:

Botte sauvage. Moccasin. The term *botte sauvage* is much older in the language than *moccasin,* and its variants, which are more literary, are mostly due to English influence.

Thé sauvage. Labrador tea.

Traine sauvage. Toboggan.

To the early French Canadians the Indian tribes were *les nations,* in the same manner as the "heathen" have been *gentes* or *gentiles* to other races, and in the earlier maps of the country such names as *Rivière des Nations, Rivière des Petites Nations, Lac des Deux Nations* appeared.

Children's songs and games are such repositories of past knowledge that it would be very strange if those of American children did not contain some reminiscences of the Indian.

As the narrative charter of a religion, myth has the specific purpose of accounting for whatever palpably exists. It is not sufficient merely to explain; the myth must integrate the troublesome phenomenon within the native culture. For this reason the "explanatory tales" offered juveniles of both races rarely became traditional with the Indians, and the mythic adaptations made by the Indians to account for white men and their culture never became popular with the whites. A fairly typical Indian accounting for the creation of white men is the short tale collected by Mary Neff in 1907 from a class of Pima and Papago children at the Industrial School then established at Tucson, Arizona. The degree of pointlessness to the white reader will vary inversely with his knowledge of Indian culture.

THE FIRST WHITE MEN*

There once lived a man who is said to have been good for nothing.

But one day he metamorphosed himself into an Eagle. He went and lived upon a high, steep mountain and, coming down, killed people every day.

One day a little man decided to kill him, and so went up; and finally, when he came to the place where the Eagle lived, the Eagle was away, but his wife was at home.

The woman told him that he must hide himself, for it was about time for the coming of the Eagle.

The little man at once transformed himself into a fly and hid himself under a pile of dead bodies.

In a few hours came the Eagle with more dead bodies. After eating his dinner, being weary from his long journey, he lay down and went to sleep.

The little man came out from his hiding place, cut off the Eagle's head, and poured warm water over the dead bodies, and they came back to life again. But some had been there so long that they turned white; and when the little man tried to talk to them, they talked a different language. So he separated them from the Indians and called them white men.

These legends are no longer believed, as the Indians are coming out of their superstition into a better knowledge.

* From Mary L. Neff, "Pima and Papago Legends." JAF Volume 25, 1912, 51-65.

The process of religious syncretism is clearer in this synopsis of "A Dakota Reading of the Creation," though there are a number of essentially disparate motifs amalgamated with the basic story of Adam and Eve and the Fall of Man. There is the matter of primogeniture, which troubled some Indians as much as it troubled some English condemned by recency of birth to go into the Church instead of the manor. The motif of the tempting serpent, an embarrassing element to Biblical exegetes, is here abandoned for a better motivated Cain and Abel—Joseph and his Brothers contention. The plum is historically a better identification of the fruit of original sin than the more traditional apple, since apples did not grow in any identifiable Garden of Eden. And what man could object to the adjustment of punishment made upon the Biblical story by the Indians? In this matter, incidentally, resides an illustration of the social function of myth—to give warrant for regulations of behavior. Woman, specifically, can be subject to man only if there is mythical charter for her subservient position, and that alone is sufficient reason for the heretical alteration of the white man's myth.

This tale has been traced to the teaching of an early missionary, one Father Bushman. It is not known what became of him.

A DAKOTA READING OF THE CREATION*

According to this narrative, among beings created by the Great Spirit, the most perfect were bears. There were two bears living together, an elder and a younger brother. The elder persecuted his weaker brother and took away from him his share of the wild plums on which they fed. The Great Spirit took pity on the younger brother and promised him that if he ceased crying he would make him his brother's master. The younger ceased weeping and fell asleep; on which the Great Spirit changed him into a man and also took a bone from his forearm, out of which he made a female helpmate like himself. As the little bear was told by the Great Spirit not to cry, Indians do not shed tears. When the little bear, having become a man, saw his helpmate, he rushed to embrace her, but the Great Spirit forbade it as immodest; wherefore Indians never caress their wives in public. The Great Spirit now told the younger brother to walk on two feet in order to show his superiority

* From "Dakota Legend," reported from *The Messenger*, Worcester, Massachusetts, July 28, 1888. Reported in JAF, Volume 2, 1889, 65.

and at the same time forbade him and his mate to eat plums, which had been the cause of the original trouble. The elder brother, seeing his brother's beauty and upright walk, became jealous and attempted to beat him but found the latter his superior in force. Therefore, he resorted to artifice, picked some fine plums, and offered them to his brother, who declined, pleading the prohibition of the Great Spirit. The bear now went to the female and showed her the fruit; when she was told that her husband had formerly partaken of the fruit, she accepted it. On account of this disobedience, the Great Spirit made her the slave of her husband. He also drove the bear into the mountains and forbade him in the future to associate with mankind.

The tale of Cinderella may be the grandest story in all the literatures of the world. Certainly no other story is so well known or so popular. Five hundred folk variants of the tale are known in Europe alone, and that does not count its modern disguises, such as the motion picture *Sabrina*. Originating in China, so far as we know, eleven centuries ago, it has spread over most of the world; but unlike the simpler story elements — motifs represented in the preceding chapter by the Magic Flight and the Pursuing Head — it had to wait for European settlement to diffuse to the Indians of the Americas. But once having established itself on these shores, it began to proliferate, adapting itself to each culture until it attained almost perfect integration.

In the first example of its naturalization, "The Tale of Cinder-Mary," the familiar Cinderella shows the conflict of cultures through which it moved before coming to the Mexican Indians. The Black Moors are ancient ogres among the Spanish; when these are joined to native Indian flying witches, the old story takes on a fearful suspense long lost in the Perrault version best known to our culture.

THE TALE OF CINDER-MARY*

Once there was a poor orphan girl who lived in an ash hole belonging to the Black Moors. One day when one of them went there to throw out the ashes, he saw her and asked her to come to their house. There they asked her name; but the poor girl did not know her own name,

*From J. Alden Mason, "Four Mexican-Spanish Fairy Tales from Azqueltan, Jalisco." JAF Volume 25, 1912, 191-198.

nor were they able to discover it. Finally they gave her the name of Maria Ceniza (Cinder-Mary). Now, the Black Moors were witches; but they did not wish Cinder-Mary to learn the fact, so they gave her a black sheepskin and a half-*real* [worth of] soap, and sent her to the river, telling her not to waste the soap, but to wash the sheepskin until it was as white as a pod of cotton.

Cinder-Mary knelt by the river and wept, because she could not wash the sheepskin as the Moors had commanded her. Suddenly there appeared a lady, who asked her why she was weeping; and Cinder-Mary replied that if she could not wash the black sheepskin as white as a pod of cotton, the Black Moors would kill her. Then the lady told her that she would bring her two white stones with which she would be able to wash the black sheepskin. Presently she returned, and soon Cinder-Mary had washed the sheepskin as white as a pod of cotton. Then the lady gave her a magic wand and told her that when she needed anything, she need only speak to the wand. Then, placing a tiny star on Cinder-Mary's forehead, she disappeared.

Now, one of the Black Moors had a daughter; and when she saw the star on the forehead of Cinder-Mary, she was very jealous and asked her mother to have a black lamb killed, that she also might go to the river to wash the skin. So, going to the river, she commenced to weep; and when the lady appeared to her and asked her why she was weeping, she replied that it was because she could not wash the black sheepskin. Then she asked her if she would not put a star on her forehead likewise, but the lady replied that she would put nothing but *mango de burro* there. Then the girl returned to the house of the Black Moors.

Another day the Moors said to Cinder-Mary that they were going to mass, and they left her behind to prepare the breakfast. "If you have not a good breakfast ready when we return, we shall kill you," they said. Then Cinder-Mary asked her magic wand to give her a dress such as had never before been seen in the world and some shoes, in order that she might go to mass. Then she followed a little behind the Moors and entered the church; and neither the Moors nor the rest of the people recognized her. When the priest saw her, he was much impressed with her beauty and thought that she would make an excellent wife for the prince; so he gave orders that double guards be stationed at the doors of the parish and that she be not allowed to leave. This, however, did not deter Cinder-Mary, who fastened some wings to her back, so that they might not catch her. The guards tried to restrain her but only succeeded in catching one of her shoes. Then she flew back to the house of the Moors and ordered her magic wand to prepare a breakfast with good food. Soon the Moors came home and began to talk about the beautiful maiden whom they had seen, with a star which illumined everything up to the grand altar; but it was Cinder-Mary.

Then the king ordered his men to search all the villages and *ranchos* for the maiden who had left the shoe behind. Soon they came to the house of the Black Moors and found Cinder-Mary's other shoe. They were about to carry the daughter of the Moor to the king, when a little dog commenced to howl, saying, "*Mango de Burro* goes, and Star of Gold remains." Then the king's retainers demanded to see the other maiden who was hidden in the house. Accordingly they left the girl who had the *mango de burro* on her forehead and carried Cinder-Mary to the king, that she might marry the prince. There was a grand wedding, and Cinder-Mary was given a castle in which to live with the prince.

Soon afterwards the Black Moors came to the castle and asked that they be allowed to louse Cinder-Mary. They came to her while she was bathing, with her hair loose, and commenced to louse her. Suddenly they stuck a pin into her head, so that she became enchanted and flew away, for they were afraid that she would denounce them because they were witches. Then they left without as much as saying goodby.

When her attendants came for Cinder-Mary, she was gone, and the only living being they could find was a dove in a cypress tree. Then they went to the head servant and asked him how much he would give them for the dove which they had found singing in the cypress tree and which said in its song that it wanted to see the king in his palace. The dove, they said, was crying piteously. The servant went at once to the king and told him about the dove. Then the king asked him how much he wanted for bringing the dove to him; and the servant replied that if he would give him five hundred pesos he would bring it. The king agreed, and the servant went and brought him the bird. While stroking its back, the king found a pin stuck in its head and pulled it out. Immediately the bird became Cinder-Mary. Then he asked her why the Black Moors had thus bewitched her; and she replied that it was because they were witches and were afraid that she would denounce them.

Then the king ordered that the Moors be brought before him, and he condemned them all to be burned to death with green wood. But Cinder-Mary entered the palace where she was to live and locked the door, so that no one might open it for five days. When at last the door was opened, it was a virgin who was shut in there.

———————————————

When Elsie Clews Parsons found the following Cinderella story among the Zuñi Indians, she supposed it to have come to the Pueblos by way of the Spanish. But it has the hand, however light, of Waihusiwa on it.

Just over a hundred years ago Frank Hamilton Cushing visited Europe with three of his Zuñi informants, one of whom was the nonpareil storyteller, Waihusiwa. Evidently the thrill of traversing the "Ocean of Sunrise" vanished in the cold mists of England, for Cushing tells us that for amusement and edification he and the Indians and their English friends told one another traditional stories. As one might imagine, the Indian contributions were more vital than the shopworn *Märchen* dimly remembered by the Englishmen. Cushing admits having contributed a particularly bad Italian story, one that would have been most politely forgotten by the Indians. Yet a year later, when the party had returned to the pueblo of Zuñi, Cushing overheard Waihusiwa narrating a re-creation of the exhausted story that can only be described as almost incredibly magnificent.

Another story re-created by Waihusiwa was one called the "Poor Turkey Girl," a tale that moves so compellingly, even in the reading, that one scarcely notices that it is at bottom the familiar story of Cinderella. Ruth Benedict, herself a poet as well as an anthropologist, said that the Zuñi retelling was "easily a better story than the original." That is extravagant praise for a story that affects to improve on the greatest story in the world, but anyone who can be emotionally moved by literature would have to agree with Dr. Benedict. No tale ever collected among the American Indians is better literature by any standards than the "Poor Turkey Girl" as Cushing gave it to the world.

The story that Dr. Parsons called the "Turkey Herd" and which I have retitled "The Unfortunate Turkey Girl" is clearly the tale told by the Zuñi master story maker. But even without the collector's intrusion of linguistic scholarship, the story has gone a long way downhill from the elevation to which Waihusiwa carried the original Cinderella. And yet even in its deterioration, it is an outstanding Indian variant of a tale told first by Europeans.

THE UNFORTUNATE TURKEY GIRL*

Long ago at Kyakima lived a girl who spent all her time herding turkeys. She never did anything for her sisters. Nobody would comb her hair. It was all in a snarl. Her sisters would tell her to cook. They would say, "Why do you so love the turkeys?" She did not answer. After her sisters had cooked, she would take the bread and go out and tend the turkeys.

At Matsaki they were dancing *lapalehakya (lapa>lapapoawe,* "parrots"; *lahakya,* "tell"). They were dancing for the third time, when the turkey girl said, "Younger sisters [*ahani*]!" The turkeys said, "What?"

The girl said, "I want to go and see the dance."

The turkeys said, "You are too dirty to go."

She repeated, "I want to go."

The turkeys said, "Let us eat the lice out of her hair!" Then each ate lice from her hair. Then an elder-sister *(kyauu)* turkey clapped her wings, and down from the air fell women's moccasins *(mokwawe).* Then her younger sister *(ikina)* clapped her wings, and down from the air fell a blanket dress *(yatone).* Then another elder sister clapped her wings, and down from the air fell a belt *(ehnina).* A younger sister clapped her wings, and a *pitone* fell down. An elder sister clapped, and a blanket *(eha)* fell down. The little younger sister *(an hani tsanna)* clapped, and a hair belt *(tsutokehnina)* fell down.

An kyauu said, "Is this all you want?"

The girl said, "Yes." She put on the moccasins and the *ehayatonana.* The turkeys put up her hair in a queue. She said to the turkeys, "I will come back before sundown." She went to her house and made a little cloth bag and filled it with meal. Then she went on to Matsaki.

Her sisters said, "Has she gone to the dance?"

One said, "Yes."

*From Elsie Clews Parsons, "Pueblo Indian Folk Tales, Probably of Spanish Provenience." JAF Volume 31, 1918, 216-255.

"She is too dirty to go."

After she reached Matsaki, as she stood there, the dance-director (*otakya mosi*) asked if she would dance. She said, "Yes." She danced all day. When the sun set, she finished dancing and ran back to the turkeys.

The turkeys had said, when she did not come, "We must not go on living here. Our sister does not love us." When she arrived, they were not there. They were on top of a little hill, singing,

> *Kyana to to*
> *kyana to to*
> *kyana to to ye*
> *uli uli uli to to to to.*

They flew down to Kyakima. They went on as fast as they could until they came to turkey tracks (*tonateanawa*). There they drank at the spring. Their tracks were from north, south, east, west. After they drank, they flew to Shoakoskwikwi. They reached a high rock. They sat on it and sang,

> *Kyana to to*
> *kyana to to*
> *kyana to to ye*
> *uli uli uli to to to to.*

When *awan kyauu* arrived, the turkeys were not there. She saw their tracks. She followed the tracks on a run. At Tonateanawa she saw where they had drunk. She ran on. Then she lost their tracks. She went back to her house. The turkeys had flown to Shoakoskwikwi, to the spring there. That is why at Shoakoskwikwi you see wild turkeys. The girl came back to her house crying. Her sisters said, "Don't cry! You did not return on time. You did not love them." The girl stayed and cooked for her sisters. Thus it was long ago.

When the Trickster, by exercising all his resources of stupidity, managed to get himself stuck fast to the Tar Baby, he was no more enraged than the various folklorists who by the same employment of intellectual resources have become trapped in the controversy surrounding the story's origin. At least one scholar, Aurelio Espinosa, dedicated his entire career to proving that the story originated in India and not in Africa, as the majority of folklorists believed. Espinosa rested his case and his efforts after he had assembled 267 variants of the tale and convinced himself at least that it had antedated even the Buddist *Jatakas,* in which it made its first appearance two thousand or more years ago.

What were the Shoshone doing with the Tar Baby? The question does not need to be asked by anyone with the slightest acquaintance with indigenous Indian mythology. Ubiquitous far past the limits of human endurance in Indian literature is the character of the Trickster, known by a dozen names at least all over the North American continent. His relation to other gods and demigods such as the Culture Hero is still a moot subject among anthropologists, but his persistence not only in Indian lore but in all the tangentially religious stories in the world argues in favor of some deep psychological need. Most persuasive is the theory that Trickster, by exercising his universal compulsions to violate all the basic mores of the people he moves among — by committing outrageous acts of incest outrageously, by engaging in inimitable promiscuity, by disregarding the simplest rules of sanitation, by flouting authority and flaunting his individuality, by stealing, killing, mutilating, and transforming his friends and enemies alike, and especially by acting brainlessly stupid — gives intense vicarious satisfaction to people whose culture would not tolerate such conduct in real life. Trickster is most popular in Indian literature because the American Indians managed to make a difficult life almost impossible. The Indian personality in the Plains, the Eastern Woodlands, the Northwest Pacific Coast, and in parts of the Oasis and Great Basin regions was ferocious, cruel, ultramasculine, egocentric, megalomaniac, hostile, fiercely competitive, extremely Dionysiac. The tensions and pressures imposed on the human body and mind by this orientation to the verities of life were frequently unbearable. In some Indian areas the difficulty was recognized and provided for; the Plains man who did not want to engage in the incessant coup-taking, raiding, and fighting could drop out and become a *berdache* — a legal woman. For the rest of the people (and the frenzied life embraced women as well in many places), the outlet was empathizing with the Trickster. Though he appears as Raven, Mink, Old Man, Finished Man, Hare, Rabbit, Wisakedjak, Sitkonski, Inkotomi, and Nanabozho in various Indian oral literatures, his most common form is Coyote.

A SHOSHONE
TAR BABY*

Coyote walked to the river to wash his eyes. Looking down he saw plenty of chokecherries below. He jumped down and did not find anything; he came near being drowned. He came out and lay down in the same place. After a short while he said, "I wonder why I can't catch them." He got nothing but sand when he went in again and nearly was drowned. He lay down on the bank exhausted, rested, rubbed his eyes, looked up, and saw the cherries above him. "I never thought of that and came near drowning." Then he got up and ate some. When done, he lay in the shade again. He went uphill and sat down. At the bottom he saw pumpkins, corn, and other eatables. He waited on the hill, saying, "I wish it would soon turn dark." Soon the sun set, and he went downhill to get some big watermelons. He made a hole and ate the biggest melon.

The garden belonged to Cottontail. He knew which were the biggest fruits and could not find them the next morning. He found the holes. "I wonder who did that?" He looked for tracks and found them. He got nothing but seeds instead of the fruits. He did not know who had stolen them but decided to catch the thief. He made a fence around the garden and a gate in it. All around the top of the fence he put big cactuses. He went into a piñon grove, got some gum, and put it on both sides of the gate.

He spoke to the gum as follows: "Catch that fellow when he comes and hold him tight."

"All right."

Cottontail stood nearby. Coyote returned the same way and found the fence, went round till he found the gate, and stepped on the gum. He tried to step back but was caught.

"Turn me loose. I want to see my brother. If you don't, I'll hit you with my left hand." He did so and it stuck fast. There was no answer. Cottontail was nearby and heard Coyote talking. "Turn me loose. I want to see my brother; I'll kick you if you don't." His leg got stuck.

Cottontail was sleeping. All night Coyote pleaded to be released. At daylight Cottontail rose, got his whip and took it with him. He approached slowly, while Coyote was still talking in the same way.

"What were you talking all night for?"

"I came to see you, but this thing caught me."

"I told you once, but you don't want to work. Don't you remember? You were too lazy to work. Why do you steal my biggest fruits? You did something bad, now I'll whip you."

*From Robert H. Lowie, "Shoshonean Tales." JAF Volume 37, 1924, 1-242.

"Don't do that, I'll never do it again." Cottontail upbraided him and whipped him; Coyote began to howl. "Brother, I'll never do it any more, let me go!" Finally Cottontail released him, telling him he should not rob any more and that he would give him one more chance.

The short myth collected by Clara True, a teacher at the Santa Clara pueblo in New Mexico, from Jose de Jesus Narangho and Francesco Narangho, is a capsule of very important Culture Hero elements. Culture Heroes, found in all religions, are personages standing halfway between humanity and the gods, who finally elect to give their power and their position over to helping mankind. For this act of treachery against divinity, they are punished by being chained to mountains where vultures eat their vitals, destroyed by assassins, or crucified. In many societies, the Culture Hero is also the Trickster—Polynesia's Maui is the classic example. In aboriginal America the Iroquois Nanabozho or Manabozho created for his people the Grand Medicine Lodge (medicine in all these contexts meaning *mana*); then he left the earth, promising to return again when he was most needed. This promise and prophecy is the second important element of the Tewa Sun myth—the promise to return. It is a frequent characteristic of Culture Heroes; most readers will remember the promise made by King Arthur on his departure for Avalon, or Lord Nelson's expected return when England is in desperate need.

In spite of his defeat by the Spaniards, Montezuma remains unsullied as the greatest of the historical Culture Heroes of Meso-America and the marginal northern region of this great aboriginal civilization. His failure is explained by the alleged, and very probably real, weakness and unworthiness of his subjects. Here that unworthiness is made most dramatic by the test devised by Montezuma.

Culture Heroes are nearly always too great to be the offspring of even extraordinary human beings. From Arthur to Abraham Lincoln, the official parentage of Culture Heroes has been questioned by the mythmakers. It is this unwillingness to allow great men common paternity that created the widespread motif of magical conception through a maiden's eating of a magical object or of her mere propinquity to a god temporarily appearing as a human being.

Myths like Montezuma's prophecy keep hope for a Messiah alive until a more forceful movement occurs.

THE PROPHECY OF MONTEZUMA*

Montezuma, the Sun Boy, had for his mother a poor and despised Indian girl. Every fall the people of the pueblo went to the mountains to gather piñon nuts. The girl and her grandmother lagged behind, knowing that they were not welcome among the others. One day, as they traveled, a beautiful vision appeared before the girl and asked, "Why do you make this journey?"

"To gather piñons," she replied.

He gave her a nut, saying, "Here is a piñon worth all the rest."

She took it and swallowed it whole.

"Do not go to the mountains. Turn about and go home," said he.

They did so; and when they arrived at the house, they found it full of new, strange, white-people's food and furniture. From that time all their wants were miraculously supplied, to the great amazement of their neighbors.

In time a baby was born to the girl—Montezuma, the Sun Boy. The people paid little attention to the lad; but before he was twelve years old, he had developed great skill—supernatural skill—with his bow; and he was always better dressed and better fed than the others. The men called him to their council meeting and questioned him about it. He said he did not know whence he got either the food and clothing or the unusual power.

"If you have the power in yourself, perform us a miracle," they said; "bring the buffalo."

"Buffalo will be here tomorrow," he replied.

The people stationed their best hunters at the four corners of the pueblo with bows and arrows. Montezuma stood on the housetop. Just as the sun came over the hilltops, the sunrise was "dirty with buffalo."

The buffalo rushed onward and trampled to death the men stationed to kill them. Regarding this as a punishment for their unbelief in Montezuma, the people elected him chief.

That was in an old pueblo where Ojo Caliente now stands.

Montezuma's rule was so wise that Santa Clara, San Juan, San

* From Clara Kern Bayliss, "A Tewa Sun Myth." JAF Volume 22, 1909, 333-335.

Ildefonso, Tesuque, Nambé, and Pojoaque put themselves under his dominion. Under him they became rich and powerful.

But at last he began to prophesy changes — the coming of new, noisy conveyances and of a strange, all-conquering race. The Indians would be subdued by a people coming from the South.

"We will resist them," said the people. "Give us your help to drive them back."

"If you can stand the test I will prepare for you, I will consent to your meeting them with force," said he.

The test took place at San Juan. He gathered all the principal men about him. Then he disappeared. Presently he reappeared, coming through the trapdoor in the roof, strangely garbed, booted, and spurred (like a Spanish cavalier). With him came an assemblage of attendants, similarly dressed; and following these came a company of beautiful women, in queer, gay attire. At sight of all this, the Indians were so terrified that they fell over each other in trying to escape from the house.

Then Montezuma came again in his own person.

"I knew beforehand," he said, "that you could not endure the test. If you are so terrified by the mere vision of the conquerors, what will you be by the reality?"

"I must leave you now," said he, "to seek a people greater in strength and numbers. Endure all things and keep the peace. You will have a long period of trouble and persecution; then will come peace and prosperity. Some time during the latter period I will return."

He went south, taking with him a wife. As they journeyed, the woman was playing with two pebbles, tossing them up and catching them. Near the boundary of Old Mexico, on the Rio Grande, the pebbles went up and came down huge boulders. They are there yet.

In the South he ruled over a more powerful people, and now and then the Pueblo people used to hear of his greatness. But at last the Spaniards invaded his domain, and though he met them in person, he could not withstand them. They pressed him so closely that he jumped into a lake and escaped through one of its subterranean passages. No one knows where he went; but he will come again, as he said he would. This is the time of peace of which he told them, and he may soon be here.

Miss True told Francesco that Montezuma had been killed by the Spaniards; and he became greatly disturbed, pacing the floor, rubbing his hair, and vehemently declaring, "It's a lie, a d — d Mexican lie! . . . If you don't believe this story, I can show you the big rocks on the Mexican border. I have seen them many times."

THE GHOST DANCE

When hope has been eroded from the messianic myths among a long-oppressed people, another phenomenon occurs, one of the strangest manifestations of polygenesis the study of man produces. This phenomenon has been variously named, though none of the names is wholly satisfactory: the nativistic endeavor, the messianic complex, the despair cult, the revitalization movement, the cargo cult. Wherever it appears, it takes uncannily the same form, even where diffusion of the fact or the stimulus is an impossible explanation.

When one culture is going down to defeat and threatened extinction before the forcible encroachment of another, superior civilization, and when all reasonable hope has vanished, unreasonable hope appears — usually among the poorest, most degraded elements of the harried society. And it appears in the person of a shaman, even when the culture has a dominant, organized, advanced religion. His shamanistic nature is often euphemistically disguised in the honorific title of "prophet," but a shaman he always is. This shaman has a vision or imagines himself actually to have been taken up (or down) into the spiritual world, where he meets God, Jesus (where the religion of the superior culture is Christianity), the Master of Life, an aboriginal god (one Amazonian nativistic shaman claimed to be a descendant on the one side of the Inca Atahuallpa and on the other of Jesus), or some recognized high deity. God tells the shaman that He is fed up with the way the world is going, and that He has chosen the people of the prophet, the shaman, to undertake management of the world. It is not going to be an easy responsibility, so the people must signify their willingness to be the custodians of the new world by dancing a sacred dance or participating in some ritual of acceptance. When the shaman returns to earth and communicates this message of the millennium to his people, the expected, reasonable reaction almost always occurs: he is told to go away and stop bothering sane people; he is ridiculed; or he is turned over to Pontius Pilate or the Indian agent—unless the shaman brings some evidence of the truth of what he says. Tenskwatawa, the Shawnee prophet, got wind of an impending solar eclipse from the whites; he then threatened to take the sun out of the sky if his people did not believe his message. They did not believe, and so he took the sun out of the sky.

But more than mere proof is needed; the implementation of the movement must be provided for. The provider can be called a "St. Paul," after the most famous example of the type. The "St. Paul" is a man who is associated with the shaman, his religion, or the dominant religion, but whose faith in his own efforts is stronger than his faith in the spirits. He is often an unscrupulous opportunist, eager to wrench the truth as the shaman sees it into a more effective means of achieving the millennium. If this St. Paul has the necessary personal qualities, he can turn the nativistic endeavor into a military movement, and the second obstacle in the path of the prophet has been overcome. But the third obstacle usually puts an end to the idea and the action: the dominant culture retaliates violently, kills the prophet and his St. Paul and all their followers that it is practicable to kill, and life goes on until another prophet appears.

The history of religion is full of examples. In fact, it can be argued that every religion begins with a nativistic endeavor. The most persistent example is Judaism, which has been going continuously since 722 B.C., when the Jews were conquered and dispersed by Nineveh, being recharged with belief by innumerable lesser shamans (all the Old Testament prophets were endeavor leaders) all the way through history. In a strong and lasting nativistic movement, other despair cults are spun off; thus Judaism produced Christianity and Christianity produced Islam as well as all the sects of Protestantism, which are producing now civil rights movements like the Black Muslims, which are producing their own nativistic heresies. And there are the Flagellants, the Quakers, the Shakers, the Ranters, the Jumpers, the Methodists, the Wilderness Worshippers, the Pillar of Fire cults, the Burning Bushers, the British Israelites, the Fifth Monarchy Men, the Cargo Cults of the southwestern Pacific islands, and in Japan after World War II the *Odoru Shukyo,* or Dancing Religion (which still has a following of three hundred and fifty thousand in Japan and some thirty thousand in thirty-two other countries).

Often the nativistic endeavor must compete with other messianic movements in its own time, and in these situations natural selection favors the strongest and most ruthless. Christianity won out over a confusion of other proletarian rebellions as the Roman Empire began to crack — Mithraism, for example, which gave Christianity much of its early mythology, and the Essenes, who were Christians before Christ.

Often the St. Pauls are better remembered than the instituting prophet. We do not know the name of the "Delaware Prophet," who set the frontier afire in 1762, but we memorialize his assistant's name by putting it on the hoods of thousands of automobiles — Pontiac. Infrequently, the prophet is his own St. Paul; the most notable example of this is Joan of Arc.

Nativistic endeavors among the American Indians produced at least three United States presidents. In 1805 the Shawnee prophet, Tenskwatawa, used his brother for his St. Paul — a handsome paragon of Indian virtues, Tecumseh. Tecumseh tried to unite all the Indians from Canada to Florida to overthrow the white man, but was defeated by William Henry Harrison in 1811. In 1835, when the Whigs were reduced to looking under flat, wet rocks for suitable candidates to oppose the Jacksonians, someone thought of old General Harrison. The Democrats justifiably ridiculed Harrison as fit only to sit on the porch of his log cabin, swigging cider. So the Whigs made log cabins and cider the basis of their campaign, and Harrison was elected by the judicious wisdom of the people. He had mercy upon his nation and died a month after assuming office, and Tyler assumed the office of the Presidency. Later in the century, when presidential candidates were similarly undistinguished, Benjamin Harrison was elected because his grandfather had been President.

But the most important of the scores of known American Indian despair cults was the Ghost Dance. Like the Essenic movement that anticipated Christianity, a Ghost Dance sprang up in 1870 among the humble Paviotso, a subtribe of northern Utes at Walker Lake in western Nevada. The prophet of this first Ghost

Dance has been arbitrarily identified as one Wodziwob. This first endeavor of the Paviotso burned out after the violent end put to the Modoc War in 1873, and because Wodziwob made both of the fatal mistakes to which nativistic prophets are prone: (1) he put a calendar date on the millennium, and (2) he died without making provisions for his resurrection.

The Ghost Dance broke out again in 1889, when a shaman variously identified as Jack Wilson, Jackson Wilson, John Johnson, Big Rumbling Belly, Koitsow, Cowejo, Kwohitsauq, Wopokahte, Wevokar, and Wovoka arose, again among the Walker Lake Paviotso. This time there were competent ethnographers on the scene to record the origin and the evolution of the religion—principally James Mooney, Indian agent and anthropologist. When the news of the Messiah (as the prophet was called by the Indians; anthropologists have settled upon the name "Wovoka" for him) reached Mooney, who was then in Oklahoma, he hurried out to Nevada to interview him. When he arrived, he found that volunteer and appointive St. Pauls were streaming in from other tribes in all directions, getting the myth from the lips of the Messiah himself and distorting it for their own purposes and for the purposes of their tribes. The apostle Porcupine, mentioned in several of the following reports, was the source of the mythic change that made Wovoka a reincarnated Jesus Christ. But Mooney's report was impeccably accurate; he even got a photograph of Wovoka (the Messiah wanted to charge Mooney $2.50 to take his picture, but vanity got the better of him when Mooney declined).

The course of the myth and its movement is documented satisfactorily in the selections that follow, for the editor of the *Journal of American Folklore* at that time was personally very much interested in the phenomenon, as well he might have been. Tribe after tribe caught the fire of the Ghost Dance; only those tribes that had a good reason for rejecting it did so. The Navaho would have nothing to do with it, because the primary prophecy of the Messiah was the return of all the dead Indians—and Navaho dislike dead folks the way they dislike fish.

The Ghost Dance came to a violent and tragic end at Wounded Knee Creek in the Sioux Badlands on December 29, 1890. That battle—or massacre—also put an end to the Indian Wars and proved that all the idealists are wrong when they insist that bullets and bombs cannot kill ideas. The last that was heard of Wovoka — the Messiah — was that he had sold himself as a sideshow attraction at the midwinter fair in San Francisco around 1893.

REPORT OF AN INDIAN VISIT TO JACK WILSON, THE PAYUTE MESSIAH*

What stands below is an authentic report of three Cheyenne Indians of the Tongue River Reservation, Montana, of what they saw and heard in presence of the reputed Indian Messiah. Their names are Porcupine, Big Beaver, and Ridge Walker, and apparently faith or curiosity impelled them to see personally the religious leader, who enjoys great popularity among the different western tribes and preaches only in his native language, the Payute. They met him, as the report states, at Walker Lake, Nevada, in the autumn of 1890. The relation of an Arapaho Indian, Sage, especially prompted them to visit the divine man.

After returning home to the Tongue River Reservation, Montana, they met there Abe Somers, a Cheyenne Indian educated at the Carlisle Training School, Pennsylvania, and recounted to him their experiences on that trip. By chance Abe Somers came to Lawrence in northeastern Kansas, in February, 1891; met there Henry Dawson North, a young Arapaho Indian then following an educational course at the Indian School of Lawrence; and gave him a circumstantial relation of what the three Cheyenne Indians had told him. North wrote down their words on the spot, and in the report given below they are reproduced verbatim from the Cheyenne language, North being equally familiar with Arapaho and Cheyenne. At present (1893) North is Arapaho interpreter for the United States Indian agent at the seat of the Cheyenne and Arapaho agency, at Darlington, Oklahoma.

Several Indians of that same reservation went from time to time on that long journey to Jack Wilson to vent their curiosity about the promised coming of the new Christ. Their names were (1) Black Bear, (2) Hänätchä-thiāk, or Sitting Bull, (3) Washee — all Arapaho Indians — and (4) one Cheyenne half-blood, Edward Geary. They started for Walker Lake from Darlington, their habitual residence, in the autumnal season of 1892, and met Jack Wilson, who claimed to be only the mouthpiece of the real Messiah and was raised by a family of white

*By Albert S. Gatschet. JAF Volume 6, 1893, 108-111.

people as one of their own children. He said that the appearance of the Messiah would occur in only four years from that time; so they had to return home rather downcast and dissatisfied.

Abe Somers himself is doubtful concerning the divine mission of Jack Wilson, as our readers may themselves gather from his report, which is here given *in extenso*. Some queer expressions may be accounted for, and excused by, the fact that the report is an almost verbatim translation from an Indian language.

ABOUT THE MESSIAH.

Dear Friends—one and all. Don't force your and others' minds on this letter, but resist it and keep your minds from it. I simply want to tell you just what I learned from Mr. Porcupine, Big Beaver, and I am sorry to say from one of them, a cousin of mine, Ridge Walker, son of Beaver Claws. I expect many of you are wishing to know, and perhaps many of you have already heard about it. I have met them face to face, and have questioned them personally when I met them; and so I learned from them some of their Messiah ideas. I try to make an account of just what I have learned from these three persons.

In the fall of the year 1890, they say, they first heard of this new Christ, at the Arapaho and Shoshone Agency, Wyoming Territory. When they and other Cheyennes of Tongue River went on a visit to said tribes in the autumn of 1890, an Arapaho Indian named Sage, who had been to the southwestern country in 1888, told them that a new Christ had arisen for the Indians; he said where he could be found and explained his doctrine to them. Farther on, Porcupine said that he and the other Cheyennes were much interested, and determined to see the Messiah; but as all could not go so far, nine of these Cheyennes were sent back to Tongue River Agency to tell the people what they had heard. Porcupine and several of the Cheyennes went on. When they arrived in Utah, they received large accessions to their caravan, Indians joining them en route at the different points, and so at last their meeting took place at Walker Lake, to hear the new Christ speak. There were many people present, including women and children.

Then Mr. Porcupine says to the Messiah: "I and my people have been living in ignorance until I went and found out the truth." He sat with his head bowed all the time, and after a while he arose and said he was very glad to see his children: "I have sent for you and I am glad that you have come, and I am going to talk to you after a while about our relations who are dead and gone. My children, I want you to listen to all I have to say, and I will teach you how to dance a dance, and I want you to dance it; get ready for the dance, and then when the dance is over, I will talk to you."

He was dressed in a white coat with stripes; the rest of his dress was that of a white man's, except that he had on a pair of moccasins. And then we commenced to dance, everybody joining in with the Christ, singing while we danced. We danced till late in the night, and he said we had danced enough. And in the morning after breakfast we went in the circle and spread grass over it on the ground, the Christ standing in the midst of us, and told us that he was going away on that day and that he would be back next morning and talk to us.

In the night, when I first saw him I thought he was an Indian; but the next day, when I could see him better, he looked different; he was not so dark as an Indian, nor so light as a white man. He had no beard or whiskers, but very heavy eyebrows; he was a good-looking man, and we were crowded up very close.

We had been told that nobody was to talk; and even if a thing was whispered, the Christ would know it. I heard that Christ had been crucified, and I looked to see, and I saw a scar on his wrist and one on his face and he seemed to be the man. I could not see his feet.

He would talk to us all day. On that evening we were all assembled again to part with him. When we assembled he began to sing, and he commenced to tremble all over violently for a while, and then sat down; and we danced all on that night, the Christ lying beside us apparently dead. The next morning we went to our breakfast; the Christ was with us again. After breakfast four heralds went around and called out that the Christ was back with us, and wanted talk with us; and so the circle was made again; they assembled and Christ came amongst them and sat down. He said they were to listen to him while he talked to us. "I am the man who made everything you see around you. I am not lying to my children. I made this earth and everything on it. I have been to Heaven and seen your dead friends, and seen my father and mother. In the beginning, after God made the earth, they sent me back to teach the people; and when I came back on the earth, the people were afraid of me and treated me badly. This is what they have done to me (showing his scars). I did not try to defend myself, and I found my children were bad, so I went back to Heaven and left them; and in so many years I would come back and see to my children, and at the end of this time I was sent back to teach them. My father told me that the earth is getting old and worn out, and the people getting bad, and that I was to renew everything as it used to be, and make it better; and he said all our dead were to be resurrected and they were all to come back to the earth, and that the earth was too small for them and us; he would do away with heaven and make the earth large enough to contain us all; and that we must tell all the people we meet about these things.

He spoke to us about fighting, and said that was bad and we must keep from it; that the earth was to be all good hereafter; that we must be friends with one another. He said that in the fall of the year the youth of all the good people would be renewed, so that nobody would be more than forty years old. The youth of everyone would be renewed in the spring. He said if we were all good, he would send people among us who could heal all our wounds and sickness by mere touch, and that we could live forever.

This is what I have witnessed, and many other things wonderful which I cannot describe. Please don't follow the ideas of that man. He is not the Christ. No man in the world can see God at any time. Even the angels of God cannot.

BIOGRAPHIC FACTS.

From information just received from Mr. James Mooney, who has seen the Payute prophet in person, I present the following biographic facts, with reference to this personage.

As near as can be ascertained, Jack Wilson is now (1893) thirty-five years old. He was called after the family name of David Wilson, the white farmer who brought him up in Mason Valley, Nevada, after the demise of his father. In the same valley, about thirty miles from the capital, Carson, he resides now. His stature nearly reaches six feet, which is more than the native Payute generally attains, and this magnitude of bodily proportions may have contributed to his success. He is a *full-blooded* Indian and was married in his twentieth year; no other language but Payute is spoken by him, and he is but imperfectly acquainted with English. There is no doubt that his religious teachings rest on a well-ordained religious system, and, in spite of the numerous false reports that are spread about him, he does not claim to be either God or Jesus Christ, the Messiah, or any divine, superhuman being whatever. "I am the annunciator of God's message from the spiritual world and a prophet for the Indian people," is the way he defines the scope of his work among men. The first revelation he received of God himself took place about four years ago, after he had fallen asleep. God admonished him to work zealously among his fellow men in promoting good morals and delegated special powers to him to this effect. Thus he considers himself a messenger of God appointed in a dream, and has, on that account, compared himself to St. John the Baptist. When he had that dream, he thought himself to be in heaven.

ACCOUNT OF THE NORTHERN CHEYENNES CONCERNING THE MESSIAH*

Mr. George Bird Grinnell, editor of *Forest and Stream* (New York), a person thoroughly familiar with Indian customs, and himself by adoption a member of the Blackfeet tribe, while at Fort Keogh, in the

* By William Wells Newell. JAF Volume 4, 1891, 61-69.

autumn of 1890, had an opportunity to learn from the chiefs of the
Northern Cheyennes their version of the origin and spread of the superstition. A statement of Mr. Grinnell's experience as given in an interview published in the New York *Tribune*, November 23, 1890, is given
substantially as follows according to the author's revision:

I spent several days at Fort Keogh, living in a camp of Cheyenne scouts
employed by the government. While there I saw and talked with two of the
principal chiefs of the Northern Cheyenne tribe, Two Moons, the war chief,
and White Bull, the peace chief. Both of these chiefs talked with me very freely
about the spread of the religious superstition among the Indians concerning
the new Messiah. Both of them felt very anxious, for they feared that the
excitement might lead to an outbreak. They told me, what I had already known,
that this supposed Messiah had predicted certain special events to come off
in September, and when these failed to happen the Northern Cheyennes lost
faith in the new doctrine. But shortly after the failure of the prophecies, some
Shoshones and Arapahos came over from Fort Washakie to visit the Cheyenne
agency, and when they got to the Cheyenne camp they reported that while
traveling along on the prairie they had met with a party of Indians who had
been dead thirty or forty years, and who had been resurrected by the Messiah.
Since their resurrection, the formerly dead Indians, so the visitors said, had
been going about just like the other Indians who had never died.

This started up the excitement again, and all the Indians at the agency began
to dance. Two Moons and White Bull were all the more alarmed because of
the trouble that the Northern Cheyennes had had last spring. That trouble
shows a trait peculiar to the Indian character. Two white men had been killed,
one of them by no one knew whom, but four or five Indians were arrested
on suspicion, were kept in jail for several months, and were then released,
not a particle of evidence having been offered against them. The other white
man was killed by two young men of the Cheyenne tribe. This one was a settler who had gone out in search of a lot of milch cows. The Indian boys were
out hunting, and one of them, stepping quickly out from behind some bushes,
frightened the cows. The settler was angry, and struck the Indian boy with a
rope. The young fellow went away and talked with his companion, and both
turned toward the settler, whose attitude was menacing. The second young
Indian raised his rifle and shot the settler dead. The boys went back to camp
and told American Horse, their chief, what they had done. They did not want
to be imprisoned and hanged, but they knew that they would have to die, and
preferred to die like warriors. So they told American Horse to send word to
the troops and the Indian police that they had fled to a hill four or five miles
away and could be captured there.

The boys dressed themselves in their best clothes, armed and painted themselves, and, mounting their horses, rode to the hill they had named. The troops
and the Indian police were told, and started out to capture the boys. Half a
mile from the hill, the boys were seen standing by their horses. As soon as
they saw the troops they mounted their horses and charged, two boys against
a hundred men. When within a range of two hundred yards the troops opened
fire, but the boys pressed on, charged clear through the troops unhurt, and
succeeded in getting a quarter of a mile beyond their enemies, when they
turned and charged back. Both boys were killed as they came on the second
time.

This irritated the Cheyennes, who are the bravest of men, Indians or white. It is clear that if people believe that they are going to be resurrected in a short time, they do not mind dying very much, and the Cheyennes are so extremely brave anyway that this belief makes them all the more dangerous and reckless. This tribe has not been treated well, as it is. They have no land excepting on the hilltops, the best land having been settled upon by the whites before the reservation was given to the Indians. Nothing will grow upon the Cheyenne lands without irrigation. Still, I do not think that the Cheyennes will go into any organized revolt. Some crazy officer of the troops, or some hotheaded settler, who may become frightened, may kill an Indian or two, and then the younger men may start in to get revenge. In this way, and in this way alone, I believe, a general outbreak may be precipitated.

I never heard of the dance of the Indians called the "Ghost Dance" until I returned to the East. In the Indian country it is known as the "Dance to Christ." The Southern Cheyennes and the Southern Arapahos were among those by whom I saw it danced. The Indians believe that the more they dance, the sooner the Christ will come. The dance usually lasts for four nights, beginning a little before sundown and continuing until any hour the next morning. The Indians, men, women, and children, form a circle, probably one hundred feet in diameter, standing shoulder to shoulder, close together. All, of course, face inward. Several men take their places in the circle and start the dance by singing a song in the Arapaho tongue. They move slowly to the left, one foot at a time, keeping in unison with the music. The scene is extremely weird when the moon is up. The Indians clad in white sheets look like so many ghosts. Their rapt and determined faces show how earnest they are. The hoarse, deep voices of the men and the shriller notes of the women mingle in a kind of rude harmony. They sing exactly together and their dancing is in perfect time to the music of the song. As I beheld it, the scene was one to thrill the onlooker.

At intervals of a few notes particular emphasis is given, and the note so emphasized is the signal to move the left foot to the left. So the circle moves around, quaint shadows playing on the turf both in and out of the circle of the dance. Frequently a few of those sitting outside the circle step into it to dance, while those who have been dancing may stop to rest. They move their heads and bodies very little, but step to the left in time with the music, so long as the song is kept up. At intervals, all in the circle sit down to rest and smoke. Even the Cheyennes sing the music of the Dance to Christ in the Arapahoan tongue. This is because the original discoverer of the Messiah was Arapaho.

I talked with "Billy" Roland, the scout who had seen Porcupine. Porcupine claimed to be the second man of the Plains tribes who had seen the Messiah. Most of the Indians now, I believe, claim to have seen him. The fact is, however, that I could find no one in the Cheyenne camp who claimed to have seen the Messiah in the flesh — that is, no one but Sitting Bull, an Arapaho. It must be understood that it is Sitting Bull the Arapaho, not Sitting Bull the Sioux, who claims to be the original prophet. This Arapaho was absent from his tribe for twelve or fourteen years with the Gros Ventres of the Prairie, a branch of the Arapahos. I think the revelations came to him when he was at Fort Washakie, the headquarters of the Northern Arapaho tribe. This tribe split up about forty years ago, one half going south as far as the Indian Territory, and the other going to the far North. They visit each other back and forth, however, and keep up a constant correspondence by letter, one of the disadvantages, perhaps, of the Indian education.

While I was at the Pawnee agency a lot of letters were received from the

Sioux, trying to get the Pawnees to unite with them. Some of the Indians came to me and asked me if I believed in the Messiah theory, and I told them, "No." When I left the Pawnees last month, there was no reason to believe that they would take part in any outbreak. There was some excitement reported among the Poncas during my stay with the Cheyennes, and many of them came to the Cheyennes to learn the Dance to Christ. At that time, too, the Caddoes were dancing according to the new doctrine. The Caddoes are a branch of the Pawnees and are too intelligent, I believe, to go into a revolt. Still, although more civilized than most of the tribes, and having farms and houses, there was more excitement among the Caddoes than among any of the other tribes. The Wichitas, Comanches, and Kiowas were also dancing in October. They are probably wilder than any of the others, but I don't think even they could be influenced to join an open revolt.

In answer to further inquiries, Mr. Grinnell informs the editor that during the autumn of 1890 he spent some time among the Southern Cheyennes, and that when he was in their camp he saw Sitting Bull, the Arapaho, who asserts that he is the chief prophet of the new religion. Mr. Grinnell has sent a fuller account of his observations among the Northern and Southern Cheyennes, written in November, 1890, and in part printed in *The New York Times*, which is given below:

Although the tribes in the Indian Territory believe that the Christ appeared to the Indians in the North, the truth is that the more northern tribes know nothing about the new religion. About the Blackfeet, Assiniboines, Gros Ventres of the Prairie, Rees, Mandans, and Gros Ventres of the Village, I can speak with great confidence, for within two months I have seen and talked with men of all these tribes. But as soon as one gets south of the Northern Pacific Railroad he begins to hear, if he goes into an Indian camp, whispers of the coming of the Messiah, or the women and children singing the songs of the worship dances. The Northern Cheyennes are interested believers in the coming of this Christ. All, or almost all, the bands of the Missouri River Sioux believe in him; so do the Shoshones, the Arapahos — north and south — the Kiowas, Comanches, Wichitas, Caddoes, and many other smaller tribes. All the above mentioned tribes hold the worship dances. The Pawnees, Poncas, Otoes, and Missourias have heard of the Messiah and believe in him, but they have not yet generally taken up the dances.

Something over a year ago an Arapaho Indian named Sitting Bull came into the Shoshone agency at Fort Washakie, in Wyoming, and told the Indians there that somewhere up north he had seen a Christ. He gave a detailed account of his journeyings up to the point where he reached the place where he saw the vision, for such it appears to have been, described the person whom he saw, told what he had said, and that he foretold a restoration of the old order of things which prevailed on the plains and in the mountains before the advent of the white settlers. The Christ told Sitting Bull of his previous life on this earth, when he had come to help the white people, of their refusal to accept him, showed the scars on his hands and feet where he had been nailed to the cross, and finally said that before long the whites would all be removed from the country, the buffalo and the game would return in their old-time abundance, and the Indians would settle down to the old life in which they depended for subsistence on game killed by the bow and arrow. After some further conversation Sitting Bull was fed on buffalo meat and then fell asleep and woke up near his own camp.

I am not at all inclined to credit the statement that this religion originated with Sitting Bull, but am disposed to think that he received the idea from other Indians, perhaps farther west. At all events, it appears quite certain that he had not been living with his tribe for ten or twelve years. Where he had been during this time is not known. Possibly with the Northern Cheyennes or perhaps with the Gros Ventres of the Prairie.

This announcement by the Arapaho received a good deal of attention from the Indians at Washakie, and some time in the winter a Northern Cheyenne named Porcupine, who was visiting there and who heard the story, made a pilgrimage to see for himself if these things were true. His story, as I received it recently when in the country of the Northern Cheyennes, was as follows: From Washakie he went to some point where he took the cars and traveled for some distance; then, leaving the railroad, he went two days in a wagon until he reached the borders of a large lake, near which is an Indian agency. Near this lake were camped a great many Indians of different tribes and some whites. When Porcupine reached there, these people told him that the Christ would be there to meet them the following afternoon. The brush, sage, and rose bushes had been cut off close to the ground over a circle perhaps one hundred feet in diameter, and in the underbrush close to this circle a little place had been cut out and a piece of canvas spread on the ground for the Christ to lie on when he should come.

The next day, as the sun was getting low, the people all assembled about this circle, and presently a man was seen walking into it. The people stood about until he had reached the middle of the circle, and then they went in to meet him. He stood in the midst and talked to them, appearing to be able to talk all languages and to make himself understood by all the tribes present. On the first occasion of his appearance he had short hair, a beard, and wore citizens' clothing — in other words, was apparently a white man. Subsequently he had long hair, down to his waist, and his skin was darker, like an Indian's. He told the people that things were going to be changed: that the game and the buffalo would be brought back; that they should again have their own country, and that the world should be turned upside down and all the whites spilled out. He closed his speech by saying that in the night he should go up to heaven to see God. Then he went to the place prepared for him and lay down and slept.

Next morning about nine or ten o'clock the people again gathered about the circle, and presently the Messiah walked in among them. He told them that he had just returned from heaven, where he had seen God. He taught the people a dance and several songs, and ordered them to hold one of these dances for four days and four nights at the full of every moon. Such is Porcupine's story.

The locality at which Porcupine saw the Christ is not known, but as nearly as I can gather, from those who claim to be best informed on the subject, it was near some lake in western Nevada, possibly Walker Lake or Pyramid Lake.

In this new dance the people form a circle facing inward and standing shoulder to shoulder, touching each other. They sing the new songs taught them by the prophets of this religion and move with a slow-stepping motion in time to the song from right to left, bending the knees slightly at each step, so that the head dips down a little. In the midst of the ring formed by the dancers usually stands an old man, who with uplifted hands exhorts them.

As the ceremony proceeds, some of the dancers become excited, and at intervals a man will break out of the ring and rush to the center of the circle, there falling stiffly on the ground, where he may lie for hours perfectly motionless. Women, too, rush to the center of the circle, but they seem to be affected less easily than the men, and will sometimes dance about for ten or fifteen minutes, crying and wailing and making strange gestures, before they fall over and lose consciousness. At a dance of Cheyennes and Arapahos that I attended a few nights ago, there were at one time in the circle three prostrate men and two men and two women on their feet. At a Caddo dance that I witnessed recently, several women broke away from the ring and danced about like intoxicated or insane persons outside the circle, finally falling apparently insensible. One of these, a young girl not more than sixteen or seventeen years old, recovered in a short time and rose and walked away.

With the Northern Cheyennes, the dance differs in one or two details from that practiced among the southern section of this tribe. Among the Northern Cheyennes, four fires are built outside of the circle of the dance — one fire toward each of the cardinal points. These fires stand about twenty yards back from the circle, and are built of long poles or logs, set up on end, so as to form a rough cone, much as the poles of a lodge are set up. The fires are lighted at the bottom and make high bonfires, which are kept up so long as the dance continues.

One of the cardinal points of faith of this religion is that those who are dead will all be raised and will again live upon the earth with their people. Sometimes during a dance a man who has been in a trance will revive and may rise to his feet and shout in a loud voice that he sees about him certain people who have long been dead. He will call these risen dead by name and say that he sees them standing or sitting near certain of the people who are looking on, mentioning the names of the latter. The people believe that he sees these long dead people and are frightened to know that they are close to them. It is not quite clear whether the living regard these persons whom they cannot see as actually resurrected but invisible, or as ghosts. As nearly as I can gather by talking with the Indians, they think them ghosts.

In connection with these dances what are regarded as miracles are not infrequently performed. For example, the other night one of the prophets announced that a number of persons long dead had arisen from the grave and had come to visit him. They had brought him, he said, a piece of buffalo meat, and that night the people should again taste their old-time food. After the dance was over this man appeared in the ring holding in his hands a small wooden dish full of meat. He called up to him the dancers, one hundred or more, one by one, and gave to each a small piece of meat out of the dish. After all had been supplied the dish appeared to be still half full.

The Cheyennes and other tribes in this territory frequently receive from the northern Indians letters touching on religious topics, and sometimes these letters contain most extravagant statements, which, however, are received by the Indians with implicit faith. A letter which came recently told of an attempt on the part of some United States troops to arrest a prophet. The soldiers approached him and tried to take hold of him in order to take him to the guardhouse, but as they reached out their hands to seize him, their arms would fall down to their sides. For a long time they tried to take hold of him, but they could not do it. He did not attempt to resist or run away, but sat there motionless. At length the soldiers gave it up for a bad job and went away.

Still more remarkable is an account which tells of a narrow escape by one of the three major generals of the army. According to this story, General Miles, with some troops, went out in person to arrest the Christ. When they came to the place where he was, he told the general that it was useless to attempt to arrest him; it could not be done, and it would be better for him not to try to do it. The general said that he had received his orders and must obey them. He then commanded the troops to take the prisoner into custody, whereupon the Christ made it rain for seven days and seven nights, and the result was that all the soldiers were drowned, General Miles alone escaping alive to tell the tale of the disaster.

The Southern Cheyennes state that the destruction of the white race will take place by its being overwhelmed in a sea of mud. The surface of the earth will become a mire in which the whites will sink, while the Indians will remain on the surface. This I believe to be a purely Indian conception, for more than one tribe believe that the giants who used to inhabit the earth, before the creation of the Indians of today, were destroyed by the Deity in just this way. In my book on the Pawnees *(Pawnee Hero Stories and Folk-Tales)*, I have stated that the Pawnees believe their predecessors on this earth to have perished in that way. The Arikaras have the same belief, which is no doubt shared by all members of the Pawnee family and perhaps by other tribes.

An account of the manner in which these spirit dances are performed is given by Mrs. James A. Finley, wife of the post trader at Wounded Knee, and is here printed as copied into the *Essex County Mercury* (Salem, Massachusetts), November 26, 1890:

This dance is participated in often by as many as five hundred Indians. In preparing for the dance, they cut the tallest tree that they can find and, having dragged it to a level piece of prairie, set it up in the ground. Under this tree four of the head men stand. The others form in a circle and begin to go around and around the tree. They will dance continuously from Friday afternoon till sundown on Sunday. They keep going around in one direction until they become so dizzy that they can scarcely stand, then turn and go in the other direction, and keep it up until they swoon from exhaustion. That is what they strive to do, for while they are in a swoon, they think they see and talk with the new Christ. When they regain consciousness they tell their experience to the four wise men under the tree. At the end of the dance they have a grand feast, the revel lasting all Sunday night. They kill several steers and eat them raw and drink and gorge themselves to make up for their fast.

The Indians lose all their senses in the dance. They think they are animals. Some get down on all fours and bob about like buffalos. When they cannot lose their senses from exhaustion, they butt their heads together, beat them upon the ground, and do anything to become insensible, so that they may be ushered into the presence of the new Christ. One poor Indian, she says, when he recovered his senses, said that Christ had told him he must return to earth, because he had not brought with him his wife and child. His child had died two years before, and the way the poor fellow cried was heartrending. At a recent dance, one of the braves was to go into a trance and remain in this condition four days. At the close of this period he was to come to life as a buffalo; he would still have the form of a man, but he would be a buffalo. They were then to kill the buffalo, and every Indian who did not eat a piece of him would become a dog. The man who was to turn into a buffalo was perfectly willing, and Mrs. Finley presumes they have killed and eaten him by this time. This lady is of the opinion that if the government lets them alone, there will be no need of troops; they will kill themselves dancing. Seven or eight of them died as a result of one dance, near Wounded Knee.

It seems evident, in a general way, that the Indian messianic excitement is the result of a combination of primitive beliefs and introduced Christian conceptions; but the task of giving a correct account of the origin, progress, and varieties of the movement is likely to be attended with much difficulty, and to illustrate the obstacles encountered by any person who undertakes, even under the most favorable circumstances, to write history; while, with regard to the relation of the original Indian ideas and dances to those now developed, the most divergent opposite views exist. The editor of this Journal has therefore prepared the following letter, to be sent to persons whose position has given opportunity for accurate observation respecting the superstition:

CAMBRIDGE, MASS., *February* 1, 1891.

DEAR SIR, — I am anxious to obtain all accessible information regarding the character and causes of the religious excitement existing among several Indian tribes, with a view to presenting a history of the matter in the *Journal of American Folk-Lore*. I would therefore request you to furnish me with any particulars which you may be able to give respecting the following points:

1. The origin and progress of the movement in your neighborhood, and anything relating to the history of the belief respecting an Indian Messiah, forms of his manifestation, revelations supposed to be made by him, etc.

2. The nature and method of the Ghost or Spirit dances, the songs used in these, with Indian words if obtainable, the ritual of preparation, fasting, acts of self-injury, etc., and beliefs relative to the dances.

3. Manifestations accompanying the phenomena, — ecstacies, visions, trances, stories of miracle and resurrection, preachings, if such exist, and legends to which the expectation has given rise.

4. The state of mind resulting from final failure, and the manner in which defeat is explained; the effect which failure has on the original belief.

5. Any other material which you may consider to be connected with the subject.

In return, I shall be happy to send to informants copies of the *Journal of American Folk-Lore* containing articles based on information received.

                    Yours very truly,
                              Editor of Journal of American Folk-Lore.

THE GHOST DANCE
REACHES THE OUTSIDE WORLD*

GHOST DANCE AT PINE RIDGE.

An interesting account of the dances near Pine Ridge Agency, South Dakota, is contributed to the *New York Evening Post,* April 18, 1891, by Mrs. Z. A. Parker. The accuracy of the description is vouched for by Miss Elaine Goodale of the agency. According to his account, the Indians at Pine Ridge began their Ghost-Dancing about the twentieth of June, selecting a beautiful location near the White Clay Creek. The white visitors found "over three hundred tents placed in a circle, with a large pine tree in the center, which was covered with strips of cloth of various colors, eagle feathers, stuffed birds, claws, and horns—all offerings to the Great Spirit." In the center, about the tree, were gathered the medicinemen and those who in visions had been permitted to hear and see departed friends. The writer observes:

I think that they wore the ghost shirt or ghost dress for the first time that day. I noticed that these were all new and were worn by about seventy men and forty women. The wife of a man called Return-from-Scout had seen in a vision that the spirits of her friends all wore a similar robe, and on reviving from her trance she called the women together, and they made a great number of the sacred garments. They were of white cotton cloth; the women's dress was cut like their ordinary gowns—a loose robe with wide, flowing sleeves, painted blue in the neck, in the shape of a three-cornered handkerchief with moon, stars, and birds, interspersed with real feathers, painted on the waist and sleeves. While dancing they wound their shawls about their waists, letting them fall to within three inches of the ground—the fringe at the bottoms. Some wore beautiful brocades, and others, costly shawls given them by fathers, brothers, and husbands, who had traveled with Buffalo Bill. In the hair, near the crown, a feather was tied. I noticed an absence of any manner of bead ornaments and, as I knew their vanity and fondness for them, wondered why it was. Upon making inquiries, I found that they discarded everything that they could which was made by the white men.

The ghost shirt for the men was of the same material—shirt and leggings painted in red. Some of the leggings were painted in stripes running up and down, others running around. The shirt around the neck was painted blue,

*From JAF Volume 4, 1891, 160-165.

and the whole garment fantastically sprinkled with figures of birds, bow and arrow, sun, moon, stars, and everything which they saw in nature. Down the outside of the sleeve were rows of feathers tied by the quill ends and left to fly in the breeze; also a row around the neck and up and down the outside of the leggings. I noticed that a number had stuffed birds and squirrel heads tied in the long hair. The faces of all were painted red, with a black halfmoon on the forehead or on one cheek.

As the crowd gathered about the tree, the "High Priest," or master of ceremonies, began his address, giving them directions as to the chant and other matters. After he had spoken for about fifteen minutes, they arose and formed in a circle. As nearly as I could count, there were between three and four hundred persons. One stood directly behind another, each with his hands on his neighbor's shoulders. After walking about a few times, chanting "Father, I come!" they stopped marching, but remained in the circle, and sent up the most fearful, heart-piercing wails I ever heard—crying, moaning, groaning, and shrieking out their grief and naming over their departed friends and relatives, at the same time taking up handfuls of dust at their feet, washing their hands in it, and throwing it over their heads. Finally, they raised their eyes to heaven, their hands clasped high above their heads, and stood straight and perfectly still, invoking the power of the Great Spirit to allow them to see and talk with their people who had died. This ceremony lasted for about fifteen minutes, when they all sat down where they were and listened to another address, which I did not understand, but which I afterwards learned was words of encouragement and assurance of the coming of the Messiah.

When they rose again, they enlarged the circle by facing toward the center, taking hold of hands, and moving around in the manner of school-children in their play of needle's eye. And now the most intense excitement began. They would go as fast as they could—their heads moving from side to side, their bodies swaying, their arms with hands gripped tightly in their neighbors', swinging back and forth with all their might. If one more weak or frail came near falling, he would be jerked up and back into position, until tired nature gave way. The ground had been worn and worked by many feet, until the fine, flour-like dust lay light and loose to the depth of two or three inches. The wind, which had increased, would sometimes take it up, enveloping the dancers, and hiding them from view.

In the ring were men, women, and children; the strong and robust, the weak consumptives, and those near to death's door. They believed that those who were sick would be cured by joining in the dance and losing consciousness. Anyone can imagine what this intense excitement, combined with the dust and fatigue, would do for them. From the beginning they chanted to a monotonous tune the words:

> Father, I come!
> Mother, I come!
> Brother, I come!
> Father, give us back our arrows!

As a result of this dance over one hundred persons remained on the ground, lying in an unconscious condition. The dancers then stopped, seating themselves in a circle, and as each person recovered from his swoon, he was brought forward and told to relate his experience. The performance was repeated three times a day, accompanied by fasting and ablutions—those who united in the dance being required to bathe every morning.

DANCE AMONG THE IOWAS.

A correspondent of the New York *Tribune* writing from Guthrie, Oklahoma, January 11, 1891, describes a dance among the Iowas. This tribe had been visited by Sioux runners, and the solemn character of the ceremony seemed to indicate a religious motive similar to the Ghost Dance. However, in this case, the dancers were made up and moved in a manner to represent the buffalo, bear, ponies, [and other animals]. The squaws did not dance but peeped from the tipis. For five hours the drum was heard, and at the close of the ceremony only three men could make the circle without falling, while at last even these succumbed.

Among causes of the movement, much stress is laid on the desire of the medine men to retain their waning power. Bishop Hare, of South Dakota, in a public address at Cambridge, Massachusetts, described the whole movement as the last effort of the heathen reactionary party. Miss Elaine Goodale, of Pine Ridge, in an article in the *Independent*, New York, has pointed out that only a minority of the Indians at the Pine Ridge Agency took part in the hostile demonstrations, while many of the Christian Indians at the time were engaged in holding services in the church at the agency, which after the action they converted into a hospital.

A writer in the *News*, Des Moines, Iowa, January seventeenth, gives the following example of messianic superstition, attributed to the Indians of the Pacific slope:

It is remembered now that in 1883 the Sanpoels, a small tribe in what was then Washington Territory, became greatly agitated over the teachings of an old chief who professed to believe that another flood was near at hand. He said that the Great Spirit had commanded him to collect tribute and build an ark that would outride the waves. His great canoe, one hundred and twelve by two hundred and eighty-eight feet, is still to be seen in an unfinished condition near one of the tributaries of the Columbia.

A Mexican merchant, visiting Sandusky, Ohio, is represented as stating that the remains of the Indian population in Mexico, in the neighborhood of the Great Mound at Cholula, are in the habit of holding regular dances in which they mourn over the past and sing of a coming Messiah. *(Register, Sandusky, Ohio, January 19).*

THE "MESSIAH CRAZE."

Several accounts printed in newspapers correspond to the statement of Lieutenant Phister, elsewhere noticed, that the Messiah was to be found in Nevada. According to a narration attributed to Sitting Bull, since slain, which went the rounds of the press, that chief is represented to have recounted the manner in which a hunting party followed a star, which guided them to a grotto in a mountain wilderness, which opened and revealed to them the deliverer.

Imposture, of course, played a part in the movement. Thus an Indian is said to have arrived in Washington Territory, coming by train, who alleged that he had been brought back to life by the Messiah (Walla-Walla *Journal,* January 9). The Kiowas are stated to have sent a messenger to Nevada, whither it was supposed the Messiah had fled. This messenger found the person he sought in a small camp and approached him with great awe, expecting to be recognized and addressed in his own tongue; but the professed Messiah asked the other through a Shoshone interpreter what he desired; on which the messenger concluded him to be an impostor, especially as he was not shown the dead relatives whom he expected to meet (*Christian Advocate,* St. Louis, Missouri, March 18, 1891). In this case the professed Messiah is said to have been a half-breed named Jack Wilson; but several papers printed descriptions of a Piute named Johnson Sides, living near Reno, Nevada, in which the latter is made to figure as a claimant to the Messiahship, which he altogether denies. The Chippewas, in January, are said to have given up their hostility to the Sioux and joined in the dance, though not believing in the coming of a Messiah (*Herald,* Los Angeles, January 10, 1891).

MESSIANIC EXCITEMENTS AMONG WHITE AMERICANS.

The New York Times, November 30, 1890, contains an article giving an interesting summary of recent religious delusions in the United States, which is quite sufficient to prove that a considerable unlettered portion of the white population stands on very nearly the same level as the Indians in respect to liability of being affected by such anticipations; we extract the following paragraphs:

It was only in the summer of 1888 that one Patterson, of Tennessee, went around preaching that a wonderful thing was to happen; and when he thought the times were ripe, he declared that the second advent of Christ had come in the person of A. J. Brown, who had served as Patterson's assistant. These two fanatics secured a large following as they went forth preaching their new doctrine, promising to forgive sins and heal all diseases. It was finally announced that Brown must go up into the mountains and fast for forty days and nights in order that he might be fittingly prepared for the mission intrusted to his hands. He suddenly disappeared, and nothing was seen of him for many days. When the prescribed period had passed, on a Sabbath morning in June, his followers went out toward the hills and suddenly he appeared before them clothed in white, with his hands uplifted. A great shout went up, and the people rushed toward him, falling upon their knees and kissing his feet. Many who were ill declared themselves healed by his touch. So great was the fanaticism of these people that one girl declared she was ready to die to prove her faith, and the nonbelievers around the town of Soddy, where these things happened, became so fearful that human life would be sacrificed that they sent for the sheriff at Chattanooga, and it required all his power to compel Patterson and

Brown to leave the neighborhood, that quiet might be restored.

A year later, in 1889, occurred that remarkable series of impositions upon the credulity of the colored people, where one man after another proclaimed himself as the Christ, promised miracles, drew crowds of excited men and women from their labors, and created consternation in those portions of the South where their performances were carried on. In one case a man nearly white, who gave his name as Bell, went among the Negroes who lived along the Savannah River and proclaimed himself as the returned Christ, crying out that those who hoped to be saved must give up everything and follow him. Hundreds believed him, left the cottonfields, the sawmills, and the turpentine stills and followed Bell, obeying his lightest word and ready to fall down at his feet in worship. So great was the disturbance that the authorities were led to arrest Bell; and when he was taken, his followers would have torn his captors to pieces and rescued him had he given the word. He told them to be patient, declaring that an angel would come to him and break his prison doors by night and that he could not be harmed. As he had some money in his possession, he was not held for vagrancy, and although thought not to be in his right mind, was soon discharged from custody. He then continued his preaching, followed by even greater crowds than before; announced that the world would come to an end on August 16; that all white men would then turn black and all black men white, and that he could supply all who wished to ascend on the last day with wings at five dollars a pair.

Bell was finally sent to the insane asylum, but a series of other successors sprang up among the Negroes and met with ready acceptance — the excitements, while they lasted, interfering with the work and business of the region. But particularly remarkable, as occurring among whites and in a class relatively superior, was the messianic delusion of Rockport, Illinois, a movement which seems to have established a sort of sect.

A very marked example of imposition upon the one side and blind credulity upon the other, the basis being a claim of the visible Christhood in the flesh, is furnished in the career of George J. Schweinfurth at Rockport, Illinois. In the cases above cited, the claimants were obscure and ignorant men, while the dupes were of the lowliest among the freedmen, who were guided only by their emotions and had no help from culture and education either in themselves or in the community around them. Vastly different was the Rockport delusion, springing up in the most intelligent section of the West at the behest of the wife of a Congregational minister, who preached that in her own person were the attributes of the risen Lord. It is some sixteen years since Mrs. Dora Beekman advanced this claim, and her followers were at first few in number, but they were strong in faith, and they located their church at Bryan, near Rockford, and went zealously to work. Mr. Beekman, not believing in the new doctrine, was torn by conflicting doctrines until finally he found relief in insanity and an asylum.

Among the converts finally came Schweinfurth, a young Methodist minister of pleasing address and appearance, and of some mental power. He was soon installed as bishop and sent forth upon mission labor. After a time, as in the case of Ann Lee, the founder of Shakerism, Mrs. Beekman's claim of immortal life was disproved by her death, and the shrewd bishop stepped into the breach, declaring that the divine spirit had passed from their former leader to himself. The claim was allowed, and today he is worshipped by hundreds, not merely as the Christ returned to the flesh, but as the maker and ruler of the earth as well.

The writer gives many examples of similar movements, in some cases leading to self-injury, in others to actual murder. Child sacrifice sometimes
appears, as in a case of a Negro mother of Springfield, Ohio, in which case,
however, timely interference saved the life of the babe.

In 1888, a certain Silas Wilcox, in Missouri, taught the doctrine that the
drinking of blood was a cure of disease, and this teaching led to the bleeding
of a number of children in order that their elders might be healed. The writer
remarks that to give an account of the delusions even of the last two years
would far exceed the space at his disposal. That the credulity is not purely
religious, but, in the absence of such enthusiasm, extends to the common
affairs of life, is shown by the recent case in Oakland, California, when the
prophecies of one Mrs. Woodworth that the coast at a given date would be
swept by a tidal wave, caused many families to abandon their homes and persons enjoying fair prosperity to sacrifice their property at a price greatly below
its actual value.

An Indian nativistic endeavor that succeeded because it manifested itself in love (or the illusion of love) instead of violence
is the peyote religion.

Anhalonium or mescal or peyote is a mild and nonaddictive
hallucinogen derived from a common spineless cactus that has
been sold in five-and-ten-cent stores as a window plant. It was
known to the Spanish priests in Mexico as long ago as the time
of the *Conquistadores,* and was in fact prohibited and condemned, along with its users, by the Inquisition in Mexico City
in 1620. It seems to have crossed the border surreptitiously
around the time of the first Ghost Dance.

Despite continuous attacks by the *Reader's Digest* and other
watchers of the ramparts, the Peyote religion still thrives. Much
of its success in opposing the will of the lawful comes from a
brilliant coup engineered by James Mooney (the historian of
the Ghost Dance) in 1918. In Oklahoma in that year Mooney
managed to secure a legal charter for the cult under the name
of the "Native American Church." This establishes the cult
as a Christian denomination and thereby immune to attacks
under the protection of the First Amendment. It is enough to
drive a moralist as mad as a peyotist.

PEYOTE JOKES*

The peyote cult or religion has become well known to students of the
American Indian through a series of excellent monographs and descrip-

* By James H. Howard. JAF Volume 75, 1962, 10-14.

tive papers. The religion, which entered the Plains area from Mexico around 1870, features an all-night ceremony in which the peyote cactus, *Lophophora williamsii,* is consumed to the accompaniment of prayers and ritual music. Although peyotists have sometimes been persecuted, and the possession of peyote is illegal in some states and provinces, the cult continues to flourish and spread in both the United States and Canada.

As has been the case with other religions, the peyote cult has extended its influence to areas of culture far outside the religious sphere. Thus, at a Plains Indian Grass or War Dance, one sometimes sees an older peyote man dressed in the costume of the religion, even though war dancing and peyotism have no formal connection. The influence of the peyote cult is also quite evident in contemporary Plains Indian art. In most peyote-using groups it has also given rise to a particular genre of humor know as the "peyote joke," which is the subject of this paper.

The usual time for telling such jokes is in the morning after the all-night ritual or meeting. In many peyote-using tribes the ceremony formally ends with a breakfast of coffee, sweet rolls, and bread, provided by those who have "put up" (i.e., sponsored) the gathering. At this breakfast participants may stand up and stretch their cramped limbs, smoke, and chat freely. In contrast to the seriousness of the previous night's worship, this is a very relaxed affair, and those present are encouraged to tell of their past experiences in peyotism, either serious or humorous. As Weston La Barre notes in his monograph *The Peyote Cult:* "Complete social informality now reigns as the food is passed to the man south of the door and thence clockwise. Much joking goes on during this meal, which has none of the seriousness of the Christian partaking of the Host."

The small collection of stories given below is a fair sample of the type of joke often heard on these occasions. Unlike the typical Euro-American joke, which depends on a terminal "punch line" for most of its effect, the peyote joke builds up slowly from one ridiculous situation to the next, and the "punch line," if present at all, appears rather weak to one accustomed to the machine-gun delivery of the television or nightclub comic. Because of this structure, a joke which is hilariously funny when told by one peyote jokester may fall flat in the hands of a less gifted raconteur. The gifted storyteller, however, can keep his audience convulsed for minutes on end, and the ability to tell amusing jokes most certainly adds to the stature of a peyote "road man" or leader.

One may wonder how these ribald and often obscene anecdotes have become attached to such an intensely devout form of worship as the peyote ritual. Perhaps the very seriousness of the ordinary peyote ceremony, lasting through some eleven hours, calls forth a release of this sort once the ceremony is ended. Likewise, they provide the peyotists with yet another body of common experience not shared by nonmembers. A familiarity with the peyote ritual is essential to the complete understanding of many of the jokes, and hence the jokes serve to bind together those whose knowledge makes the circumstances of the joke intelligible.

Many peyote jokes find their humor in human miscalculation and error, and in this respect are similar to certain Euro-American jokes. La Barre cites two jokes of this type:

"A Comanche told me a Kiowa ate a lot of peyote once and tried to sing a Comanche song. He sang the wrong words, which meant *Mentula exposita est, Mentula exposita est!*

Likewise:

"Koshiway (Oto) told a joke in the morning about a partially deaf man's misunderstanding the song 'Jesus in the glory now, *he ya na ha we,*' and singing 'Jesus in Missouri now.' Jack said laughing, 'He must be getting close; He's just over the river now!'"

A story heard by the writer among the Prairie Potawatomi in Kansas involves not human but animal error. As told by a Potawatomi peyotist, the story went as follows:

"It used to be the custom at meetings down here for the road man to gather up everybody's feathers [wands of feathers carried by peyotists in the meeting] just before closing. He would put them down in a pile behind the altar, pray, and then sing the quitting songs. After the meeting everyone would come up and get his feathers back.

"Well, this one time they were having a meeting at a place out in the country here, a place where they raised chickens. It was just getting light and the road man had gathered up all the feathers and had them in a pile beside him. There was a little banty rooster running around in the yard outside. It would crow a little, scratch around a bit, then wander in a little closer to where the temple [the peyote tipi] was set up. Finally it saw the big pile of feathers by the road man and mistook it for a hen. It gave a big run and jumped right on top of the feathers. Boy, you've never seen such a disappointed rooster in all your life!"

Several peyote jokes, however, do more than recount a comic mischance, and go on to point a moral. La Barre cites a story of this type, told by O. W. (Comanche) to E. R. (Delaware):

"The leader of a Wichita Easter meeting had a fine watch, costing from $150 to $200. At daylight, before water time, wanting to display it, he put it down by the feathers. A man to the north was singing and making vigorous punches toward the peyote. When he looked at his watch later, 'it was just a mess of works in there loose, and the hands dropped off,' though nobody touched it. 'It don't pay to go in there and then try to show off.'"

Many peyote jokes tell of serious devotional acts being interrupted by some ludicrous occurrence. Perhaps the jokes of this type reflect an unconscious resentment of the hardship and the composure which attendance at a ceremony entails. Here is an example from the Kiowa:

"Once some young men in our tribe decided they wanted to hold a peyote meeting. None of them owned a tipi, so they just built a windbreak, about waist-high, using old blankets, pieces of canvas, and sticks. The young man sitting chief [i.e., acting as the leader of the ceremony] was pretty good at peyote talk. When he prayed to the Almighty, everyone sat up and listened.

"Well, the meeting was just getting underway, and this young man was praying. There was a young drunk wandering around outside, and he came stumbling up just at that time. He stood right behind the moon [altar] and leaned over the windbreak, gaping down at the leader and breathing wine fumes on his neck. The leader didn't notice him at first, and he was praying, 'Our Father, Who art in heaven—' and just then he turned a little, and saw the drunk, and said, without even pausing for breath, 'What in *hell* are *you* doing here?'"

Stories frequently have to do with strange happenings resulting from one or another individual suffering from "peyote effect" after eating an unusually large number of "buttons" (the dried tops of the peyote cactus). La Barre notes that "Jonathan Koshiway (Oto) laughingly told me of a meeting in Kansas where the singer's jaw became locked; the whole meeting was upset while they shook and fanned him with cedar incense until his jaw 'came back.'"

La Barre comments that this may have been the effect of the strychninelike alkaloids in peyote. Another story concerning "peyote effect" was told by William C——— (Ojibwa), about an old man he had seen at a Potawatomi meeting in Kansas. This old man wandered from group to group the morning after a peyote meeting. At each stop he would tell the first part of a peyote joke, but due to the amount of peyote he had eaten, he would always forget to finish. After telling a part of each joke, he would laugh loudly and walk on to the next knot of people and begin again.

A classic peyote joke from the Pine Ridge Reservation in South Dakota, and one told in several versions, involves the interruption of a religious procession. It was apparently the custom when peyote first reached Pine Ridge for the adherents to stage these processions, perhaps in imitation of Roman Catholic processions. Various peyotists would take the parts of biblical characters. One such procession which took place in the twenties involved many individuals still prominent in the cult in that area. A male leader took the part of Christ, swathed in a white sheet and riding a mule. Close behind was the Virgin Mary, played by a female devotee. Others were dressed to resemble shepherds, Roman soldiers, and so on. The shepherds, who followed closely behind Christ and the Virgin, had several sheep and a goat for added realism.

The procession wound impressively through the hills near Pine Ridge until it neared an Indian cabin. Just as it was passing this cabin, a large dog chased a cat directly under the mule ridden by Christ, causing it to buck the rider into the dust. Worse yet, every time the rider attempted to stand up and remount, the goat would butt him over again from behind. Soon the entire procession was in an uproar, with horses bucking, sheep bleating, and the biblical characters cursing and swearing as they attempted to bring order out of chaos.

Later an old Indian woman, scolding the owner of the dog and cat for not keeping them under control as the "holy" procession went by, commented: "It was bad enough when Christ got bucked off his mule, and the billy goat butted him in the rear end. But when the Holy Virgin tore her dress on the barbed wire fence, that was a *terrible* thing!"

More typical of the jokes told at the present time is one currently making the rounds. A young Indian (variously described as a Potawatomi, a Winnebago, or an Omaha) has just come into a bit of money from a land sale and decides to go "girling" in Oklahoma. He buys himself a new suit of clothes and hops the first bus to Anadarko.

Getting off the bus, he sees an old Indian man, obviously of the old school, standing on the corner. The old man wears his hair in braids, neatly wrapped with blue and green yarn, has a dark shirt and trousers, moccasins, and a white sheet wrapped around his waist in lieu of a blanket. The young man thinks, "Aha, here is an old-timer who can help me out. These old-timers know all about love medicines, and that's what I want right now."

Accordingly, he approaches the old man, introduces himself, and in Indian fashion invites the old man to a restaurant for a fine meal. "Order the biggest steak in the house, Uncle," he urges. "Way ahead! [i.e., good]," answers the old-timer, and does as suggested. After the main course the young man says, "How about pie *à la mode,* Uncle? Wouldn't that go good about now?" Again the old Indian gratefully accepts. Then, "Would you like a cigar to top off your meal?" Again the old man gladly accepts.

"You have been very nice to me, Nephew," he comments at last. "And I appreciate what you have done for a poor old man. Now in our Indian way that might mean that you want me to help you out in some way."

"That's true, Uncle," the young man replies, "I do need your help. I am down here for social purposes, and I know you old people are wise in these old Indian medicines. Could you get hold of some love medicine for me?"

At this point the old man smiles, reaches under the sheet around his waist and into his trousers' pocket. Pulling out four peyote "buttons" he hands them to the young man, saying, "Here, take these and love *everybody!*"

AN EPILOGUE AND A PROPHECY*

Among those who came out from the cave worlds first were the Americans, so said our ancients. Now while we were yet journeying, before we settled where now we get being, our older brother left us and journeyed toward the land of the sun. (So said our ancients.) And when our older brother (the Americans) separated from his younger brother (the Oraibi), the younger brother commanded him, saying, "Brother Older, you go toward the country whence comes out the sun. Toward the country of great rivers and great trees you go. There you will find a home. Many men's ages shall pass while we are apart. Your children shall increase, and mine. Your children shall fill the world whither you go. Then you shall turn back to the place of your birth, seeking a country more spacious wherein to dwell. It is then that you will meet me again. You will find me poor, while you will return in the grandeur of plenty, and in the welfare of good food. You will find me hungry and offer me nourishment; but I will cast your morsels aside from my mouth. You will find me naked and offer me garments of soft fabrics, but I will rend your raiments and trample them under my feet. You will find me sad and perplexed, and offer me speeches of consolation and advice; but I will spurn your words, I will reproach, revile, and despise you. You will smile upon me and act gently; but I will scowl upon you and cast you aside as I would cast filth from my presence. Then will you rise and strike my head from my neck. As it rolls in the dust you will arrest it and sit upon it as upon a stool-rock. Then, nor until then, may you feed my belly or clothe my body. But a sorry day will it be for you when you sit upon my head as upon a stool-rock, and a glad day for me. For on that day you will but divide the trail of your own life with the knife which severs my head from my body, and give to me immortal life, liberty, and surcease from anxiety."

*From Frank Hamilton Cushing, "Origin Myth from Oraibi."
JAF Volume 36, 1923, 163-170.

AND A JUDGMENT*

Almost everything was Coyote's way. The Indian planted the apple. When he planted it, he said for all the Indians to come and eat. When he told them that, all the people came.

The white man was a rattlesnake then, and he was on that tree. The white people have eyes just like the rattlesnake. When the Indians tried to come to eat the apples, that snake tried to bite them. That's why the white people took everything away from the Indian; because they were snakes. If that snake hadn't been on the tree, everything would have belonged to the Indian. Just because they were snakes and came here, the white people took everything away. They asked these Indians where they had come from. That's why they took everything and told the Indians to go way out in the mountains and live.

* From Isabel T. Kelly, "Northern Paiute Tales." JAF Volume 61, 1938, 363-437.

V

Cowboy Songs

THE ERA OF THE COWBOY lasted less than half the lifetime of a man. Not until 1870 had it recognizably begun; by 1895 it was all over, except for those marginal survivors of every movement who exist only to give archaeological testimony of dead cultures. In space, too, the range of the cowhand was restricted; only that narrow and desolate corridor running along the eastern slope of the Rocky Mountains knew the genuine working cowboy. Even his profession was an economic negligibility; all the cattle driven from range to market in those twenty-five years numbered less than a tenth of the unsung buffalo they displaced.

The cowboys themselves were far less in the reality than they were in the legend. They were at the top of their caste, it is true; but it was the lowest economic caste. As an itinerant worker, the cowboy was technically a hobo, one notch above the tramp (the itinerant nonworker) and two notches above the bum (the sedentary nonworker). There was little below the cowboy but the cow. The railroads that stitched the coasts together, after the Civil War, brought in settlers to occupy their right of way, and the cowboy came to supply meat for these unheroic folk.

The culture of the cowboy was the half-culture of the pastoral nomad. From their spurs to their battered hats (which only rarely were Stetsons), they depended for survival on the outsiders on whom they looked down. They were badly supplied by the outsiders, for whom the cowboy's thirty-five dollars a month was no compelling mercantile stimulus. The cowhand never was arrayed in the glory of Roy Rogers; his outfit could have come unlaundered from the Goodwill Industries. A cavalry surplus hat, perhaps; certainly the jacket of a discarded suit; monstrous great chaps with a gap in front that demanded the re-invention of the codpiece for the sake of decency — in this raiment the cowboy (himself mustachioed like Andy Clyde) offered himself to history. He was not a likely candidate for literary immortality. Mere caretakers of ambulatory steaks, cowboys should not logically have inspired legend any more than the butchers for whom they indirectly worked.

But logic has very little to do with human affairs, and in story fact is just the seed of fancy. The mature growth of truth is no more like its factual beginning than the oak tree is like the acorn. In this matter we have listened too attentively to our literary critics, who have always proved themselves peculiarly hypermetropical when they are caught standing in the middle of a movement. They seldom recognize present story as future legend, though the materials of their profession demonstrate the evolution continually. Today they shoot fish in television's barrel, debunking both the cowboy of reality and the cowboy of fantasy, just as the literary critics of centuries past condemned the Arthurian Legend when that great treasure trove of story was in the making. "Open manslaughter and bold bawdry," Roger Ascham said of it almost half a thousand years ago, and three hundred years beyond that, the arch-Victorian Lord Tennyson condemned it as having been "touched by the adulterous finger of a time that hovered between war and wantonness." Except for the archaic rhetoric, these could have been modern criticisms of the immorality, violence, and unreality of the television cowboy.

Time will burnish the legend of the cowboy, as it did the legend of Arthur. There is as much fact in the screen cowboy as there is in the Arthuriad, but we are fourteen centuries beyond the facts of Arthur, and that makes the difference. When he first appeared at the dim Battle of Mount Badon near the start of the sixth century, Arthur was an unnamed warrior fighting for a doomed cause against his country's invaders. But only leaders of lost causes become heroes, and heroes go with the land, not with the people; so the Celtic Arthur's Germanic enemies made him their own, and Germanic he remained until the French adopted him after the Conquest. As he grew, he gathered; other heroes joined him as his subordinates, just as every television marshal brings into his story most of the known good men and bad of the legendary West. Arthur's wise man, Merlin the magician, goes back farther in Celtic legend than Arthur himself, but Merlin never had star quality. Gawain, once the Celtic sungod Gwalchmei, brought Arthur his service and his sword, for he too lacked the charisma to carry a series. Arthur's archenemy, Modred, was another old Celt before he entered the legend as Arthur's illegitimate son and nephew (try that morality on television!). Guenevere was the swan-maiden wife of the great Irish hero Cuchulain five centuries before she became Arthur's queen and Launcelot's lover. Tristram may be oldest of all; he can be traced to a Pictish legend of one Drostan, a swineherd who falls in love with his uncle's wife. The Holy Grail is pagan if it is anything, and if it existed, it had no place to stand until the Anglo-Norman poet Wace invented the Round Table six hundred years after Badon. The lastest comer was Launcelot, created by the Frenchman Chrétien de Troyes to displace the rough and rugged Gawain, whose image did not sit well in the era of Courtly Love and Courtly Lovers. And chivalry? Why, it never existed anywhere, anytime, any more than the Ponderosa existed.

Some day, when viewers and critics are dust, literary archaeologists of a more dissociated and objective age will unearth the story of the American Arthuriad. They will be able to show their students, as we cannot now show ours, exactly how the shotgun ambush behind the saloon rain barrel evolved into the confrontation on Main Street at High Noon. They will rightly find us wanting for not having recognized the greatness of the story begun by these ignoble, horny-handed and horny-minded men who drove meat for the tables of railroad immigrants.

The Arthurian legend was made in prose and verse; the legend of the cowboy began in song. It would be gratifying to say that the early folklorists caught these lyrics and their significance as they were made, but it is not so. They were men of their time, as we are, and their time saw no great value in what cow-tenders sang. Some songs did manage to slip into the *Journal of American Folklore* unnoticed among the Indian myths, and sometimes there was a bit of background knowledge accompanying them. More often they came encased in error and ignorance, which only recently are being dispelled.

John I. White, easternized now in Westfield, New Jersey, is a modern scholar dedicated to finding the facts about the old songs, an indefatigable detective of who made them and when and how. In his article "A Montana Cowboy Poet," White hurries time into burnishing the memory of D. J. O'Malley, whom the identity-erasing folk process threatened with oblivion.

The most tenacious characteristic of the true folksong is this resistance to individual possession. The claim-jumping compulsion of the folk is so overwhelming that once upon a time, and not so long ago, folklorists used to think that no one wrote a folksong. Either a song was just found, like babies, under a cabbage leaf, or the folk put it together in a mass conspiracy around a campfire. Of course, every work of creation is the product originally of an individual artist, however much the folk tamper with it later. ("The Old Chisholm Trail" is an example of too many cooks improving the soup.)

One ubiquitous method of tampering is the jumped claim. The first lesson a young folklorist learns is that the good informant is the bad informant, for such a person's imagination carries him too far from the truth too fast. Few young folklorists can resist showing the claim-jumper that the song for which he asserts authorship was made before either of them was born — and thereupon the novice learns his second lesson: do not confront the folk plagiarist with evidence of his theft, for the invariable reaction of the composer-thief is to become abusive. With cowboys this could be dangerous.

For all the obscuring factors, human and cultural, the real composer of a folksong stands somewhere back in the dark corridor of time, and diligent scholarship can occasionally find him. This is what John White did when he re-examined the claims of D. J. O'Malley for "When the Work Is Done Next Fall" and several other classic cowboy songs. But it was the old story. The doubting Thomases who keep our profession honest heard O'Malley and dismissed him (as White shows us in the case of the very influential J. Frank Dobie). After White's article appeared, all doubting stopped, for all the good that did O'Malley, who was dead — dead and buried.

A MONTANA COWBOY POET*

Miles City, Montana, at the confluence of the Yellowstone and Tongue rivers, once was a rip-snortin' cow town. It boasted a real cow town weekly newspaper, the *Stock Growers' Journal,* which devoted its news columns largely to events and statistics of special interest to cattlemen. Much of the advertising space described saddles, harness, railway cattle cars, and other items essential to the business of stock-raising, and included notices about horses that had strayed from home. In addition, the entire back page and a few inside columns were crammed each week with drawings of beeves displaying brands of the many cow outfits operating in eastern Montana.

Fortunately for those of us who enjoy singing or listening to cowboy songs, during the early 1890's the *Journal* had editors who liked to run poetry. It was a rare issue that failed to carry at least one, sometimes two, poems either lifted from other papers or composed by local rhymsters. In fact, the editors seem to have encouraged verse-making on the subject of cowboy life. Luckily, some of this grass-roots poetry by Montana cowhands had enough substance to catch on with range troubadors of the period. As a result, it was passed on by word of mouth from one singer to another, often being polished up in the process, and today we find variants of some of the items which originated in the *Journal's* columns ranking high among what western historian David Lavender recently described as "America's very limited, truly indigenous folk music."

The most persistent contributor of original verses to the *Journal* was Dominick J. O'Malley (1867–1943), who, at the age of fifteen, following the disappearance of his soldier-stepfather from Fort Keogh adjacent to Miles City, had gone to work as a horse wrangler for the

* By John I. White. JAF Volume 80, 1967, 113-129.

Home Land & Cattle Company, operated by the Niedringhaus brothers. In a very short time the young wrangler with a flair for versifying had become proficient at the cowpuncher's unique and often dangerous trade, which he followed for nearly twenty years. Three trips up the trail with Texas cattle bound for northern ranges, the last in 1891, were among his unusual experiences.

Perhaps the most famous bit of verse to which Mr. O'Malley appears to have a clear title usually is known among ballad singers as "When the Work Is Done Next Fall." When it appeared in the *Stock Growers' Journal* on October 6, 1893, its writer called it "After the Roundup" and modeled it on "After the Ball," the Charles K. Harris waltz-time song hit of 1892. Here are Mr. O'Malley's lines exactly as they were printed almost three-quarters of a century ago. The *Journal's* compositor, apparently not up on the latest song hits, set the eight lines of the chorus flush to the left and neglected to label them "chorus." Therefore they look like a bobtailed second stanza.

AFTER THE ROUNDUP

A group of jolly cowboys
Discussed their plans at ease,
Said one; "I'll tell you something
Boys, if you please:
See, I'm a puncher,
Dressed most in rags,
I used to be a wild one
And took on big jags.
I have a home boys,
A good one, you know,
But I haven't seen it
Since long, long ago.
But, I'm going home, boys,
Once more to see them all;
Yes, I'll go back home
When work is done this fall.

"After the roundup's over,
After the shipping's done,
I'm going straight back home, boys,
Ere all my money's gone.
My mother's dear heart is breaking,
Breaking for me, that's all;
But, with God's help I'll see her,
When work is done this fall.

"When I left my home, boys,
For me she cried,
　　Begged me to stay, boys,
For me she'd have died.
　　I haven't used her right, boys,
My hard-earned cash I've spent,
　　When I should have saved it
And it to mother sent.
　　But, I've changed my course, boys,
I'll be a better man
　　And help my poor old mother,
I'm sure that I can.
　　I'll walk in the straight path;
No more will I fall;
　　And I'll see my mother
When work's done this fall."

　　That very night this
Cowboy went on guard;
　　The night it was dark
And 'twas storming very hard.
　　The cattle got frightened
And rushed in mad stampede,
　　He tried to check them,
Riding full speed;
　　Riding in the darkness
Loud he did shout,
　　Doing his utmost
To turn the herd about.
　　His saddle horse stumbled
On him did fall;
　　He'll not see his mother
When work's done this fall.

　　They picked him up gently
And laid him on a bed.
　　The poor boy was mangled,
They thought he was dead.
　　He opened his blue eyes
And gazed all around;
　　Then motioned his comrades
To sit near him on the ground:
　　"Send her the wages
That I have earned.

> Boys I'm afraid that
> My last steer I've turned.
>   I'm going to a new range,
> I hear the Master call
>   I'll not see my mother
> When work's done this fall.
>
>   "Bill, take my saddle,
> George, take my bed,
>   Fred, take my pistol
> After I am dead.
>   Think of me kindly
> When on them you look—"
>   His voice then grew fainter,
> With anguish he shook.
>   His friends gathered closer
> And on them he gazed,
>   His breath coming fainter,
> His eyes growing glazed.
>   He uttered a few words,
> Heard by them all:
>   "I'll see my mother
> When work's done this fall."

Today "When the Work Is Done Next Fall" usually is sung as a simple ballad with four lines to the stanza:

> A group of jolly cowboys, discussing plans at ease.
> Says one, "I'll tell you something, boys, if you will listen, please.
> I am an old cowpuncher and here I'm dressed in rags,
> I used to be a tough one and go on great big jags."

The ending, too, has been improved as the song was passed from one singer to another over many, many years. John A. Lomax, the first collector to put it between the covers of a book, gave it this way in his notable volume *Cowboy Songs and Other Frontier Ballads*:

> Fred, you take my saddle; George, you take my bed;
> Bill, you take my pistol after I am dead;
> And think of me kindly when you look upon them all,
> For I'll not see my mother when work is done this fall.
>
> Poor Charlie was buried at sunrise, no tombstone at his head,
> Nothing but a little board; and this is what it said:
> "Charlie died at daybreak, he died from a fall,
> And he'll not see his mother when the work's all done this fall."

In the original edition of the Lomax book, published in 1910, no tune was given. The revised and enlarged edition, issued in 1938 and reprinted many times, includes both words and music, the tune resembling that in Carl Sandburg's *The American Songbag,* published in 1927. First to put the song on a phonograph record was Fiddlin' John Carson, who recorded it on an Okeh disc early in the 1920's.

Among the odd incidents connected with this famous western ballad was its issuance in sheet music in 1929 by the F. B. Haviland Publishing Company of New York, with words and music attributed to one R. O. Mack. When Mr. O'Malley heard about this he nearly had a stroke. All the rest of his life he saw red every time he thought of the fat profits he was certain were being made on his brain child by someone else. Mr. Sandburg might have seen red, too, or perhaps have just been amused, had he run across Haviland's publication. The Mack version (both words and music) and that in *The American Songbag* are identical twins, even to the peculiar spelling of the words "here" and "hear" in the first and fourth stanzas respectively.

An even greater oddity is the David Guion arrangement of "When the Work Is Done Next Fall," published in sheet music by Carl Fischer Inc. in 1931. Although presented in a perfectly straightforward fashion, this carries the hard-to-believe subtitle "Humorous Cowboy Song."

I was fortunate enough to meet D. J. O'Malley in 1933 and to carry on correspondence with him for a good many years thereafter. I also was able, through advertising, to obtain seven copies of the *Stock Growers' Journal* containing verses signed by him. These covered the period from August 3, 1889, to April 7, 1894. He signed his work "D. J. White" or with the initials "DJW" because at the time he went by the family name of his stepfather, Charles White. The latter was a member of Troop E, Second Cavalry, and in 1877 brought his family to the fort on the Yellowstone named for Captain Myles Keogh, an officer who had died with Custer at the Little Bighorn the year before. In 1881 Charles White disappeared, and his stepson had to go to work to help support his mother and a sister. Mr. O'Malley believed White deserted and went to Canada; a saddle mule wearing Uncle Sam's brand went AWOL from Fort Keogh at the same time.

Throughout his life Mr. O'Malley liked to be known as Kid White. In 1934, when he attended a big cowboy reunion at Miles City, the other old-timers usually referred to him that way. While the record is not clear, it appears that he probably took his own father's name of O'Malley officially in 1909 when he met a girl from Eau Claire, Wisconsin, married her, and settled down there. The rest of his life was spent in Eau Claire except for a three-year period, 1921–1924, when he returned to Montana to work as a guard in the state penitentiary at Deer Lodge. During his later years in Eau Claire he worked in a factory, making tires for the vehicle that put the horse out of business. In his spare time he wrote more poems and many historical sketches for Montana newspapers. His last wish, which was carried out by his family, was to be buried among his old cowpuncher friends at Miles City.

I first heard of Mr. O'Malley thirty-five years ago when I was a moonlighting singer of western ballads over the radio in New York. He had written to *Western Story Magazine* (issue of January 1932) complaining about R. O. Mack having taken credit for "When the Work Is Done Next Fall." I wrote him, and in 1933, because I happened to be making a trip through the West, I arranged to visit him at his home in Eau Claire and have a look at his remarkable scrapbook. Impressed with his sincerity and the printed evidence of his work, I wrote a brief article about him for the February, 1934, issue of *Frontier Times,* published by Marvin Hunter at Bandera, Texas. Shortly thereafter I put together a twenty-page pamphlet titled *D. J. O'Malley; Cowboy Poet.* Most of the two hundred copies printed were given to O'Malley for distribution to his old friends in May, 1934, at the Golden Jubilee of the Montana Stock Growers' Association at Miles City. A few were sent to folklorists around the country. This pamphlet was the basis for the comments on Mr. O'Malley in *Anglo-American Folksong Scholarship Since 1898* by D. K. Wilgus, published in 1959.

On July 22, 1934, Mr. O'Malley wrote me that he was born April 30, 1868, at San Angelo, Texas, and I once published this information. Recently his two daughters informed me that when he attempted to obtain a birth certificate in order to qualify for an old-age pension, he learned to his surprise that he had been born in 1867 at New York City. His father was a New Yorker and a member of a New York regiment during the Civil War. After the war he re-enlisted, and at one time was stationed at Fort Concho near San Angelo. When his son was about four years old, the elder O'Malley died while undergoing an operation for the removal of a Confederate bullet.

In 1894 the *Stock Growers' Journal* printed what has since become another well-known cowboy song — a humorous ballad for a change — titled "D-2 Horse Wrangler," and signed "R. J. Stovall." Mr. O'Malley claimed credit for this one, too, maintaining that he wrote the verses, but because an acquaintance who was the subject of the tale wanted to surprise his wife by blossoming out as a poet, the latter was allowed to sign his name. There was one consideration — a five-dollar hat, said by Mr. O'Malley to be the most he ever received for a set of verses.

Variants of "D-2 Horse Wrangler" have found their way into numberless printed song collections and onto numerous phonograph records under the titles "The Horse Wrangler" or "The Tenderfoot." According to Mr. O'Malley, it was written to be sung to the tune of an old Irish-American comic ballad called "The Day I Played Baseball." Incidentally, making up new western poetry to fit the tune of a well-known song was by no means unique with Mr. O'Malley. Back in 1904 the late Joseph Mills Hanson wrote the famous cowboy song "Railroad Corral" to be sung to the Scottish air "Bonnie Dundee." The unknown ranch poet who composed "Whoopee Ti Yi Yo, Git Along Little Dogies," first recorded in 1893 by Owen Wister at Brown-wood, Texas, almost certainly had "The Rose of Tralee" in mind.

The model for "D-2 Horse Wrangler" began this way:

> My name it is O'Halloher,
> I'm a man that's influential,
> I mind my business, stop at home,
> My wants are few and small.
> Some blackguards 'tother day did come,
> They were full of whiskey, gin and rum
> An' they took me out in the broilin' sun,
> To play a game of ball.

Here is the *Stock Growers' Journal* offering for February 3, 1894:

D-2 HORSE WRANGLER

> One day I thought I'd have some fun,
> And see how punching cows was done;
> So, when the roundup had begun,
> I tackled a cattle king;
> Says he: "My foreman is in town;
> He's at the MacQueen, his name is Brown;
> Go over, and I think he'll take you down";
> Says I: "That's just the thing."
>
> We started for the ranch next day,
> Brown talked to me most all the way,
> He said cowpunching was only fun,
> It was no work at all;
> That all I had to do was ride,
> It was just like drifting with the tide,
> Geemany crimany, how he lied;
> He surely had his gall.

He put me in charge of a cavard
And told me not to work too hard,
That all I had to do was guard
The horses from getting away.
I had one hundred and sixty head,
And oft times wished that I was dead,
When one got away Brown he turned red.
Now this is the truth, I say.

Sometimes a horse would make a break
Across the prairie he would take
As though he were running for a stake,
For him it was only play.
Sometimes I couldn't head him at all,
And again my saddle horse would fall
And I'd speed on like a cannon ball
Till the earth came in my way.

They led me out an old gray hack
With a great big set fast on his back,
They padded him up with gunny sacks
And used my bedding all.
When I got on he left the ground
Jumped up in the air and turned around.
I busted the earth as I came down,
It was a terrible fall.

They picked me up and carried me in
And rubbed me down with a rolling pin:
"That's the way they all begin,
You are doing well," says Brown.
"And tomorrow, morning if you don't die,
I'll give you another horse to try."
"Oh! won't you let me walk?" says I.
"Yes," says he. "Into town."

I've traveled up and I've traveled down,
I've traveled this country all around,
I've lived in city, I've lived in town,
And I have this much to say:
Before you try it go kiss your wife,
Get a heavy insurance on your life,
Then shoot yourself with a butcher knife,
It's far the easiest way.

Considering the general excellence of the rhyming in the above, the poor rhyme in the third line of the second stanza probably can be blamed on an unpoetic printer who had to decipher a handwritten manuscript. Obviously the writer intended "He said cowpunching was only play."

The MacQueen mentioned in the opening stanza was Miles City's leading hostelry and headquarters for stockmen. Its *Journal* advertising of the day played up its electric lights, electric bells, and steam heat. A news item on November 18, 1893, read: "The bathrooms at the MacQueen have recently been renovated, and to those who bathe, Mr. Tracy will be pleased to explain the valuable properties of the artesian water used for that purpose." The old landmark went up in smoke in 1897.

"Cavard" (third stanza) is a corruption of a Spanish word meaning a herd of horses. A "set fast" (fifth stanza) was a saddle sore that never quite healed.

Mr. O'Malley's scrapbook yielded one other newspaper clipping that could well be part of the history of another very famous song, one commonly known as "The Cowboy's Dream" or "Grand Roundup" and sung to the tune of "My Bonnie Lies Over the Ocean." Before describing the O'Malley contribution, I should point out that the authorship of "The Cowboy's Dream" has been ascribed to more people than any other song I ever heard of; also that any reader interested in going into its ramifications will find an entire chapter devoted to it in a scholarly new book, *Songs of the Cowboys,* by Austin and Alta Fife of Logan, Utah.

The O'Malley clipping, unfortunately, has no date and the verses are not signed. However, the editors inserted this one small clue at the top in capital letters:

BY ONE OF THE COWBOYS OF MONTANA, FORMERLY OF LYNN

In 1934, when Mr. O'Malley and I were preparing the pamphlet already described, he wrote me concerning his recollection of the song.

This was written in 1887 while our wagon was working the North Fork of Sandy Creek. I was wrangling horses for the outfit. One of the boys at the wagon whose name was Tom Phelps was a great hand for singing old Sunday School songs. About three fourths of the time he was singing "The Sweet Bye and Bye" and often he would finish a verse with "I wonder if ever a cowboy will get to that sweet bye and bye?"

One night after supper I had unrolled my bed and was lying on it and that line of Phelps's kept running in my head and I began to try to add enough to it to make a verse, which I did before I rolled in. It was the first verse, and the next day I kept at it, and in three or four days I had written all of it. Tom Phelps was the first to sing it.

At the request of some of the boys I sent it to the Miles City paper but wouldn't let them put my name on it as I was afraid I'd be joked at by the boys. We got mail for a while at a ranch P.O. called Lynn and the editor credited the poem to "one of the cowboys of Montana, formerly of Lynn." Lynn had been discontinued in the fall of '86. I had written a couple of other pieces before I did this but never got up courage enough to have them printed.

Here are the stanzas Mr. O'Malley claimed he wrote in 1887 at the age of twenty.

SWEET BY-AND-BY REVISED

> To-night as I lay on the prairie,
>   Looking up at the stars in the sky,
> I wonder if ever a cowboy
>   Will go to that sweet by-and-by.
>
> For the trail to that bright mystic region
>   Is both narrow and dim, so they say,
> While the broad one that leads to perdition
>   Is posted and blazed all the way.
>
> Now I wonder whose fault that so many
>   Will be lost at the great final day,
> When they might have been rich, and had plenty
>   Had they known of the dim narrow way.
>
> I hear there will be a grand roundup,
>   When the cowboys, like others, will stand,
> To be cut by the riders of judgment,
>   Who are posted and know every brand.
>
> Then perhaps there may be a stray cowboy,
>   Unbranded, unclaimed by none nigh,
> To be mavericked by the riders of judgment,
>   And shipped to the sweet by-and-by.

Another extremely interesting chapter in the history of this same song was contributed by Will C. Barnes—cowboy, author, forester, legislator, and holder of the Congressional Medal of Honor for bravery in action against the Apaches. The Barnes version, which conceivably could have been a working over of Mr. O'Malley's, was widely cir-culated almost three-quarters of a century ago. I quote it below for comparison with the verses given above and because interested schol-ars will not find it in the Fife book just mentioned.

In an article "The Cowboy and His Songs" in *The Saturday Evening Post* for June 27, 1925, Mr. Barnes, who had never heard of Mr. O'Malley, had this to say:

I first heard this song in 1886 or '87 on the Hash Knife Range in Northern Arizona. A half-breed Indian boy from Southern Utah sang about four verses which he had picked up from some other singers. He knew nothing of the authorship. I wrote these four out in my calf-branding book one evening. Later on, a boy from down Pecos way drifted into our camp and sang the four with slight variations with two new ones, one of which he claimed as his own work. I wrote another and eventually picked up three more, until I finally had ten verses in all.

With the idea of using it as the motif for a cowboy story, I rewrote two or three verses, changed the words of several, added the chorus, and cut the ten down to six verses. These were published with one of my earliest Western stories — The Stampede on the Turkey Track Range. So far as I have been able to run it down, this was the first time the words ever appeared in print. Since that time the song has been printed in almost every volume of cowboy songs which has been published.

In his short story, printed in *Cosmopolitan* for August, 1895, author Barnes has his verses being sung by a cowboy on night guard circling a herd of cattle. The chorus he mentions is missing.

> Last night as I lay on the prairie,
>   And looked at the stars in the sky,
> I wondered if ever a cowboy
>   Would drift to that sweet by and by.
>
> The trail to that bright, mystic region,
>   Is narrow and dim, so they say,
> But the one that leads down to perdition
>   Is staked and is blazed all the way.
>
> They say that there'll be a great round-up,
>   Where cowboys like dogies will stand,
> To be cut by those riders from Heaven,
>   Who are posted and know every brand.
>
> I wonder was there ever a cowboy
>   Prepared for that great judgment day,
> Who could say to the boss of the riders,
>   I am ready to be driven away.
>
> They say He will never forsake you,
>   That He notes every action and look,
> But for safety you'd better get branded,
>   And have your name in His great tally-book.

> For they tell of another great owner
>   Who is nigh overstocked, so they say,
> But who always makes room for the sinner,
>   Who strays from that bright, narrow way.

Shortly before Mr. Barnes died in 1936 he wrote to me and added an amusing sidelight to his *Saturday Evening Post* account of his song.

Several years before it appeared in the *Cosmopolitan* I had sung it in public during the first political campaign I was in, in Arizona in 1888. I and another cow person made the campaign with a buckboard and a little folding organ. I played and we sang cowboy and Mexican songs all over northern Arizona, and were terribly defeated. However, in 1890 we came back with the same organ and songs and were both elected.

Like D. J. O'Malley, Will C. Barnes obviously was a cowboy who liked to sing — which leads to an interesting question: was there a great deal of singing by the rough, tough men who followed the longhorn cow? For years I have saved clippings and references on the subject, and I would say the answer is *yes*. As to evidence from a real, live ex-cowboy, my files show that on December 29, 1934, I stirred up Mr. O'Malley on this with the following:

Some day when you haven't anything better to do, I wish you would write me a paragraph or two on just how much and what kind of singing was done in the old days by cowboys on roundups or when driving cattle up the trail. A man from West Texas once told me that in his outfit they didn't sing at all. After a day's work, all they wanted was some sleep.

He came right back on January 6 with the following, written in the present tense although the events described took place half a century before.

I can't imagine what sort of an outfit that man from West Texas worked with who told you cowboys didn't sing on the roundup or trail. Maybe they were all dummies. Why, there is more singing on the trail than on the roundup. The boys all sing on night guard, and almost every evening until first guard comes off some will be around the fire singing. I'll admit that on the general or spring roundup there isn't as much of it as on the beef work for the reason that breakfast usually is about 4 a.m. and from daylight till dark it is just work, and then two hours guard, and a hand does usually catch a few snores whenever he can. There is a big circle in the morning, dinner along about 9 a.m., then the roundup is to be worked, cows and calves to be cut out and all the calves to be branded. But on the beef work there are not many calves to be branded, the moves are not as long, and beeves have to be handled slowly. The herders go on at noon and all the boys but the herders are in camp till late in the afternoon when camp is moved just far enough so the beef herd can feed in to the bedground. And then the boys gather around and sing a lot, play the mouth harp, too, and maybe a banjo, but seldom a guitar as all the radio cowboys do now. Maybe that man [from West Texas] worked on only one general roundup and thought the whole works was the same.

When I thanked him and said I was surprised to hear about banjos being so popular in cow camps, he sent this additional comment on January 14:

I never saw a bunch of cowhands at a camp where there wasn't someone singing unless it was on the Spring work when days were so long and so much work. There would often be nights when the boys were too tired to sing in camp, but you'd sure hear the night guards at it, tired or not. Yes, the banjo was in the majority on the range. I think the guitar came into use on the radio and phonograph from the fact that the cowboy was associated in the minds of the people with Mexicans. And it is well known the guitar is their instrument. But I can honestly say that where I saw one guitar in a cow camp I saw twenty banjos and about double that number of mouth harps, and once in a while a violin.

Two other signed O'Malley poems in the *Journal* that appear never to have been taken up and perpetuated by rangeland troubadors are worth quoting as early portraits of cattle-country life painted by a genuine working cowboy. These were called "The Cowboy Wishes" and "Cowboy Reverie." The former appeared on April 7, 1894. According to its composer, it was written during a meeting of the Stock Growers' Association when Miles City was full of young fellows seeking jobs as cowhands.

They were all dressed up with no place to go. Big hats, spurs, leather cuffs, six-shooters. And 95 per cent of them had never punched a cow in their lives unless it was some old milk bossie in the barn they had punched with a pitchfork handle while they were feeding her.

Mr. O'Malley explained that to make a "Winter play" was to keep busy in sight of the boss in order to be considered when the scarce off-season jobs were handed out. To "catch a regular" meant to take a nap on day herd while the cattle were lying around on water. The word "rep" (last stanza) was an abbreviation for "representative," a highly responsible cowpuncher who often worked outside the home range, checking on stray cattle and otherwise looking after his company's interests. Mr. O'Malley was just a mite proud of his own long service as a "rep" for the Home Land & Cattle Company, whose principal brand was *N-Bar-N*.

THE COWBOY WISHES

I want to be a cowboy
     And with the cowboys stand,
With leather chaps upon my legs
     And a six-gun in my hand.
And, while the foreman sees me
     I'll make some Winter plays,
But I will catch a regular
     When the herd's thrown out to graze.

I'll have a full-stamped saddle
     And a silver-mounted bit,
With conchos big as dollars,
     And silvered spurs, to wit;
With a long rawhide reata
     And a big Colt's forty-five
I'll be a model puncher
     As sure as you're alive.

I want to be a tough man,
     And be so very bad,
With my big white sombrero
     I'll make the dude look sad.
I'll get plumb full of bug juice
     And shoot up the whole town
When I start out to have a time,
     You bet I'll do it brown.

I want to be a buster
     And ride the bucking horse,
And scratch him in the shoulders
     With my silvered spurs, of course.
I'll rake him up and down the side,
     You bet I'll fan the breeze.
I'll ride him with slick saddle
     And do it with great ease.

I want to be a top man
     And work on the outside
So I can ride within the herd
     And cut it high and wide.
Oh, a rep is what I want to be,
     And a rep, you bet, I'll make.
At punching cows I know I'll shine;
     I'm sure I'll take the cake.

The following stanzas appeared in the *Journal* over Mr. O'Malley's name on May 14, 1892.

COWBOY REVERIE

Tonight as I rode 'round my cattle
    I thought of my once cozy home,
So full of the little one's prattle,
    And wondered how I came to roam.

To leave the dear home of my childhood
    Cost my poor heart a great deal of pain,
But now my mind's fixed on one happy thought,
    I'll soon see my dear ones again.

No more will I be a wild cowboy
    But I'll live like a man ought to do,
And sit by the stove when the chilly winds blow
    And not freeze myself through and through.

No more will I ride on the night guard
    When loud Heaven's thunders do roar.
No. I'll pound my ear down on a goose hair
    And think me of third guard no more.

No more will the cook's call to "grub pile"
    Cause me from my hard bed to creep.
No. I'll wait till the gong sounds at seven
    To rouse from my innocent sleep.

No more festive calves will I wrestle
    So close by the hot branding fire.
I'll have no hide knocked off my knuckles,
    For that always did rouse my ire.

When the rain's coming down, my slicker I'll have
    And not leave it lying in camp.
For in herding without one when Fall rains are here
    A cowboy most always feels damp.

Now look at that long-horned son-of-a-gun,
    Up that draw, now he's going to sneak.
I wish I could run him plumb off that cut-bank
    And break his blamed neck in the creek.

Get back in the bunch, blame your trifling hide,
    Or with you it will go mighty hard.
What's that, Jim? Ten minutes of twelve did you say?
    Well, go in and call up the third guard.

In his autobiography, *Adventures of a Ballad Hunter,* John A. Lomax, in discussing the famous song "Whoopee Ti Yi Yo, Git Along Little Dogies," stated: "So far as I can discover, the word 'dogie' was first printed in *Cowboy Songs"* (the noted Lomax collection of Western ballads first issued in 1910). Author Andy Adams could have disputed this, for seven years earlier on page 313 of *The Log of a Cowboy,* he quoted two lines from the same song and used the word "dogie." True, an eastern typesetter who must have thought the animal referred to was canine rather than bovine spelled it "doggie." And Mr. Barnes, of course, put it in the third stanza of "The Cowboy's Dream." But D. J. O'Malley was several jumps ahead of all of them. On November 28, 1891, the *Stock Growers' Journal* printed "Cowboy's Soliloquy," signed by him, which mentioned "dogies" in both the first and third stanzas.

In 1934 Mr. O'Malley supplied me with this account of the circumstances that inspired the verses printed below.

I was with a trail herd from the Texas Panhandle in 1891. We left the Canadian River in early March and crossed the Yellowstone onto the N-Bar-N range the middle of September. We were to drive them to the Little Dry and turn them loose, but two days before we got to where we were to ride off from them we got word to hold them along the Dry until further orders. We didn't get away from them until the 14th of October—just about eight months looking at the same dogies. Every day grew so monotonous we scarce knew what to do with ourselves. Just day herd and night guard.

Half a dozen writers have given half a dozen explanations of the origin of the word "dogie." It all seems to boil down to this: dogies were range cattle, usually young range cattle.

COWBOY'S SOLILOQUY

I am a cowpuncher
    From off the North Slide,
My horse and my saddle
    Are my bosom's pride;
My life is a hard one,
    To tell you I'll try
How we range-herded dogies
    Out on the Little Dry.

The first thing in the morning
    We'd graze upon the hill,
Then drive them back by noontime
    On water them to fill.

Then graze them round till sundown,
    And I've heaved many a sigh
When I thought "two hours night guard"
    After night fell on the Dry.

The next day was the same thing
    And the next the same again,
Day-herding those same dogies
    Out on the Dry's green plain;
Grazing them, then bedding them,
    One's patience it does try
When you think "now comes our night guard"
    After night falls on the Dry.

They're all right in the daytime,
    But our Autumn nights are cold,
And the least scare will stampede them,
    And then they're hard to hold.
How many times I've "darned" the luck
    When dusk I would see nigh,
And say, "I wish you were turned loose
    E're night falls on the Dry."

For a large bunch of cattle
    Is no snap to hold at night,
For sometimes a blamed coyote howl
    Will jump them in a fright,
Then a man will do some riding,
    O'er rocks and badlands he will fly;
A stampede is no picnic
    After night falls on the Dry.

Then should my horse fall down on me
    And my poor life crush out,
No friendly hand could give me aid,
    No warning voice could shout;
They'd hardly give one thought to me
    Or scarcely heave a sigh,
But they'd bury me so lonely
    When night fell on the Dry.

Lomax, by the way, thought enough of Mr. O'Malley's claims to authorship to correspond with him for several years and to mention him three times in the 1938 edition of *Cowboy Songs*. Fellow Texan J. Frank Dobie, on the other hand, took a dim view of the whole thing, insisting in correspondence with me during 1934 that D. J. O'Malley was a Johnny-come-lately, that the songs discussed here originated much earlier. The late Mr. Dobie had very positive ideas on the origin of "When the Work Is Done Next Fall," based purely on hearsay. He spoke his piece at least twice in print. A comparison of his statements reveals a striking inconsistency.

In 1927, when writing in *Texas and Southwestern Lore,* a publication of the Texas Folklore Society, Mr. Dobie quoted a Confederate veteran, W. W. Burton of Austin, Texas:

We had in our company during the Civil War a fellow named Marshall Johnson from Waco, who was the greatest hand to make songs and speeches that I have ever known. Poor fellow, he got killed in a stampede one fall early in the seventies, up on the Bosque River, and the well known cowboy ditty When Work Is Done This Fall was made on the occasion.

Thirty-two years later, in *Western Folklore* for October, 1959, Mr. Dobie stated that W. W. Burton told him Marshall Johnson made up the song to commemorate the death near Waco of a cowboy known as "Arkansaw."

There are two other rather interesting pieces which, like "D-2 Horse Wrangler," Mr. O'Malley claimed but could not supply positive proof of authorship. One of these, "A Busted Cowboy's Christmas," was printed in the *Stock Growers' Journal* on December 23, 1893, signed with an obviously fictitious name, "Iyam B. Usted." The same issue of the *Journal* stated that the town's "tin horn gamblers" also were having a rough Christmas, twenty of them having been told by the chief of police to leave Miles City or else. The editor must have been up against it, too, because he announced that the office would be open on Christmas Day to receive delinquent subscriptions.

A BUSTED COWBOY'S CHRISTMAS

I am a busted cowboy
    And I work upon the range;
In Summer time I get some work
    But one thing that is strange,
As soon as Fall work's over
    We get it in the neck
And we get a Christmas present
    On a neatly written check.

Then come to town to rusticate,
　　We've no place else to stay
When Winter winds are howling
　　Because we can't eat hay.
A puncher's life's a picnic;
　　It is one continued joke,
But there's none more anxious to see Spring
　　Than a cowboy who is broke.

The wages that a cowboy earns
　　In Summer go like smoke,
And when the Winter snows have come
　　You bet your life he's broke.
You can talk about your holiday,
　　Your Christmas cheer and joy;
It's all the same to me, my friend,
　　Cash gone — I'm a broke cowboy.

My saddle and my gun's in soak,
　　My spurs I've long since sold;
My rawhide and my quirt are gone;
　　My chaps — no, they're too old;
My stuff's all gone, I can't even beg
　　A solitary smoke.
For no one cares what becomes of
　　A cowboy who is broke.

Now, where I'll eat my dinner
　　This Christmas, I don't know;
But you bet I'm going to have one
　　If they give me half a show.
This Christmas has no charms for me,
　　On good things I'll not choke,
Unless I get a big hand-out —
　　I'm a cowboy who is broke.

The other, according to Mr. O'Malley, was written in 1897 at the request of a cowpuncher friend named Green Johnson, who had suffered a hip injury. Because he could no longer ride, Johnson had become a sheepherder. To quote Mr. O'Malley:

... he was camped about eight miles from where I was camped holding some bulls for my outfit, and I rode over to see him on several occasions. He was a good cook and neat about his camp. One day I found him pretty grouchy. He said he didn't care who came to his camp nor how much they ate of what

he had cooked up but he'd be damned if he didn't think they ought to clean
up the dishes they dirtied and not leave them for him to do after he'd been
with the sheep all day. And he said, "Kid, write me a verse to leave in sight;
maybe it will do some good." I said I'd try, and when I came to see him again
I had written these verses. Green sent them to the *Stock Growers' Journal*
in Miles City, saying he had found them on his mess box. Ed Butler, one of
the editors, asked me if I wrote them, as they sounded like me, and I told him
I did and why. He wrote quite an article in his paper on passers-by at a camp
leaving dirty dishes after feeding themselves.

I am sorry to say I never have found the issue of the *Journal* said to
have carried Mr. Butler's comments and the following gem of western
Americana.

FOUND ON A SHEEP HERDER'S MESS BOX

You stranger, who comes to my tent,
I hope you'll ride away content.
Eat all you want, my only wishes
Are, when you're through you'll wash the dishes.

The fare is plain, I will allow,
But you are in a sheep camp now;
So bacon fried you'll have to go,
With flapjacks made of sour dough.

There's coffee made and in the pot,
Placed on the stove 'twill soon get hot.
You cannot ask for pie or cake,
For they take too much time to make.

So, stranger, please be kind enough,
Don't try to treat the herder rough;
Eat all you want, eat all you can,
But tie my tent and wash the pan.

Yes, stranger, of a sin beware,
Don't make the poor sheep herder swear;
But please respect his only wishes,
Eat of his grub but wash his dishes.

It accords poorly with the emerging image of the cowboy that
he was as likely to sing hymns as bawdy songs — neither of which
are commonly published as being properly in his repertoire. And
when he was well and truly oiled, the cowhand would weep

over the soppiest songs as readily as any homesick prairie physician. There seems to be something about the cattle industry
that turns its practitioners into sentimental idiots, for in Australia, too, where the history of cattle parallels our own, the least
hint of melancholy would send the stockmen into paroxysms
of grief and self-pity. The only difference is that in Australia
the cowhands are afraid of being disturbed in death by the dingo
instead of the coyote.

"Oh, Bury Me Not on the Lone Prairie" is the most maudlin
of the soppy songs, and like "Home on the Range," its origin
goes back into the unrecoverable mists. Like so many of the
western songs, this has an eastern origin. Eloise Hubbard Lin-
scott, in her book *Folk Songs of Old New England,* says this was
an adaptation of "The Ocean Burial," which was "written by
the Reverend Edwin H. Chapin (1814–1880), a famous Univer-
salist clergyman, and published in the *Southern Literary Messenger* in 1839. It was set to music by George N. Allen, and
sung in public at the concerts of Ossian N. Dodge and in innumerable homes." This original is in fourteen stanzas wherein
the sailor dies as slowly as a stabbed opera singer. The cowboys
speeded things up a bit.

OH, BURY ME NOT ON THE LONE PRAIRIE*

"Oh, bury me not on the lone prairie."
These words came low and mournfully
From the pallid lips of a youth who lay
On his dying couch at the break of day;
Who had wasted in time till o'er his brow
Death's shades were closely gathering now.
He thought of home and the loved ones nigh,
As the cowboys gathered to see him die.

"Oh, bury me not on the lone prairie,
Where the wild cy-ote will howl o'er me,
In a narrow grave just six by three, —
Oh, bury me not on the lone prairie.
I always hoped to be laid when I died
In the old churchyard by the green hillside.
By the bones of my father, oh there let me be, —
Oh, bury me not on the lone prairie."

*JAF Volume 14, 1901, 186.

"I wish to lie where a mother dear,
    And sister's tears can be mingled there,
    Where my friends could come and weep o'er me, —
    O, bury me not on the lone prairie."
    It matters not, so we oft him told,
    Where the body lies when the heart grows cold:
    "But grant, oh grant this boon unto me, —
    Oh, bury me not on the lone prairie."

"Oh, bury me not — " and his voice failed there,
    But they gave no heed to his dying prayer;
    In a narrow grave just six by three
    They buried him there on the lone prairie.
    Where the dewdrops close and the butterfly rests,
    Where wild rose blooms on the prairie crest,
    Where the cy-ote howls and the wind blows free,
    They buried him there on the lone prairie.

UVALDE, TEXAS.   *Mrs. Annie Laurie Ellis.*

G. F. Will wrote a short article, with almost no commentary of his own, for the *Journal of American Folklore* in 1909, entitled simply "Four Cowboy Songs." It escaped the notice of most subsequent researchers, though three of the four songs were of first interest to folklorists later.

Will's first interest was the Indians of North Dakota, on whom he wrote a half dozen articles in specialized journals. He collaborated with George E. Hyde on a book that did not find any wide popularity — *Corn among the Indians of the Upper Missouri,* in 1917. Will's remarks in his *Journal* articles show that he knew very little about the provenance of the songs he collected, but he does record that in 1909 cowboy songs were being fast forgotten, dying out in the saloons where once they were part of what he called "celebrations," at the campfires, in the ranch house at stag dances, and during night-guard rides.

THE TEXAS COWBOY*

I am a roving cowboy just off the Texas plain,
My trade is cinching saddles, and pulling bridle-reins;
    I can throw a lasso, I can throw it with my ease,
I can rope a broncho, and ride him where I please.

*From G. F. Will, "Four Cowboy Songs." JAF Volume 26, 1913, 185-188.

My bosses they all like me, they say I can't be beat,
For I gave them all the bold stand-off, — you know I've got the cheek.
It's true I work for wages, I take my pay in gold,
But I'm bound to follow the long-horn cows until I get too old.

I once did love a little girl, I loved her with my heart,
I would have worked and supported her, and taken her for my part;
But when I made a little stake, and married thought we'd be,
The prettiest girl in this wide world went square back on me.

It almost broke my heart when she was taken away,
She fell in love with another gent, and cursed be the day!
But I will cheer up my courage now, and love another one,
But I'll punch the cows on the Lone Star trail until my race is run.

Adieu, kind friends, I'll leave you now,
You see I am bound to roam, leave my dear old sweetheart,
    Two sisters and a home.
But when I am on the Lone Star trail, I'll ofttimes think of thee,
I will ofttimes think of the pretty girl that went square back on me.

BISMARCK, N. DAK.   *Arthur Bivins.*

Just as the character of a nation is established by its first influential settlers, so the character of a legend is set by all who participate in its beginning. If their view of the situation is skewed by any factors that distort reality, so the legend will be skewed — and by the anthropological process of transculturation, the stereotype will be self-fulfilling. There were others perhaps more knowledgeable than John Lomax collecting folklore among the cowboys toward the end of the last century, but it was Lomax's *Cowboy Songs* that took the cowhand's songs out of the cattle corridor and gave them to the nation to admire. Lomax had a bias toward occupational songs, and so the evolutionary direction of the legendary cowboy turned in that line. Before this idea was driven back into the mind of the cowboy himself so that he too began to mistake ideality for reality, he sang things that no one would accept as cowboy songs today.

"The White Captive" seems doubly wrong, for it skews the Indian also. It was Henry Rowe Schoolcraft who first portrayed the Indian as a sentimental, Roussellian noble dashing about the forests hand in hand with his lady love, looking for cliffs to leap off. The Indian never saw himself that way—and he certainly never acted that way—but then Indians don't buy romantic novels about Indians. The cowboys knew the Indians well enough, and in point of fact they were still killing one another when "The White Captive" was being sung by cowboys. And sung it was in the old days, for variants of the ballad were picked up all over cowboy country. Perhaps the cowboys thought eastern Indians were different.

Phillips Barry in *The New Green Mountain Songster: Traditional Folksongs of Vermont* says, "'The White Captive' was written in his youth by the Reverend Thomas C. Upham, afterwards ... Professor of Moral Philosophy at Bowdoin College .... It was first printed for the author in the *Columbian-Sentinel,* Boston, September 19, 1918." And so once again a prominent folklorist misses an earlier printing in the *Journal of American Folklore.* The first printing of the song was by G. F. Will, whose destiny it seemed was to go unheralded and unread, in 1909. That variant was rather fragmentary; this fuller version appeared in the *Journal* three years later. Peabody and Will both found a Texas variant, though Will's came to him indirectly from Otis Tye of Yucca, North Dakota, who said he learned it from a Texas cowboy. Peabody's guess that the conflict embedded in the ballad was the massacre of Wyoming, Pennsylvania, in the Revolutionary War, and remembering the orgy of Roman adoration rampant in the young colony (even George Washington wanted to reform the Army according to the Roman plan, with centurions and such-like), one is persuaded that he was right. But it is, for all its unlikeliness, a genuine cowboy song.

THE WHITE CAPTIVE*

The sun has gone down o'er the hills in the west,
And its last beams have faded o'er the mossy hill's crest;
The beauty of nature, the charms of the fair,
A maiden was bound with her white bosom bare.

At the foot of the mountain Amandia did sigh
At the hoot of an owl or a catamount cry,
At the howl of some wolf from its long granite cell
Or the crush of some dead [forest] tree as it fell.

---

*From Charles Peabody, "A Texas Version of 'The White Captive.'"
JAF Volume 25, 1912, 169-170.

The camp-fire was kindled and fanned by the breeze,
And its red embers shone o'er the evergreen trees;
But fierce was the looks of that wild savage scene,
The light o'er their features in entrance did gleam.

The watch-fire was kindled, and its red light did glare.
This maiden was bound with her white bosom bare.
Around her stood this mercerless throng,
Impatient to join in the war-dancing song.

They brought out then the captive all friendless, forlorn,
Her face bathed in blood and her garments all torn.
She counted vengeance in the face of the foe,
And sighed for the time when her suff'rings might close.

They waited a moment while they gazed on the fair,
Whose dark hazel eyes were uplifted in prayer.
And down on her bosom her dark locks did flow,
Which hid from the gazers her bosom of snow.

The chief of these warriors, young Albion, drew near
With an eye like an eagle and a step like a deer.
"Forbear," cried young Albion, "your freedom to crave,"
Gave a sigh for her suff'ring, and a tear o'er her grave.

"Forbear," cried young Albion, "your tortures forbear!
This maiden shall live, by the heavens I swear!
To-night if a victim shall burn at your tree,
Young Albion, your leader, your victim shall be."

At the dawn of the evening, at the close of the day,
A birch-tree canoe was seen gliding away.
Swifter than the wild duck that skims o'er the tide
Young Albion and Amandia together did ride.

At the dawn of next morning a white cot was seen
With its blue curling smoke o'er the wild willows green,
But great was the joy when she stepped on the shore
To embrace her kind father and mother once more.

But all that he asked was kindness and food,
From the parents of Amandia to the chief of the woods.

One reason G. F. Will did not imprint his name in the history
of the cowboy's legend was his ignorance of the drama behind
the evolution of the songs he collected. Ignorance is bliss; had he

known how the song he dismissed as suggesting "strongly a parody on some of the English ballads" came to be, he would have been most regretful indeed for his dismissal.

In his earliest days "The Dying Cowboy" (now better known as "The Streets of Laredo") was the unhappy Irishman, "The Unfortunate Rake." His earliest days were the close of the eighteenth century, and as a character, his days were not long, for he was a young man dying of what most euphemistically was called a social disease. The early folklorists did not admit the existence of such things in mixed company, and so the song, a broadside (a city-bred version of the more noble ballad, printed by the yard on rolls of paper and hawked by yardage, like a bolt of cloth), had opportunity to develop on its own without attention or interference of the scholars. It came with the Irish and English immigrants to America, and there split into three distinct variants, depending on what folk group it fell among. In the southern white hillbilly society, the Rake changed sex and became "The Bad Girl's Lament." Some versions of this genus are as beautiful as any song on such a theme can be; the variant collected in 1953 in the Virgin Islands (a strange place for the Rake to turn up, considering the nature of his affliction) is the best of all.

Among the southern Negroes the song weakened in melody and strengthened in rhythm, becoming the classic lament, "St. James Infirmary" (the Irish original had the Rake dying of venereal disease most incongruously in London's St. James' Hospital, which had been founded in commemoration of fourteen chaste, honest, but leprous maidens).

And finally, the ballad migrated to the West, recovered its melody perhaps through the Spanish, and became "The Streets of Laredo." Some of the variants of "The Streets of Laredo" have the Rake visiting first the unidentified establishment owned by one "Rosie," whose profession we can guess, but he is always shot some place or other, a circumstance of ballad change that suggests some delicacy on the part of the adapting composer. Among the real cowboys, of course, either means of fatality would have been equally likely.

Curiously, this song in Australia (where stockmen followed much the same recreational habits as the American cowhand) is derived not only from "The Unfortunate Rake," but from the

Rake's affinal relative, another eighteenth century broadside called "The Tarpaulin Jacket." There one can hear in the performance of those wandering troupes providing "good, clean family entertainment" variants of "The Dying Stockman," whose original malady has also been obscured. In Australia the Rake falls off a horse, and it serves him right.

THE DYING COWBOY*

As I rode down to the theatre, the theatre,
As I rode to the theatre one day,
I met a young cowboy all dressed in white linen;
All dressed in white linen, all fixed for the grave.

Chorus.

Go play the fife lowly and beat the drum slowly,
And play the death march as they carry me on;
Take me to the prairie and lay the sod o'er me,
For I'm a young cowboy, I know I've done wrong.

When once in the saddle I used to go dashing,
When once in the saddle I used to be gay;
I first took to drinking and then to card playing,
Got shot through the lungs and am dying to-day.

Chorus.

Go write a letter to my gray-headed mother,
And break the news gently to sister dear;
But there is another more dear than a mother,
Who'd bitterly weep if she knew I were here.

Chorus.

Go gather around me a group of young cowboys,
And tell them the story the cowboy has said,
And tell them take warning before they go farther,
And stop the wild roaming before it's too late.

Chorus.

Go bring me a cup, a cup of cold water,
A cup of cold water the dying man said;
But ere they returned the spirit had got him,—
He'd gone to the giver, the cowboy was dead.

* From G. F. Will, "Songs of Western Cowboys." JAF Volume 22, 1909, 256-261.

The genuine folksong of protest, ignored for centuries by influential members of the several Establishments who did not encourage rocking of the socioeconomic boat, has again fallen upon hard times through the misbehavior of dropouts from their schools and their culture who sing protest against affluence. The genre, however, goes back in English at least to the fourteenth century, and has a long and legitimate, if not a noble, tradition. Certain professions in which there was much exploitation and actual oppression never developed songs of protest; all of these have been trades entered voluntarily. Like the trade of tending cows. To do it at all, one needed to want to do it, and one had to go out of one's way socially and spatially to get into it. So cowboy songs of protest are nearly nonexistent; even the best known of these few, "Buffalo Skinners," is a transplant from northeastern occupations.

Yet G. F. Will found his cowboys singing "The Shanty Teamsters' Marseillaise." The explanation is simple though unsatisfying: some of the cowboys had experience in the lumber camps before finding their true calling in life. And then, too, cowboys would sing anything for a drink.

SHANTY TEAMSTERS' MARSEILLAISE*

Come, all ye gay teamsters, attention I pray,
    I'll sing you a ditty composed by the way,
Of a few jovial fellows who thought the hours long,
    Would pass off the time with a short comic song.

Chorus
    Come, cheer up, brave boys, it is upward we go
    Through this wretched country, the Opeongo.

As it happened one morning of a fine summer-day,
    I met Robert Conroy, who to me did say,
"Will you go to my shanty and draw my white pine,
    I'll give you good wages and the best of good time."

"For to go to your shanty we do feel inclined,
    To earn our good wages and be up in good time;
To our wives and our sweethearts we'll bid all adieu,
    And go up to York Branch and draw timber for you."

*From G. F. Will, "Four Cowboy Songs." JAF Volume 26, 1913, 185-188.

There assembled together a fine jovial crew
    With horses well harnessed, both hardy and true;
All things being ready, we started away
    From fair Elmer town about noon of the day.

The road led o'er mountains, through valleys and plains,
    In a country where hardship and poverty reign,
Where the poor suff'ring settler, hard fate to bewail,
    Is bound down with mortgage, debts due, and claims.

At a place called York Branch, where Conroy holds his rules,
    There assembled together his hack-knaves and fools,
And old Jimmy Edwards, that cut-throat and spy,
    Would try to deceive you by advices and lies.

Not long at the farm we're allowed to stay,
    But escorted by Jimmy we're hurried away,
Where Frenchmen and Indian, their living to gain,
    Were abused by a brute, Jerry Welch was his name.

We read of the devil, from heaven he fell,
    For rebellion and treason was cast down to hell;
But his son Jerry Welch remains here below
    To work deeds of darkness, cause sorrow and woe.

With the eyes of a demon, the tongue of a knave,
    These two villainous traitors should be yoked in a sleigh;
And Jerry's old squaw, for a teamster and guide,
    To tip up the brutes of the Branch for to drive.

At length we commenced the white pine to draw;
    It was Jerry's intention to put us square through,
To break down our horses, and show no fair play;
    And he ordered brave Jimmy to drive night and day.

But the teamsters consulted, and made up a plan;
    Since fair work won't do, to go home every man.
So we left Conroy's shanty, and Jerry the knave;
    For true loyal teamsters ain't born to be slaves.

So we are at home and surrounded by friends,
    We are thankful for favors that Providence sends;
We'll sing our adventures, and our shantying is o'er,
    And we'll never go up the York Branch any more.
              Chorus
    Come, cheer up, brave boys, we plough and we sow,
    And adieu evermore to the Opeongo.

Walter Prescott Webb, author of *The Great Plains* and *The Texas Rangers* as well as a number of articles on Texas folklore, was among other things a good friend of Frank A. Hamer, the Texas Ranger who gunned down Bonnie and Clyde. Evidently he was not a violent man himself, but he liked to see violence done, for his interest was in the wilder parts of the Old West. In "The Bee County Iliad" he extracts a lyric biography of a man named Floyd Canada, an outstanding member of the Negro community around Beeville, Texas, when to be outstanding one had to be pretty agile with a razor.

Prescott implies that Canada composed — or at least constructed — this short life of a natural man, but one would like more evidence for the implication than the assertion. What this song consists of are pertinent selections from that great amorphous mass of maverick couplets long drawn upon for various named blues. This "Iliad" is nearly unique in that it tells a coherent story; most blues deal with one approach to one emotional situation.

When the white man discovered this enormous disordered storehouse of memorable couplets, he expanded them into narrative songs. Readers conversant with hillbilly song will recognize in some of the "stanzas" the seeds of entire songs in the repertoire of white, folk entertainers. For instance, the second stanza of part one — "The Wanderlust and the Long Freight-Train" — became a decade later the hillbilly "Cannonball Blues" on the records of the famous Carter Family; stanza four was made by the great Jimmie Rodgers (see my article, "Jimmie Rodgers — A Folksong Catalyst," in Chapter Six) into his "Blue Yodel Number Five," and stanza ten into his "Train Whistle Blues."

The evolutionary line of the cowboy legend has excluded the Negro (his return in the last year or so is an intrusion prompted by external events and fashions), but many of the old cowhands and trail drivers were tanned more deeply than the sun could have accomplished. J. Frank Dobie in his book *Cow People* tells about several Negro cowboys, among them Al Jones, a memorably handsome man who had driven up the trail thirteen times, four times as boss. There was genuine integration in the cowboy era, in all its aspects; it can no longer be chronicled, however, that Clell Miller of the Jesse James' gang was a Negro.

THE BEE COUNTY ILIAD*

The material presented in the following notes was gathered around Beeville, Texas. Beeville is in Bee County, a cattle country, now becoming agricultural, and is located ninety miles south of San Antonio, about midway between there and Corpus Christi. It is near the Nueces River, and within thirty miles of the historic old Goliad of Texas-Mexican fame.

The best field of folklore is found in the strong Irish element in the population around Beeville, who are always stored with local legends and superstitions, and who are highly gifted in spinning these into interesting tales for all who will come and listen. Next there is the Negro, an animated body of superstition and song. Then there are the war stories and ballads, here as well as wherever the veterans may be found. Three other fields are to be found in the railroad songs, cowboy songs, and the mass of Mexican superstition and legend.

Any one of these fields offers inexhaustible resources to the gleaner of folklore. The material seems to increase with the effort to get it. This paper will not deal with the cowboy songs, for others have covered that subject too ably, nor shall I attempt the Mexican lore. I shall give some local tales and legends and some Negro songs.

There is an interesting story regarding the peculiar properties possessed by the waters of the Nueces River. This river must be sacred to Ananias, for it is said that he who drinks of its waters loses all desire to tell the truth thereafter.

Tradition also accounts for the name "Marysville," which Beeville had before it was given its present name. Away back in the days of Spanish dominion, before there was an American settlement in southwestern Texas, two beautiful *señoritas* lived with their father in a *cabana* (cabin), under a large *mott* (grove) on the site of Beeville. Maria was the younger daughter, says tradition, and the most beautiful woman in all the Spanish settlements. She was the typical Spanish maiden, with the characteristic dark eyes, olive complexion, and a wealth of beautiful long dark hair, which made her the envy or admiration of all. Tradition tells how the Indians came once when the father

*From W. Prescott Webb, "Notes on Folk-Lore of Texas."
JAF Volume 28, 1915, 290-299.

and sister were away and murdered her for her beautiful hair. The
father had her buried beneath the largest tree and near his favorite
smoking-place. Here he and the grief stricken lover would come and
watch in the twilight and darkness over her grave. The lover carved
her name on the tree in large Spanish letters, which could be seen until
recent years. Later the missions in Texas were abandoned. When the
Americans came and found the mysterious tree with the strange word,
they made a settlement and called it Marysville. The tree still stands
in a yard in the center of Beeville.

There are stories of buried treasure left by the pirate and buccaneer
Jean Lafitte. A certain Steve Pipkins was instructed by a "spirit"
to go to a [certain] tree on the San Antonio River, and from it to step
twenty-five feet south, one foot east, and one foot north, and then to
dig down three feet. "Then," said the spirit, "you will find a square
iron box left by Jean Lafitte." The man did not believe in spirits or
buried treasure, and refused to go; but his wife urged and insisted
until he had to [go] for the sake of [domestic] peace. When he arrived
at the place, he found — no, not the box, but the hole from which it
had just been removed, and around which the dirt was still fresh.

The wolves around Beeville are noted for cunning, and it is said
that they can catch chickens out of the highest trees on any night when
there is a bright moon. The wolf comes up directly under the tree in
which the coveted chicken roosts. He makes a noise and wakes the
chicken and gets its attention. Then the wolf begins to chase his own
tail, slowly at first, then faster and faster. The chicken, watching the
whirling wolf, becomes dizzy, and falls out of the tree — an easy prey.

On an expedition for collecting folklore, I made the most valuable
find of my collection — a Negro song which I have with conceit named
"The African Iliad." I came upon it in this manner:

One morning I heard a schoolboy singing a snatch of a Negro song.
I said, "Harry, where did you learn that [song]?"

"From a Negro here in town," he replied.

"Do you know it all?" I [then] asked.

"No," he laughed, "there is more to that song than I could learn
in a week." That sounded interesting.

"Who is that Negro?"

"Floyd Canada," he answered.

"Well, Harry," I said, "don't you think we could look Floyd up and
get all that song?"

"I don't know, sir, he's in jail now for shooting craps."

That made the quest even more fascinating. But Floyd's jail sentence soon expired; and I located him, through Harry, over across
the railroad track, in a Negro pool hall. We found him with a band

of his comrades, including the hotel waiter, making merry with guitar, banjo, harp, and song—as merry as though a jail had never been. When we told Floyd what we wanted, his black face was cleft with a broad grin from one big ear to the other. But in a small town one cannot spend much time in a pool hall, and especially a Negro pool hall. The nearby depot offered the solution, for it is the common meeting ground of all the races; and to the depot I invited Floyd. I had expected in him an old Negro, but found instead a man of about twenty-seven. He was very modern, too. He had seen several states from the sidedoor of a freight car and still more from the rods, as his song will indicate, and had a detailed knowledge of the interior of more jailhouses than churches. Floyd knew the world, evidently.

In the corner of the depot Floyd dictated to me the "Iliad," and I wrote it down. The song tells no connected story, any more than the ruins of Rome tell a story, or the grave of an American Indian, with its bones, arrowheads, beads, and pottery, tells a story; but a story may be drawn from it—the story of the modern Negro. It contains an account of practically every phase of his life; and if the race should be blotted out and its history lost and forgotten, much of it could be reconstructed from this ballad. We could learn what the Negro held to be of highest importance; we could learn of his desires and aims, his love and hate, his ethical and chivalrous ideas, his philosophy of life, code of morals, and idea of the future. And it is for this reason that I have named it "The African Iliad."

It is remarkable, if for no other reason, because of its length, for it is among the longest ballads in existence. It contains eighty stanzas of four lines each, rhyming in couplets. While the song has little narrative unity, it has a certain unity of subject matter. Pervading nearly every line is a spirit of restless wandering—the *Wanderlust* and desire for a long freight on which to ride away from trouble. It, like all the popular ballads, sings itself. Floyd says it is sung to the tune of "The Dallas Blues." The subject matter of the song falls into five more or less well-defined groups. I have attempted to arrange these in some order. The first division deals with his wanderings and the call of the road; the second treats his mother, whose advice he has ignored, and of home, which he imagines as does every prodigal, he will never leave when he reaches it once more. In the third canto he sings of his sweetheart, the delights of love, and the pangs of jealousy. In the fourth he is evidently married, for he sings of domestic troubles and family quarrels; but, strange to say, not one note does he utter of domestic happiness. In the fifth and last he deals with trouble, is sentenced to death by the law for a crime, and concludes by making provisions for the final disposition of his body. Following are selections:

THE RAILROAD BLUES

I. THE WANDERLUST AND THE LONG FREIGHT-TRAIN

Every time you hear me sing this song
You may know I've caught a train and gone.
I get a letter, and this is how it read:
Stamped on the inside, Yo lover's sick in bed.

Give me my shoes and my Carhart overalls,
Let me step over yonder and blind the Cannon Ball;
That's the long train they call the Cannon Ball,
It makes a hundred miles and do no switchin' at all.

Train I ride doan burn no coal at all,
It doan burn nothin' but Texas Beaumont oil;
That's the long train they calls the Cannon Ball,
It makes a hundred miles and do no stoppin' at all.

If you ever had the blues, you know jus' how I feel,
Puts you on the wonder, and make you want to squeal;
When you take the blues and doan know what to do,
Jus' hunt you a train and ride the whole world through.

Big Four in Dallas done burned down,
Burned all night long, burned clean to the ground;
But give me my shoes, and press my overalls,
If you doan min' my goin', baby, I'll catch the Cannon Ball.

I'm worried now, but I won't be worried long,
This north-bound train will certainly take me home.
Number Nine is gone, Number Ten's switchin' in the yard,
But I'm goin' to see that girl if I have to ride the rods.

I got the railroad blues, but I haven't got the fare,
The company sho' ought to pay my way back there.
The train I ride is sixteen coaches long
Dat's de train done take yo' baby home.

I'm a goin' away, it won't be long;
When I hit Houston, I'll call it gone.
When I git to Houston I'll stop and dry;
When I hit San Tone, I'll keep on by.

How I hate to hear the Monkey Motion blow,
It puts me on the wonder, and makes we want to go.
Dat passenger-train got ways jus' lak a man,
Steal away yo' girl, and doan care where she land.

I may be right an' I may be wrong,
But it takes a worried woman to sing a worry song;
When a woman's in trouble, she wring her hands and cry;
But when a man's in trouble, it's a long freight-train and ride.

II. HOME AND MOTHER

I went to the depot wringin' my hands and cryin'
Everybody's bound to have trouble some time;
If I'd a listened to what my mother said,
I'd been at home lyin' in my foldin' bed.

When I git home, mother, I'm sure goin' to stick an' stay;
Mother, you may beat me, but you'll never drive me away;
When I leave agin, hang crepe all on yo' doah;
If I ain't daid, I ain't comin' back no mo'.

When I git home, mother, I'll tell you the truth;
I love you, an' I ought'n't left yo' roof;
You tol' me befo' I left yo' doah,
Many nights I'd sleep on the cold hard floah.

My mother's daid, my sister's gone away,
That's the reason why I'm wanderin' around to-day.
I followed my mother right to her buryin'-ground,
You ought to a heard me cryin' when they let her down.

I went to the graveyard, peeped in my mother's face,
Ain't it sad to see you, mother, in this lonesome place!
Doan never leave yo' mother old and gray,
You'll be bothered, man, troubled all the day.

III. LOVE

If you mistreat me, you certainly won't agin;
You can tell jus' how your trouble begin;
When you're in love, you can't control yo' min',
Single man bound to git drunk any time.

I got one girl, an' I'm goin' to git me two;
You look so sweet, baby, no tellin' what you'll do.
If you don't love me, please don't dog me around;
Be true with me, and I'll not leave the town.

If I feel to-morrow like I feel to-day,
I'm gwine to ride the last train away;
If I had all you women's hearts in my hand,
I'd show you how to treat yo' nice black man.

I'm goin' away, it won't be long;
You're gwine to miss me when I'm daid and gone.
You are my lover, turn the light down low,
I got somethin' to tell you just befo' I go.

It's hard, man, but still it's true
To love some woman that never cares fo' you.
When you git one girl, you better git you two,
For there ain't no tellin' what the girls'll do.

There's lots of trouble here, and more on down the road,
You always will find trouble, no matter where you go;
Trouble is a thing that never worries my mind;
But if you're in love, it'll worry you some time.

I'm goin' to town now, what you want me to bring you back?
I'm in love with you, baby, jus' anything you like;
Lemme tell you, girl, please doan wear no black;
'Cause when you think I'm daid, I'll come easin' back.

Red River's on the boom; Guadaloupe's standin' still;
Brown woman on the train; black one on the hill.
You brown-skin woman, let me be yo' Teddy Bear,
Put a chain on my neck, an' I'll follow you everywhere.

I'm a goin' to tell you what the Mexican tol' me,
I no lika you, you no lika me;
All I want in this wide worl'
Is a pocket full o' dollars an' a Creole girl.

I sent my girl to have her fortune told;
She come walkin' back with her mouth chock full o'gold.
Come, go with me, get your mouth filled with gold!
I wouldn't mistreat you to save nobody's soul.

IV. MARRIAGE AND DOMESTIC TROUBLES

If I get drunk an' down, who's goin' to take me home?
For yonder stands my babe with a hobble on.
My babe sees me standin' in the barroom door,
An' I swore to her I'd never git drunk no more.

Ain' it hard when yo' wife puts you out of doors,
Leave you standin' cryin', you ain't nowhere to go;
You get the blues so bad, you can't control yo' mind;
You love yo' wife, but she'll worry you some time.

You can always tell when she doan want you 'round,
Yo' meals ain't ready, and yo' bed's turned upside down;
Then you stay out late, git yo' name straight,
Befo' you come agin to yo' baby's gate.

My heart is forever breakin'
Children in the do' screamin',
It may be cloudy an' a rainin',
Keep me worried an' a singin'.

V. TRIAL, DEATH AT HANDS OF THE LAW, AND FINAL WILL

I ain't a goin' to die, jus' goin' to sleep away,
To-morrow's goin' to be my trial day;
Yonder comes my girl, a hundred in her hand,
Sayin', Please spare my man, Judge, if you can.
I went to the court-house an' stood right on the stage,
Tol' the judge to give me justice, to let me have my way.
He read my papers, I was guilty of my crime;
Then I axed for 98, but he give me 99.

I went to the jail-house; first thing I spy,
Jail-house key, and you ought 'o hear me cry.
Look here, woman, can't stand to see you go, —
Hang my case, Judge, an' I'll meet you further down the road.

When I die, ship me to my mother;
If my ma doan want me, ship me to my pa;
If my pa doan want me, bury me in the sea,
Where the whales and de sharks'll make a fuss over me.

In all this ballad the Negro has sung nothing about the white man's advantage of him, and nothing of his having to work hard for a living. He loves, gambles, loafs, bribes the courts, and beats his way on the freight. He turns his thoughts inward; he is extremely self-centered. He may be elated to the point of ecstasy, or depressed to the point of self-effacement, but he is in any case concerned only with himself — his love, his trouble, his own interest at all times. He seems to have some regard for his mother, but this is only when he is in trouble. He mentions his father but one time and that is with regard to his burial.

Nothing could be greater than the difference between this song of the modern Negro, and the songs sung by the antebellum darky on the old plantation. The difference in the song indicates the corresponding difference in the singers. The old Negro lived a simple life on the plantation and in the dusk of the evening twanged his banjo and sang of hard times, the white man's greed, and of the wild animals. He, too, sang of his love—about the only thing the old Negro and the modern one, like Floyd, have had in common.

———————————

One of the cowboys from whom John Lomax collected his great canon of cowboy songs, R. S. Scott, of the Little Missouri River, wrote him,

Nearly every well established ranch had for its own individual song a set of verses of its own making. Some "smart" cowboy would lead off composing these verses, which the outfit would take up, chorusing in whenever the song was sung. When a puncher from another outfit drifted into camp, he was expected to sing any new song he might know or new stanzas to an old song, and to teach them to the camp he was visiting. In exchange he took the novelties his hosts knew. Thus songs like "The Old Chisholm Trail" became of interminable length.

What Scott described in these words is the typical process of folk transmission. In the prisons of the South, certain great folksingers and musicians left so strong a mark of their own personalities on the prison songs that folklorists whose specialty is this area of folksong can tell from a singer's style exactly where he did his time. On a slightly higher social level, archaeological crews make up songs so distinctive in style that similar identification can be made by collectors of archaeological folksongs.

"El Cancion del Rancho de los Olmos" is an example of what Scott was talking about. It was collected by the last of the truly fabulous links with the era of the cowboy, J. Frank Dobie. Dobie died four years ago in Texas, "where he was born and reared and remained green," as Stith Thompson said of him in his *Journal of American Folklore* obituary. He was fabulous, for fables were told of him, and like other fabulous figures he had a centripetal force upon good stories that originated with lesser people, though he told many good stories of his own creation. He was a folklorist "in spite of himself," for he lived beyond the time of his true destiny, when it was no longer possible to do the things folklorists could only study. His father and his uncles were cowmen, each with an idiosyncrasy that students of the legend expect in the great practitioners; Dobie's father, for instance, worked cattle with a white handkerchief tied over his nose, a habit that surely must have filled strangers with apprehension. J. Frank managed the 256,000-acre ranch of his Uncle Jim in the early twenties, but by that time he was already committed to herding students at the University of Texas, where he was to spend the whole of his turbulent life. While teaching, collecting folklore, and writing eighteen books, Dobie became, as we say, "a legend in his own time." Not always was the legend a peaceable one. Dobie was as cantankerous as a man in his position can be. When the University built its great skyscraping tower of learning out in the middle of a prairie where space was the cheapest commodity, the administration thought at last it had done something of which Dobie might condescend to approve. Dobie's considered observation was, "It would be all right if they laid it on its side." To Dobie serious scholarship was the process of "transferring bones from one graveyard to another," so he made sure that the material he wrote about was alive, even if he had to fix it up a bit to give it that animation.

EL CANCION DEL RANCHO DE LOS OLMOS*

El Rancho de los Olmos is in Lasalle County, Texas, in the Rio Grande border country. Like other ranches of the border country, it is worked by Mexican *vaqueros;* and while they drive their herds, or build tanks with scrapers, or burn the thorns off the prickly pear in drouthy times for the cattle, or sit around the camp at night, they are great hands to sing. Sometimes there is an improviser in camp; often a *corrido* (cow outfit) has a song of its own. I knew one Mexican whose horse played out one day while he was running a *ladino* (outlaw) steer in the brush. The steer was almost played out too. The *vaquero* could almost catch the steer but not quite. Finally he got down and led his horse and followed the steer at a distance until the latter entered an impenetrable *magote* (area of thick brush). Then he stopped under a mesquite tree,

*From J. Frank Dobie, "El Cancion de los Olmos." JAF Volume 36, 1923, 192-195.

unsaddled his horse, and while he let him rest, composed a song on his experience. It became known as the song of the *"Caballo Fragado"* (the "Broken Down Horse") and was for a long time sung by the hands of the ranch on which he worked, El Rancho de las Animas. However, I was never able to get the song memorized or written down.

I did, however, get the Olmos Ranch song. It was occasioned by the swimming of a herd of cattle across the Nueces River when that stream was up. Placido Salinas was afraid to swim; he returned to camp. He was the best-natured fellow in the world. While he waited for the *corrido* to come in, he began his composition. That evening when the other *vaqueros* came and began taunting him, he sang what he had composed. Others entered into the composition and the singing until almost every man of the outfit was represented in a stanza. At least, this is the account of the origin of the song as it has been given me by two or three of the *vaqueros* present. An interesting point is that at least eight years after the date of composition the song was still being sung with gusto by the men on the Olmos Ranch. I am sorry that I cannot give the music of the song. To hear, though, the Mexicans sing it at night, while the coyotes howl in refrain out on the hills around, is to realize the romance and beauty of folksinging.

1

El dia diecinueve de Marzo,
¡Qué dia tan señalado!
Que en la pasta de Martinez
Don Plácido se ha rajado.

1

The nineteenth day of March it was,
A day to be remembered by all,
When in the pasture called Martinez
Don Placido's bluff had a fall.

2

Decía Don Adolfito
Como hombre muy decidido:
—Déjenme venir, muchachos,
Que hay que pasar los novillos.

2

Said there Don Adolfito,
A man of decision and mettle:
"Let me go on, my boys,
For we've got to cross these cattle."

3

Decía Manuel Hinojosa
En su caballo trigueño:
—Yo lo sigo, Don Adolfo,
Déjeme quitar el freno.

3

Said there Don Manuel Hinojosa,
Who was riding his horse of brown,
"I'll follow you, Don Adolfito,
But let me take my bridle down."

4

Decía Joaquin Villareal
En su caballo Borracho:
—Aquí se rajó un amigo,
¡Qué lástima de machacho!

4

Said there then Joaquin Villareal,
Who was riding his horse Borracho,
"Here a friend is certainly bullying;
What a pity about this muchacho!"

5

Decía Placido Salinas
Paseándose en el barranco:
—Aquí los espero yo;
De veras, me los espanto.

5

Said there Placido Salinas,
Pacing up and down the river:
"Here, I'll await you fellows;
In truth, there's trouble in my liver."

6

Felis era aventador
Por toda la ria del rio,
Y Lupe era atajador
En su caballo tordillo.

6

Now Felis was *abentador*,
All along the river side,
And Lupe was *atajador*
On his iron grey horse astride.

7

Cuando venían de vuelta
Manuel pensó diferente
De volverse al Camerón
Con toditita su gente.

7

That evening when rode towards
    home
The men who had crossed the river,
They seemed to the boss of the
    Camerón
An outfit not quite familiar.

8

Lupe no carga chivarras,
Anda muy bien abrigado
Y de tanto que se mojó
Se le desbarrato el calzado.

8

Lupe wore no leather leggins,
Though his skin was well protected;
Lupe was not wearing shoes
And his wet toes could be detected.

9

Lupe cargaba su capa,
Que era un purito rajón,
Y se quedó en el Camerón,
Secando su pantalón.

9

What he wore was his old slicker,
From tail to collar a long split,
And when he got to the Camerón
He began to dry his breeches a bit.

10

Miguelito de caballo
Estaba trayendo un macho,
Y lo quería pa' cortar
Porque se atenía el muchacho.

10

As a boy, Miguel had learned to ride
On a mule that was his crony—
Oh he was fine for cutting cattle!—
Miguel rode him for a pony.

11

Aquí va la despedida,
Sentádose en un cajón,
Y aquí se quedan cantando
Los versitos del rajón.

11

And now to this we'll say so-long,
Sitting on an old board box,
And now for a while we'll sing in
    song
Some verses about the coward.

Notes: 1. Martinez is the name of a pasture on the Nueces. 2. Don Adolfo was *segundo* in the outfit to Manuel Hinojosa, the *caporal.* 3. Bridles are frequently removed from horses in order to enable them to swim better. 4. Borracho was the name of the horse. 6. The *aventador* is the pointer or lead man of the herd; the *atajador* rides along the side of the herd at the point, though sometimes the swing men are all called *atajadores.* 7. Camerón is the name of a ranch included in the limits of the Olmos holdings. 8. *Chivarras* is the name on the border always used for leather leggins, rather than the word *chaparejos* which seems to be used farther west and north in the old Spanish-American cow country. 9. *Capa* is used exclusively to mean slicker. 10. The mule which Don Miguelito had ridden as a boy had a reputation; he could not be worked in harness, but was good as a cutting animal. His age is implied by the fact that Don Miguelito was a little old man near eighty! 11. The *cajón* was a feed trough, a popular setee.

The song is so colloquial and so local, frequently so nearly nonsensical and incoherent, that I have essayed a translation that does not altogether betray the original, I hope.

John Avery Lomax, born a hundred and one years ago, followed the trail of cowboy songs for most of his eighty years. He has no rivals in the history of scholarship in the cowboy legend, and his personality and accomplishment loom just as large in the chronicle of the workers in every field of American folklore. He was twice president of the American Folklore Society, he was one of the founders of the Texas Folklore Society, and with his son Alan he established the Archive of Folk Song at the Library of Congress. His classic collection, *Cowboy Songs*, was followed by a number of other books on folksong of comparable stature.

But like other great men, John Lomax does not stand up well under close scrutiny. Jack Thorpe, who began collecting cowboy songs in 1889 and who published *Songs of the Cowboys* in 1908, accused Lomax of rustling *Cowboy Songs* out of his work. Lomax's defense was to ignore Thorpe. The standard history of folksong scholarship in this century, D. K. Wilgus' *Anglo-American Folksong Scholarship Since 1898*, scours Lomax for having been "extremely careless and inefficient in documenting and preserving his field materials," and for imposing his own views upon the legend of the cowboy at a time when the legend was so malleable as to be shaped by such influences. We are told even by his friends that Lomax in a fit of pique destroyed his first collections of material; 203 of the 250 Edison phonograph cylinders that substantiate his work have vanished; and many of his assertions elicit the scholarly condemnation, "puzzling." He often committed the unpardonable offense of making up standard texts out of fragments found God knows where. Even worse, he claimed having done so even when he hadn't. And all of this means nothing at all, for, like all great men, Lomax fulfilled the only requirement of a great man: to be great.

The selection that follows is from Lomax's presidential address to the American Folklore Society in 1914. It is an epitaph for the era of the cowboy, the certification by its greatest student that the reality of the cowboy was no more, and that the time of legend-making had begun.

The song with which Lomax ended his address will be the subject of an article soon to be published in the *Journal of American Folklore* by John I. White, "Owen Wister and the Dogies." John Lomax wrote in his notes to *Cowboy Songs*, "The tune of this song was given me at the Texas Cattlemen's Convention, Fort Worth, Texas, 1910, by Mrs. Trantham, a wandering gypsy minstrel. The words were woven together from five fragments." "Whoopee Ti Yi Yo'" is known to have been put in print as early as 1903 in Andy Adams' *The Log of a Cowboy,* and folk genealogists have traced its ancestry to "The Old Man Rocking the Cradle"; but most interesting are the entries made by Owen Wister, whose book *The Virginian* was the greatest of all cowboy novels, in his recently discovered diaries. An entry written by Wister at Brownwood, central Texas, early in 1893 notes, "I have come upon a unique song . . . and I transcribe it faithfully. Only a cowboy could have produced such an effusion. It has the earmark of entire genuineness."

THE DECLINE AND FALL
OF THE COWBOY BALLAD*

A ballad has been defined by Professor Kittredge as a story told in song, or a song that tells a story. This general definition of a ballad has been made more specific by various limitations. For instance, it is said that a genuine ballad has no one author; that, instead, some community or some group of people is its author. It is therefore the expression of no one mind: it is the product of the folk. Furthermore, the ballad has no date. No one knows just when the most treasured of the English and Scottish ballads were composed. For generations before Percy made his first collection of them — and no one knows just how many generations — they were handed down by word of mouth, as is the Masonic Ritual. A ballad, finally, is impersonal in tone; that is, it is the expression of no individual opinion. It might have been written by anyone. A ballad, then, is a story in song, written no one knows when, no one knows where, no one knows by whom, and perhaps, some may think, no one knows "for why." Notwithstanding, as the spontaneous poetic expression of the primitive emotions of a people, ballads always have had and always will have the power to move mankind.

Have we any American ballads? Let us frankly confess, that, according to the definitions of the best critics of the ballad, we have none at all. There has, however, sprung up in America a considerable body of folk-song, called by courtesy "ballads," which in their authorship, in the social conditions under which they were produced, in the spirit that gives them life, resemble the genuine ballads sung by our English and Scottish grandmothers long before there was an American people. We recognize and love the new ballad, just as we love the old, because the real ballad, perhaps as much as any other form of expression, appeals to our deepest, most intimate, and most elemental associations. Our primitive instincts yet influence us. You and I, living in the heyday of civilization under the conventions of cultured people, are yet, after all, not so far removed from a time and from a folk that spoke out their emotions simply and directly. A ballad is such a fresh, direct, and simple expression — not of an individual, but of a people — upon a subject that has a common interest and a common appeal, because of its common association to all of that people; and the emotions it expresses are the abiding experiences of the human heart. I contend that American ballads that have caught the spirit of the old ballads,

*From John A. Lomax, "Some Types of American Folk-Song."
 JAF Volume 28, 1915, 1-17.

however they may be lacking in impersonality, in form, and in finish, do exist and are being made today.

The making of cowboy ballads is at an end. The big ranches of the West are being cut up into small farms. The nester has come and come to stay. Gone is the buffalo, the Indian war-whoop, the free grass of the open plain; even the stinging lizard, the horned frog, the centipede, the prairie dog, the rattlesnake, are fast disappearing. Save in some of the secluded valleys of southern New Mexico, the old-time roundup is no more; the trails to Kansas and to Montana have become grass-grown or lost in fields of waving grain; the maverick steer, the regal longhorn, has been supplanted by his unpoetic but more beefy and profitable Polled Angus, Durham, and Hereford cousins from across the seas.

The changing and romantic West of the early days lives mainly in story and in song. The last figure to disappear is the cowboy, the animating spirit of the vanishing era. He sits his horse easily as he rides through a wide valley enclosed by mountains, with his face turned steadily down the long, long road — "the road that the sun goes down." Dauntless, reckless, without the unearthly purity of Sir Galahad, though as gentle to a pure woman as King Arthur, he is truly a knight of the twentieth century. A vagrant puff of wind shakes a corner of the crimson handkerchief knotted loosely at his throat; the thud of his pony's feet mingling with the jingle of his spurs is borne back; and as the careless, gracious, lovable figure disappears over the divide, the breeze brings to the ears, faint and far, yet cheery still, the refrain of a cowboy song:

Refrain.

Whoopee ti yi yo, git along, little dogies;
    It's my misfortune and none of your own.
Whoopee ti yi yo, git along little dogies;
    For you know Wyoming will be your new home.

As I was walking one morning for pleasure,
    I spied a cow-puncher all riding along;
His hat was throwed back and his spurs was a jinglin',
    As he approached me a-singin' this song.

Refrain.

Early in the spring we round up the dogies,
    Mark them and brand them and bob off their tails;
Drive up our horses, load up the chuck-wagon,
    Then throw them dogies up on the trail.

Refrain.

It's whooping and yelling and driving them dogies;
    Oh, how I wish you would go on!
It's whooping and punching and go on little dogies,
    For you know Wyoming will be your new home.

Refrain.

Some boys goes up the trail for pleasure,
    But there's where you've got it most awfully wrong;
For you haven't any idea the trouble they give us
    While we go driving them all along.

Refrain.

Oh, you'll be soup for Uncle Sam's Injuns;
    "It's beef, heap beef," I hear them cry.
Git along, git along, git along little dogies,
    For the Injuns'll eat you by and by.

VI

Songs of the Old Country, Songs of the New

THE NEED FOR ART'S EMOTION is in every human being, though the need and the accomplishment vary more from one person to another than almost any other quality. Some can be satisfied by merely receiving passively the emotion made by some other man's art; some are driven to their own creation. One man may not be satisfied unless he can make a better "Moses" than Michelangelo; another can be satiated watching a master quarterback going beyond what is expected of him.

In either case—Michelangelo or the quarterback—*art is the extension of craftsmanship to communicate emotion.* Unless the craft has been mastered, no art can result. This is the one re-

229

liable touchstone for determining the genuineness of what is truly art and what is spurious — whether the artist is folk or sophisticated.

Almost none of the western settlers were trained to the labor they had to take up for the rest of their lives in the New Country. The mastery of craft that allowed artisans like Paul Revere to communicate emotion through silverwork was rarely possible where the entirety of life had to be put into the fight against the environment. Few folk enclaves developed to the point where craftsmanship transmuted to creativity, as it did with the New York Shakers or the Pennsylvania Dutch.

The only expression of emotive creativity the Western settlers had in any significant quantity was their song. Songs took up little room in the wagon and handcarts of the pioneers, and so everyone had a pack of remembered lyrics and melodic stories to build upon in their new homeland. And songs kept alive the memory of the Old Country and the Good Old Days.

Perhaps in a larger view what has been said here for the West could be said for all of America. Every nation seems to have a limited store of artistic energy, to expend in achieving a mediocrity of universality or superlativeness in one genre. The Dutch put their art into painting, the Italians into sculpture, the English into writing. But we can still ask as Sydney Smith did a hundred and fifty years ago, "In the four quarters of the globe, who . . . looks at an American picture or statue?" The United States chose to put its energy into technology, a craft that perhaps never will be mastered so long as it is vital, and therefore may never produce art.

For the country as well as the region, our accomplishment in art has been in song. Conditioned to limit the province of art to piano playing and painting and similar elevated expressions of the spirit, we are most grudging in accepting what the rest of the world accepts without formal admission — that American folksong and American popular music have displaced the folk and popular music of almost every other country on earth. If we are made to see this fact, we are annoyed and distressed by it. Why, we ask, must the rest of the world be so perverse? Why will it not import our democracy or Edward Albee or Andy Warhol or Leonard Bernstein?

As an anthropologist with a specialty in ethnomusicology, I

have heard American hillbilly music in Old Stone Age Australia and in New Stone Age Melanesia, sometimes among people who have never heard a radio or seen a television or motion picture. But somehow the folksong, the popular song, the hillbilly song have penetrated where nothing else of our culture has made any impact. And one must not get the idea that other peoples sing our songs to please us. No one outside the transmitting range of Navaho radio stations has heard the astounding adaptations these Indians constantly make of our vulgate music — three parts indigenous Indian vocables and one part popular lyrics, like:

> *Wey ah hey ah e yan ah*
> *Ta e ah hey ya e ah, Ya e ah hey ya e ah, Ya e ah hey*
> *ya e ah,*
> *Wey a heyn ee ya ah*
> *Ya e ah hey ya e ah, Ya e ah hey ya e ah, Ya e ah hey*
> *ya e ah,*
> *Wey a heyn ee ya ah*
> *Weh an a ye hyah ha ah e weh an a yahn*
> *a weh heyn ah ah*
> *Yan a* sugar in the morning
> Sugar in the evening
> Sugar at suppertime
> *A weh ah hey ah e yan ah*
> Be my little sugar
> And love me all the time *ah wey ah hey e ha ah*

Of all the world's musics, viable or moribund, none compares with the American vulgate for anthropological interest, even if the artistry is questionable. All the songs that follow, whether they are patent importations from the ultimate homelands of their singers or made up on the spot for a local purpose and a limited subject, are the result of centuries of commingling influences, elements, forces — diffusions of fact, or stimulus — all transmuted in the alembic of the New Country to something rich and strange. The strangeness is wonder on the part of the folklorist to find the most casual expression of his folk the end product of centuries of molding and polishing. "He came to us on the edge of evening," said an old Pennsylvania Dutch woman to Cornelius Weygandt, "selling stoves."

Norman Cazden mentioned in the seventy-seventh volume of the *Journal of American Folklore* an allusion in Jacques Handschin's study *Der Toncharaketer* concerning the ninth century Irish scholar John Scot:

Once Charles the Bald, whom he sat facing at dinner, brusquely called out to John, "Just what is really the difference between a Gael [Scotus] and a fool [sottus]?" Whereupon the quick-witted philosopher retorted, "Indeed, there is only the table between the two."

A thousand years later the Arkansas squatter made the same distinction across the fence from the Arkansas traveler.

The *contre danse* evolved to the *quadrille*, one species of which was sung (the *singing quadrille*) and this in turn spawned the Kentucky Running Set, which developed such local sub-species as the New England Quadrille and the Cowboy Square Dance. It will take a discouragingly long time before Americans acquire enough confidence in their own culture to see the imaginative caller, with his mastery of the craft of directing a floor full of dancers, as an artist to be compared with the conductor of an orchestra of serious musicians, but the possibility of such a thing should be allowed to enter our minds. Visualize the mass choreography of a barn-full of dancers moving intricately to the chanted directions of Kizzie Nelson's cousin, back in Yarrow, Missouri.

A MISSOURI DANCE CALL*

All to your places
And straighten up your faces.
Join eight hands and circle to the left,
And when you get around, remember the call.
Take a chew tobacco and spit on the wall.
First gent balance to the second couple.
Swing the girl with the possum jaw.

*By Ruth Ann Musick. JAF Volume 69, 1946, 323-324.

And don't forget your taw.
Everybody swing.
First gent balance to the second lady.
Swing the girl with the run-down shoe,
Balance to your partner; you know what to do.
Balance to the third couple.
Swing the girl in the calico.
Balance to your partner; don't be so slow.
Whoopee, here we go!

Second gent balance to the first couple on the right.
Swing the girl in the run-down shoe,
And don't forget old Aunt Sue.
Balance to the next.
Swing the girl with the fuzzy head,
And don't forget the girl that is almost dead.
Balance to the next.
Swing the girl dressed in blue.
Don't forget your partner, you know what to do.
Third gent balance to the couple on the right.
Swing the girl that is half tight.
And swing your partner, before you have a fight.
Balance to the next.
Swing her high; swing her low;
Swing her away down on the Ohio;
And don't forget your partner, you know.
Grey lady dance as pretty as you can;
The fourth gent balance to the couple on the right.
Swing the girl dressed in yellow,
And watch your partner that she don't get another fellow.

Balance to the second couple.
Swing the girl that is big and fat.
And watch your partner, she might smack you flat.
Balance to the third couple.
Swing the girl dressed in red;
And don't forget your partner, or you might wish you were dead.
Join hands and circle to the left.
All jump up and never come down.
Eight hands up and here we go;
Way down the river on the Ohio;
Everybody dance as pretty as you can;
Why in the world don't you left hand a man?
Right hand your partner and right and left grand;
Come to your partner once and a half, and promenade back.
First couple balance to the couple on the right.
Pen the pig three rails high;
Pig jump out and the hog jump in,
Three hands around and circle again;
Hog jump out and four hands around;
Ladies docee and the gents, you know,
Swing by the right, and right and left go.

The songbag of folk whose traditional roots were in the eastern mountains does not vary much wherever it is found — not because each seedling community has taken the same selection from the parent stock, but because the entire treasury of song is well known to the commonality. The folk informant who cannot produce several hundred traditional songs in a few days of singing is not a good representative of her culture. I say "her" in this sentence because my thoughts run back to Aunt Molly Jackson, who like the people described in the following article, by Asher Treat, was a Kentuckian. She composed her first song at the age of four; she ran messages for her father's miners' union at five, she went to jail first at the age of ten (where she wrote a song called "Mister Cundiff, Won't You Turn Me Loose," so much appreciated by the townsfolk who visited her at the jail-house window that she came out "with $38 in money and 27 plugs of Cup Greenville" tobacco), and spent the whole of her long life using songs in her fight against the oppressors of her people, real and imagined. She knew hundreds of songs from the traditional songbag, and she composed scores of others for whatever purpose was at hand when she clubbed the Muse. She admired Robin Hood and filled out the gaps in his life with additional ballads where the ancient narratives were lacking. Once she began singing for me "The Gest of Robin Hood," which goes 456 stanzas. Unhappily, that was back in the days when one could not afford to expend so much recording tape on one song. She is gone now, and so is the song.

Aunt Molly knew all of the songs in Asher Treat's article. And it would take little searching in any western community even today to duplicate them. What the ladies of the Jacobs clan sang to Asher Treat is a cross-section of the repertoire brought by the westering settlers from the Old Country, in this continent or beyond. The contention may be established by considering the genealogy of these songs, so far as we can trace it. And thereby hangs an apology and an explanation: in the days of gold it was a common if dangerous question among the milling herd of prospectors, "What was your name in the States?" So it is with the songs Treat gathered; they had changed their names, and in comparing the following notes with those he appended, you will see that in a disturbing number of cases, the songs successfully concealed their identity.

"I WILL NOT MARRY A FARMER"

In the States the name of this fragmentary lyric comparing the several disadvantages of possible bridegrooms was "The Roving Gambler." Sandburg found it in one of those old intriguing songsters (like *Merchant's Gargling Oil Songster*) as "The Gamboling Man." But there is no question that originally this was a boast of a gambler, not a railroader at all; the young lady is described thus:

> *She took me in her parlor, she cooled me with her fan,*
> *She whispered low in her mother's ear, "I love this*
>   *gambling man."*

Moreover, he was an Englishman, more's the pity, before his ruffled shirt was roughened.

"WELL MET, WELL MET, MY OLD TRUE LOVE"

One of the great ballads, this is best known in America as "The House Carpenter." Known to folklorists as "James Harris" or "The Daemon Lover," it is Number 243 in the Child Collection. It appears first in the collection of Samuel Pepys, where it is dated 1685. It got into print in Scott's *Minstrelsy* in 1812. This magnificent song's peregrinations defy any summary, its artistry defies any analysis. It must be heard as a great experience in folk music.

"MY OLD HEN'S A GOOD OLD HEN"

Treat says in the note to the first song in this selection that he doubts that this is of mountain origin. He is correct; it is sung in England as a genuine, living nursery rhyme — not one of the defunct Mother Goose fossils prised into the minds of helpless children. There they sing,

> *Oh, I have a good old hen;*
> *She lays eggs for gentlemen.*

But the Jacobs ladies came by the song honestly. Frank Proffitt, who brought "Tom Dooley" to the outside world from the North Carolina mountains about the time the Kingston Trio was teething, says "Cluck Old Hen" (as he calls it) was known to every banjo-picker in the mountains. Its melody demands a banjo imitation of a clucking hen.

"LAST SATURDAY NIGHT I ENTERED A HOUSE"

Genealogy untraceable and best untraced, since its origin is an elusive broadside — elusive because it has undergone so many transformations that any original found is simply the earliest found. Every situation of protest has used this as a parodial vehicle. Aunt Molly Jackson made her own — "Hard Times in Colman's Mines." And a protest song against Mayor LaGuardia was called "Hard Times in the Subway." Both the latter songs were derivative of a variant line, whose best known representative is "Hard Times in Cryderville Jail." Watch for this to turn up as a marching song of the Mormon Battalion.

"NO, BROTHER, I'LL NEVER BE BETTER "

Speaking of the Mormons, Rosalie Sorrels found this ballad, correctly titled "Christine Leroy," to be ambivalently popular among old Mormon ladies, to whom it was a tragic tale of polygyny. Though it derives from the *post bellum* sentimental era, there is no question about its status as a folksong, in spite of Treat's disclaimer.

THE SINGING KENTUCKS MOVE WEST*

It is not a long time since the loggers left northern Wisconsin, but it will be a long time before they come again. Drive eastward or northward from the town of Antigo and you may see why. Stump-studded, brush-choked acres line the road for miles on either side. They stretch far back among the rough little hills until interrupted perhaps by a clear creek, a peat bog, a spring-fed lake, an abandoned railroad, or a paved highway to the resort region farther north.

There is some second growth hardwood, much poplar and birch, which helps to preserve the water level and serves as shelter for small game, occasional wolves, foxes, deer, and bear. Where the land has been partially cleared, you may see a plentiful scattering of glacier-borne rocks; but the soil, even when freed of stumps and stones, is not very fertile. The natural obstacles to cultivation – the shortness of the growing season, and the severity of the winters – combine to discourage any but the most stubborn attempts at farming.

The lumber companies, however, with these worthless and tax-encumbered wastes on their hands, told quite a different story to their prospective buyers. Many poor immigrants parted with a lifetime's savings, only to find themselves stranded in a godforsaken wilderness where they faced the choice of starving to death or making the land support them.

*From Asher E. Treat, "Kentucky Folksong in Northern Wisconsin."
JAF Volume 52, 1939, 1-51.

Some of the victims were Polish and Bohemian peasants; some were native Americans in more or less distant parts of the country. Ten or twelve years before the turn of the century a stream of migrants began to flow northward from eastern Kentucky. Most of them came from Powell, Wolf, and Breathitt counties, some from Elliott and Carter, and a few from Rowan and Greenup. By 1903 or 1904 there were well-established colonies of these people in the Wisconsin backwoods, and the flow of newcomers had just about ceased. A virtual island of mountain culture had been formed, with a population in Forest and Langlade counties of perhaps two hundred families.

"Kentucks," they were called. Some, perhaps most, were like my friends the Jacobses: honest, diligent, of high native intelligence, and with the most engaging qualities of hospitality, gentleness, good humor, and inborn dignity. Others were shiftless, quarrelsome, lawless, and highly resistant to any modifying influences. The term "Kentuck" is not always a complimentary one as it is heard in the mouths of the Wisconsin farmers and villagers of other than Kentucky ancestry.

Perhaps their tenacity to their southern way of living contributed to the cultural isolation of these people. They had known backwoods life before. They knew how to hunt, fish, cut timber, and scratch the cheap land enough to raise a little corn, a few hills of beans, and maybe some potatoes. But a certain uneasiness and distrust toward them was often manifested by their northern neighbors. Their names, their speech, their manners, their cookery — many things made them seem different from the others; and even now, when many are of the second or third generation of the Wisconsin born, some of those differences persist.

My own early impressions of the Kentucks, which I got as a small boy in the town of Antigo, were mostly from rumors and frequent newspaper stories of shooting or stabbing brawls in the village of Elton, generally involving moonshine liquor in one way or another. Those were Prohibition times, and the newspapers found plenty of copy in the periodic raids on "the Kentucky moonshiners." About their participation in the social life of the areas and settlements in which they lived I have little information. I believe that such participation was limited. Whatever had been their habits in Kentucky, most of the migrants were not regular churchgoers in their new environment. Their children went to the local schools, but attendance was often irregular or infrequent.

Assimilation into the general population of the area is already extensive, of course. Intermarriages are common. Intercommunication and access to the larger towns are no longer matters of difficulty. Even the poorer families could not easily dispense with their cars and radios. The neighborliness of the other inhabitants is increasing. There is a county zoning ordinance restricting the future use of the less arable land to forest and recreational purposes. All these things tend to bring the Kentucks out of the "bresh" and into the farm areas and cities. But while the cultural unit is noticeably less compact than it was even a few years ago, there are some localities where things remain pretty much in the same condition as that which characterized the days of the early migration—where the speech, manners, and mode of life are largely transplants from the southern mountains. These remnants are unlikely to survive the older generation by more than a very few years.

The singers of the songs recorded in this collection are all members of one family whose original home was near the town of Grayson, in Carter County, Kentucky. It was there that Madison Green Jacobs married Ollie Jacobs, thus uniting two of the three apparently unrelated Jacobs families who lived in that neighborhood. It was in Carter County, also, that seven of the twelve children were born. In 1906 the family moved to a small farm near the village of Bryant, Wisconsin, about nine miles northeast of Antigo. When most of the children had grown up and moved elsewhere, Mr. and Mrs. Jacobs took another place, also near Bryant, and lived there until Mr. Jacobs died, a few years ago. Mrs. Jacobs is now seventy-six years old. She spends most of her time with her children, five of whom live on farms or in villages within an hour's drive of Bryant, four having children of their own.

Mrs. Jacobs is regarded by all her children, and indeed by everyone who knows her, with the greatest respect and affection. Her difficult life and the fortitude with which she has lived it are to be read in every line and contour of her handsome face. She is painfully crippled with arthritis, so that a movement of any kind is often a veritable ordeal for her. Nevertheless, she insists upon taking active and effective part in the housework and is never known to utter a complaint or to be otherwise than cheerful and lovable.

Pearl Jacobs, now Mrs. Rodney Borusky, is a daughter of Mrs. M. G. Jacobs and the mother of two children. She is tall, thin, and dark, with a high forehead, high cheekbones, large, expressive eyes, and a thin, sensitive mouth. She possesses the same gentle and cheerful dignity which appear in the other members of the family and are reflected in her two children. During the past few years she has learned the importance of collecting and preserving the songs which form so intimate a part of her and her people's experience. She has become accustomed to singing the songs phrase by phrase, so as to make the notation of them easy; and she has gone to much trouble to refresh her own extensive memory by conferring with her relatives and writing down the words to many of the songs in advance of my infrequent collecting trips.

Maud Jacobs, a sister of Pearl, received high school training while still living in Kentucky, and has since then lived for several years in fairly large cities, where she has naturally acquired somewhat more of the urban outlook than have the others. Nevertheless, her memory of the songs is very vivid, so that she has been able to supply words to many verses which her relatives had forgotten. Several of the songs might have escaped notation entirely except for her diligent and continual searching of her memory for them. I am also indebted to her for much of the factual material given above. Although she has sung many of the songs for me, almost all were taken from the singing of Mrs. Jacobs or Pearl.

Others of the brothers and sisters have aided the work by expanding or correcting the material given me by the principal singers. These others are probably no less musical than are Mrs. Jacobs and Pearl, but for one reason or another they have been less accessible to me.

My acquaintance with the Jacobs family goes back to the year 1921, when I entered high school in Antigo as a classmate of Mrs. Jacobs's youngest son, Paul. He and I became friends; but it was not until after his death in 1925 that I came to know the rest of the family. Since that year I have visited them almost every summer and have learned to have the deepest regard for all of them. The songs have been taken a few at a time since I first heard some of them sung in 1932.

While it might be anticipated that the transplanted musical culture of the Kentucky immigrants would have undergone modification in the new surroundings and would show the influence of the neighboring groups, it is my impression that this has not happened. I have done a small amount of collecting among other people of the same locality and have found little that I could interpret as evidence of such influence. On the contrary, comparison of certain of these tunes with those collected by Cecil Sharp and others has led me to suspect that in the Wisconsin songs we have material which has been protected from contamination, perhaps to an extent even greater than has the culture of the present day mountain folk themselves. Until the introduction of the radio, there was little opportunity for the Wisconsin Kentuckians to hear singing by others, and it appears unlikely that other versions of the same songs would have been sung by any of the people with whom the migrants came into contact. Mrs. Jacobs and her older children learned the songs while they were still living in Kentucky and have sung them continuously among themselves ever since.

The singers themselves believe that the songs have undergone no modification. They can distinguish carefully and accurately between their own versions of tunes and texts and those which they have sometimes heard on the radio. For example, they sang the ballad of "Barbara Allen" for me on two separate visits, at one time specifying that they were then singing it "the way Bradley (Kinkaid) does," and at another time, "the way we heard it in Kentucky." Radio performances have occasionally reminded them of songs which they had temporarily forgotten; but they are not indebted to the radio for any of the tunes or words given here. Almost all of these they regard as of Carter County ancestry. It may be worth noting here that none of Cecil Sharp's collecting was done in Carter County.

The tunes of all of the songs have been transmitted to and among the Jacobses purely by vocal tradition. No member of the family has any knowledge of musical notation. They would have been unable to read the melodies even if they had seen them printed. Mrs. Jacobs, however, reports that her mother possessed a scrapbook containing clippings from country papers in which she found the words of certain verses which she had not previously known, or had forgotten. The custom of keeping such scrapbooks was apparently a rather general one. The texts of the ballads would be requested by a reader in one issue of the farm journal and supplied in a later issue by another reader who happened to remember them. The particular book to which Mrs. Jacobs refers was destroyed by fire many years ago.

So far as I know, the songs were not communicated to the children by any deliberate process of teaching. When asked where a tune has been learned, Pearl usually responds, "O, I heard mother sing it." Singing was, and still is, among these people an almost inevitable, though often subconscious, accompaniment of housework. On occasions such as funerals, prayer meetings, or parties it might take on a more deliberate or formal nature; but as is probably the case with musical people generally, scarcely a moment passes during which some tune is not either in the head or on the lips. It was not necessary for the children to "commit" the songs to memory; they learned them without effort, simply by hearing them often. A good thing to see is that Pearl's two children, Claire and James, know a number of the songs and are learning more.

The notation has been done under a variety of circumstances. Some was made at the second Jacobs farm near Bryant. The farmhouse there was of logs covered with tar paper. There was a single large room, with a loft above which served as a bedroom for those of the family who still lived at home, and with a small alcove at one end where Mrs. Jacobs slept. The large room was the kitchen, dining room, and general family headquarters. A big wood range stood in one corner, supplied with cordwood from a box beneath the south window. Over and around the stove hung long strings of "leatherbreeches"—that is, dried string beans. The furniture included a large folding table, a few chairs, and a long bench.

I would sit on a chair between the woodbox and the stove, as far out of the way of cooking operations as good hearing would permit. Five or six people might be busy about the room, mixing biscuits, making gravy, or frying chicken. There was plenty of conversation, and the work of taking dictation was not always easy; but it seemed better not to wait for more favorable circumstances. When a song had been sung once or twice, or through a few verses, I would ask to hear it a little at a time. Mrs. Jacobs soon learned about how much I could conveniently get before it was necessary to interrupt, and from then on she would sing a phrase, or a few notes at a time. While I was busy writing down what I had just heard, she would continue her work and conversation until I asked for more. Then with surprising lack of hesitancy, she would resume singing where she had left off.

I WILL NOT MARRY A FARMER

Sung by Maud Jacobs and Pearl Jacobs Borusky, September 6, 1938. Cf. Sharp, "Soldier Boy For Me" (A). Professor Leland Coon of the University of Wisconsin has suggested that "My Old Hen's a Good Old Hen," may not be of mountain origin, since "section men" were probably not people familiar to the mountain folk. In this connection it is interesting that this song of railroaders was unknown to Mrs. Jacobs.

> I will not marry a farmer.
> He's always working in the dirt.
> But I will marry a railroader
> That wears—a striped shirt.
> A railroader, a railroader, a railroader for me!
> If ever I marry in this wide world,
> A railroader's wife I'll be—

There are other verses about the disadvantages of gamblers and others.

LAST SATURDAY NIGHT I ENTERED A HOUSE

Sung by Mrs. M. G. Jacobs, September, 1933. Mrs. Jacobs learned this song from Walter Justice in Kentucky.

> Last Saturday night I entered a house
> And thru the darkway I crept like a mouse.
> I opened the door and went straightway
> Into a room where the girls—all stay.
> And it's hard times!

Such laughing and chatting as we did keep!
We waked the old widder up out of her sleep,
And in a few words she did address me,
"Such an impudent fellow before me I see!"
And it's hard times!

"O, widder, O, widder, you'd better keep cam [=calm]
Until you find out who I am.
I'm Johnny the Carpenter I go by that name.
A-courting your daughter, for that purpose I came."
And it's hard times!

"O, daughter, O, daughter, O, daughter," said she.
"To think that my daughter would go before me
When I am so old and you are so young.
You can get sweethearts and I can get none."
And it's hard times!

"O, widder, O, widder, O, widder at large,
If you are an old widder you are a great charge.
O, widder, O, widder, O, widder by name."
She up with a broomstick and at me she came.
And it's hard times!

Such fighting and scratching! At last I got clear,
I mounted my horse and for home I did steer,
The blood running down, my head being sore.
There stood the old $\left\{ \begin{array}{l} \text{devil} \\ \text{widder} \end{array} \right\}$ with a broom in the door.
And it's hard times!

Come all young men, take warning by me,
And never a widder's daughter go see.
For if you do, t'will be your doom.
They'll fight you like Satan and beat you with a broom.
And it's hard times!

NO, BROTHER, I'LL NEVER BE BETTER

Sung by Pearl Jacobs Borusky, September, 1932. The folk origin of
this song seems highly questionable to me.

> No, brother, I'll never be better,
> 'Tis useless in telling me so;
> For my poor broken heart's just awaiting
> A resting place under the snow.

I only was dreaming, dear brother,
Of our bright happy home filled with joy,
When a serpent crept into our Eden
In the fair form of Christine Le Roy.

I was dreaming again of our bridal
One year ago only tonight,
As I stood with the gas lights above me
Robed in jewels and garments of white.
She came with the smile of an angel,
And wished us a lifetime of joy,
That beautiful, radiant creature
'Twas beautiful Christine Le Roy.

The jewels shone bright in her tresses,
Parted back o'er her white marble brow,
And they gleamed like the stars in the gas light
On her fingers as white as the snow.
When she gave her hand to my husband,
Tho' I knew he was only a boy,
I trembled with fear at the glances
From the bright eyes of Christine Le Roy.

Now brother be kind to your sister,
Whose poor heart grows weary and faint
From the ways and the wiles of a demon
With the beautiful face of a saint.

When I sleep 'neath the snowdrifts of winter,
Where no sorrow or sin can destroy
O, tell them they murdered me, brother,
My husband and Christine Le Roy.

WELL MET, WELL MET, MY OLD TRUE LOVE

Sung by Mrs. M. G. Jacobs, September, 1933, and again, September 6, 1938. Cf. Sharp, "The Daemon Lover." Mrs. Jacobs learned this song from her mother.

"Well met, well met, my old true love.
Well met, well met," said he.
"I have just returned from the salt, salt sea;
And 'twas all for the sake of thee."

"I once could have married a king's daughter fair,
And she would have married me.
But I refused that rich crown of gold,
And it's all for the sake of thee."

"If you could have married a king's daughter fair
I'm sure you're much to blame,
For I am married to a house carpenter,
And I think he's a fine young man."

"If you'll forsake your house carpenter
And go along with me,
I will take you where the grass grows green,
⎧On the banks of the Sweet Willee ⎫ „
⎩On the banks of the Sweet Liberty ⎭.

"If I forsake my house carpenter
And go along with thee,
What have you got for my support,
And to keep me from slavery?"

"I have six ships sailing on the sea,
The seventh one at land,
And if you'll come and go with me
They shall be at your command."

She took her babe into her arms
And gave it kisses three,
Saying, "Stay at home, my pretty little babe,
For to keep your father company."

She dressed herself in rich array
To exceed all others in the town,
And as she walked the streets around
She shone like a glittering crown.

They had not been on board more than two weeks,
I'm sure it was not three,
Until she began to weep
And she wept most bitterly.

"Are you weeping for your houses and your land,
Or are you weeping for your store,
Or are you weeping for your house carpenter
You never shall see any more?"

"I'm not weeping for my houses nor my land,
Nor I'm not weeping for my store,
But I'm weeping for my pretty little babe
I never shall see any more."

They had not been on board more than three weeks,
It was not four I'm sure,
Until at length the ship sprung a leak,
And she sank to arise no more.

"A curse, a curse to all sea men!
A curse to a sailor's life!
For they have robbed me of my house carpenter
And taken away my life."

MY OLD HEN'S A GOOD OLD HEN

Sung by Pearl Jacobs Borusky, July 13, 1938. This was another of
Madison Green Jacobs's songs.

My old hen's a good old hen. She lays eggs for the section men.
Sometimes one, sometimes two, sometimes enough for the
    whole damn crew.
Cluck, old hen! Cluck, I tell you! Cluck, old hen, or I'm agoin'
    to sell you.
Cluck, old hen! Cluck, I say! Cluck, old hen, or I'll give you
    away.

A folk society is one that has been isolated from the generality
of its surrounding culture. The isolating factors are innumerable,
but when a group separates itself by choice, the motivation is

most commonly religious. And that makes the inevitable cultural lag doubly great, for religion itself is a strong force for conservatism.

This is to say that the Mormons are backward, and that is to say far too much for one's health and welfare in the West. I will leave the rest of the saying to Levette J. Davidson, once a dear friend of mine, who has gone to a place beyond the power of even the immortal Saints of these Latter Days to injure him.

MORMON SONGS*

Social groups have, most frequently, developed a characteristic folk-lore when they have been united by common interests and by some sort of isolation. From the beginnings of Mormonism over a century ago, Latter-Day Saints have regarded themselves as a chosen people, set apart by their religion from the "Gentiles," a classification which included all non-Mormons. The migration of the Saints to the Salt Lake Valley in 1847 and the years following, resulted in a geographical isolation which permitted cultural inbreeding and encouraged communal life. Only in recent times have communicants of other beliefs ceased to regard Mormons as queer and even malevolent. But the contemporary decay of doctrinal emphasis among Mormons and non-Mormons, the frequent population movements since World War I, which have mixed believers and nonbelievers of all sorts—even in Salt Lake City—and the universal pressure toward standardization have removed some of the conditions which permitted Mormon culture to flower in its own peculiar way. Surviving from earlier times are, however, some traditions which repay examination.

The history of Mormonism from the days of the prophet Joseph Smith down to the "manifesto" abolishing polygamy in 1890, and even later, can be traced in song. Mormons called themselves "Latter-Day Saints"; the following examples indicate that "Singing Saints" would be equally appropriate. Aside from the hymns of the Church, however, there seems now to be little knowledge of the songs that were popular in the early days. Wallace Stegner, for example, observed in his otherwise informative *Mormon Country,* "The Mormons are a singing people and always have been, but their creative energy seems to have spent itself on hymns, which are often folksy enough."

The volume devoted to Utah in the "American Guide Series" is a bit more aware of the variety of songs, but gives no examples beyond

*By Levette J. Davidson. JAF Volume 58, 1945, 273-300.

hymns and one verse and chorus from "The Handcart Song." The compilers wrote:

> With the Mormons, in the days of the settlement of Utah, when pioneers sang to keep their courage up, music played a more important part in community cultural life than any other art. It was a humble music, inclined to hymns, ballads, sentimental songs, reels, and, where instruments were available, to martial airs; but it was a folk music gathered, as were the rank and file of the Church, from every State in the Union and from half the countries in Europe. The Mormons played or sang with very little restraint; indeed, their authorities encouraged them to do so and the Church sponsored secular singing and dancing. . . . Moreover, purely secular songs written to commemorate important events were scarcely distinguished from the contents of their hymn book. There were songs (sometimes serious, frequently satiric, and occasionally almost ribald) to celebrate a convert from Sweden or the planting of mulberry trees in the southern colonies, to "josh" sheep skinners or to lampoon turncoats who deserted the army to marry Mormon girls.

The following pages will serve at least to amplify and to illustrate these statements from the Utah Guide.

MORMON HYMNS

The history of Mormon hymnology has been written by George D. Pyper in *Stories of Latter-Day Saints Hymns, Their Authors and Composers*. "Sister" Emma Smith, wife of the Prophet Joseph Smith, made the first collection in 1835, enlarging it in 1841. Most of the hymns were those already in use in Protestant churches; but several were soon written which "expounded the truths of the newly revealed Gospel." The revised hymnbook issued by Brigham Young, Parley P. Pratt and John Taylor, in Manchester, England, in 1840, went through twenty-five editions. Often Mormon words were set to old music, and even "war and sentimental tunes were commandeered to fit inspirational hymns."

An early commentator on the Mormon settlement in Utah, the anonymous author of a History of the Mormons, says that the hymn beginning, "Yes, my Native land, I love thee," was "sometimes sung on shipboard in Liverpool prior to the departure of Mormon emigrants." According to this writer, "Many of their fugitive hymns and songs, not included in their hymn books, are adapted to popular tunes sung as 'The Sea, the Sea, the Open Sea,' 'Away, Away to the Mountain's Brow.' . . ."

The following hymn was, he noted, sung "to the tune of 'The Rose That All Are Praising.'"

A CHURCH WITHOUT APOSTLES IS NOT THE CHURCH FOR ME

A church without a prophet is not the church for me;
It has no head to lead it, in it I would not be;
But I've a church not built by man,
Out from the mountain without hand,
A church with gifts and blessings, oh, that's the church for me,
Oh, that's the church for me, oh, that's the church for me.

The God that others worship is not the God for me;
He has no parts nor body, and can not hear nor see;
But I've a God that lives above,
A God of Power and of Love,
A God of Revelation, oh, that's the God for me.

A church without apostles is not the church for me;
It's like a ship dismasted afloat upon the sea;
But I've a church that's always led
By the twelve stars around its head,
A church with good foundations, oh, that's the church for me.

The hope that Gentiles cherish is not the hope for me;
It has no hope for knowledge, far from it I would be;
But I've a hope that will not fail,
That reaches safe within the vail,
Which hope is like an anchor, oh, that's the hope for me.

Other hymns peculiar to Mormonism refer to the prophet Joseph Smith. Such is "We Thank Thee O God for a Prophet," written to the tune of "The Officer's Funeral," which William Fowler, the composer, had heard from his father, who had been sent by the English government to Australia and was present at the officer's funeral for which the melody of this song had been composed.... On the long journey across the plains, to strengthen the faith of his fellows and to prove his devotion to the cause, William composed the words. "Joseph Smith's First Prayer" is a song describing a miraculous vision that came to the prophet-to-be. Perhaps the best loved hymn is "Come, Come, Ye Saints," composed by William Clayton at the request of President Brigham Young, on April 15, 1846, for use of the pioneers on their difficult trek to the Salt Lake Valley. The tune was that of the old English song "All Is Well."

Probably the most prolific of hymn writers was Eliza R. Snow, often called the "Mormon Poetess." Her popular "O My Father" suggests the possibility of a pre-existence to earthly life and of a Mother God as well as a Father God in Heaven. Her compositions include "The World's Jubilee," "In Our Lovely Deseret," "Zion Prospers, All is Well," "Through Deepening Trails," "O Awake! My Slumbering Minstrel," and "Our Prophet, Brigham Young." Some of the peculiar doctrines of Mormonism, such as celestial marriages, baptism for the dead, the destruction of the Nephites, the revelations in the Book of Mormon, and polygamous marriages are used as themes in several of the songs included in the older editions of the hymnal. Two stanzas from one advocating many marriages follow:

> Through him who holds the sealing power
>   Ye faithful ones, who heed
> Celestial laws, take many wives,
>   And rear a righteous seed.

> Though fools revile, I'll honor you,
>   As Abraham, my friend;
> You shall be Gods, and shall be blest
>   With lives that never end.

The following stanza from Eliza R. Snow's "In Our Lovely Deseret" explains part of the Mormon discipline:

IN OUR LOVELY DESERET

> That the children may live long,
> And be beautiful and strong,
> Tea and coffee and tobacco they despise,
> Drink no liquor, and they eat
> But a very little meat;
> They are seeking to be great and good and wise.

Another song for children contains the following:

> I'll be a little Mormon
> And seek to know the ways,
> Which God has taught his people
> In these—the latter days,
> By sacred revelation
> Which He to us hath given,
> He tells us how to follow
> The sacred road to Heaven.
> Though I am young and little,
> I, too, may learn forthwith
> To live the precious gospel
> Revealed to Joseph Smith.

It is interesting to note that just before the mob attacked the jail in Carthage, Illinois, and assassinated Joseph Smith and his brother Hyrum on June 27, 1844, John Taylor sang at the request of the prophet, "A Poor Wayfaring Man of Grief." This was a favorite of Joseph Smith and popular in Nauvoo.

CAMPAIGN SONGS

Dissatisfied with the attitude toward the Mormons taken by the announced candidates for the presidency of the United States in 1844, Joseph Smith himself sought that office. His murder by the mob in Carthage ended Mormon hopes of political success.

Of the numerous campaign songs which sprang up, pro-Mormon and anti-Mormon, only a few fragments have survived, such as the following:

> Kinderhoos, Kass, Kalhoun, or Klay,
> Kan never surely win the day.
> But if you want to know who kan,
> You'll find in General Smith, the man.

and

> Come, then, O Americans, rally to the standard of Liberty,
> And in your generous indignation, trample down
> The tyrant's rod and the oppressor's crown
> That yon proud eagle to its height may soar
> And peace, triumphant, reign forever more.

SONGS OF THE MIGRATION

After the expulsion of the Mormons from Nauvoo in 1846, they moved to a temporary camp on the Missouri River on the outskirts of the present Omaha. Here in "winter quarters" they prepared for the great migration of 1847 to the Salt Lake Valley. In the years which followed additional companies made the twelve-hundred-mile journey to the Promised Land. Since many of the converts to the new faith were too poor to buy teams and wagons for the overland trek, Brigham Young recommended that they make the journey on foot after building handcarts upon which to draw their supplies. Five companies crossed in this way during 1856, and a total of ten before 1861, by which year the

Utah settlers were able to supply enough stock for wagons and other transportation. A number of handcart songs were made up and sung along the way, including the following.

A. THE HANDCART SONG

Ye Saints that dwell on Europe's shore
Prepare yourselves with many more
To leave behind your native land
For sure God's Judgments are at hand.
Prepare to cross the stormy main
Before you do the valley gain
And with the faithful make a start
To cross the plains with your handcart.

Chorus

Some must push and some must pull
As we go marching up the hill
As merrily on the way we go
Until we reach the valley, oh.

The land that boasts of liberty
You ne'er again may wish to see
While poor men toil to earn their bread
And rich men are much better fed,
And people boast of their great light,
You see they are as dark as night.
And from them you must make a start
To cross the plains with our handcarts.

But some will say it is too bad
The saints upon their feet to pad
And more than that to push a load
As they go marching up the road.
We say this is Jehovah's plan
To gather out the best of man,
And women too, for none but they
Will ever gather in this way.

As on the way the carts are hurled
'Twould very much surprise the world
To see the old and feeble dame
Lending her hand to push the same.
The young girls they will dance and sing
The young men happier than a king,

The children they will laugh and play
Their strength increasing day by day.

But ere before the valley gained
We will be met upon the plains
With music sweet and friends so dear
And fresh supplies our hearts to cheer.
Then with the music and the song
How cheerfully we'll march along
So thankfully you make a start
To cross the plains with our handcarts.

When we get there amongst the rest
Industrious be and we'll be blessed
And in our chambers be shut in
While Judgment cleanse the earth from sin.
For well we know it will be so,
God's servants spoke it long ago,
And tell us it's high time to start
To cross the plains with our handcarts.

B. HANDCART SONG

(Tune: "A Little More Cider")

Oh, our faith goes with the handcarts,
    And they have our hearts' best love;
'Tis a novel mode of travelling,
Devised by the God above.

Chorus

Hurrah for the Camp of Israel!
    Hurrah for the handcart scheme!
Hurrah! hurrah! 'tis better far
    Than the wagon and ox-team.

And *Brigham's their executive,*
    He told us the design;
And the Saints are proudly marching on,
    Along the handcart line.

Who cares to go with the wagons?
    Not we who are free and strong;
Our faith and arms, with right good will,
    Shall pull our carts along.

C. HANDCART SONG

Obedient to the Gospel call
We serve our God the all in all
We hie away to Zion
We do not wait to ride all day
But pull our handcarts all the way
And Israel's God rely on.

To Zion pull the handcart
While singing every day
The glorious songs of Zion
That haste the time away.

Our prayers arise to greet the sun
And when his shining course is run
We gather round the camp fire
To talk of God and all his ways
His wondrous work of Latterdays
Until the dancing blaze expires.

We climb the hills and far away
Then down where sleeping valleys lay
While still the miles onward roll
Till Zion rises on our sight
We pull our handcarts with our might
Triumphant then reach the goal.

And those we left beside the way
To dream where summer breezes play
Saw in the camp fire's vivid blaze
Fair Zion with her golden skies
Grand temples there that stately rise
And satisfied rest always.

The following song was composed by Eliza R. Snow in honor of President Brigham Young and his men, who had located the place for the Mormons to settle. According to tradition, Brigham Young and his "pioneer band" made the official entry into the Salt Lake Valley on July 24, 1847. This date is celebrated annually as Pioneer Day throughout Mormondom, with reunions, programs, and singing.

TO PRESIDENT B. YOUNG AND CAMP

Hail! ye mighty men of Israel
   Who the hiding place have found;
The eternal God has blest you
   You have stood on holy ground.

Chorus

Praise the Lord! we're glad to meet you;
   Welcome welcome, on your way —
Yes, O yes, with songs we greet you,
   Pioneers of Latter-day.

A choice land of old appointed
   For the House of Israel's rest,
You have found and consecrated —
   Through your blessing 'twill be blest.

Holy, free, and unpolluted
   Will that land for us remain
While the sacred laws of justice
   There the Saints of God maintain.

Go, return to Winter Quarters —
   Go in peace and safety too;
There the purest hearts are beating,
   Warm with hopes of seeing you.

We will onward to the Valley —
   Speed your way — make haste and come,
That ere long, with joy and gladness,
   We may bid you *welcome home.*

The following stanzas are selected from another of Eliza Snow's compositions encouraging the migration:

A JOURNEYING SONG FOR THE PIONEERS TO THE MOUNTAINS

The time of winter now is o'er —
   There's verdure on the plain;
We leave our shelt'ring roofs once more,
   And to our tents again.

Though Camp of Israel, onward move;
   O Jacob, rise and sing;

Ye Saints, the world's salvation prove —
　All hail to Zion's king.

We go to choice and goodly lands,
　With rich and fertile soil,
That by the labor of our hands
　Will yield us wine and oil.

We leave the mobbing Gentile race,
　Who thirst to shed our blood;
To rest in Jacob's hiding place,
　Where Nephite temples stood.

Another of the songs which cheered the Saints on their westward journey is the following. To the Mormons, "Upper California" was a term denoting the area west of the Rockies.

The Upper California, Oh, that's the land for me;
It lies between the mountains and the great Pacific sea;
　The Saints can be supported there,
　And taste the sweets of liberty
In Upper California — Oh, that's the land for me!
　Oh, that's the land for me.

We'll go and lift our standard, we'll go there and be free!
　We'll go to California and have our Jubilee;
　A land that blooms with beauty rare,
　A land of life and liberty,
With flocks and herds abounding — Oh, that's the land for me!
　Oh, that's the land for me.

We'll burst off all our fetters and break the Gentile yoke,
For long it has beset us, and now it shall be broke;
　No more shall Jacob bow his neck,
　Henceforth he shall be great and free
In Upper California — Oh, that's the land for me!
　Oh, that's the land for me.

We'll reign, we'll rule and triumph, and God shall be our King;
The plains, the hills, and valleys shall with hosannas ring;
　Our towers and temples there shall rise,
　Toward the great Pacific sea,
In Upper California — Oh, that's the land for me!
　Oh, that's the land for me!

We'll ask our cousin Lemuel to join us heart and hand,
And spread abroad our curtains throughout fair Zion's land;
   Till this is done, we'll pitch our tents
   Toward the great Pacific sea,
In Upper California—Oh, that's the land for me!
   Oh, that's the land for me!

Then join with me, my brethren, and let us hasten there;
We'll lift our glorious standard and raise our house of prayer;
   We'll call on all the nations round
   To join our standard and be free
In Upper California—Oh, that's the place for me!
   Oh, that's the place for me.

Still another of the overland journey songs is a rousing diatribe against Mormon persecutions, set to the tune of "Old Dan Tucker."

According to the note accompanying "The Dying Californian," in *Pioneer Songs,* this was an adaptation of "The Dying Sailor" and was composed in honor of one member of the Mormon party of immigrants who had sailed from New York under Samuel Brannan on the ship *Brooklyn.* This young man had died before the ship reached San Francisco Bay, on July 31, 1846.

SONGS OF THE MORMON BATTALION

When the Mexican War broke out in 1846, President Polk accepted the offer of the Mormons to contribute troops. Some five hundred of the Saints, encamped at Council Bluffs, were enlisted in July. After accompanying General Kearney to Santa Fe and then to California, they were mustered out. A number of them stayed in California; some went to Salt Lake, which had become in 1847 the Mormon Promised Land.

In the midst of their hardships the members of the Mormon Battalion were cheered by song. According to Sergeant Daniel Tyler, ". . . our cheerful camp singer, Levi W. Hancock, oftentimes amused and entertained us while around the campfires and often composed songs to fit the occasion as the following will show.

The two examples which Tyler prints would in a preliterate age have been handed down orally, perhaps becoming a part of the anonymous folklore of the Mormons. At any rate they illustrate the circumstances under which popular verse sometimes was composed. To conserve space only a few stanzas of each are given.

THE DESERT ROUTE

While here, beneath a sultry sky,
Our famished mules and cattle die;
Scarce aught but skin and bones remain
To feed poor soldiers on the plain.

Chorus

How hard to starve and wear us out,
Upon this sandy, desert route.

We sometimes now for lack of bread,
Are less than quarter rations fed,
And soon expect, for all of meat,
Naught less than broke-down mules, to eat.

Our hardships reach their rough extremes,
When valiant men are roped with teams,
Hour after hour, and day by day,
To wear our strength and lives away.

A Doctor which the Government
Has furnished, proves a punishment!
At his rude call of "Jim Along Joe,"
The sick and halt, to him must go.

Both night and morn, this call is heard;
Our indignation then is stirr'd,
And we sincerely wish in hell,
His arsenic and calomel.

THE BULL FIGHT ON THE SAN PEDRO

Under command of Colonel Cooke,
When passing down San Pedro's brook,
Where cane-grass, growing rank and high,
Was waving as the breeze pass'd by,

There, as we gained ascending ground
Out from the grass, with fearful bound,
A wild ferocious bull appear'd,
And challenged fight, with horns uprear'd.

"Stop, stop," said one, "just see that brute!"
"Hold!" was responded, "let me shoot."
He flashed but failed to fire the gun—
Both stood their ground but would not run.

The man exclaimed, "I want some meat,
I think that bull will do to eat";
And saying thus, again he shot
And fell'd the creature on the spot.

But lo! it did not end the fight—
A furious herd rushed into sight,
And then the bulls and men around,
Seemed all resolved to stand their ground.

In nature's pasture, all unfenc'd,
A dreadful battle was commenc'd;
We knew we must ourselves defend,
And each, to others, aid extend.

Whatever cause we did not know,
But something prompted them to go;
When all at once in frantic fright,
The bulls ran bellowing out of sight.

And when the fearful fight was o'er,
And sound of muskets heard no more,
At least a score of bulls were found,
And two mules dead upon the ground.

Numerous other songs were composed in honor of the faithful services of the Mormon Battalion, notably those by Thomas Morris and Eliza R. Snow, also printed by Tyler. Those by the men who served in the battalion are closer to folk expression. Such is the song by Azariah Smith, "composed when quartered at San Diego, in the service of the United States," to the tune of "Hard Times." The first three and the fifth of the thirteen stanzas follow.

SONG

In forty-six we bade adieu
To loving friends and kindred too;
For one year's service, one and all
Enlisted at our country's call,
    In these hard times.

We onward marched until we gained
Fort Leavenworth, where we obtained
Our outfit—each a musket drew—
Canteen, knapsack, and money, too,
    In these hard times.

Our Colonel died — Smith took his place,
And marched us on at rapid pace;
O'er hills and plains, we had to go,
Through herds of deer and buffalo,
   In these hard times.

At length we came to Santa Fe,
As much fatigued as men could be;
With only ten days there to stay,
When orders came to march away,
   In these hard times.

ANTI-FEDERALIST SONGS

When the state of Deseret was admitted as the Territory of Utah in 1850, difficulties developed. President Fillmore appointed Brigham Young as governor, but included three non-Mormons among the territorial officials. Conflict between the Mormons and federal forces broke out when Brigham Young was replaced by Governor Cumming. A military force of twenty-five hundred troops under General W. S. Harney, later replaced by Colonel Albert S. Johnston, came out in 1857 to support the non-Mormon governor. The Mormons began drilling an army of their own and sent out detachments to destroy army supply trains. Actual bloodshed was avoided through the intervention of Colonel T. L. Kane as mediator. Through agreement with Young, the troops entered Salt Lake City in the summer of 1858 without opposition.

The following songs were an outgrowth of this Mormon War. The first "Mormon Army Song," given below, seems to have been set to the tune of "Yankee Doodle." Mrs. Grace A. Woodbury, of Salt Lake City, wrote to me as follows: "Sister" Freliegh, who has been dead about thirty years and who lived to be ninety plus, used to sing it at the Pine Valley celebration of July 24; I can still recall her shrill, quavering rendition of it."

MORMON ARMY SONG

When Uncle Sam he did send out his army to destroy us,
He thought the Mormons we will rout, so they cannot annoy us.
The force he sent was competent, to "try and hang" for treason,
That is, I ween, it would have been, but there was a good reason.

Chorus

There's great commotion in the East about the Mormon question
The problem is, to say the least, too tough for their digestion.

As they went marching up the "Platte," they sang a catchy ditty,
And boasted we'll do this and that, when we reach Salt Lake City.
And right they were when they got there, they made the Mormons
    stir, Sir,
That is, I swan, they would have done, but, say, they didn't get
    there.

Then they returned with wildest tales, said: "Mormons beat the
    devil,
They ride up hill and over rocks as fast as on the level.
And if you chance to shoot one down, and you are sure he's
    dead, Sir,
The first you know he's on his horse, and riding on ahead, Sir."

Then on Ham's Fork they camped awhile, saying we will wait
    longer,
'Till Johnston and his troops come up, and make our forces
    stronger.
Then we'll advance, take Brigham Young and Heber, his
    companion,
That is, they would have done, but were afraid of Echo Canyon.

The next is a parody on Stephen Foster's "Camptown Races."

There's seven hundred wagons on the way,
    Du dah!
And their cattle are numerous, so they say,
    Du dah; du dah day!
Now, to let them perish would be sin,
    Du dah!
So we'll take all they got for bringing them in,
    Du dah; du dah day!

Chorus

Then let us be on hand
By Brigham Young to stand;
And if our enemies do appear
We'll sweep them off the land.

Old Sam has sent, I understand,
    Du dah!
A Missouri ass to rule our land,
    Du dah; du dah day!
But if he comes we'll have some fun,
    Du dah!
To see him and his juries run,
    Du dah; du dah day!

Old Squaw-Killer Harney is on his way,
    Du dah!
The Mormon People for to slay
    Du dah; du dah day!
Now, if he comes, the truth I'll tell,
    Du dah!
Our boys will drive him down to hell,
    Du dah; du dah day!

The entry of non-Mormons, or "Gentiles," into the Salt Lake Valley during the Civil War period caused additional friction. Federal troops under Colonel Patrick E. Connor set up headquarters at Camp Douglas, on the eastern outskirts of Salt Lake City. His commission was to protect the Overland Trail, but he also encouraged non-Mormons to enter the valley and to search for mineral wealth. He even permitted his soldiers to prospect; and, after his release from the army, in 1866, he became an outstanding mining man in the region. The completion of the transcontinental railroad in 1869 brought additional Gentiles to compete with the Mormons.

The English traveler Ludlow was in Salt Lake City at the time Colonel Connor's regiment was camped just outside the city. He described one service which he attended in the Tabernacle at which numerous hymns were sung "by the whole congregation with abundant fervor under the leadership of a small choir near the stage accompanied by a melodeon and a violin." He reported that some of Connor's bluecoats were present and nearly broke up the meeting by singing the original words instead of the Mormon hymn which had been set to the tune of "The Star-Spangled Banner."

"Young men!" said a venerable biship, sternly, from the rostrum, "you forget that you are in the house of the Lord."

"Not a bit of it, old horse," one of the boys spoke right out in meetin'. "What in thunder dije want to sing such all-fired nice tunes for, if you want a feller to sit still and bust himself?"

When President Brigham Young was put under arrest in January, 1872, accused of murder, many anti-Mormons thought that he had run away. According to Edward W. Tullidge, "A doggerel song was sung about this with much anti-Mormon applause, running thus:

> Where now's the Prophet Brigham?
> Where now's the Prophet Brigham?
>   Down in Kanab.
> By and by we'll go and fetch him
>   Down in Kanab."

Contrary to the expectation of the United States prosecuting attorney, Brigham Young returned to the city voluntarily and applied for bail.

Still other songs celebrating the conflicts between Mormons and non-Mormons exist, but enough has been given to indicate the popular nature and the small literary value of these effusions.

GENTILE SONGS RIDICULING THE MORMONS

Probably the best known and most opposed of all the Mormon doctrines was the one advocating polygamy. Although not publicly announced until 1852, this practice was reputed to have been sanctioned by Joseph Smith before his death. After many anti-polygamy crusades had been organized by Gentile women in Salt Lake and throughout the nation, Congress outlawed it in 1882. Federal marshals and courts vigorously prosecuted offenders, but it was not until 1890 that the president of the Mormon Church issued a "manifesto" directing all Mormons to "refrain from contracting any marriages forbidden by the law of the land."

Many satirical and ribald verses were made up and sung concerning this "peculiar practice." The following verse, for example, was added to the popular song, "The Man That Knows It All."

> There's shiploads of Mormonites coming o'er,
>   Coming o'er, bound for Utah;
> Oh, each has five wives and they shout for more;
>   What d'ye think of it now?
> Oh, that's an old wrinkle in Solomon's time;
> Not in mine; I'm much inclined
> To take but one trick boys, not five of a kind;
> I'm the man that knows it all.

Somewhat similar is "The Mormon Coon," which sounds as if it had been used by Negro minstrels.

THE MORMON COON

Young Abraham left home one day
Nobody knew just why he went away
Until a friend of his received a note
It was from Abe and this is what he wrote:

I'm out in Utah in the Mormon land
I'm not coming home, 'cause I'm a living grand
I used to rave about a single life
Now every day I get a brand new wife.

I got a big brunette
I got a blonde petite
I got 'em short, fat, thin, and tall
I got a Zulu pal
I got a Cuban gal
They come in bunches when I call

Now — that ain't all
I got a homely few
I got 'em pretty too
I got 'em black as the octoroon
I can cut a figure eight
I must ship them by freight
For I am a Mormon Coon.

There's one girl that ain't married yet, they say
I'm saving her up for a rainy day
If for every girl I had a single cent
Then the picture gallery I could rent.
I got me many of a homely lot
I keep the marriage license door bell hot
If a wife upon the street I chance to run
I have to ask her, "What's your number, Hon?"

The two following selections were included by Vardis Fisher in his somewhat unsympathetic picture of the Mormons' *Children of God.*

In the Mormon beds out West,
There the concubines do rest,
While their husband visits Emily and Jane!
Oh, the babies do abound

In tens of thousands all around,
While the husband now slips in to see Elaine!

and

Oh-ho, there goes pa
Back to Washington,
But he won't take ma!
Oh-ho, here comes pa
Back from Washington!
Too much ma.

A curious survival is "The Mormonite Preacher"; it was sung and played on an eight-string guitar by George Vinton Graham, of San Jose, California, and recorded by Sidney Robertson, December 3, 1938. Graham said that he had learned it from his mother when he was a boy in Iowa and that his aunt from Ohio also sang it. It tells of the way in which the Mormonite preacher stole some bacon from a man named George and, when asked what he had tied up in a bag, replied that it was his Bible containing the secrets revealed by Joseph Smith.

More comic than satiric is the song entitled "Bishop Zack, the Mormon Engineer," the engineer on the Denver and Rio Grande Railroad who had a wife in every town. It is, no doubt, an imitation of the famous "Casey Jones."

BISHOP ZACK, THE MORMON ENGINEER

Zack Black came to Utah back in Eighty Three,
A right good Mormon and a Bishop, too, was he,
He ran a locomotive on the "D'n' R. G.,"
And Zack was awful popular as you will see.

Chorus

Hear him whistle!
He ran a locomotive on the "D'n' R. G."

Zack he had a wife in every town,
He numbered them from twelve 'way down to number two,
Oh, in his locomotive he'd go steaming 'round,
And when he'd pass each wifie's home his whistle blew.

Zack he always said he loved 'em all the same,
But wifie number twelve he loved her mighty well,
He had her picture mounted in his engine cab,
And when he passed her home he'd always ring the bell.

Listen ev'rybody, 'cause this story's true,
Zack had a wife in ev'ry town his train passed through.
They tried to shift Zack over to the old "U.P.,"
But Zack demurred, 'cause he preferred the "D'n' R. G."

The following "Mormon Love Serenade" could hardly be expected to win the hearts of fair ladies, but it no doubt brought laughs to the Gentiles.

MORMON LOVE SERENADE

Say, Susan wilt thou come with me, in sweet community to live
Of heart and hand and home to thee,
A sixteenth part I'll freely give,
Of all the love that swells my breast,
Of all the honor of my name,
Of worldly wealth by me possessed,
A sixteenth portion thou shalt claim.

Nay, tell me not too many share the blessings that I offer thee,
Thou'lt find but fifteen others there,
A household happy, gay and free.
A mod'rate household, I may say,
My neighbor has as many more
And Brother Brigham, o'er the way,
Luxuriates in forty-four.

I'll give thee whatso'er thou wilt, so it but be a sixteenth part;
'Twould be the deepest depth of guilt,
To slight the rest who share my heart.
Then wilt thou not thy fraction yield,
To make complete my perfect bliss?
Say "yes" and let our joy be sealed,
With just the sixteenth of a kiss.

SOCIAL SONGS OF THE PIONEERS

Among the songs which were popular in Utah in the early days are many that were common throughout other frontier communities. Mrs. Grace A. Woodbury, of Salt Lake, recalls hearing the following in her childhood: "The Big Sunflower"; "The Frog A-courting He Did Ride," a Billy Emerson minstrel song; "Sadie Ray," who "lived in a cool and shady woodland," and "Annie Lyle," both of whom died in or near the last stanza; "Johnny Sands and Betsy Sprague," in which Betsy, who proved to be "a terrible plague," was drowned; "Kicking Mule"; "The Mighty Ram," who rambled till the butchers cut him down; "Some Day I'll Wander Back Again to Where the Old Home Stands"; and "Come Back to Our Cottage So Lonely." Mrs. Woodbury wrote, "Aunt Sarah Jane used to sing a very sweet song, 'Down by the Gate Where the Lilacs Bloom,' but I never heard anyone else sing it."

Several descendants of the Mormon pioneers have told me that various of the old-timers were great singers, but that no record was kept of what they sang. Mrs. LeRoy R. Hafen, of Denver, cherishes the memory of the childhood experience of listening to her father sing many songs while they rode on a load of hay the seven miles back from the fields at evening to their home in St. George. Miss Marguerite Sinclair, secretary of the Utah State Historical Society, wrote me that one of the members of her board, who lives in Cedar City, told her of an old custom in Southern Utah.

It was the practice to make up long verses to the tune of the old minstrel song, Dandy Jim from Carolin, about the different ones in town. For instance, if a man came in from herding sheep all winter and attended a dance, someone would immediately begin singing verses made up to the above-mentioned tune, about most everyone, for the one who had been away so long, to acquaint him with the latest gossip—of who had jilted Mary Ann, or who had been wed, or who had had a quarrel.

Still popular is "The Merry Mormons," sometimes called "The Mormon Father," or "Daddy, I'm a Mormon."

THE MERRY MORMONS

(*Tune: "The Bonnie Breast Knots"*)

What peace and joy pervade my soul—
What sweet sensations o'er me roll;
And love predominates the whole,
    Since I became a Mormon.

Chorus

Hey the merry, ho the merry,
    Hey the merry Mormons;
I never knew what joy was
    'Til I became a Mormon.

At night the Mormons they convene,
To chat a while, or sing a hymn,
Or perchance repeat a rhyme
    They've made about the Mormons.

To Sabbath meetings they repair —
Both old and young assemble there,
The words of inspired men to share —
  No less will suit the Mormons.

As ancient Israel's youths denied
To wed with those whom Heaven defied,
So modern Israel's youths have cried —
  We'll marry none but Mormons.

The Mormon father likes to see
His Mormon fam'ly all agree —
The prattling infant on his knee
  Cries, Papa, I'm a Mormon!

O, be our home, — the Mormons cry, —
Our place of birth, and where we die —
Celestialized and purified —
  The earth for perfect Mormons.

HUMOROUS DREAM SONGS

One of the most delightful of the folk songs once popular in Southern
Utah is the following:

CARROT GREENS

The other night I had a dream,
I dreamt that I could fly,
I flap't my wings like a buzzard
And I flew into the sky.
And there I met St. Peter
I met him at the gate.
He asked me in to dine with him
And this is what we ate:

Chorus

Oh, — carrot greens,
Good old carrot greens.
Corn bread and butter-milk
And good old carrot greens.

The other night I had a dream,
I dreamt that I had died;
I flap't my wings like an eagle,
And flew into the skies.

And there I saw Moroni,
A-sitting on a spire;
He asked me up and said we'd sup
On this most humble fare:

The following dream about St. Peter was included by Maurine Whipple in her Mormon novel, *The Giant Joshua.*

I dreamed as I lay on my bed of sweet slumber
That Saint Peter, who bosses the gate and the keys,
Refused to admit quite an army in number
Because of their lives of most indolent ease.

An old Dixie Pilgrim next made his appearance.
With rag-tattered jeans and a broken straw hat;
Meekly bowing, he asked for a ticket of clearance,
Said Peter, "You need no such ticket as that."

Said Peter, "Good friend, we are all well acquainted
With all Dixie Pilgrims and loved Rastus Snow—
They are worthy to enter and will surely be sainted"—
As he passed through the gate, Peter bowed very low.

Requiem

He rests from his labors, from dread chills and fever,
His long-handled shovel he left down at Price;
He heeds not the roaring of old Virgin River.
He's fumbling his grub-sack 'neath the tree of Paradise.

Another vision song, to the tune "Vilikins and his Dinah," was printed in the Salt Lake City humor magazine, the *Keepapitchinin*, April 1, 1870. Only one of the seven stanzas is given below, but the story tells of how St. Peter came to John with the offer to get him suckers. The merchant got out a bottle of brandy, and the two sat on the floor and drank together. The identity of the merchant has been lost.

THE VISION THAT JOHN SAW

There was a rich merchant in this city did dwell,
He had a great vision—he saw quite a spell;
His name is well known; he's scarce fifty years old
With a very large fortune of greenbacks and gold.
    Singing ritooral, liooral, lioorallalla,
    Riooral, liooral, lioorallalla (*ter*)

TOPICAL SONGS

Several Mormon songs were composed as records of important events.
One of the best is "The Boys of Sanpete County." It was composed to
the tune "Just Before the Battle Mother," by members of the group
who survived the tragedy. It tells of the catastrophe which overtook a
party sent out from Sanpete County to bring immigrants to Utah. Attempting to ferry the Green River in June, 1869, they were swept
overboard when the cattle stampeded, and six men were drowned.
Another, entitled "Our Leaky Tents," is a soldier's lament over hardships encountered during the Blackhawk War in 1865, against the Indians. It is set to the tune "Tramp, Tramp, Tramp."

The building of the Pacific railway gave employment to many Mormons, for Brigham Young took a contract for the section across Utah.
The following was sung by the Mormon workers:

ECHO CANYON

At the head of great Echo, there's a railroad begun,
And the Mormons are cutting and grading like fun;
They say they'll stick to it until it's complete,
For friends and relations are longing to meet.

Chorus

Hurrah! hurrah! the railroad's begun,
Three cheers for our contractor his name's Brigham Young,
Hurrah! hurrah! we're honest and true;
And if we stick to it, it's bound to go through.

Now there's Mister Reed, he's a gentleman too,
He knows very well what the Mormons can do;
He knows in their work they are lively and gay,
And just the right boys to build a railway.

Our camp is united we all labor hard,
And if we work faithfully we'll get our reward;
Our leader is wise and industrious too,
And all things he tells us we're willing to do.

The boys in our camp are light-hearted and gay,
We work on the railroad ten hours a day;
We're thinking of the good times we'll have in the fall,
When we'll take our ladies, and off for the ball.

We surely must live in a very fast age,
We've travelled by ox teams and then took the stage,
But when such conveyance is all done away,
We'll travel in steam cars upon the railway.

The great locomotive next season will come,
To gather the saints from their far distant home,
And bring them to Utah in peace here to stay,
While the judgments of God sweep the wicked away.

Two other railroad songs follow, but the circumstances under which
they were composed are unknown to me.

THE RAILROAD CARS, THEY'RE COMING

The great Pacific Railway,
  For California hail!
Bring on the locomotive,
  Lay down the iron rail,
Across the rolling prairie,
  'Mid mountain peaks so grand,
The railroad cars are steaming, gleaming, through Mormon land.
The railroad cars are speeding, fleeting, through Mormon land.

The prairie dogs in Dogtown,
  Will wag their little tails,
When they see cars a-coming,
  Just flying down the rails,
Amid the sav'ry sagebrush,
  The antelope will stand,
While railroad cars go dashing, flashing, through Mormon land.
While railroad cars go dashing, flashing, through Mormon land.

THE IRON HORSE

The Iron Horse is coming here,
From out the East he's drawing near,
And we will at attention stand,
To welcome him to Mormon land.

Across the plains the iron steed,
Into our valleys soon will speed,
He travels where he has a mind,
And draws a string of cars behind.

The Union railroad now is here,
And to the River brings us near,
No more for months and months we'll wait,
For mules and ox-teams slow-poke gait.

The Iron Horse snorts sparks and fire,
And drinks ten barrels, (and I'm no liar,)
At twenty miles an hour he flies,
He runs a race on rails and ties.

THE ARTISTRY OF MORMON SONGS

Little originality is to be found in the musical aspects of Mormon songs. In fact, most of them were composed to familiar tunes, borrowed from wide ranging sources. There is much testimony, however, to the enthusiasm and the energy with which the Mormons performed their hymns, their satirical songs against non-Mormons — especially the federal authorities — and their humorous songs about pioneer conditions. The traditional emphasis on music in the Church has been maintained from the beginning. Today the Mormon Tabernacle Choir and the great organ which accompanies it are world famous.

A study of Mormon songs, does, however, reveal much of interest in regard to the customs, the attitudes, and the tastes of one of the few religions which originated in the United States. Its comparatively recent development may account, in part, for the lack of authentic folk music. Since most of the Mormon songs were the product of a literate people, they were soon put into print and the names of the composers preserved with them. Certainly they were in many respects of the folk, and should be known by students of American folklore.

The two concluding articles in this survey of American folk-song from the pages of the *Journal of American Folklore* are concerned with a subject that was deliberately ignored by early scholars — the matter of who makes folksong. For many years the Cabbage Leaf School of folksong origin dominated scholarship, and in its time any song whose authorship could be established was by the existence of that knowledge disqualified from further examination. It was a ludicrous position, as every folklorist acknowledges today, but still the prejudice continues. Now, however, the song of known composition is rejected for other reasons, nearly always specious. But having been forced to give any reasons means that the old prejudices are dying.

The two articles explain their subjects sufficiently well to make the point of the composers' importance and their place among the folk.

JIMMIE RODGERS, A FOLKSONG CATALYST*

On May 26, 1954, in Meridian, Mississippi (according to an account in the Meridian *Star* of the next day), Governor Frank Clement of Tennessee, Senator J. O. Eastland of Mississippi, Hy Raskin, Deputy Chairman of the Democratic National Committee, W. P. Kennedy, President of the Brotherhood of Railroad Trainmen; H. E. Gilbert, President of the Brotherhood of Locomotive Firemen and Enginemen; and fifty thousand constituents gathered to hear Adlai Stevenson commemorate the twenty-first anniversary of the death of a man — unknown to many folklorists — who nevertheless had a most pervasive if not profound effect on American folksong. From the time of his first phonograph recording in 1927 until his death in 1933 this man, Jimmie Rodgers, sold more than twenty million records of his sentimental songs and rowdy blues. The records were bought by country folk who turned up for the next twenty years as folk informants, even in the Archive of American Folk Song.

His "Blue Yodel Number One ('T for Texas')" has been collected and published as genuine folksong by Henry as well as by Brown and his editors; his "Blue Yodel Number Four ('California Blues')" and "Blue Yodel Number Five" by Brown; his "Blue Yodel Number Eight ('Mule Skinner Blues')" by Leach and Beck; his "Soldier's Sweetheart" (though this song raises special problems of provenance) by

*By John Greenway. JAF Volume 70, 1957, 231-234.

Henry, Hudson, and Randolph; his version of Kelly Harrell's "Away
Out on the Mountain" and his "Waiting for a Train," and possibly others — Laws, the most carefully restrictive classifier since Child, admits
a stanza with the note "No one, so far as I know, has attempted to trace
the history of this ballad." And before his death Jimmie Rodgers, like
Charlie Chaplin, had been admitted into perhaps the purest folklore of
all, children's folksay. Yet of these folklorists, only Randolph mentions
Rodgers' name — and he misspells it.

There are understandable reasons for this general unacquaintance
with Jimmie Rodgers. First of all, no one considered him to be a folksinger; to the folklorists he was at best merely infrafolk, at worst just
another radio practitioner of commercial hillbilly degeneration; to Jimmie Rodgers himself, he stood, like Jelly Roll Morton, in a higher
stratum than that of the amateurs who sang for the Library of Congress'
aluminum discs. But more important, his best work was so thoroughly
saturated with Negro folksong fragments that a collector might easily
miss the hand of the conscious artist at work. Belden and Hudson were
as right as anyone unacquainted with Jimmie Rodgers could be when,
in their headnote to "It's Raining Here," they remarked, "As we have
it here it is clearly a Negro blues song"; yet the song is Rodgers' "Blue
Yodel Number Five," word for word as he sings it on Victor Record
22072.

Jimmie Rodgers composed and recorded twelve "blue yodels" and
a number of blues of similar pattern for which he was paid royalties as
his original work, yet of this great mass of song there is scarcely a word
that cannot be traced to song and sung phrases of hoboes and Negro
railroad workers. This does not imply that Rodgers performed no vital
part in the making of his songs. Despite Coleridge, there is really no
imagination, only fancy; one and one do not make three, or two plus,
or a star, but two; a man can work only with the materials at hand. In
molding the fragmentary, ephemeral phrases of the Negro folksinger
into a fixed form, which has become a pattern for not only his commercial followers but, the folk, Jimmie Rodgers gave us an opportunity to see how folksong evolved through the ages. The incoherent, in-
articulated, ubiquitous song phrases — maverick stanzas — of which
Newman Ivey White gives so many examples in his *American Negro
Folk Song*, no doubt would have found a pattern without Jimmie Rodgers. Indeed, the "blues" form was evolving when he began to pick up
the phrases from the road gangs on the Mobile and Ohio Railroad in
the first decade of the century. Jimmie Rodgers' function was to be the
catalyst that accelerated the process.

Rodgers' material came firsthand from the folk. He was born with
the new century in the railroad town of Meridian, Mississippi, into a

family of railroad men. His first job was as a waterboy to the Negro gandy dancers, who taught him the railroad jargon. One of the first bits of formal education he attained was the knowledge that a train crew consisted of "a hoghead, a swellhead, two empty heads, and a baked head"; he also learned their work songs, and how to play the banjo. At fifteen he became an "empty head" for the New Orleans and Northeastern, and worked as a railroadman until tuberculosis forced him to try professional singing as a desperate expedient. From his first singing job as a blackface banjoist with a medicine show, he progressed through the usual painful stages until in 1928, in the acoustically perfect Camden Trinity Baptist Church, where Caruso sang and Sir Harry Lauder had his purse stolen, Jimmie Rodgers made his recording of his first "blue yodel" — "T for Texas." From that date until 1933 he led the Victor best-seller lists with records of his sentimental songs, cowboy songs, lullabies, love songs, and above all, his "blue yodels." Several of his last compositions were about his struggle with tuberculosis, and though he had been "fighting like a lion," in 1933 he died of "that old T.B."

His miscellaneous and sentimental songs are of little interest to folklorists. Only "The Soldier's Sweetheart" has managed to get into collections of folksong, and there is doubt whether Rodgers had anything to do with its composition. It is through his "blue yodels" that Rodgers comes into American folksong. The twelve numbered "blue yodels" and the half-dozen derivative pieces are little more than extensions of his first "Blue Yodel Number One ('T for Texas')" — which may therefore be taken as typical of the series, both in tune and verbal pattern:

> T for Texas, T for Tennessee;
> T for Texas, T for Tennessee;
> T for Thelma,
> That gal that made a wreck out of me.

Refrain (yodel)

O-la-ee-oo La-ee-oo La-ee.

If you don't want me, mama, you sure don't have to stall;
If you don't want me, mama, you sure don't have to stall;
'Cause I can get more women
Than a passenger train can haul.

I'm gonna buy me a pistol just as long as I'm tall;
I'm gonna buy me a pistol just as long as I'm tall;
I'm gonna shoot poor Thelma
Just to see her jump and fall.

I'm goin' where the water drinks like cherry wine;
I'm goin' where the water drinks like cherry wine;
'Cause the Georgia water
Tastes like turpentine.

I'm gonna buy me a shotgun with a great long shiny barrel;
I'm gonna buy me a shotgun with a great long shiny barrel;
I'm gonna shoot that rounder
That stole away my gal.

Rather drink muddy water, sleep in a hollow log;
Rather drink muddy water, sleep in a hollow log;
Than to be in Atlanta
Treated like a dirty dog.

The identifying characteristics of the "blue yodel" are (1) the slight situational pattern, that of a "rounder" boasting of his prowess as a lover, but ever in fear of the "creeper," evidence of whose presence he reacts to either with threats against the sinning parties or with the declaration that he can get another woman easily enough; and (2) the prosodic pattern, the articulation of Negro maverick stanzas dealing with violence and promiscuity, often with double meaning, and followed by a yodel refrain.

In this "Blue Yodel Number One" it will be seen that the first stanza is the only one not ubiquitous in Negro badman—badwoman songs that were old long before Jimmie Rodgers began singing publicly. White, for example, reports "Kentucky water drinks like sherry wine" from Georgia in 1915; and from Alabama in the same year, "Gona get me a pistol with a shiny barrel / Gona kill the first fellow [sic] / Fooling with my long haired girl." Localization is not important here; like folklorists, railroad men are of national repute and influence. What is significant, however, is that no song corresponding to the "blue yodel" form has been collected before 1927, when Rodgers made his first recording in Bristol, Tennessee.

What is true for the "blue yodels" is true for several of his other songs. Laws, for instance, allows "Ten Thousand Miles from Home" ("Waiting for a Train") entrance to his *Native American Balladry* and consequently to authentic American folksong on the basis of its inclusion in six collections, but the earliest of these was published in 1931. And so for the other side of the coin: even Jimmie Rodgers' personal and pathetic "T. B. Blues" is not wholly original, for its central stanza, "Well the graveyard must be an awful place / Lay a man on his back and throw dirt in his face," was published by W. C. Handy several years before Rodgers "composed" it.

Rodgers' work is useful not only for helping us understand some of the changes undergone by folksong but also for permitting the recovery of original phraseology which has since become corrupt. For example, it seems fairly apparent that "'Where wuz you, Sweet Mama, / When de boat went down?' / 'On de deck, Baby, / Hollerin' "Alabama boun'!'" is a humorous adaptation of an earlier, more meaningful question resembling Rodgers' "'Where was you, mama, when the train left the shed? / Where was you, mama, when the train left the shed?' / 'Standin' in my front door, / Wishing to God I was dead'" (from "The Brakeman's Blues"). And Rodgers' "'If that's your mama, you better tie her to your side; / If that's your mama, you better tie her to your side; / 'Cause if she flag my train, / I'm sure gonna let her ride'" (also from "The Brakeman's Blues") seems to have been expurgated in the folk version to "I had a good woman, but the fool laid down and died; / I had a good woman, but the fool laid down and died; / If you get a good woman, / You better pin her to your side."

It would be repetitious and merely corroboratory to probe these generalizations through the other "blue yodels." However valid this retrograde analysis may or may not be, however much influence Rodgers has demonstrably had in American folksong, there is a caution for collectors in all of this. Everything is grist for the folk mill, and Jimmie Rodgers is not the only commercial hillbilly whose records are almost as common in many otherwise isolated folk communities as the five-string banjo. To eliminate consideration of these people on esthetic grounds is to apply dubious criteria at best.

W. C. Handy once admitted to Dorothy Scarborough that all of his blues were either based on a Negro folksong or were "a composite of racial sayings." To collect the "blue yodels" without reference to Jimmie Rodgers is precisely like collecting as folksong the "St. Louis Blues" without reference to W. C. Handy.

WOODROW WILSON GUTHRIE (1912-1967)*

On the third of October death came for Woody Guthrie, a mercy delayed for the full term of 13.7 years allotted Huntington's choreics between the onset of their disease and its fatal termination. Now begins the legend of Woody Guthrie.

It will be a legendary process of compelling interest for us. As students of past legendry, we are not often privileged to observe mythopoeic forces beginning their work of creation. It is even more rare to

*By John Greenway. JAF Volume 81, 1968, 62-65.

have one of our own become legend. And since no group of persons outside our society knows so well and so dispassionately both Guthrie and the forces remolding him, we have a responsibility to attend upon the process, for there are no others to hold the truth of Guthrie above the other considerations working upon his image.

There are already two legendary Guthries. One was made out of innocent necessity by the popular press, building a foundation upon that most useless of hypocrisies, *de mortuis nil nisi bonum.* Woody Guthrie in McLuhanland is a good and simple man who brightly sang his sound of music through the agonies of the Dust Bowl Exodus and the Great Depression like an unwanted child of the Trapp Family. But how else could the mass media equate the real Guthrie with the man who composed what is perhaps the greatest affirmation of America yet put into song?

The other Guthrie is darker in visage and longer in the making. This is Woody Guthrie, Hero of the Proletariat, long needed to fill the place of that first shaker of singing fists, who died by the bullets of Utah's ring squad in 1915. Joe Hill's factitious legend was kept alive as long as determination could help it, but when he said "I never died," it was just the last of his lies.

If he had never written his songs, Guthrie's life would be only an exercise in the banality of tragedy. He was born in the boomtown of Okemah, Oklahoma, in the year Woodrow Wilson became President. His father courted and won ineffectuality – he had arthritis, but he became a pugilist; he was a Socialist, but he became a real estate speculator. Woody's mother was a beautiful woman – until that dread insanity of the muscles burst out of its latent heredity. "I used to go to sleep at night and have dreams," Woody wrote in his great autobiography, *Bound for Glory;* "I dreamed that my mama was just like anybody else's. I saw her talking, smiling, and working just like other kids' mamas. But when I woke up it would still be all wrong."

Fires pursued Woody throughout his life. Two of them destroyed his homes in childhood; another burned his sister to death; and a last fiery tragedy sent his mother to the insane asylum and his badly burned father into terminal apathy. Woody and his brother Roy were left alone in their family's decayed two-room shanty, orphans of living parents. Woody took to the road, and that was his real home for the rest of his active life. He had talents, but his feet were too fast for his hands. When he had work, he was a hobo; when he was idle, he was a tramp. He married – once, twice, three times? He had children – two, three, more? One was burned to death in an electrical fire during her parents' absence. But neither wives nor children could keep him from his compulsive, aimless rambling.

At the end of America's Red Decade he drifted into New York, drawn by that strange centripetal force that brought together such disparate rebels as Aunt Molly Jackson from the coal mines of Kentucky and Pete Seeger from the classrooms of Harvard. There they hammered folk songs into weapons of subversion. There were others far more sophisticated and intelligent than Guthrie, and they persuaded him that bad luck was a by-product of capitalism. He was a victim of deceit, but he was a willing victim, and he led others into the same entrapment. He composed a dozen execrable songs to help Howard Fast lure thousands of dupes up to Peekskill, New York, to have their heads broken in the glorious cause of Communism. Guthrie also wrote a regular column for two Communist newspapers, in which he explicitly advocated the composition of songs to fan the flames of discontent. But he was only a limp leftist at best, a born deviationist, and those in his group who remain to this day ever faithful to political infidelity condemned him and his work until fourteen years ago, when he nearly burned off his hand in a gasoline fire and entered the hospital for his long wait for death. Then he became useful to them and worthy of the apotheosis they are conferring upon him with their legend.

Legend-making begins with the breaking of paradoxes into simplicities. Next, the useful simplicities are built into a structure that surrounds the real man as a scaffold surrounds a great statue. But unlike art, legendry breaks the statue away and leaves the scaffolding to represent reality.

But what is reality in Woody Guthrie? Among the fourteen hundred songs he claimed to have written, only 10 per cent are songs of protest, yet these are the whole for the image of the proletarian hero. He also wrote songs of quite unprintable obscenity, but no mythmakers have as yet seen any use for them. In both the world of McLuhan and the world of Lenin, obituaries have recalled his hatred of a "song that makes you think that you're not any good," but no one else ever wrote songs of such venomous scurrility against people he did not like. His songs of protest scorch the irresponsibility of cops and capitalists, yet he was a man of monumental personal irresponsibility. His indictment of those who would "rob you with a fountain pen" will live as long as his legend, but as visitor to your home he would walk off with your guitar or your wife with equal want and willingness. He could write songs as infernally bad as "Kloo Klacka Klambo" and as supernally good as "Deportees." He was well enough read in revolutionary literature to write paeans to Gerhard Eisler, yet he never left the folk.

Scholarship might resolve some of these paradoxes if the existent documents were available, but they are not. Some of Guthrie's songs, letters, and other writings are in the hands of a dubious group called the "Guthrie Children's Trust Fund," who let no one outside their own purposes see them. The rest are in the possession of his antepenultimate-penultimate wife, who guards them with equal fervor.

If fear has any place in their motivation, these people are fearing without cause. Guthrie is as safe from his writings as Jesus Christ is safe from the Dead Sea Scrolls. What will matter after all of us are gone is what the culture chooses to matter, and that will be the truth for our culture. There is no doubt that Guthrie the proletarian hero will vanish as certainly as Joe Hill. What will endure are a handful of magnificent songs—the songs of the Dust Bowl, the songs that children grow on, the songs that schoolchildren of the Pacific Northwest sing about the dams at Bonneville and the Grand Coulee, and the song that all America will sing long beyond our memory, "This Land Is Your Land." And since these will endure, their composer will endure, and he will be the man he must have been to write them.

When Leslie Fish was a little girl across the Hudson in New Jersey, taking ballet lessons from a woman named Marjorie Mazia, she remembered that one day a wiry little man with dark curly hair came in and sang songs to the children. In later years Leslie came to know that Marjorie was Woody's wife, and she then set out to learn all she could about that strange man. She was one of the very few to visit him regularly in the extremity of his suffering, and she sang to him songs of his own composition and hers as long as he was able to understand them. One that warmed him until the end was her "Song for Woody."

SONG FOR WOODY*

> Hey there, Woody, are you rambling again?
> Hey there, Woody, are you rambling again?
> If there's a place in this land you ain't been,
> Well, I'd like to go there and see.
>
> Hey there, Woody, now where do you roam?
> Hey there, Woody, now where do you roam?
> If there's a state that you've never called home,
> Well, I'd like to go there and see.

*By Leslie Fish. JAF Volume 81, 1968, 66-67.

Hey there, Woody, what are you singing now?
Hey there, Woody, what are you singing now?
If there's someone you ain't sung of somehow,
Well, I'd like to go there and see.

Hey there, Woody, what you scribbling tonight?
Hey there, Woody, what you scribbling tonight?
If there's many folksongs can match those you write,
Well, I'd like to go there and see.

Hey there, Woody, will you sing Reuben James?
Hey there, Woody, will you sing Reuben James?
If there's a folksinger ain't heard your name
Well, I'd like to go there and see.

Hey there, Woody, all needings must end,
Hey there, Woody, all needings must end,
But if there's a good man who wasn't your friend,
Well, I'd like to go there and see.

You sang of our rights and you sang of our wrongs,
You sang of our rights and you sang of our wrongs,
If there's someone never heard of your songs,
Well, I'd like to go there and see.

You're all of this country rolled up in one man,
Yes, you're all of this country rolled up in one man,
It's your songs we're singing all over this land,
And I'm going to go there and see—
Yes, I'm going to go there and see.

VII

The Days of Gold
and the Days of Dross

THE DAYS OF GOLD LASTED one third of the half a man's lifetime given by history and circumstance to the era of the cowboy. Less than that, perhaps; much less, if we conclude the romantic days of gold as the time gold could be won with a pick and a pan from the surface of the bountiful earth. Within ten years from the time that the Mormon elder Sam Brannan set insanity loose in San Francisco with his quinine bottle full of gold dust, it was all dross and disillusion for the prospector without capital for hard-rock mining:

> *I've been to California and I haven't got a dime;*
> *I've lost my health, my strength, my hope, and I have lost*
>   *my time.*
> *I've only got a spade and pick, and if I felt quite brave,*
> *I'd use the two of them there things to scoop me out a grave.*

But as someone observed, it was the presence of the prospector and not his production that developed the West. The gold brought them out, even if they brought out little gold. Fifteen thousand hopefuls went to California around the Horn in 1849; forty-five thousand that year trekked across the central trails and another ten thousand came over the southern trails. In that first year of migration five thousand left their bones along the way, dead of Asiatic cholera; they are unknown, they left no folklore. Those who made it washed ten million dollars out of the thin California streams in the first year of mining. Three years later the miners had to go underground and process gold out of quartz, and mining became mere wage labor for the majority. Eighty-one million was extracted by eastern capital in that peak year; thereafter production dropped to a fairly steady fifteen million, and what money was made by the ordinary man was made in work he could have done back east. He pursued the bitch goddess to more remote parts of the West—to the Rockies and beyond to the Great Plains, to the plateaus, to Alaska, even to Australia.

The miner's production of his only art—his song—was as meagre as his gold. The bulk of gold songs seems much larger than it is, because those that are known are known by everybody. There are few so unfamiliar as to puzzle the song prospector for their origin and identification, as there were in Asher Treat's collection of migrant Kentucky songs. And of the few that do exist, not many qualify as genuine folk songs.

There is a reason for this curious situation, and even more curious, it is the reason so few folk songs emerged from the Australian gold rush, which followed the California strikes by only two years. In America's case it was John A. Stone who liked to be known as "Old Put"; in Australia it was Charles Thatcher. Both were music hall entertainers, composers, and singers whose proper environment was the city. Each had an astounding facility for writing songs as fast as they could be printed, on every subject the miners had any interest in. And they were good songs, nearly all of them; good enough, at any rate, to discourage the working miner from trying his own hand at lyric composition. Old Put spoke for both himself and his Australian counterpart when he wrote in the Preface to his *Original California Songster,*

Having been a miner himself for a number of years, he has had ample opportunities of observing, as he has equally shared, the many trials and hardships to which his brethren of the pick and shovel have been exposed, and to which in general they have so patiently, so cheerfully, and even heroically, submitted. Hence ever since the time of his crossing the Plains, in the memorable year of '50, he has been in the habit of noting down a few of the leading items of his experience, and clothing them in the garb of humorous though not irreverent verse.

Many of his songs may show some hard edges, and he is free to confess, that they may fail to please the more aristocratic portion of the community, who have but little sympathy with the details, hopes, trials or joys of the toiling miner's life; but he is confident that the class he addresses will not find them exaggerated, nothing extenuated, nor aught set down "in malice."

That was in 1855, but as early as his arrival Stone was serving his function with great popularity on the goldfields. But Old Put was known as an identity; he was a man of the sophisticated city joining a society that vanished before it was isolated long enough to become a genuine folk, and so, while his compositions entertained folklorists as well as they had the miners, they were well outside the fence dividing folk from conscious art. They did indeed fail to please the aristocratic portion of the scholarly community, and they pleased the class he addressed, so folklorists had little to show for their years of rocking the placer cradle in California.

Although most of Old Put's wonderful compositions must languish forever in the old songsters for those with knowledge, taste, and perseverance to find and enjoy, at least one song probably of his authorship (though claim of composition has been made by and for others, including John Derby, John Woodward of Johnson's Minstrels, Johnson himself, Frank W. Smith, Frank Swift, and Mark Twain) got firmly into oral tradition as a genuine folk song. That is the sad ballad of one Joe Bowers, who left his lady-love to search for shining gold, only to find the only color resulting from the expedition was the red in the hair of his sweetheart's baby, a red suspiciously like that in the hair of the butcher who stayed home. In weaker versions, the suspected father is a cowboy, properly married to the faithless Sally.

JOE BOWERS

1

My name is Joe Bowers,
  I have a brother Ike,
I came here from Missouri,
  Yes, all the way from Pike.
I'll tell you why I left there
  And how I came to roam,
And leave my poor old mammy,
  So far away from home.

2

I used to love a gal there,
  Her name was Sallie Black,
I asked her for to marry me,
  She said it was a whack.
She says to me, "Joe Bowers,
  Before you hitch for life,
You ought to have a little home
  To keep your little wife."

3

Says I, "My dearest Sallie,
  O Sallie! for your sake
I'll go to California
  And try to raise a stake."
Says she to me, "Joe Bowers,
  You are the chap to win,
Give me a kiss to seal the
    bargain,"
  And I throwed a dozen in.

4

I'll never forget my feelings
  When I bid adieu to all.
Sal, she cotched me round the
    neck
  And I began to bawl.
When I begun, they all
    commenced;
  You never heard the like,
How they all took on and cried
  When I left old Pike.

5

When I got to this here country
  I hadn't nary a red,
I had such wolfish feelings
  I wished myself most dead.
At last I went to mining,
  Put in my biggest licks,
Came down upon the bowlders
Just like a thousand bricks.

6

I worked both late and early
  In rain and sun and snow,
But I was working for my
    Sallie,
  So 'twas all the same to Joe.
I made a very lucky strike,
  As the gold itself did tell,
For I was working for my
    Sallie,
  The girl I loved so well.

7

But one day I got a letter
  From my dear brother Ike;
It came from old Missouri,
  Yes, all the way from Pike.
It told me the goldarndest news
  That ever you did hear.
My heart it is a-bustin',
  So please excuse this tear.

8

I'll tell you what it was, boys,
  You'll bust your sides, I know;
For when I read that letter,
  You ought to seen poor Joe.
My knees gave way beneath me,
  And I pulled out half my hair;
And if you ever tell this now,
  You bet you'll hear me swear.

9

It said my Sallie was fickle,
  Her love for me had fled,
That she had married a cowboy
  Whose hair was awful red.
It told me more than that,
  It's enough to make me
    swear,—
It said that Sallie had a baby,
  And the baby had red hair.

10

Now I've told you all that I can
    tell
  About this sad affair,—
'Bout Sallie marrying the
    cowboy
  And the baby had red hair.
But whether it was a boy or
    girl
  The letter never said,
It only said its cussed hair
  Was inclined to be red.

———

In the gold rush the preoccupation and the occupation of its participants were to find gold; some were there—and these eventually fared best—to get the gold by one means or other from those who found it. There were none whose interest was to find out what mass of beliefs, customs, superstitions, and lore was being created in this new environment. And that for one fairly sensible reason: there was no money in that kind of endeavor. There is not much money in it now, but a person with a surfeit of education and a deficit of acquisitiveness can earn enough to make the doing worth the doing. Thirty years ago Wayland D. Hand made the investigation in the Utah silver mines that our profession wishes could have been made a century or so earlier in California; but for California, nothing is left for us now but archaeology.

Gold was found in Utah before it was found in California, but the Mormon leaders wisely realized there was no health for a struggling settlement in gold frenzy, so the discovery was kept privy from the world. In 1862 Utah was under the control of the federal government; and its representative, Colonel Patrick E. Connor, saw in the presence of gold, silver, copper, and lead the device by which the troublesome Mormons might be swamped out of power by a rush of Gentile settlers. In his newspaper *Union Vidette* Colonel Connor broadcast the news of mineral discovery in Bingham Canyon, and the rush was on.

Other areas yielded their wealth in fast succession. Silver was found in Little Cottonwood Canyon by soldiers in 1864; in 1869 gold, silver, and lead deposits were found at what is now Park City; in 1870 the silver mines at Silver Reef began producing. And so it went. Connor's idea was sound, if unethical. Vice followed the prospectors as fast as vice can move. The silver mining town of Alta had five thousand residents supplied by two breweries and twenty-six saloons, whose names, it can be fairly assumed, did not suggest that Mormon morality was being supported — The "Bucket of Blood," for example.

Utah gold gave out by 1870, and in 1893 the price of silver dropped that metal into an economic slump from which it never recovered. Nevertheless, mining persisted and a folk community gradually built up, with its own lore — here described by Professor Hand.

FOLKLORE FROM UTAH'S SILVER MINING CAMPS*

The survival of a few waifs of folklore among the hard-rock miners of Utah has an antiquarian interest not only for the collector of American popular traditions but also for the compiler of local social and economic history. These survivals are typical specimens of the fast-dwindling body of western mining lore that awaits the hand of the collector — lore without which no chronicle of the human side of western mining can be complete.

Miners in Utah as well as mining itself have changed greatly since the sixties and seventies of the last century, when the vast mineral resources of the state were discovered. To understand the changes in the social orientation of the miner from these early beginnings — and now I can speak of miners everywhere — it is not necessary to review in detail the part that has been played by the introduction of all kinds of mining machinery and improved working methods. By common consent the changes wrought by mine industrialization are salutary, insuring for the worker, in spite of immediate or tributary drawbacks of one kind and another, two values of overwhelming moment: better working conditions (shorter hours, better conditions of health and safety) and better pay. These benefits are a matter of common knowledge and require no further elaboration. Viewed from the standpoint of the individual miner as a craftsman, however, they do not represent clear gain. Specialization has robbed the miner, who in olden days

*By Wayland D. Hand. JAF Volume 54, 1941, 132-161.

worked by hand and not infrequently alone, of a resourcefulness of hand and mind that would be the envy of many a modern "shifter." With this versatility and hardihood, exemplified by the old-time prospector, who took his chances—often to a point of physical privation—of making a strike or improving his "diggin's," have been lost much of what is tritely called the glamour and romance of mining. Gone, for instance, is prospecting in its traditional forms. Even the "buckboard prospector," who won the genial contempt of the real sourdough for inspecting his properties in a rig, has given way to the prospector who commutes to his claim in an auto. Gone, or all but gone, are the great boarding houses which offered surcease from the day's toil and provided an easy comfort for the review of the events of the day in the various mines of the camp. Gone are the rowdy saloons and other places of amusement where blowhards, wrought upon by liquor and egged on by their comrades, spun their tall tales. Gone are many of the business and social institutions which catered to a population made up of many races and of people who had come from all walks of life in pursuit of quick wealth. Gone, in short, is the old-time mining camp which was certainly, as Helen L. Moore and many others think, the most picturesque phenomenon on the American frontier. With the passing of these institutions much of the off-the-job contact of the miners has been lost. It is not easy to estimate the far-reaching effects of these changes, for better or for worse, in terms of the *esprit de corps* of the miners themselves, and well nigh impossible to assess the resultant losses in their characteristically abundant lore. For these changes in the social background of mining, the automobile, of course, is chiefly responsible. It is a common sight at quitting time to see motorcars loaded with miners departing in all directions. Many miners, for example, travel distances of over forty miles a day to and from Park City, and lesser distances to the mines of the Tintic, Ophir-Mercur-Stockton, and Bingham districts. To these commuters, coming from rural as well as urban communities, the old-timers who still haunt main street, watching the cars as they come and go, have tendered the opprobrious title of "farmers."

It is from these old-time miners, who still follow the progress of the "diggin's" from their numerous haunts on and off main street, as well as from those who, although they have taken to easy chairs in surrounding towns and settlements, still have fresh memories of the old days, that I have collected this folklore from Utah's three principal lead and silver mining districts: Park City, Ophir-Mercur-Stockton, and Tintic. I also collected considerable material from the Bingham district which is principally a copper producing area with open-cut mines.

Much material has come also from many active miners living in and out of camps, and from prospectors "up in the hills." My investigations took me to a score or more of small towns in these districts and elsewhere, where I talked with numerous old miners who had flocked to the thriving Utah camps in the early days. Among these old timers were many second-generation Irish and Cornish miners who remember hard-rock mining in Utah in its early phases, i.e., roughly prior to 1890. The fathers and uncles of these men were among the first miners to drive tunnels and sink shafts in the state. Although the "Cousin Jacks," as the Cornish miners are affectionately known, have long since ceased to be a dominant force in these districts, vestiges of their methods and mining lore are still to be found in all camps.

Since the material I have gathered is quite varied and in part nondescript, I propose to treat it under a number of descriptive headings.

LOCATING OF MINES

The discovery of ore-bearing bodies of rock is the chief task of the prospector. Much of this work today is done by men trained in geology, but there are still many men "up in the hills" hunting for a precious "ledge" who have only the most rudimentary knowledge of geology, if any at all. These men usually rely only on the thoroughness with which they comb a region and on their luck. Experienced miners can regale one with tales by the hour of prospectors who "stuck it out" until they came across an ore body. One of the best tales of this kind in Utah concerns the prospector of the old Shoebridge Bonanza Mine. After numerous unsuccessful trips he threw away his pick in despair. As it struck the ground, it exposed to view a rich vein of silver. Many are the tales of such accidental discoveries. A well known one concerns a lucky teamster named Allen, whose government mule accidentally kicked up a piece of rock that revealed the presence of gold. The founding of the Mercur Camp traditionally dates from this discovery. Another such story concerns the accidental finding of a ledge near Fish Springs in Juab County by a sheepherder. As he was riding through a narrow pass, the stirrup of his saddle chanced to break off some rock which glistened in the sun. Miners are reported to have passed through this same defile many times, but none had ever noticed the outcropping.

The more successful prospectors are often referred to as being able to "smell the ore." Down in the mine this term is also applied to miners with keen judgment in picking up trails of ore that have "pinched out." In mines of consequence, of course, the workings are determined by mining engineers and geologists, but even their success is often humorously explained in terms of their "smell for the ore."

Old time miners recall the use of divining rods of various kinds and even the use of the compass in locating ore bodies. I can form no idea of how widespread the use of these contraptions was in early days. Today one encounters an occasional divining rod operator. These practitioners employ everything from the traditional forked stick, usually the willow, to mechanical contraptions of one kind and another. The term "doodlebug" is often applied to the latter gadgets.

From olden times there have survived certain popular notions and practices in the locating of ore bodies by nongeological surface indications. Some miners believe, for example, that ore-bearing ground will not hold snow. This notion may be a borrowing from the more widely current belief that snow will not overlie oil-bearing shale. The most unusual surface indicator of this nature that I have heard about in Utah is the so-called "lead flower," which is supposed to betray the presence of lead bodies below. This account I obtained from an old German miner in Highland Boy, who in turn heard it from a countryman. The flower in question, I think, is the common sego lily, Utah's state flower. Inquiries elsewhere brought no corroboration that this flower or, for that matter, any other plant is believed to indicate the presence of mineral wealth below, although it is quite generally known that experienced prospectors watch the stands of timber in various areas as indicators of mineralization.

Well known among mining folk, of course, is the help afforded by burrowing animals, particularly groundhogs and gophers, in turning up ore. Their "dumps" are carefully examined for traces of mineral. Horn silver, valued at a dollar a pound, was taken from gopher mounds on the Eureka Mining Company property in 1870, and there are numerous less well known instances. The tradition of housewives' watching the craws of domestic fowls, so widespread in California, is little known in Utah.

DREAM MINES

The location of mines following dreams is one of the most unusual phenomena in Utah's mining history. Mines discovered in this way are generally referred to as "dream mines." The most famous mine in Utah thus to be located is the now inactive "Humbug" in the Tintic district, discovered in August, 1896, following a dream by the late Jesse Knight. He is supposed to have envisioned in a dream a rich body of ore beneath a certain sagebrush. The unusual name given to the mine is the word that one of Knight's technical associates, John Roundy, is reputed to have uttered when Knight made known to him the curious circumstances of the dream. Knight, who gained almost instant wealth, later acquired a whole string of mines along the east slopes of the Godiva range in the Tintic district. He was a shrewd mining man as well as an unusually successful financial operator. From his son, J. Will Knight, Jr., I learned that this famous old mining figure rarely, if ever, went down into his mines, preferring to direct operations from the surface.

If the dreams of Jesse Knight were to bring him and his associates wealth, those of John Koyle, head of the locally famous Salem Dream Mine, have as yet, after almost half a century, not been so destined. This venerable gentleman's dreams date from about 1894. He has had them periodically since, and his mine, located in a non-metalliferous range in the southern part of Utah county, is still being worked with varying fortunes. Many people financially interested in the mine believe that Providence is withholding its bounties until a time when the Mormon church will have become financially imperiled. Jesse Knight's great munificence toward the church in the churchwide financial crisis during the incumbency of President Wilford Woodruff, may serve, to a certain extent, as a basis for this belief. Supposedly, under the terms or instructions given in the dream, only hand implements may be used in the operations. This primitive way of mining has occasioned, for instance, the laborious hoisting of ore and rock by hand windlass to eleven landings, hand-drilling exclusively, and the like. The driving of tunnels, moreover, has been accomplished without surveys. One more or less legendary guide to the direction of the main tunnel is the old Koyle home in Leland, some five miles distant. A workman employed at the mine some thirty years ago told me that as long as men could see this landmark from the face of the tunnel they knew themselves to be proceeding in the right direction.

A religious devotion, reminiscent of that found in mines of some of the countries of Europe, has characterized the Salem Dream Mine workers. There have been over the years, whenever the mine was working, prayers night and morning for the safety of the miners and the successful prosecution of the work, but there is not provided, as in the case of mines in certain European countries, a chapel within the mine for this purpose. Abstinence from strong drink and tobacco, as required by the teachings of the church was, and still is, enjoined on the miners, as well as the living of a blameless Christian life. Nowhere among the miners of Utah did I find the practice of communal devotions among miners, practiced either in the mines or above ground. Religion today seems not to have kept its hold on the hearts and lives of the miners as it once did. One Cornish miner, whose memory reaches back almost to the seventies, deplored the carefree and frivolous spirit with which the average miner approaches his work today. Such censure is hardly admissible, of course, because of the old miner's failure to divorce the old superstitious notions of his day from religion. As a class, miners, as far as I can learn, are as religious as any other group. In the matter of real Christian charity, as I point out at the end of this article, they are exemplary.

There are a few other dream mines in the state, none of which have been, to my knowledge, profitably worked. Since Norman C. Pierce is compiling for early publication a history of the dream mines of the state as a counterpart to his unpublished history of the Salem Dream Mine, I shall confine myself to a brief mention of them. The Amazon Mine in Logan canyon was located following the dream of a man by the name of Curtis. Alma Merrill dreamed of a coal mine in the hills between Richmond and Smithfield, worked for years on the property but was never able, my informant says, "to dig up anything that would ignite and keep burning." The dream mine of Ben Bullock east of Santaquin and that operated by Ben Holten in Sardine Canyon are only locally known. An elderly mining engineer in northern California has linked the name of D. C. Jackling, famous western mining figure, with a dream mine somewhere in Utah, but I am sure that my informant's account, elaborate though it is, rests on mistaken identity, a phenomenon very common, as is well known, in the processes of oral tradition.

Numerous dream mines actually never reach the stage of a "mine," but remain rather mere "dreams," which linger in fancy or prompt the one so wrought upon to make only a cursory search. A good example of this type of lore is a story which I obtained from the German miner alluded to above. He once grubstaked a miner who had a prospective zinc mine in the southwestern part of the state near Caliente, Nevada. Trudging along over the wastes with the prospector whose memory became increasingly indistinct, he at length asked the man where the mine was, only to learn that the venture was based wholly on a dream. The one comfort the German could derive from his experience was that he had not been wilfully hoaxed; his companion had simply had a dream, and an honest one. Mines found and operated by spiritualists are rare. From the collectanea of Dr. Austin E. Fife I learn that Johns [William?] Barbee relied on a spiritualistic medium, Tom McNally, to help him locate and work the famous Silver Reef Mine in southern Utah, but on this point the *Utah State Guide* is silent.

LOST MINES

Utah has its share of "lost mines." This term usually applies (1) to mines that were actually worked and then "lost" in some way before their resources were fully exploited, or (2) to mineral deposits that were glimpsed, hastily marked and mapped, and then lost before the prospector could get back from filing his claim or provisioning himself for the work. To the former classification belong such famous lost mines as the Lost Josephine Mine near Monticello, the Lost Rifle-Sight Mine near Hite, the Lost Jack Wright near Moab, and the Bullet Mine in Uintah County. The legendary material about these and other lost mines gathered by the Utah Writers' Project has been generously placed at my disposal. Since this material is to be fully treated in a forthcoming book on mining, I prefer to give here for illustrative purposes one typical story of lost mines from my own collection. This legend is apparently a badly broken-down and abbreviated variant of that of the "Bullet Mine," but I give it just as I heard it. An old man in eastern Utah watched gophers throw up particles of gold in their mounds. He located a mine on the property in this remote area and proceeded to mine gold for use in the Salt Lake Temple. He always approached his mine from a different direction, so as not to betray its location to the Indians. The Indians, however, found the mine and finally killed him, but there was a big cave-in in the mine, and they stayed away from it because of a superstition that a bad spirit hovered near. A variant of this tale gives in detail the ruse employed to prevent discovery of the mine by others, viz., the miner (a Mexican) rides backward on a mule away from the mine.

An old desert rat who was murdered near Lofgreen during the spring of 1940 used to tell a curious tale about a hidden or lost mine somewhere in the vicinity of Green River, Wyoming. The legendary workers or guardians of the mine were occasionally seen at dusk riding off up into the hills, but every attempt to follow their phantom cavalcade — I think they rode white horses, but I am not sure — proved abortive. This legend, unless it be based upon the wildest fancy, might be explained as some sort of *Nebelsage*. Localized in mining country, these mists could easily be associated with miners riding white horses. I have tried in vain to obtain other variants of this tale, comprehending, as it does, not only many different motifs of miners' folklore but also certain cardinal features of the etiological legend.

Some of the stories about lost mines have references to ancient hieroglyphics and to crude drawings of mules entering a mine empty and coming out laden. The finding of old mining artifacts of any kind in remote areas often starts anew tales of lost mines. Bishop Koyle, for example, appears to have placed some credence in old hieroglyphics or pictures that he is supposed to have found near his mine.

The second kind of lost mine is, as defined above, one that really hasn't been located and worked at all. These tales are almost as numerous as fishermen's tales of "the big one that got away," but they are invariably told as fact, and often are instrumental in getting other miners to take up the search for the lost treasure. There are many explanations of how "strikes" are lost, and they are usually believed. It is not uncommon for miners to hunt for some lost ledge until their dying day. The case of old man Buys is typical. Contesting for the one-thousand-dollar prize offered by Brigham Young for the first seam of coal found in the new territory, the old prospector located an outcropping east of Bountiful in the hills. He marked the seam by placing a knife in it. Then he hurried to town to get provisions, but before he could get back a rainstorm had caused a slide. Later snowslides came, and by spring the contour of the hill had completely changed. Disfigurations of the landscape of this kind are quite typical in tales of lost mineral outcroppings.

MYSTERIOUS SOUNDS

The belief in spirits of dead men or of ghostlike characters, man or beast, in the mines is not so prevalent as it used to be; in fact, it is difficult to get enough lore of this kind to piece together a fabric of fact and fancy that will give an adequate idea of how widespread the belief in these supernatural beings was in early days. As is well known, legends and superstitions are often based on faulty vision or hearing, or upon a misconstruction of some phenomenon validly observed. Thus many of the noises and sights that strike fear into the miner can be plausibly accounted for. In all camps one hears tales of miners who have heard strange noises emanating from unworked sections of a mine, or even from the face of a drift or from the side walls as they work. These noises range from human speech "coming right out of the rocks," as one miner told me, to sounds of one kind and another that simulate various types of work in the mine, most usually the striking of the single jack against the drill. An investigation, undertaken cautiously and not without trepidation some hours, or even days, later, is likely to reveal nothing more than the dripping of water on a hard surface, the falling of particles of rock, or the like. At an old mine in Gold Hill, there is a legend that a dead miner can still be heard, or could be some years ago, at certain times at night "single jacking" in the face of the drift. I have heard other variants of the tapping of the dead miner. Many of the tales of this kind were introduced, no doubt, by the Cornishmen with their stories of the "Tommy Knockers" and

"Tommy Knockin'." Thirty years ago one might have expected almost any miner to be conversant with these terms. Today, strangely enough, they are little known. There are two prevailing notions about them, viz., that they are (1) little dwarflike creatures, essentially benign, but occasionally given to vindictiveness when they were neglected or abused, and (2) that they are the spirits of dead miners or sinister forces at work in the mine. The latter notion of them I found more prevalent in the Utah camps, and Anthony Fitch has given it excellent embodiment in his ballad, "Tommy Knockers." Although "Tommy Knockin'" is usually thought to portend evil for an individual miner, it may likewise portend bad luck for an entire group. From a man who formerly mined in Eureka I have obtained a rather unusual variant showing the beneficial nature of such a message. When a sleeping miner is awakened by a "Tommy Knocker" between midnight and two in the morning, so the story goes, he will come upon a strike if he moves in the direction of the knock. "Tommy Knockers" are also referred to occasionally as "ghosts" or "mountain ghosts." Now and then pranks are played, in which "Tommy Knockin'" and its equivalents figure. The perpetrators listen intently as the victim gravely describes the knocking. In rather rare cases, though always humorously, the term is applied to the signals exchanged between miners in adjacent workings, and even to the exploratory tapping for cavernous areas ahead. Miners using the term in these connotations have in most cases, to be sure, not forgotten its original meaning and intent.

STRANGE SIGHTS

Although "Tommy Knockers," as noted above, appear to have been more often heard than seen, they are occasionally conceived, along with various other ghostlike characters, as having some sort of corporeal existence. Accordingly, I have heard old Cornishmen refer to them as "mountain ghosts," a term which classifies them as standing somewhere between mere invisible forces, on the one hand, and the friendly "little men," on the other.

In one of the mines of the Tintic district, the miners used to believe in a dwarflike character with a beard to the floor who chased the miners in a playful sort of way. There was current in Park City in early days a belief in a dwarf with arms long enough to remove his sandals without stooping and powerful enough to pull himself up ladders without the aid of his feet. The feet of this wicked dwarf were used to kick out the rungs of ladders, thus blocking the escape of entrapped miners. This legend appears to have been current especially among Mexican miners. Reported in the same issue of the *Park Mining Record* is a Mexican variant of an Indian mine legend concerning the habits of Indian miners in climbing up notched tree trunks in mines in place of ladders. This denizen of the mines, a so-called "Step Devil," gouged out notches in the trunks of trees and timbers with an enormous and powerful toenail as he climbed.

In the Grand Central Mine in Eureka, miners are reported to have seen a dog-faced man roaming in the workings, but I could not learn what function, if any, this strange creature performed.

More numerous are the tales dealing with headless miners. These stories seem to have wide currency, being known in most of the mining camps of the West. One old-timer claims that stories of this kind were brought to the western camps by Pennsylvania coal miners. In the Leadville (Colorado) camp such a headless miner was observed by other miners as he got into the hoist. One common form which this story has assumed is the motif of the "headless rider," who climbs aboard the train of cars for a ride. He usually boards the train at a point in the mine where he had been killed, months, or years before, riding along for a few hundred feet without speaking a word to the muleskinner or the tram driver. I have heard references to this story in all the camps, but never with any elaboration. The headless miner simply rides along, says nothing, and then mysteriously vanishes. The only explanation of the phenomenon that I have heard is that the dead miner feels himself a part of the working crew, riding along only by force of habit. A variant of this tale obtained from an old lady in Silver City, tallies with the general type in every regard except that the rider is not headless. There is, so far as I can learn, no sinister meaning attached to the presence of such riders.

There are other stories in which dead miners are merely seen. One of the better ones of this kind concerns a dead "Bohunk" in one of the mines in Tintic. He is supposed to have appeared in the stope in which he was killed some time later, wearing the same clothes and the same old money belt. Such experiences occasionally rest on misconstructions. In one of the coal mines in Carbon County a miner imagined he saw a ghost of one of his companions whom he thought killed in a cave-in. When the person in question arrived at the spot from a different direction, the man "could not believe his eyes."

Another strange sight reported by miners in most camps, but particularly current in Park City, is that of a white horse, moving phantom-like through the workings of the mine. Often a mule is substituted, and occasionally a headless white mule. The appearance of these phantom animals in mines struck terror into the miners, and often after a report of such an incident, many a man would quit his job rather than face the bad luck that was regarded as sure to follow. Some miners believed white horses and white mules of this kind to be an embodied spirit of a dead miner. Belief in such transformations is on the whole rare and, of course, difficult to trace because of the fact that explanations are readily dropped or altered. On one recorded occasion some miners employed the ruse of a white horse to force some undesirable miners to quit, but when this became known the whole crew in the workings was fired. One of the most unusual stories of this kind concerns a beautiful woman riding on a white horse on the two hundred foot level of the Zev shaft in the old Alliance Mine in Park City. An Irish miner by the name of Quinn is supposed to have seen her two or three times in remote sections of the level. This beautiful creature with long blonde tresses and radiant white flesh was reported to disappear as soon as he began to question her. He was greatly puzzled about her reason for being there, but never did learn. Other people have sought to explain her presence by saying that she was hunting her husband who had been crushed in the mine years before. This is a common explanation for a woman's going into the mine, and is likely at the heart of the widespread superstition that it's bad luck for a woman to be in a mine, which I treat below.

Beliefs in helpful unseen forces or in friendly embodied spirits, such as the *Berggeist* of the miners of the Erzgebirge, for instance, are not nearly so numerous. Of the former variety I have collected but two examples. Both of them were brought to Park City in the early days by miners from Montana. "Candlestick Dan" Sullivan mucked out forty cars about four hundred feet along a slight decline, pushing them in the regular way. On the return trip (slightly uphill) the cars moved along without any pushing, and "Candlestick" naturally attributed this to a friendly unseen force. A similar experience befell one of the oldest retired miners who is still living in Park City when he was a young man working in the mines of Montana. An unseen force moved his car, and six or seven terrified miners who saw this unusual sight wanted to quit their jobs.

WOMEN IN MINES

One of the most common of all miners' superstitions is that of the bad luck associated with a woman's going down into the mine. This superstition is quite as common in coal mines as in metal mines. Negro coal miners are particularly superstitious in this regard. This superstition is not limited, as we shall see, to women down in the mines, but applies to their presence near the collar of a mine and on other properties as well. In many mines the hoistman, knowing the feelings of the miners in this regard, often refused to lower women into the mine. Such, for instance, was the practice of the hoistman at the old Ben Harrison in Stockton. Only rarely could he be prevailed upon to make an exception to this rule. If women are perchance allowed to go down into a mine, many miners will leave when they appear, believing that some mishap will attend. The appearance of a woman at the collar of a shaft is considered a bad omen. Her presence there is usually taken to reflect her anxiety about the safety of her husband. One miner of a practical turn of mind sought to explain this fear to me in terms of a safety placard formerly exhibited in the coal mines: "Your wife and family await your safe return." The presence of a woman at the mine betrayed, as he explained it, a feeling that there might not be a safe return. This same miner, who had worked in various coal camps, as well as in some of the camps with which this article is mainly concerned, claims that the superstition refers particularly to a woman appearing singly. My own interviews do not bear out this contention. That this superstition is not as widespread as it used to be is proved by the fact that women are from time to time taken down into mines. Some miners explain the reluctance to permit women in the mine as being due to a natural proclivity to ask a great many questions about mining and thus keep the miner from his work. Others, in turn, have been known to welcome women into mines because of the cheer that they bring. These last two reasons must be viewed as exceptions. Many miners think that a woman's presence in the mine will change the luck, for better and for worse.

One of the most unusual kinds of stories involving "women at the shaft" has to do with the widows of dead miners who appear at the shaft from time to time, months, or even years afterward, hoping to meet their husbands as they come off shift. The fact that their husbands were brought out after some disaster and properly buried, seems not to dispel the hope that the men "will be acomin' off shift." These are the most touching stories of the devotion of a miner's wife that one hears in any mining camp. Many such stories may get in circulation following mining disasters in which the bodies of miners are not recovered for days or weeks. In such cases the wives often keep a constant vigil at the shaft, or make frequent trips to it. A typical example of such devotion occurred at the Centennial Mine in Eureka in 1914 in which about a dozen miners were entombed. One German woman insisted that her Jake would come out alive, because he had previously escaped entombment in Colorado. Surely enough, Jake was the only one to escape.

Almost every mining camp has its tale or tales about "the woman in black." This type of tale, as we shall see by the examples below, bears some slight resemblance to the tale of the woman in white in the mine. Each type has as its underlying idea, perhaps, the concern of a widow for her dead husband. White, as well as the customary black, may figure as a funereal color. On or near the road to the Silver King Mine overlooking Park City, so the story runs, a woman garbed in black was occasionally seen about dusk wandering slowly back and forth along the barren terrain, apparently bent on no particular goal. Children and others who saw her were naturally frightened. No one apparently knew who she was, but it was suggested that she might have been a lonely widow haunting the area. A story localized between Highland Boy and Bingham is the same in many particulars—a woman in black hovering near a cave at dusk—but the reason is somewhat different. She is thought to have been improperly buried (in black), and thus bent on haunting the place until she could be properly interred, presumably by her husband. This tale reverses the relationship of the dead to the living. A sensational story from Eureka about the "woman in black" dates from the early 1920's. She was unlike the other two mentioned in that she was a real person, rather than either a wraith or a revenant. She would lurk behind trees and buildings, stepping out from the shadows at night to terrorize women and girls. Officers could never locate her, because she operated in one part of town and then another. She confronted men only twice, one of them knocking her down. On one other occasion she drew a gun on a man, asking him if he were so and so. When he replied, "Good God, no!" she replied that she had made a mistake and left without parley. This is all that is known of her. Perhaps the last encounter contains some hint as to the reason for her skulking about, *viz.*, she might have been hunting some man who had done her grievous harm, perhaps her husband

or some lover. The scaring of women and girls might have been per-
petrated with some knowledge of the fear of "the woman in black" in
other camps. This strange motif may not be necessarily peculiar to
mining camps, but it appears to have found there a rather hearty
acceptance.

Graveyard stories are frequently heard in mining camps. The cemetery is usually located near the camp and is therefore a familiar landmark to residents. Often in a bad state of repair, but always somber
and awesome, it makes an ideal setting for some of the macabre spec-
tacles reported. The best of these that I have heard concerns the old
graveyard at Alta. The person relating the tale claims it happened about
1900. On certain dark and stormy nights in the summer time, he said,
the residents were accustomed to see the bodies of the dead lying on
the surface of the ground. Since this local legend is a good example of
an *Erlebnissage,* as this term is used by von der Leyen and Ranke,
I prefer to allow my informant to tell his own story. "One night as I
was taking a short cut through the little old cemetery about midnight—
and was it raining and dark!—Well, just as I got to the cemetery here
were the bodies lying on the surface. I was too frightened to attempt
to touch them with my foot, not to say my hand, and broke into a run.
After getting out of the cemetery nothing special happened, and I was
too timid to tell of my experience for a long while." This legend, and
others like it, need not necessarily have a mining camp as a locale,
but once more it must be noted that the mining folk have given them a
receptive ear. Another curious tale centers about the cemetery at
Alta. In 1873 a mysterious stranger offered to resurrect some men
killed in altercations over claims, and a sum of twenty-five hundred
dollars was quickly subscribed to induce the man to leave town rather
than create the complications that would arise were the men brought
back to life.

SUPERSTITIONS

There are numerous miners' superstitions that have to do with the men
in the mines as well as with their families at home. Close indeed are the
ties that bind a miner to his family. The thoughts of the wife and children are always centered in the safety of the family provider, a feeling
which he naturally reciprocates. The stirring ballad, "The Avondale
Mine Disaster," relates better than mere words can do the tragedy that
ensues when these ties are suddenly broken.

All is not tragedy of course, as some of the humorous anecdotes
below bear out. One Bingham miner claimed that accidents always
happened to him on days when he had quarreled with his wife and left

the house in a huff. The snuffing out of a candle in a mine was usually thought by "Cousin Jacks" to betoken something of an untoward nature at home. If a man's candle went out three times, some other man was thought to be molesting his wife. The dying out of a candle flame is a very unusual occurrence, and the staying alight of one after blasting is almost unparalleled. For this reason unusual significance is attached to the fact. Con O'Neil, colorful Irish foreman of the Silver King Mine, who has worked in the big camps all over the West, tells a tale of a candle that stayed alight after an eighteen-shot blasting in Leadville years ago. The only possible explanation, he says, is that the candle was sheltered by a ledge. This explanation, however, did not satisfy one miner who immediately wanted to quit.

Accidents in mines are popularly supposed to occur in series of three, as are also fires in the mining camps. After some accident or fire, therefore, people can be heard to remark that there are "two more to come."

Whistling in a mine is generally thought to be unlucky. This is an English superstition and was likely introduced to western mines by the Cornishmen. An account of the dire misfortune that followed whistling in a mine is reported in the *Park Mining Record* of February 2, 1882. A shaft was abandoned and as the miners were leaving, one of their number began to whistle. The others remonstrated with him, but to no avail, for he only whistled faster and louder. In the midst of a tune a rustling noise was heard, and the miners were imprisoned in a cave-in. All but the offender escaped. It was explained that whistling dispels the "good spirit." From a mining operator of considerable experience in the famous Alta district, I have obtained the following short treatise on whistling: "It is a well known fact, and I have never seen it to fail in all of my mining experience since the turn of the century, that something terrible happened almost immediately; and it has been demonstrated to me several times that the ore body would pinch out or be cut off by a fault or become too low grade to mine, the moment anyone whistled underground near where the stoping operations were being carried on; and in more than one instance the mine caved in, or it was hit by a sudden inrush of water. In no instance did I know of a death caused by a whistle underground, but almost everything else happened that could cause bad luck in the mine."

The dropping of tools and the falling of miners' clothes out of his locker or from the hammock on which they are attached to a cable are signs of bad luck. Some miners refuse to work the rest of the day, believing that their own falling down shafts and other mishaps are thus foreseen and forestalled. Certain common superstitions are interpreted in mining camps as applying especially to miners. The howling of a dog at night, for instance, moved one old lady in one of the camps to observe that some miner would be hurt the next day. Miners fear black cats, especially if one passes in front of them when they are bound for work.

A very common superstition, resting apparently on fact, has to do with the wrenching loose of miners' boots in falls down shafts. To this phenomenon has been applied the readily understood term "falling out of his boots." Boots and shoes are commonly thought to become disengaged from the legs and feet during the fall and to be found in the sump or somewhere near the shaft "all laced up." Four miners out of five working in the mines today will vouch for this phenomenon as a fact, although few have themselves actually witnessed the sight. It is indeed rare to come upon a miner who has never heard of "falling out of one's boots" in some connection. I have talked with a few men who have recovered the bodies of men who have fallen to their death. Their testimony authenticates, almost without exception, this common bit of miners' lore. One informant, for instance, told me that he was at the bottom of a shaft during such a fall, and that he heard the shoes tumbling down some seconds after the body had landed. One miner, on the other hand, who had fallen twenty-three hundred feet is reported to have landed "in his boots."

BURIALS

The Christian burial of miners used to be looked upon by Cornish miners, and others, as a necessity before operations in a mine could resume after accidents. This practice was especially punctiliously observed by south Europeans working in the Utah coalfields. Speaking of this custom in the early days one may observe that, wherever practicable, the entire shift was dismissed for the remaining part of the day and often the following one. More extended layoffs were never in order in the Utah camps because of the menace of water in many mines. As the mines increased in size and in the number of operations, and as greater numbers of men were employed, the practice of quitting a shift died out altogether. Nowadays only two or three of the dead miner's closest associates accompany the body to the undertaker's. One old Cornish miner, who mined in England before coming to this country, deplored this lack of reverence for a departed comrade because of cold financial considerations. In the English mines of his day, he said, one miner was appointed to go to all the workings of a mine and inform the workers of a death. The mine was thereupon shut down for twenty-four hours or so. In case of big accidents in the mines here, it has always been a practice not to allow miners in any of the workings until bodies are recovered and the workings pronounced safe.

There are many superstitions about parts of miners' bodies which are not recovered and properly buried. The spirit of the departed one is supposed not to rest until the lost members are properly interred. This is likewise true of men who have lost limbs or other parts of their bodies in mine accidents. Their wounds either never heal completely or there are recurring after-effects unless the dismembered parts are properly committed to mother earth. One miner in Ophir, for example, lost three fingers, and since the pain would not cease, he often wandered about in the mine at night hunting them with a view to a proper interment. There are also two rather unusual stories of this kind found in Park City, the second one being an especially good example of an etiological tale. In a fight in one of the stopes of a mine, one of the combatants lost an arm. Thereafter the arm could occasionally be seen dangling in the stope where it was lost. The other story deals with a Mexican who met with a fatal blasting accident in the Judge-Daly Mine. Miners passing a fungus growth simulating human hair somewhere near the spot where the miner was killed were unable to account for this strange growth. The explanation finally arrived at, and soon spread abroad, was that the man's scalp had been blown against the round, green stull with such force that the hair began to grow.

Spots where miners are killed are usually well remembered because men pass by them many times every day. New miners are casually informed of such places, but gradually come into possession of all the known facts about the accident and any and all lore that may have sprung up. The only case I know in which anything like a ceremony or memorial is indulged in has come to me from one of the mines in Eureka. Catholic miners riding in a skip up and down a raise habitually crossed themselves at a point where a comrade had met death. Pierre van Paassen relates a case of a Croatian miner in a Canadian gold mine crossing himself before going into a dangerous working.

UNLUCKY DAYS

Certain days and certain times of the day are regarded by miners as being more unlucky than others. Friday the thirteenth, is, of course, an unlucky day, and some miners even today are accustomed to lay off shift on such a Friday. By association with this especially unlucky day, any Friday has come to be thought of as unlucky. Certain south-European miners in some of the coal camps, for instance, habitually lay off Fridays. Although I cannot match this superstition in one of the metal-mining camps, I can cite an example of a "Cousin-Jack" foreman in Mammoth who refused to hire new men either on Friday or on Saturday, or to begin new operations on these days. Monday is sometimes regarded as an unlucky day, and the fancied extra number of accidents falling on this day is often explained by the fact that the miners are more logy from carousing over the weekend than they otherwise might be. I have not tried to support this notion by resort to accident statistics, since the notion is not widely held. Yet, oddly enough, miners, with rare exceptions, do not object to working Sundays. This is a rather curious fact, since there is a general prejudice in Utah against Sunday work. Moreover, miners from the west of England brought with them a strong prejudice against working on the Sabbath day.

When the mines used to run full time there were ordinarily only two holidays—Christmas and the Fourth of July, but some miners were accustomed to lay off on certain other holidays. To show that one cannot lay great stress on these facts, I point to a coal miner who claimed he had worked many a Christmas but never on New Year's day. From one of the Tintic mines there comes a story of an Italian miner who hurt his hand on May 1. Forever after he laid off on this day. This anniversary strangely coincides with that of one of Utah's greatest coal mine disasters. For years after the Winterquarters explosion of May 1, 1900—in fact until the mine shut down, some twenty years later—men refused to enter the mine on this day. This was in tribute to the scores of dead miners, but mainly because the day was regarded as unlucky. Similar holidays have been observed at disasters at other Utah mines.

The most dangerous and unlucky time of the miner's day is the period between midnight and two o'clock. This is almost universally held and is generally explained by the fact that at this time the "ground is working" or the "mountain is working." Some miners believe that twelve midnight and twelve noon are equally dangerous times. Accidents are supposedly most frequent just after midnight. Men on graveyard shift always feel safer, therefore, when this hour is past.

HUNCHES

Miners' hunches concern a variety of things connected with mining and with a miner's life: hunches that a body of ore lies in a certain place, hunches that all's not well at home or with one's fellow miners, hunches that accidents impend. In every camp one can hear dozens of tales of miners who, having a presentiment of some misfortune, followed their hunches and were saved. One miner in Stockton told me that something told him to "go to supper." It wasn't time, but he went anyway and found, upon returning, that there was a big cave-in just where he had been working. Often men go right up to the shaft in the morning but decide on the spur of the moment not to go down. On such days the man's partner is either badly hurt or killed, together with the substitute miner. Thus, ironically enough, many miners are caught working shifts and in parts of mines in which they ordinarily would not be. Among the "Bohunks" in the coal camps the phrase, "I've got the hunch," was a statement that was taken at face value and demanded no further elaboration. The man simply laid off for the shift, and that was that. All was forgotten the next day. One of the most interesting stories of hunches concerns a dog which was a mascot in the Winterquarters Mine. Although the dog was accustomed to go into the mine the first thing every morning, it stayed outside and howled on the morning of the big disaster. Several miners, including some who were on the ground at the time, have attested this in my hearing. One of the most pathetic of such stories encountered in any camp concerns the man who decides to quit working in a mine on a certain day, announcing with light spirits to his comrades every once in a while: "Next Monday (or any specified day) will be my last shift." Such statements often turn out to be prophetically tragic, for the man is killed on the very day he intended to quit.

One hears stories of a miner or of some member of his family dreaming of accidents. Dreams of this kind are as sure of dire fulfillment in the popular mind as are hunches. One example of this type of dream will suffice. The wife of a miner who was killed in the Winterquarters disaster saw the accident in a dream and pleaded with him not to enter the mine. He went, saying that he needed his "monthly wages."

Apart from hunches, which fall into a rather easily defined category, there are other happenings of a miraculous nature in all mines, as, for instance, curious accidents in which men escape almost certain death, and providential intervention of various kinds. Miners come to look upon these benefices with gratitude, just as they face the vicissitudes of tragedy and sorrow with unfailing courage. These strange accidents, though they actually happen, are retold so many times that they become hallowed legends. One of the most unusual stories of a miner's being saved from almost certain death concerns a mine in Leadville, but it is pertinent here. A man being lowered down a shaft on an old-fashioned bucket hoist was caught on a spike at the nape of the neck, and dangled there until the bucket was raised again. His plight was unknown to the hoistman who, for some reason, raised the bucket somewhat more slowly than usual. In another miraculous rescue, this time from a burning mine in Silver City, a man by the name of Wells was entrapped a short distance from the mouth of the tunnel. Another man on the outside, who had never heard the doomed man's name, audibly called it out and assisted him to safety. The rescuer, according to the variant of it I obtained, apparently had no business at the mine. Neither could I learn whether he was an ordinary miner working in the area or some strange ministrant such as, perchance, one of the Three Nephites. Reported miraculous assistance by these undying messengers is not an unusual phenomenon in Utah and surrounding states.

ANIMALS UNDERGROUND

The cleverness of horses and mules working underground is a subject of much interest among miners who have worked with these animals. These stories are of special interest in view of the fact that most animals in the mines have long since been replaced by motorized equipment. Many tales concern the extraordinary sense of sight possessed by these animals, their judging of weights and loads, and their sense of danger. Tales commonly heard concern wise old mules who pull seven cars, but not eight; mules who pull trains thousands of feet without a light; and mules who can tell to the minute when it is quitting time. For this reason a new skinner invariably finds it a difficult job to take over a mule trained by another skinner. Any cruelty to mules in a mine is bound to call forth the sternest of rebukes from other miners.

Miners have a similar affection for rats and mice, because of their helpfulness in sensing danger. These creatures are fed and often given nicknames. Their movements are closely watched, and experienced miners know that when these creatures begin to move out of a workings that a cave-in or the like will follow. This axiom has found expression in the proverbial apothegm, "When the rats move out, so does the miner." Any harm to them inflicted by a greenhorn is certain to bring a rebuke from someone in the crew. I know of a case in which a young Slav killed a mouse. An older miner summarily slapped his face and then explained in detail the usefulness of the creature.

The most curious story of this kind that I have heard concerns a rat in a mine in Marysvale, which, being unable to wake a sleeping miner, implanted its fangs in his glove and tugged until he was awakened. Both escaped a cave-in just in time. Other miners to whom I later told this story, expecting thereby to elicit a snicker, accepted it without question. More than one miner regarded it as possible and likely in view of the way that such creatures are often made pets. There is an account, which may be apocryphal, to the effect that mice and rats left the mine days before the Winterquarters disaster. This hardly squares with the great stock ordinarily taken in their movements. The tricks of pack rats in removing candles and other things are not viewed with too much vexation.

Occasionally wild animals of one kind and another wander into tunnels, causing fear and commotion. Green miners are often prankishly informed of the presence of animals such as mountain lions and cougars. One such tale concerned not a mountain lion but a skunk that had wandered in. Another prank, typical of the many which miners are fond of playing, concerns a frog dressed up in red. The animal was released in the face of a drift, and as a miner returned to his work there he came running out, claiming that he had seen the devil.

Dangerous pranks are not as common as they used to be. Everything possible has been done to relieve the tension under which men in this hazardous profession work. Tampering with lights and equipment is a serious offense that always beings severe disciplinary measures. One still hears, however, of pranks of the more harmless variety. Greenhorns are sent for a variety of nonexistent gadgets such as "left-handed monkey-wrenches," "skyhooks," used for fastening to the tops of tunnels and stopes, and "timber stretchers." "Mine salting," of course, is a prank of an entirely more serious nature. Fine particles of ore are forced into the seams of a worthless mine to simulate the presence of ore and thus defraud investors. Every camp has a few stories of this kind. Most mines, nowadays, in view of the severe penalties involved, are "salted only with the tongue," that is, represented as being richer than they actually are.

TALL TALES

With the passing of many of the colorful miners who wandered from one camp to another all over the West has passed also most of the body of the tall tales that they carried with them. The tales of characters like "Pie Face" Leary, "Ten-Day" Kelly, "Box-Car" Anderson, "Sunrise Slim" Carlson, "Black Jack" Murphy, and men of that kind will likely never be told again. Their stories ranged from feats of legendary strength, to feats of drinking, gambling, and fighting. They told tall tales of lucky strikes of ore, lost mines, strange sights in mines and out. Tales of this kind, alas, will never be told again with the same lavish and exuberant sense with which the old-time itinerant miner told them. Similar tales were also told by and about townspeople and others not intimately connected with mining. There was in Eureka, for instance, an old-time mine blacksmith who would throw his anvil up in the air so high that he could run around his shop in time to catch it before it hit the ground.

CUSTOMS

There are certain customs connected with mining that have been observed for decades in the mines of Utah. It is traditional for shift bosses to precede the men to the workings. This is done especially in coal mines to determine the fitness of any portion of the mine for men to work. In accidents and rescue work it is traditional for the boss to surpass the members of his crew in valor.

A customary sign for the lowering of the cage is made by the cage rider. He makes a gesture of cutting his throat, which means, in effect, to "cut the rope and lower the cage." Signals in individual mines vary, of course.

Miners have a variety of greetings and prosaic references to things. These range from the more or less formal greeting of European miners, such as "Good bye, by Jingo," an English miner's leave-taking salute, to expressions such as "another one finished," repeated after a miner has taken his bath and is leaving the mine for the day. Another English miner's parting salute is: "I'll take off now." Prosaic Americanisms of this sort are: the inevitable, "another day, another dollar," "there's another one to the rest," and "she's deep enough." This last phrase may mean that the mine is deep enough for the day—that is, it is time to quit—but generally it means that the miner has decided to quit his job in that particular mine. Failure to return a common greeting such as "good night" or "good day" apparently is not believed in the Utah mines to presage an accident for the offender, as this oversight was believed to do in the west of England.

MINERS' SONGS

Everywhere I went I made inquiries about miners' folksongs, but no miners could remember that distinctively miners' songs were sung in the mines themselves, and the old-time songs heard in boarding houses, saloons, and public entertainments have in the main been forgotten. I see little or no hope of obtaining these songs from the lips of old Utah miners, and the prospect of turning them up in old song books, programs of entertainments, old pamphlets of different sorts—all of them rare and hard to get—seems little brighter. Only a public appeal for old pocket songsters, and other old documents of song through the columns of the local papers and other channels will bring these old miners' songs to light. They should be published, if in no other way, as a civic enterprise, because they will reflect, perhaps better than anything else, the spirit of the men and women who made mining in Utah the daring and thrilling American adventure that it is.

MINING FOLK

Undue emphasis on the lust for wealth has distorted the view of the miner and in many cases robbed him, in the common mind, of some of the finer human virtues. Among the miners of Utah, who are quite typical of those in other western camps, one may generally expect to find people of true human worth and dignity. There is no class of people anywhere, certainly, that excels mining folk in friendliness and liberality. The spirit of sharing and sharing alike, born of common necessity in early days, is still to a certain extent a guiding principle of social conduct. This spirit of fellowship is seen, for instance, in the old tradition of "giving a shift or two" to the widow of a comrade, even though workman's compensation has largely obviated this need. It is a matter of common knowledge that in the early days following fire and other disasters, homes were rebuilt and households restored by common subscription. Any miner of character today, even though "prospecting's dead and gone to hell," can usually manage to obtain a "grubstake" from someone. The regard for the "regular fellow" is as high, and the contempt of the "claim jumper" and his ilk is as bitter, as it ever was. Although many miners live in a sort of glorious past and find it hard to adjust themselves to conditions during times of *borasca*, they must be regarded as among the most valued citizens of the great western empire. They are proud of their camps, those who still live there, and justly proud of their profession and its fine traditions.

It was in Utah in 1914 that the mines produced the greatest figure in the martyrology of American labor. As such things so often do, the incident that led to the apotheosis of Joe Hill was not made of the stuff of greatness. Toward midnight on the tenth of January in that year, two masked men robbed a Salt Lake City grocer and killed him. The grocer's son fired at the men and shot one in the chest. Salt Lake City was a smallish community fifty years ago, and so when a man bleeding heavily from a chest wound staggered into a nearby physician's surgery a short while after the robbery, circumstance pointed guilt's finger at the man. The man was Joe Hill, his defense was absurd (he maintained that he was shot fighting over a woman, whose name he would not utter out of concern for her reputation), and after a trial of unique drama, Hill was blown by the rifles of the state's firing squad into labor immortality.

Hill was, before his immolation, a nonentity who, among other things, was a sometime member of the most militant organization in American labor history, the Industrial Workers of the World. Hill said that he was in Utah laboring in the copper mines at Park Hill. (The I.W.W. at first said it knew nothing about his presence there and in fact disbelieved it.)

The "Wobblies" — as the I.W.W. called themselves — were there, however. From 1913 they had been agitating, striking, and sabotaging the ailing copper mines until the people of Utah, individually and collectively, were eager to lynch all Wobblies on which anything could be pinned. Not only Utah, but the surrounding states as well. Big Bill Haywood and George Pettibone were kidnapped in Denver and taken to Idaho to be tried for conspiracy in the death of Frank Steunenberg, the former governor of that state, murdered by Wobbly triggerman Harry Orchard as the culmination of more than a score of murders for the I.W.W. But Haywood got soft-headed Clarence Darrow for the defense and later jumped bail to escape to Russia.

The I.W.W. was built into "One Big Union" out of two ineffectual political parties, the Socialist Labor Party and the American Labor Union, and one very effectual labor union, the Western Federation of Miners. The W.F.M. later pulled out, along with the wherewithal, shortly after the foundation of the amalgamation in 1906. The "Red" syndicate won the idealistic jurisdictional dispute, and quickly the Wobblies became the first instrument of effective direct action (their motto was DYNAMITE — THAT'S THE STUFF) and protest singing.

They are nearly all gone now, the old Wobblies, and not even the F.B.I. takes much interest in them. I knew one of the greatest of them well — Harry "Mac" McClintock, one of the small band who turned the I.W.W. into a singing movement, and who will always be remembered as the composer of "Hallelujah, I'm a Bum." One could not help sharing in their enthusiasm if not in their philosophy; hearing Mac tell how he laid out the light-heavyweight champion of the world, Stanley Ketchell, when Stan was making a little money on the side doing some scabbing in Nevada (Mac got him from behind with a beer bottle), made one see what made this band of "rebel boys" cohere.

Mac is gone now, and so is the last of the articulate old Wobblies, John Neuhaus. But before his death, Neuhaus passed his memories and his notes along to Archie Green. Green is a folklorist who came to his profession the hard way; like myself, he was first a carpenter, putting down the hammer for the pen later in life.

JOHN NEUHAUS: WOBBLY FOLKLORIST*

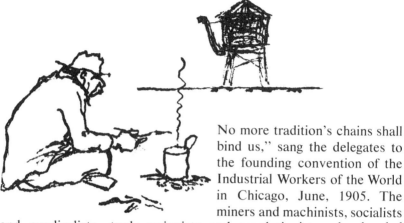

No more tradition's chains shall bind us," sang the delegates to the founding convention of the Industrial Workers of the World in Chicago, June, 1905. The miners and machinists, socialists and syndicalists, trade unionists and revolutionists who banded together to organize all workers, regardless of craft, origin, or status into One Big Union were soon to be labeled "I.W.W.'s," "Wobs," and "Wobblies." There is no evidence that the pioneer Wobblies in their formative years were aware of the turn-of-the-century stirrings in ballad scholarship, folklore, and cultural anthropology. The I.W.W. organizers knew only from their personal experience as workers and as dreamers of a new society the weight and strength of tradition's chains.

President William R. Bascom, at the American Folklore Society's 1953 meeting, stated, "... folklore is an important mechanism for maintaining the stability of culture." He went on to say that among its plural functions folklore is used to provide members of society with "... a compensatory escape from 'the hardships, the inequalities, the injustices' of everyday life." The Industrial Workers of the World scorned all the mechanisms and artifacts of "compensatory escape" used by workers. But in spite of their mockery and vituperation, they developed, in time, their own body of traditional lore — song, tale, custom, aphorism — and within the enclave of the dominant society

*By Archie Green. JAF Volume 73, 1960, 189-217.

they abhorred, they used this folklore to transmit their own cultural values. Notwithstanding their post-World War I decline as an effective force in the labor movement, they lived to see in the late 1930's many of their own traditions conveyed by the folk process outside their isolated goup to the giant industrial unions of the New Deal period.

Much of the history of American folklore study is the enlargement of scope and probing in depth as the scholar casts his net to include new groups — "spatial, occupational, linguistic, religious, or racial." Strangely, no folklorist has come to grips with either the labor or radical movement in the United States. George Korson knows trade unionism more intimately than any folklore scholar, yet in his excellent studies he has avoided general union songs not specifically connected with coal mine minstrelsy. John Greenway surveyed such labor songs as met his thematic criterion — protest; however, his basic interest was not whether labor unionism as an institution or movement was sufficiently stable and isolated to permit its members to develop a body of traditional material. The reason for these lacunae is complex and, properly, the subject for separate research.

There died in San Francisco, California, on June 29, 1958, an unsung folklorist, John Neuhaus, who made his life's work the study of Wobbly tradition. It was my fortune to know him well. I have set my memorial to him in the form of an essay on his scholarship in this challenging area of folklore study.

A trait John Neuhaus held in common with his fellow workers was a constant and ingrained use of special slang characteristic of the labor movement. In a very real sense this oral vocabulary is part of labor folklore. It conveys values from old members to new; it makes for group cohesion; it carries messages with greater and more economical impact than print. Trade union expressions come from a bewildering variety of sources: job argot, industrial relations terminology, events in union history, and the general matrix of colloquial speech. Curiously, there is no adequate glossary of labor language developed either on etymological or folkloristic lines. Henry L. Mencken noted that slang dictionaries gave only cursory notice to the picturesque language of the trades. In his glossary of occupational cant, he included an all-too-brief section on "Union Men in General." Mencken's perceptive separation of the unionist's class allusions from his craft catch-phrases is a valuable guide in laborlore exploration. The present essay employs some labor language used by Neuhaus and his fellow Wobblies.

At the time of his death, John Neuhaus was a member of Lodge 68, International Association of Machinists, and Industrial Union 520, Industrial Workers of the World. John liked to sound the full titles of his unions. Each name conveyed a rich pattern of meaning and tradition known to him. In the most literal sense of the word he was a dual unionist – a member of rival organizations far apart in goals and actions. His two unions had hammered each other long before John took up his trade, and he was aware of their differences. Yet he lived a serene life, loyal to both groups, striving always to balance the everyday pragmatism of the Machinists with the social idealism of the Wobblies. Without affectation he symbolized the century-old conflict in the American labor movement between business unionism and radical unionism. His years of work and wandering had taught him that both streams often ran together, and that the distinction between job and class consciousness was sharper in books than in life.

But John did not think of himself as a balancing force or symbol. He was aware of his loyalty and dedication to the whole trade union body, and for the last years of his life chose as a personal task the preservation of the song lore of the labor movement. John was a folklorist and ballad scholar without degree, publications, or classroom forum. He understood the nature of the folk process and oral transmission in folk-song development and sought constantly to distinguish sophisticated change from folk change. He did not live long enough to see into publication his extensive collectanea on Wobbly songs, but he left enough material to indicate the depth and range of his study. His file of song-books and scrapbooks provides tools of analysis to enlarge the boundaries of American labor lore.

I knew John only in his last five years. A friendly librarian had brought us together while he was on his never-ending quest for trade union song. My own interest in labor history and industrial folklore paralleled his. We became friends. On his constant visits to our home, his amulet was an ordinary shopping bag. For me there was always a book or pamphlet; for my children, candy. People who knew him only as a quiet listener at public meetings marveled at the mystery of his bag and called him "Shopping Bag John." But like his namesake of earlier years, Johnny Appleseed, Neuhaus scattered seed from his bag – little red songbooks, yellowed sheet music, old folios, carefully handprinted texts to obscure ballads, clippings on labor language, notes on remembered anecdotes of his craft.

Cancer cut him short before his work in the world was done. A few machinists from his last shop, a few companions from his I.W.W. branch mourned him. They knew him as a warm and generous friend and an intelligent scholar. While alive, John refused to make any tape recordings of his repertoire. He effaced himself in favor of his beloved music. Hence his memorial must lie in the telling of his work.

John Neuhaus was born in York, Pennsylvania, in 1904, of German immigrant parents, and was raised in Joliet, Illinois. Before finishing public school, he began his apprenticeship in the machine shop of the Illinois Steel Company. Big Steel had been open shop since Homestead, and there were no union buttons worn in the mill, but John was a strong unionist from the beginning. He was far too reserved to be a good joiner. He never related when he first joined the I.A.M., nor how many times he fell by the wayside and rejoined during boomer days, but he humorously recalled meeting in his youth the walking delegate in a saloon, and forever after associating beer and business unionism. He related that the machinists in his shop walked out during the 1919 Great Steel Strike.

Not all unionists display devotion by dramatic action or continuous membership. John counted himself fortunate that his loyalty could be measured in creative terms. From childhood he knew songs from home and church. When the depression uprooted him, he took to the road. In San Francisco, in 1930, he joined the Industrial Workers of the World, and for the first time was caught up by the excitement of labor song.

John's duality as a Machinist and One Big Unionist, as well as a worker and student, was of long standing. In his anecdotes he integrated and synthesized his experience. The I.A.M. solved his bread-and-butter problems, made the job tenable, and gave him dignity as a craftsman. The I.W.W. described the future he longed for — industrial democracy. He was not much concerned with political action, for he seemed to think of himself mainly as a worker or producer. He labeled himself an anarcho-syndicalist. He organized his life from the lathe. It was characteristic that he related how he could never eat a dish of porridge without becoming conscious of his countless hours in the shop that produced the milling machinery for Quaker Oats.

When he learned that I was collecting industrial slang expressions of an ethnic cast such as "Irish confetti," "Portugee lift," and "Mexican dragline," he added "German planer" to my list. He knew the word from earliest apprenticeship, and said it was a semi-humorous term for a file. He related: "When I served time, the native-born Americans were the skilled pattern-makers, electricians, and maintenance men, while the furnace men, billet men and laborers were Bohunks. The old-time German immigrants were halfway between. They were hard workers and had the patience to do by hand what an American would expect a machine to do. The boss figured a German would work like a horse. If he had a rough casting he'd yell, 'Hey, Fritz, get out your "German planer."' The boss expected the German mechanic to be willing to file all day, like an ox. Once an American demanded his time when the boss asked him to use the 'German planer' on a fitting." John guessed that the expression was known since the 1880's because all the old hands used it. He cautioned me that the term did not reflect on a mechanic's skill, but only on the supposed German willingness to work hard.

Neuhaus summed up his pride in craft by relating that of all his jobs in steel mill, roundhouse, arsenal, shipyard, foundry, and jobbing shop he liked his time with a Tulsa Geophysical Research Company best, for there he had a chance to work with geologists and engineers in perfecting new oil-drilling equipment. The use of scientific techniques in the shop excited him tremendously.

John was chary of personal detail, but quite direct in describing his evolution as a student of folksong. His mother sang old country ditties, and in church he heard Lutheran hymns when he was a boy. His sisters enjoyed the parlor ballads of the day. In later years he taught himself the rudiments of musical notation in order to couple the words and melodies of labor songs. In addition he kept a scrapbook of personal favorites. Among these were two that had been with him from before his tenth year: "The Orphan Girl," learned from the singing of a sister, and a bawdy variant of "The Girl I Left Behind Me," learned from a neighborhood playmate.

Probably he was unaware of just when he became a conscious collector, but World War II tied him down in the Mare Island Naval Shipyard at Vallejo, California, and he sensed that his booming had ended. He began to collect the I.W.W. songbooks with the provocative subtitles: "Songs of the Workers, On the Road, In the Jungles, and In the Shops — Songs to Fan the Flames of Discontent." By 1939 the twenty-seventh edition had been published. Its price was still ten cents. It contained half a hundred pieces. But where could one obtain the earlier editions to search out forgotten numbers and note changes in text and ideology? University libraries had few copies. I.W.W. headquarters in Chicago had only recent copies, for their files had been scattered by fire, vandalism, and the hostile fingers of government agents in the post-World War I onslaught on radical and nonconformist thought.

Patiently John began to query old Wobs, haunt bookstores, advertise, frequent meetings and gatherings of labor enthusiasts. His shopping bag always contained the current edition for distribution. His eye always was peeled for early editions. When he was fortunate enough to get an old-timer who had sung in jail or jungle, John asked him to recall the forgotten melodies. In his room he kept a miniature piano. Gradually he began to fill his scrapbooks with coupled texts and tunes. He was not bold enough to use the term folklorist, but in 1953 he wrote to two friends, "For nearly seven years already I have been powerful much interested in parodies. Much of my leisure time is given to putting the poems and music together. That is the reason for the toy piano in my room."

Gradually a clear pattern emerged. Since almost all Wobbly pieces were set to popular song hits of the 1900-1915 period, or to familiar gospel and revival hymns, John would collect the sheet music, song folios, and hymnals that had been the actual sources for the labor bards, even though he knew that they had often obtained their melodies orally, or were musically illiterate. John stressed in his comments that Joe Hill, Dick Brazier, Ralph Chaplin, T-Bone Slim, and the other minstrels did not consciously seek out folk-music. They were remote from the reservoirs of native folksong—Southern Appalachia, rural New England, the agrarian South. Furthermore, the days of middle-class intellectual and urban folk-music revivals were yet to come. That some of the Wobbly melodies were both popular and folk, and that some of their compositions later became folk songs, was coincidental. It was not until after the final parody, a 1929 hard times ballad, "Boom Went the Boom"—was entered in a Wobbly songbook that persons in the American labor movement made a conscious study and utilization of native folksong material.

John was still gathering books, sheet music, and folios, and entering lyrics and melodies in his dozen huge scrapbooks, at the time of his fatal illness. In his own eyes the heart of the collection was a little metal machinist's toolbox holding twenty-six of the twenty-nine editions of the red songsters. He moved heaven and earth to find the missing three and placed upon me the heavy responsibility of adding them to his collection.

W. H. Westman, General Secretary-Treasurer of the I.W.W., was exceedingly helpful to Neuhaus in gathering the ephemeral books. John reciprocated with generous financial contributions to the cause. In his act of contributing he utilized two personal techniques that endeared him to his friends. His gifts were often in the form of neat packets of two dollar bills. If he requested information from a correspondent, he enclosed a self-addressed envelope posted with six separate one-half-cent stamps.

In his studies he began to reconstruct the sequence of I.W.W. songbook editions, for the early books were undated and unnumbered. John explained that the pioneer members of the General Executive Board who printed the literature were far too busy organizing in a climate of hostility and struggle to worry about edition numbers. The builders of a new society were not bibliographers. Yet John knew that the time had come to put the story of Wobbly song in a folkloristic and historical context.

For Neuhaus, acquisition was not an end in itself. His goal was to issue a master songbook based on the twenty-nine editions published between 1909 and 1956. He wished to couple lyrics and music for all the songs. It is a commentary on his values that he looked deeply for evidence that an included poem had been sung either by the original contributor or by later singers.

Of a Ralph Chaplin piece he noted, "Some of the poems in the I.W.W. songbooks were never written with the idea of their being sung, but were just written as poems. 'Mourn Not the Dead' is such a sonnet. It was written one sleepless night on the wall of his cell in 1917 in Cook County Jail, Chicago, Illinois." When John studied Chaplin's elegy, "Wesley Everest," honoring the murdered martyr of Centralia, Washington, he indicated that its tune was "In the Shade of the Old Apple Tree," although no Wobbly songbook so marks the poem. Neuhaus attempted to delineate the boundary between poetry and folksong, in part because he knew that labor poetry was often preserved in print, whereas labor song went uncollected and unrecorded. When Frank Little was lynched at the trestle in Butte, Montana, August 1, 1917, Phillips Russell offered a poem in his honor. In his early notes on the piece John wrote, "Can be sung to 'Old Black Joe,'" but in his final manuscript he left out the Stephen Foster reference, for Neuhaus could find no evidence that it had ever actually been sung to music.

Something of John's effort in musical research is seen in the song, "Organize," by James Ferriter. The tune was indicated as "The Green Fields of Dunmoor." John wrote in 1956, "I have so far been unable to find any song by the above name. My inquiries in this country as well as England, Scotland, and Ireland have thus far led nowhere." Therefore, he added that the song could be sung to the tune of the familiar "America the Beautiful." This was John's suggestion and not the composer's intent.

Before the First World War the piece "Tie 'Em Up," with words and music by G. B. Allen, appeared in an I.W.W. songbook. In 1956 John wrote with controlled frustration, "Thus far have been unable to get the music of this song. Only one fellow worker have I met who knew the song, but his singing was so bad, I was unable to get the tune. Also no trace of G. B. Allen as yet." Of the Joe Hill song, "Should I Ever Be a Soldier," John wrote, "Tune—'Colleen Bawn,' an American popular song, copyright 1906, words by Ed Madden, music by J. Fred Helf. This tune is not to be confused with the folksong by the name of 'Colleen Bawn' or the 'Colleen Bawn' from the 'Lily of Killarney' opera by Jules Benedict."

These few citations from his scrapbooks and manuscripts tell both his attachment to the songs and his depth of study. In 1955 we visited a good union printer for estimates on the proposed book. The cost was considerable, particularly since John had already poured all of his funds into gathering raw material. He never gave up the idea of publishing a complete musical I.W.W. songbook, but actually he altered his plans and began to prepare a manuscript of texts alone with headnotes on melodic antecedents. John knew that only a few of the songs still lived in oral tradition free of the printed page, but felt that a complete gathering of all pieces would cast light on the origin and development of the labor movement's beliefs and values.

It was his goal to issue his master compilation of texts as the thirtieth edition, and as late as March, 1958, he was laying out front and back covers and selecting his cartoons and drawings from earlier numbers. Black cats, wooden shoes, stopped clocks, braying donkeys, and overalls-clad monkeys all were to reappear in his new edition. Tradition belongs to the eye as well as the ear.

Neuhaus was not articulate enough to influence persons in labor education or the professional world of industrial relations. The fact that much of his collecting took place during the Cold War era, with labor officials and academic folklorists casting a cold eye on radical song, did not deter John. He was convinced that the labor movement would in time cherish all its heritage. If he had lived long enough, and his earning power had held up, he would probably have financed his thirtieth edition. In my time with him I learned something of his perception and insight. Much of his knowledge he conveyed to me in conversation. Some information I wrote down as we sat together in my library; some I noted after each visit. Some I reconstruct now, from memory and his manuscripts.

Is there a labor singer who does not know Joe Hill's classic, "The Preacher and the Slave" ("Pie in the sky")? It was an early hit and entered hobo tradition. Carried by the folk stream throughout the land, it reappears in contemporary language and literature. It is, of course, a reminder of the rivalry between Wobblies and the Salvation Army for the souls of migratory workers. In its original form it contained an anti-clerical stanza, deleted in current I.W.W. songbooks. Carl Sandburg printed the original version in his *American Songbag* (New York, 1927).

In 1954, Joe Glazer, labor singer, made the first commercial phonograph record of the songs of Joe Hill. He altered the now suppressed stanza. Some years later John Neuhaus met Joe Glazer. He thanked him for his efforts in preserving labor songs, added several fine variants to his repertoire, and chided him, "You shouldn't have changed the lines. It's all right for a worker who hears a song and forgets part of it to make a change. He can't help it. But you can read and write, and you know how to find sources. Your change is out of order."

The Wobs inherited a singing tradition from their predecessor radical movements. The practice of tailoring a labor song to political or philosophic models even before it had a chance to enter oral tradition is an old one and continues to this day. At times both political and folk change take place simultaneously.

To their songs Wobblies also added parodies – humorous, offbeat or ribald. John was fond of singing such variants and retained a final stanza to Joe Hill's "The Tramp." He had learned it from old-timers and entered it in his manuscript, for to his knowledge it had never been printed in a little red songbook. At gatherings he would conclude "The Tramp" with:

> In despair he went to Hell,
> With the Devil for to dwell,
> For the reason he'd no other place to go.
> And he said, "I'm full of sin,
> So for Christ' sake, let me in!"
> But the Devil said, "Oh beat it, you're a 'bo."

John was gratified to note that Barrie Stavis and Frank Harmon in their chapbook, *The Songs of Joe Hill,* included the old-time last verse, and regretted that he did not know their source.

Neuhaus was conscious of musical as well as textual tradition. In 1955 he distributed many copies of the Stavis and Harmon book, but in his private copy he penciled above the headnote to the music of "Scissor Bill," "Joe Hill wrote his parody to the tune of 'Steam Boat Bill' but these buzzards don't know the difference between 'Steam Boat Bill' and 'Casey Jones' as they have the song here to 'Casey Jones.'" The melodic difference between "Casey Jones" and "Steam Boat Bill" seemed so obvious to him that he could not comprehend two sophisticated writers making the error.

The last recital John ever attended was given by a University of California graduate student, Bill Friedland, who knew a host of labor songs from his own days on the line as a Detroit auto worker. Friedland introduced "The Commonwealth of Toil" by stating that it was to be sung to the tune of "Darling Nelly Gray." He then proceeded to sing it to the tune of "Little Log Cabin in the Lane." This had happened previously. Neuhaus had spoken to Friedland, identifying the melody he was actually using, and singing for Bill the music to "Darling Nelly Gray." At the final recital John whispered to me with a smile: "It's still wrong. He sings by ear. That's how he learned it."

John correlated song texts not only with music, but with study in history and linguistics. His notes on the colloquial language used in

Wobbly songs were extensive. In his last years he met an etymologist, Peter Tamony. Both were present at a Glazer sing in San Francisco, when someone inquired if Joe Hill originated the term "scissor-bill." At John's urging, Tamony prepared an extended analysis of the usage. John submitted it to the *Industrial Worker* for December 28, 1957, and felt a real sense of achievement on seeing it in newsprint. John had wanted Peter Tamony to delve into all the Americanisms in the songs.

I have left for the last the stories of two rediscovered songs in the Neuhaus collection. He had obtained all but three of the twenty-nine Wobbly songbooks. He lacked only the second, eleventh, and twelfth. From his twenty-six books he concluded that there had been one hundred and seventy-six songs and poems selected for publication. He knew that there were many hundred more printed in I.W.W. papers, but his initial task was to collate and preserve the one hundred and seventy-six.

Few editors can resist the temptation to add choice pieces to their collections. John was no exception. In the final draft for his proposed thirtieth edition, I found that he had added a handful of songs from sources other than the little red books. We can only guess at his standards of inclusion. Neuhaus was not a capricious or arbitrary craftsman. His machinist's calipers and feelers were ever at his side. He was a careful worker, precise and exact. One of his new songs, "The Kitten in the Wheat," demands attention.

A sab-cat and a Wobbly band
A rebel song or two;
And then we'll show the parasites
Just what the cat can do.

From early spring till late in fall
We toil that men may eat,
And "All for one and one for all,"
Sing Wobblies in the wheat.

And have you fixt the where and when
That we must slave and die?
Here's fifty thousand honest men
Shall know the reason why.

The sab-cat purred and switched its tail
As happy as could be.
They'd better not throw Wobs in jail
And leave the kitten free.

The sab-cat purred and twitched its tail
And winked the other way.
Our boys will never rot in jail
Or else the plutes will pay.

What is the meaning of this song? So many labor songs are turgid, didactic, rhetorical, that it comes as something of a pleasant surprise to find a piece of I.W.W. folk poetry that is subtle and understated. Why did the Wob minstrel hide his message? When did he fashion his literary images? How conscious was his ambiguity?

Parasites and plutes were known to all the Wobblies as the enemy — the master class. The sab-cat was the symbol of sabotage. The extent to which sabotage was used as a technique in bringing the strike onto the job and to slow it down is disputed by historians and sociologists to this day. Some workers, brutalized by an environment beyond the limits of human decency, responded with savagery of their own. During the anti-I.W.W. trials of World War I, the sabotage pieces were deleted from their publications. John felt it proper to replace a few to tell all the story. He knew that the kitten in the wheat was the black cat's offspring — the rock in the sheaf to break the threshing machine gears — the match or the phosphorus in the bundle to fire the stack. The kitten was not turned loose often — some Wobblies contend not at all — and the song may have been sung as much to appeal for cream for kitty as to incite action.

It never entered John's mind to censor a song because the conditions out of which it arose had passed, or because the organization had shifted its ideological line. He knew that "The Kitten in the Wheat" was the best and most singable of its group, and was drawn to it like a ballad hunter to an antique lay.

Neuhaus' source for "The Kitten" is *The Literary Digest*, April 19, 1919, but where the unnamed reporter found the song is left to future scholarship. Another mystery remains. No melody was indicated in the story. Yet John entered it in his manuscript as sung to "The Girl I Left Behind Me." How did he know? Had he heard the song in his boomer days in the Midwest? Had he interviewed a fellow worker who remembered the tune? Did he make an educated guess solely from the feeling he had for poetry and parody?

A final reminiscence concerns the last song John passed on to me. Bill Friedland and I had been collecting material from a building trades-man and former Wobbly, Joe Murphy, in Occidental, California. Joe sang us a fragment he remembered from his active days as a Wob organizer in the Northwest in the 1920's. It began "The dehorn's nose is deepest red," and he identified the tune as "The Red Flag." Neither Bill nor I had seen it in print or had heard it sung.

That week I questioned John about "The Dehorn" on the telephone. He laughed and sang it into the mouthpiece. We were to meet in a few days for a visit to Berkeley. Page Stegner, a Stanford University student, accompanied us, and high over San Francisco's Bay, John sang the parody once more. He regaled us with a fascinating account of dehorns and dehorn squads, hijacks and hijack squads, smilo joints, Missouri bank rolls, and harvest stiffs and hijackers greasing the rails. Much of his tale came from his own time on the road in the bleak and dismal years of unemployment.

When I jotted my notes for Neuhaus' "Bay Bridge Story" early Sunday morning, April 27, 1958, I did not know that it was his final gift to me.

Any worker under the influence of liquor, narcotics, games of chance, or wild women, was a dehorn, for he was literally as harmless as a steer dehorned by a cowpuncher. During a strike a band of tough, disciplined, or puritanical Wobs would be selected to close the saloons, gambling joints, and whorehouses in order to dehorn the dehorners. If necessary, a bar or brothel might be dismantled by the committee.

The portrait of the irresolute dehorn gave John the opportunity to indulge in his favorite pastime, a leisurely journey into musical history. "The Red Flag," he related, was one of the first I.W.W. songs taken over intact from the British labor movement. It was composed during the London dock strike of 1889 by James Connell, an Irish socialist. Although Connell's original tune was "The White Cockade," "The Red Flag" soon became attached to "Maryland, My Maryland," itself derived from "O Tannenbaum," which went back at least to a medieval German drinking song, and hence gave the Wobbly hymn an ancient lineage.

"The Red Flag" was an I.W.W. song known to wide sections of the labor movement. On May Day, 1920, Eugene Debs was still in Atlanta Prison. During morning exercises he gathered the class-war prisoners and led the singing. Only when the closing refrain, "Come dungeons dark, or gallows grim, This song shall be our parting hymn," broke the courtyard silence, did the rest of the prisoners sense the momentary exultation of the group.

Long before my query about "The Dehorn," Neuhaus had drilled me on how Wobblies selected their music. "The Red Flag" was known from the first songbook and it became a melodic source for "Joe Hill in Jail," "Harvesters," "I.W.W. Prison Song," and "November Nineteenth." John puzzled out this process in a scrapbook headnote for John Nordquist's "November Nineteenth," a song memorializing Joe

Hill's execution in Utah in 1915. Neuhaus wrote: "This is another case where a fellow worker knew the tune to a parody ('The Red Flag'), but maybe did not know the name of the song ('O Tannenbaum'— 'Maryland, My Maryland') to which the parody was written, so in sending in his parody ('November Nineteenth') he simply states that it is to be sung to the song he knows by that name, not knowing that it is a parody to a parody." Neuhaus, of course, was developing his own understanding of the manner in which lyrics and melodies entered the folk stream to be eroded and altered.

Some "Red Flag" derivatives made the little songbooks; others did not. Perhaps "The Dehorn" was kept out because it lacked dignity, or because it was a direct burlesque of a serious song. We do not know if it ever saw print in an I.W.W. newspaper. The author, too, is unknown at the present. Apparently it has not been collected by any folklorist. John, himself, was careful to tell Page Stegner and me that he learned it from Louis Gracey, a West Coast shovel stiff and fellow worker, who had taught it to him in the Oakland, California, I.W.W. Hall in 1947. John had noted the words and had never passed them along until Murphy's singing of a line or two stimulated my curiosity.

"The Dehorn Song" is no lyric masterpiece, but it reveals facets of labor folklore. It also shows that the Wobbly could poke fun at himself; he possessed a strain of humor sadly lacking in other sections of the radical movement. The song flays the drunkard, but not in the saccharine tones of a temperance tract, for behind the portrait lay the militant dehorn squad—an instrument of social control developed by outcasts consciously dedicated to rebuilding society. The text follows:

THE DEHORN

The dehorn's nose is deepest red,
The one bright spot on his empty head.
To get his booze he begs and steals,
Half naked he goes without his meals.

Chorus

Oh dehorn, why don't you get wise,
And quit the booze and organize?
A sober mind will win the day,
The One Big Union will show the way.

And when the dehorn gets a job,
He's satisfied, the dirty slob.
A pile of straw will do for a bed
On which to rest his wooden head.

> To stick around and fix the job,
> It never pierced his empty nob.
> For fifty cents will get him drunk,
> And fifty cents a lousy bunk.
>
> And when the dehorn gets stakebound,
> He starts to dream about the town.
> He kicks about the rotten chuck,
> And never saw such a sticky muck.
>
> Oh point to him with nose so red
> With tangled feet and soggy head.
> For all this life to him will yield
> Is just a grave in potter's field.

John Neuhaus knew that some labor songs met the generally recognized criteria of folksong definition—age, life in oral tradition, evidence of change—and that some did not. Like many fellow workers and boomers, he put public libraries to extensive use. Here he read Child, Sharp, Lomax, Sandburg, Barry, Cox, Korson, and their companions. In John's planned master songbook he did not divide folksong from broadside. We do not know if he would have come to such a consideration in time. His main task was to preserve all the songs and to present them in a continuum of history. He had read the tentative comments on "Casey Jones" by folklorists Duncan Emrich, William Alderson, and Wayland Hand. He knew that without his collected material they and their colleagues would not have the empirical data to penetrate deeper into this area.

Normally, judgment is reserved on the inclusion of a topical piece in the corpus of folksong until several variants are collected from oral tradition over a period of time. What happens when collectors overlook or bypass a field? John Harrington Cox gathered a rich treasure in *Folk Songs from the South* (Cambridge, 1925), and his headnotes are monuments in ballad scholarship. In the early 1920's he passed through West Virginia bituminous mining counties where coal-diggers were locked in bitter industrial war. No echo of trade unionism sounds in his book. Were there no labor songs in his informants' repertoires, or did he avoid such material? We do not know.

There is first hand evidence, but not from the pens of ballad scholars, that Wobbly song entered oral tradition a half century ago. Carleton Parker is best remembered as the University of California economist who pioneered in psychological studies of casual labor. Early in 1914 he met hundreds of migrants, bindle stiffs, and fruit tramps. Of eight hundred hoboes whom he observed, he wrote that half "... knew in a rough way the—for them, curiously attractive—philosophy of the I.W.W. and could also sing some of its songs.... Where a group of hoboes sit around a fire under a railroad bridge, many of the group can sing I.W.W. songs without the book. This was not so three years ago." How much richer would American folklore be today had those songs sung "without the book" been noted by a Barry, a Korson, a Neuhaus?

"The Kitten in the Wheat" and "The Dehorn Song" were probably sung in many a jungle, and to my knowledge, they never were printed in the little red songbooks. Both can be dated in the decade 1910-1920. They can only be compared for oral change with their variants if intense collecting is undertaken from living Wobblies in the few years ahead. It may well be that I.W.W. songhunting will remain fragmentary and sporadic, and that it will not go much beyond Neuhaus's scrapbooks and manuscripts. But even if little collecting is done and if no neat or final label—folk or broadside—can be assigned to any particular piece, it still may be possible for future students to generalize about Wobbly folksong.

No social group that sang as much as did the Wobs could have escaped affecting American tradition; yet the number of songs gathered by folklorists and printed in their writings is minuscule. In 1927 Carl Sandburg printed three I.W.W. songs, only one of which had clearly come to him orally. Three years later, George Milburn in *Hobo's Hornbook* (New York, 1930) included several more I.W.W. songs without distinguishing sources. Apparently between 1905-1960 only two such songs collected in the field have been printed in academic folklore journals. To date, John Greenway has published the most extensive data on Wobbly song with his actual selections coming from "in print" little red songbooks. In spite of this meager representation, the songs did circulate and were subject to the folk process. How do we know and where do we seek evidence?

Something of the strident tone of Wobbly song got into radical fiction in the 1920's and 1930's. Upton Sinclair, John Dos Passos, Robert Cantwell, Josephine Herbst, and others heard song, absorbed lore, and gave it back in their writing. Library of Congress field recordings also preserve some Wobbly material in full dimension. Comments on the use of singing are found in the anti-I.W.W. trial reports, as well as in governmental agency proceedings of the World War I and post-war attack on the movement. Curious hobo variants of "Pie in the Sky" were recorded commercially about 1930 by hillbilly stars—Carson Robison, Frank Luther, and Vernon Dalhart. Other hobo phonograph records may reveal I.W.W. influence. Many of the obscure sectarian and splinter groups on the radical left have issued ephemeral songbooks, offering Wobbly songs selected from the memory of the compilers and unknowingly preserving significant variants. The Communist movement with its interest in "people's songs" retained and extended Wobbly lore. Folklore collected in industrial cities between 1936 and 1940 by the W. P. A. Federal Writers' Project may reflect I.W.W. tradition. In the years since World War II a number of universities have undertaken local oral history projects involving taped interviews with old trade unionists. Echoes of Wobbly tradition are heard on these tapes. Urban singer-collectors of the 1950's have picked up stray fragments of Wob songs previously overlooked or ignored. And finally, the extensive I.W.W. publications have yet to be examined by a trained folklorist in the way that George Korson searched the *United Mine Workers Journal.*

From all these sources a story may be gathered to reveal the real impact of I.W.W. lore — sardonic, humorous, visionary — on American society: a narrative that is not only fascinating in its own right, but part of the whole complex of "studies that illuminate the American mind." John Neuhaus went about his work in collecting Wobbly tradition with skill and devotion. Without formal training he brought together a valuable body of material in an unexplored area. He combined a song hunter's zeal with a scholar's instincts. American folklore study is enriched by his contribution.

The emotion does not appear in the reading, but anyone who has ever heard "The Days of Forty-Nine" sung in a reflective, bold, and grave Dorian mode would agree that there is no traditional song of the miners to challenge it as a proper threnody for that golden age. Fittingly, too, its composition has been persuasively attributed to the Homer of that golden age, John "Old Put" Stone.

THE DAYS OF FORTY-NINE*

We are gazing now on old Tom Moore,
    A relic of bygone days;
'Tis a bummer, too, they call me now,
    But what cares I for praise?
It's oft, says I, for the days gone by,
    It's oft do I repine
For the days of old when we dug out the gold
    In those days of Forty-Nine.

*From John A. Lomax, "Some Types of American Folk-Song."
 JAF Volume 28, 1915, 1-17.

My comrades they all loved me well,
   The jolly, saucy crew;
A few hard cases, I will admit,
   Though they were brave and true.
Whatever the pinch, they ne'er would flinch,
   They never would fret nor whine;
Like good old bricks they stood the kicks
   In the days of Forty-Nine.

There's old "Aunt Jess," that hard old cuss,
   Who never would repent;
He never missed a single meal,
   Nor never paid a cent.
But old "Aunt Jess," like all the rest,
   At death he did resign,
And in his bloom went up the flume
   In the days of Forty-Nine.

There is Ragshag Jim, the roaring man,
   Who could out-roar a buffalo, you bet;
He roared all day and he roared all night,
   And I guess he is roaring yet.
One night Jim fell in a prospect hole, —
   It was a roaring bad design, –
And in that hole Jim roared out his soul
   In the days of Forty-Nine.

There is Wylie Bill, the funny man,
   Who was full of funny tricks;
And when he was in a poker game
   He was always hard as bricks.
He would ante you at stud, he would play you at draw,
   He'd go you a hateful blind, —
In a struggle with death Bill lost his breath
   In the days of Forty-Nine.

There was New York Jake, the butcher boy,
   Who was fond of getting tight;
And every time he got on a spree
   He was spoiling for a fight.
One night Jake rampaged against a knife
   In the hands of old Bob Sine,
And over Jake they held a wake
   In the days of Forty-Nine.

There was Monte Pete, I'll never forget
　　The luck he always had;
He would deal for you both day and night
　　Or as long as he had a scad.
It was a pistol-shot that lay Pete out,
　　It was his last resign,
And it caught Pete dead shore in the door
　　In the days of Forty-Nine.

Of all the comrades that I've had
　　There's none that's left to boast,
And I am left alone in my misery,
　　Like some poor wandering ghost.
And as I pass from town to town,
　　They call me the rambling sign,
Since the days of old and the days of gold
　　And the days of Forty-Nine.

VIII

Bad Men and Big

ONE DOES NOT SPEAK OF ROPE in the home of a hanged man. Nor does one speak of Colonel Chivington in the old homes of Denver, or of John D. Lee in the old homes of Utah. These are subjects avoided for the delicacy of the situation, not because of the simple inference that these men were bad. Such an inference is possible only to one whose opinions were formed in the safety of his remoteness from the hard questions Chivington and Lee solved for their people. Their people are sensitive about the matter only because they understand how profitless it is to argue the difference between a bad man and a big man.

I make no judgment about the persons who move through this chapter. I leave the inference for the reader to make. I will say only that all of the men herein are either bad or big. Perhaps they are both.

It is safe to say, however, that there is a powerful movement afoot to "peaceify" the West and improve its image before the world. Jack Schaefer, repenting the stern reliance upon force exhibited by his hero Shane, has been escalating nonviolence in recent years with writings like *Heroes without Glory: Some Goodmen of the Old West,* in which people like John A. Thompson, the skiing mailman, are held to outclass the badmen "thirty to one," whatever that means.

Things at least were pretty bad in the Old West. Hanging Judge Parker, who dangled dead men like Christmas tree ornaments around Fort Smith in the last quarter of the nineteenth century, has suffered a steady decline in respect and reputation in a society where criminals can no longer be convicted if they confess to a crime before they are asked. What the "see-gooders" overlook about Judge Parker's severity is the recorded fact that during his tenure of office as a judge, sixty-five of his deputies were killed. Even the goodmen were often badmen. Bob Dalton was once chief of the Osage Police. And the badmen were often goodmen. The last time anyone saw Frank James, he was working as a shoe salesman in St. Louis.

Where on the scale does one put Boston Corbett? He shot John Wilkes Booth, and that was a Good Thing. But on another occasion he took his pistol and held up the entire Kansas House of Representatives.

If the bad guys write bad poetry, are they to be twice condemned, or is their art to be taken as a saving grace? Bonnie Parker was handy with the poetic pen as well as with the pistol. What about Black Bart, who left at the scenes of his crimes verse like this:

> *Now I lay me down to sleep*
> *To wait the coming morrow,*
> *Perhaps success perhaps defeat*
> *And everlasting sorrow.*
> *I've labored long and hard for bread*
> *For honor and for riches*
> *But on my corns too long you've tred*
> *You fine haired sons of bitches.*

Certainly there must be some mitigation of punishment for that last rhyme. But on the other hand, Wells Fargo was held up three hundred and thirteen times in fifteen years, which is a bit much.

Is the judgment to be a matter of which side was he on? Take Randy Runnels, for instance, whom nobody on television seems to have heard of. Randy was a caution, he was. Wells Fargo hired him on to see what he could do to clean up the Yankee Strip, that passage through Panama that some daring migrants chose in preference to the long trip around the Horn. Runnels did the job. He gathered a few others like himself, and in a matter of weeks he had hanged hundreds of highwaymen, leaving their bodies along the path as a *memento mori* to all who came thither.

And Texas Ranger Captain Frank A. Hamer, who has been in the pictures lately. His official biography, *I'm Frank Hamer*, attests to his having engaged in a hundred gunfights in which he was wounded seventeen times while killing fifty-three men (and one woman). Hamer himself was more modest; elsewhere he is quoted as cutting all these figures in half. But most of his violence was literally slapping desperadoes into unconsciousness with a grizzly swipe, a blow much more effective than the popular pushing punch favored by ordinary American pugilists. See him in *Bonnie and Clyde*. It's a great picture.

It all boils down, if that is the proper expression, to whose head is in the bottle. Whose head *was* in the bottle, incidentally, when Captain Harry Love's vigilantes went out after Joaquin Murrieta and his associate, Three-Fingered Jack, and came back with a head and a hand pickled in whiskey?

Since I wrote my last word on Robin Hood and his disreputable descendants four years ago, nothing has happened to change the facts about these heroes, or the lack of facts about them, or my opinion about them, so the word can be repeated here for those who are not conversant with the background of this putative Anglo-Saxon patriot and national benefactor:*

Robin Hood appeared first in literature in a snide reference in *Piers Plowman* at the end of the fourteenth century, when Slobbering Sloth admits ignorance of his Pater Noster, but says he can make up for it by

---

* *The Inevitable Americans* (New York: Alfred A. Knopf, 1964), 149-151.

reciting "rymes of Robin Hood and Randolf, erle of Chestre," another person of dubious morality. The antiquarian Bishop Stukely in his *Paleographia Britanniae,* written about the middle of the eighteenth century, gives Robin Hood a noble pedigree by claiming him as the son of Waltheof, Earl of Northumberland and Huntingdon, and Judith, niece of William the Conqueror, thus making him sibling to Malcolm and Donalbain, of famous memory. Of this, Charles Parkin in his "An Answer to, or Remarks upon, Dr. Stukeley's *Origines Roystonianae"* said: "His pedigree of Robin Hood is quite jocose, an original indeed." Joseph Ritson's version of Robin's origin (1795) is more popular: "Robin Hood was born at Locksley, in the county of Nottingham, in the reign of King Henry the Second, and about the year of Christ 1160. His extraction was noble, and his true name was Robert Fitzooth, which vulgar pronunciation early corrupted into Robin Hood. He is frequently styled and commonly reputed to have been Earl of Huntingdon, a title to which in the latter part of his life, at least, he actually appears to have some sort of pretension."

Ritson actually appears to have some sort of pretension to verisimilitude, but his biographical sketch of Robin Hood is wholly imaginative. The turn of the eighteenth century was not a time of outstanding scholarly probity, but as we shall see presently, folklore is not limited to the folk; there are, distressingly, many cases of irrational belief even in scientific bodies. It would be profitless to summarize the numerous pseudo-historical vaporings about the true life of Robin Hood; however, they all generally agree that he was a Saxon who took to the woods of eastern England after the Norman Conquest, and there he carried on a campaign of altruistic pillage. The western territory, meanwhile, was held by another retaliatory hero, one Hereward the Wake, putative son of Lord Leofric, whose wife, Godiva, made a public exhibition of herself in protest against her husband's tax policies, an act which doubtless had some influence in shaping young Hereward's later demeanor.

The most literate of contemporary iconoclasts, Lord Raglan, does an admirable job of destruction on the historical Robin Hood in his delightful book, *The Hero.* He shows that Saxons had no surnames, and not before the sixteenth century did Normans take hereditary last names; that "of none of the families in which earldoms were created from 1066 until 1442, when John, Lord Talbot, became Earl of Shrewsbury, is there a legitimate descendant in the male line"; that there is no such place as Locksley either in Nottinghamshire or Yorkshire; that the long bow did not come into use in England until the end of the thirteenth century; that the earldom of Huntingdon was held from 1185 until 1216 by David of Scotland; that there were no friars in England,

Tuck or other, until the year 1224; that "Little" as in "Little John," did not in Norman times refer to one's physique but to one's character; and, as a final humiliation, that the names of Robin (diminutive of Robert) and all his merry men (and his merry maiden Marian) except the miller, Much, were Norman. Furthermore, he adds, "the first Wake to be christened 'Hereward' was born in 1851." But come back two hundred years from now and see who is better remembered — Robin Hood or Lord Raglan.

ROBIN HOOD AND THE AMERICAN OUTLAW*

The most familiar characterization of our American outlaws is that they are "Robin Hoods." References to the prototypic bandit are conventional for both biographers and folklorists. In fact, such references are inevitable. Not only does the Robin Hood legend have the authority of age, but it is still regarded as the classic formulation of the outlaw tradition. Yet folklore scholars have not detailed the numerous parallels which presumably justify this classic allusion, nor have they demonstrated why the legends of such homegrown heroes as Jesse James or Sam Bass should be viewed as variants within the parent tradition. Some analysis of these presumed parallels, by means of a comparison of the historical and folkloric elements in the legends, would therefore seem to be in order.

The continuity of outlaw traditions over both space and time has intrigued many observers, including a president of the United States. Theodore Roosevelt noted that "there is something very curious in

*By Kent L. Steckmesser. JAF Volume 79, 1966, 348-355.

the reproduction here on this continent of essentially the conditions
of ballad growth which obtained in medieval England, including, by
the way, sympathy for the outlaw, Jesse James taking the place of
Robin Hood." These conditions would seem to be fairly predictable.
They would involve a recurrent social situation, namely, one in which
the law is corrupt. In Anglo-Saxon tradition "law" and "justice" are
assumed to be one and the same. On occasion, however, the two are
divorced. The law becomes the tool of a "gang" which must be over-
thrown, or it comes to represent a social system in which injustice is
the rule. In such situations the outlaw, though technically a criminal,
may become a folk hero by serving the higher cause of justice. Robin
Hood, Jesse James, and Billy the Kid are all thought to have emerged
from such situations.

Like most outlaws of folklore, Robin Hood is viewed as the champion of the socially and economically oppressed classes. The folk of
medieval England idolized him as the symbol of resistance to a corrupt
priesthood and nobility. The Sheriff of Nottingham and the Abbot of
St. Mary's are the stock figures who personify the evils of a system in
which the poor are exploited and oppressed. The vitality of the Robin
Hood ballads in British oral tradition is usually seen as evidence that
Robin's victories over the law were widely applauded.

Unfortunately, the actual origins of the Robin Hood legend do not
match the classic model. The historical records of this period are too
scanty to permit definitive conclusions, but enough evidence exists to
enable historians to question the folk version of Robin Hood's career.
There is for example the familiar and troublesome question of whether
Robin Hood was an actual person or, as Francis James Child claimed,
"absolutely a creation of the ballad muse." The fact that we cannot
find the Sheriff of Nottingham or the Abbot of St. Mary's in history
tends to prove that Professor Child was right. The actors in this particular legend belong not to history but to tradition. In addition, Robin
Hood's first appearance (in Langland's *Piers Plowman*) does not make
him the hero of the socially and economically oppressed; this appears
to be a later folk infusion. We have no evidence that the presumed
perversion of justice by the legal authorities of thirteenth-century
England was resisted by an outlaw who set out to correct the evil.
Folklore insists that in such circumstances an outlaw of the Robin
Hood type does emerge, but history is silent.

American folklore places Jesse James and Billy the Kid in the same
classic situation. Jesse and Frank James return from Confederate
guerrilla service in the Civil War to find their home state of Missouri
overrun with carpetbaggers, Radicals, and other vindictive Unionists.
In the folklore version these persecutors attack Jesse's father, put his

mother in jail, and savagely beat him with rope ends. The law itself has become a weapon of the Yankee oppressors. To secure justice for himself and his friends, Jesse must live outside the law. Once again, an undesirable social and political situation breeds an appropriate outlaw hero.

History, however, fails to support the folk interpretation. There is no record of the mistreatment of Jesse's father (Dr. Samuel), of the retention of his mother in jail, or of the attack on Jesse himself. "Persecution" of the innocent is a basic folk explanation of outlawry, being applied to both the Jameses and the Younger brothers. Many Missourians, however, refused to accept this excuse. A letter in the St. Louis *Globe* of March 13, 1875, signed CONFEDERATE, pointed out that the James boys could have returned to their homes in peace like the rest of the Confederate soldiers, but had deliberately chosen to be highwaymen and killers. From the historian's point of view, it seems likely that the "persecution" episodes like those above were invented and applied to Jesse James to fit him into the Robin Hood pattern. Certainly the journalistic apologists for the gang were constantly praising their "Robin Hood" characteristics.

Although Billy the Kid has only borderline status as a folk hero, his legend being largely literary in origin, it should be noted that his social environment seemed to meet all the requirements for outlaw legendry. The usual picture of southeastern New Mexico in the 1870's is that of helpless farmers ruled by a corrupt political machine which hand-picked the judges, sheriffs, and legislators. When the Englishman John Tunstall attempted to compete with this machine, he was assassinated. The Kid then became the agent of retribution for his employer's death. But since Tunstall's slayers were shielded by the law, opposition to the established system became the only path to true justice.

The actual situation was rather different from the black-and-white picture of popular tradition. While Tunstall's opponents were allied with a known political machine, the "Santa Fe Ring," he was himself trying to form such a ring. Tunstall was an ambitious and aggressive person, quite different from the refined and sensitive idealist known to legend. His ambition brought the two rival gangs into open warfare, with both sides attempting to use the legal machinery for their own ends. The Kid was simply the paid gunman of one faction, and the issue of justice for oppressed farmers was a distinctly minor consideration.

The tales and ballads which embody the outlaw traditions also tend to fall into a standard pattern, one feature of which is that the outlaw is a "friend of the poor." The one constant element in popular conceptions of Robin Hood is that he "steals from the rich and gives to the poor." He tells his men to rob only knights and abbots, never "good yèman." The ballad of Jesse James informs us that "Jesse James was a man and a friend of the poor." The James boys continued to be relatively popular in Missouri because "they didn't ever cause farmers any trouble. Mostly they robbed banks and railroads and express companies that had plenty of money." Sam Bass was favorably known to the squatters and farmers of east Texas for his presumed generosity with twenty-dollar gold pieces stolen from the Union Pacific. And Billy the Kid "was good to Mexicans. He was like Robin Hood; he'd steal from the white people and give it to the Mexicans, so they thought he was all right."

The folk tradition of Robin Hood's generosity to the poor rests upon very slender foundations indeed. Only one of the ballads, the "Gest of Robyn Hode," is specific on this point:

> Chryst have mercy on his soule,
> That dyed on the rode!
> For he was a good outlawe,
> And dyde pore men moch god.

In view of such meager evidence, the origins and evolution of this particular legend are worth serious study. Historical evidence confirming the generosity of American outlaws is also lacking. After the robbery of the Kansas City fairgrounds in 1872, a letter from one of the James gang appeared in the Kansas City *Times* (October 15). Signed JACK SHEPHERD, DICK TURPIN, CLAUDE DUVAL, it proclaimed that "we rob the rich and give it to the poor." No evidence shows, however, that any of the money from the Kansas City robbery, or from any of the gang's other robberies, ever found its way into the pockets of the deserving poor.

Demonstrating the essential falsity of such "friendship for the poor" traditions does not mean that they will be rejected by the poor people who perpetuate them. The Jesse James ballad has flourished among the poor whites and southern Negroes, and in fact one theory on the authorship of this ballad attributes it to a Negro convict. Mexicans have remembered the legend of Billy the Kid, much to the disgust of the dominant "Anglos." Pretty Boy Floyd has been the hero of a Robin Hood tradition among Oklahoma farmers. In the classic development of such legends, one can safely predict that the downtrodden will idolize the outlaws.

The anecdotes which exemplify the outlaw's generosity and sense of justice are often similar. Robin Hood lends four hundred pounds to Sir Richard of Lee, to enable him to pay his debts to the grasping Abbot of St. Mary's. When the Abbot's clerk (in later versions the Abbot himself) rides through Sherwood Forest shortly thereafter, Robin Hood holds him up and takes eight hundred pounds. When a poor widow (in various locations) is threatened with the loss of her property to a heartless banker, Jesse James lends her eight hundred dollars to meet the debt. While the banker is on his way home, Jesse holds him up and recovers the money. This floating anecdote is also assigned to Sam Bass, who ranks just below Jesse as an American Robin Hood.

Most likely the widow episode never occurred. It cannot be pinned down to any particular location or specific date. The story first appeared in print in 1897, fifteen years after the death of Jesse James, although it was undoubtedly current in oral tradition before then. The Hopkins *Journal,* published in Nodaway County, Missouri, reported that it occurred in "that part of the state." In 1899, Jesse James, Jr., told the story in his book, *Jesse James, My Father,* placing the incident in Tennessee. The historian must classify this appealing anecdote as folklore.

Tales of this type may involve restraint rather than positive action. Large classes of the population are exempt from the outlaw's exactions. Robin Hood never interferes with yeomen, with women, or with monks who are honest about the amount of money which they are carrying. Jesse James never robs preachers or ex-Confederates. In one story, he returns valuables to a preacher, explaining that "we never take from preachers, widows, or orphans." Sam Bass is buying clothes from an honest clerk when he glimpses a pile of money in the store safe. Instead of robbing the store, Sam warns the clerk to be more careful.

Such praiseworthy acts indicate that idealization of the outlaw's character is understood to be an integral part of the tradition. In the ballads it is always "jolly Robin"; and as one ballad says with unconscious irony: "So curteyse an outlawe as he was one / Was never none yfounde." The basic decency of the outlaws' character is proved by their religious orthodoxy. According to tradition, Robin Hood was notably pious, holding three Masses every day. Jesse James was a devout Baptist who taught in a church singing school. Both bandits robbed only the purse-proud clergy who exploited the commoners. Biographers tell us further that the James boys never looted, never touched whiskey, and were always "polite, deferential, and accommodating." Sam Bass's ballad proclaims of him: "A kinder-hearted fellow you seldom ever see." Billy the Kid was a laughing, likable boy, who would "give a friend the shirt off his back." Assignment of the Robin Hood tag to any American outlaw implies such an idealized character profile, and outlaws who lack these ideal traits are excluded from the tradition.

Once again it must be noted that these are traditional rather than personal attributes of the individual involved. The medieval world was one of bald stereotypes, and certainly Robin Hood has few identifiable personal characteristics. He is simply an abstraction of Good, while the Sheriff of Nottingham is an abstraction of Evil. Aside from a rough sense of humor and snatches of piety, the Robin Hood of the ballads reveals little that would be useful in a character sketch. But the American outlaws are similarly typecast, a process which seems to be inevitable when a particular outlaw becomes the symbolic champion of justice or any other favored cause. J. Delange noted that this development marked the difference between the outlaw traditions of Iceland and England: "In Iceland the main interest centered around the individual and his fate, and in England the outlaw represented to the people the champion of freedom or their jealously guarded liberties. In other words, he became a social type."

We are close enough to the historical sources to know that most of the popular lore about the American bandits is unhistorical. The belief that Jesse spared preachers clashes with the facts of the Hot Springs stage robbery, in which he took a minister's watch on the grounds that "Jesus Christ never carried one." The sentimental touch which has Jesse leading a church singing school melts before the family reports which tell us that he could not carry a tune. While the Sam Bass of folklore is a "kindhearted fellow," the Sam Bass of history was, according to contemporary reports, a "confirmed gambler, a horse racer, a guzzler of whiskey, a brawling desperado, a horse thief." The gap between history and folklore in the case of the American outlaws might lead us to look for identical phenomena in other outlaw traditions, even those like Robin Hood's, in which the historicity of the central figure is itself an issue.

This is especially true of another familiar aspect of folk glorification of the outlaw – the belief that he is never the aggressor, that he "shoots only in self-defense." According to the sixteenth-century English historian John Major, Robin Hood never killed unless he was attacked or resisted – a rather broad category. A noted biographer of the James brothers claimed that "they do not kill save in stubborn self-defense. They have nothing in common with a murderer." The "boys" themselves made the same claim in a letter to the Kansas City *Times* (October 15, 1872). Billy the Kid shot only to protect himself, and those he did kill "deserved what they got."

Such claims, at least for the American outlaws, do not stand the tests of historical analysis; they may be recognized as standard apparatus of the tradition. In robbing banks or trains Jesse James committed several cold-blooded murders, and he never asked his victims whether or not they were Yankees. The Winston train robbery (July 15, 1881) was especially brutal; the conductor and a passenger were killed without reason. On April 1, 1878, Billy the Kid and fellow gang members shot down the sheriff and deputy sheriff of Lincoln County from behind the cover of an adobe wall. In the face of such evidence, the folk belief in "self-defense" appears to be wishful thinking.

The bandit hero of the Robin Hood tradition outwits his opponents in a variety of trickster tales, many of which feature the disguise theme. Robin Hood appears in Nottingham so successfully disguised as a butcher that the Sheriff's wife invites him to stay for dinner. On other occasions he masquerades as a beggar, a woman, and a potter. Sam Bass liked to go into towns posing as a Texas Ranger and ask farmers for their opinions of his outlaw career. Jesse James assumed the dialect and manner of a country bumpkin and joined a posse which was searching for himself. He also liked to reverse the shoes of his horses to throw pursuers off the trail.

Most of these trickster tales are borrowed stock, coming from folk tradition rather than from history. Tales of disguise predate Robin Hood, although Americans know little or nothing of Hereward or Eustace the Monk. Posing as a potter was the classic disguise of all medieval outlaws. When three of these outlaws so disguise themselves, it seems safe to conclude that the device is being borrowed from tradition. The story of Jesse's disguise as a country bumpkin seems to have been invented, although it should be mentioned that in escaping from the Northfield bank robbery the boys did pose as law officers. The reversal of horse shoes goes back before Robin Hood to Eustace and Hereward, although Robin Hood himself does not use the trick.

The individual legends within the Robin Hood tradition are united also by the theme of betrayal. An informer or turncoat is as familiar in the *persona* of the outlaw narratives as are detectives and Merry Men. If a betrayer did not exist, folklore would invent him. Robin Hood dies through the treachery of his cousin, the prioress of Kirklees. Jesse James was betrayed by Robert Ford, a "dirty little coward" according to the ballad interpretation, and a "traitor of the worst order, a veritable snake in the grass," according to Jesse's biographers. Sam Bass was sold out by one Jim Murphy, and the ballad predicts: "Oh what a scorching Jim will get when Gabriel blows his horn." Billy the Kid is shot down by a onetime friend turned Judas, Pat Garrett. For the outlaw hero to die by any means other than treachery is unimaginable.

Objectively considered, none of the outlaws was "betrayed." Betrayal implies promises, but no promises were made to these bandits. Proposals of an amnesty for Jesse James were made, but neither Jesse nor the Missouri Legislature ever took them seriously. Governor Lew Wallace did make a deal with Billy the Kid, who was to surrender himself and stand trial for his crimes. But the Kid broke his arrest and thus prevented Wallace from carrying out his part of the bargain. He thereby became fair game for the agents of the law.

Theoretically the disposal of the bandit, whatever the method used, should be welcomed by society. But folk psychology has its own rules. Because society's law is frequently seen as venal or corrupt, the death of a popular outlaw symbolizes the defeat of all hopes for true justice, at least for the poor. And death by treachery rather than by "fair" means serves as the justification for further glorification of the hero. The parallels between Robin Hood and Jesse James in this respect indicate the continuity of this admiration for the man outside the law.

It appears then that in the Robin Hood tradition we are dealing with a basic folk narrative, that is, one largely divorced from history. Robin Hood and his American descendants are all actors in a classic drama, the major theme of which is man's struggle against corruption and injustice. However, the plot, the actors, and the general circumstances involved in these folk dramas do not resemble much that the historian is able to recognize. While historical circumstances of a certain kind, namely the existence of oppression and injustice, might seem to bring forth outlaw heroes, such situations must be examined with care. In the first place, the historical situations recede, and we then know the outlaw only through folkloric statements. In the second place, the existence of oppression may be the folk version rather than the historical truth. Thirdly, the outlaws of history seldom fulfill the functions which folklore assigns to them. They are not out for social justice, but for a fast buck.

Of course the American outlaw legends can all be tied more closely to history. Unlike Robin Hood, the actual existence of Jesse James or Billy the Kid is undoubtable; in newspapers and court records we can learn of the enormity of their crimes. The American outlaws are grimmer and more violent characters than the Robin Hood of the ballads. Robin's half-friendly bouts with friars and plowmen bear little resemblance to the inevitably fatal gun battles which mark the careers of American outlaws. As the New York *Illustrated Times* of April 22, 1882, said in its obituary of Jesse: "Claude Duval, Robin Hood, and Brennan-on-the-moor, were effeminate, sun-flowered aesthetes compared with the Jameses and their sworn confederates." Furthermore, the American bandits do not ultimately make peace with the law as did Robin Hood; they are all unrepentant sinners to the moment of death. And the supporting characters in the American outlaw narratives are actual persons, not symbolic figures drawn from popular plays or the May games.

But similarities in plot and character are enough to justify continued use of the classic reference. The outlaw hero, from Robin Hood to Sam Bass, is a thoroughly folkloric product. His concern for the poor, his exemplary character, his cleverness, his "betrayal" by a traitor are all aspects of legend rather than of history. The historical biographers aid in this folkloric process, perhaps unconsciously, by molding their heroes to fit the Robin Hood stereotype. Journalists also make significant contributions in the "Robinhooding" of American outlaws. But even without the assistance of biographers and journalists, the people will transform the facts of outlaw biography into legend. The similarities between Robin Hood and the American outlaws are clearly owing to the uniformity of folk belief across the centuries.

It is the perspective one gets in observing a primitive society and its culture that sends many dedicated students of man into anthropology, for the behavioral reactions and the culture processes are the same no matter what people are being watched. Whatever it is in our deepest minds that constructs barriers against unbearable reality prevents us from seeing ourselves as others see us. Jesse James and Sam Bass and even Billy the Kid are Americans at least, and therefore at least human. One can deceive oneself into seeing them in their own mold and agreeing that heroism is after all a matter of perspective. One can even make up jokes about them. There's the story about the effeminate passenger on a train about to be robbed by Jesse James. "I'm going to rape all the men and rob all the women!" announced Jesse. An eagerly apprehensive lady corrects him: "Don't you mean you are going to rob all the men and rape all the women?" The sweet young man turns on her sharply: "Oh, I say, do you *mind?* Who's robbing this train — you or Mister Jesse James?"

It's all very funny, and no one likes that dirty little coward who shot Jesse when Jesse wasn't expecting it. So we can empathize with Jesse and his mob.

But look at it another way. Read B. Traven's *Treasure of the Sierra Madre* again. Remember that chapter in which the bandits, disguised as *mestizos*, enter the train? How did you feel about the terror that swept ahead of them as they marched up the aisles, shooting the soldiers, trainmen, and passengers?

Remember the hysterical women, "moving about as if they had been blinded"? Did that scene burn itself into your mind, when some of the women "ran against the muzzles of the guns and held them against their breasts, begging to be shot"? "The killers served them all as they wished. Women were on their knees, some praying to the Holy Virgin, others simply shrieked and tore their hair and mutilated their faces with their fingernails. ... Not women alone, but also men were crying like little children. Without begging for mercy, they were not even attempting to hide themselves. They seemed to have lost all sense. Many of them made faint efforts to fight, with the hope of ending it sooner. Their nerves had given way. With their war cry: *'Viva nuestro rey Cristo!* Long live our king Jesus!' the bandits had started the slaughter. With the same cry the signal was given to begin plundering."

That is a Mexican train robbery. These men are heroes, Robin Hoods, James brothers.

Fear is the spur that keeps such creatures elevated in esteem, that causes the victims to identify with the monsters. Bruno Bettelheim, who kept his own sanity in a German death camp by observing as a psychiatrist the behavior of his fellow Jewish prisoners, noticed that after a critical period of time, the doomed Jews began one by one to imitate their guards, piecing together their rags to look like Nazi uniforms, ordering one another to hang themselves (which they who were so ordered did), beating one another. In Chicago more recently five nurses were murdered one by one. They might have lived had they fought, but in situations of stark terror, there is no power in the muscles or the mind beyond what is required to do all one can to please, please, please the man who is about to kill you. If you have time, make him into a hero, write songs about him, sing his praises as a benefactor of humankind.

The Texas Rangers go back in time to the establishment in 1826 by Stephen F. Austin of a border guard of twenty to thirty men. Nine years later, during the Texas revolution, the guard became the law enforcement agency to convince the Mexicans and Indians that they were dealing with a nation, and a tough nation.

In those earliest days their quarry, especially the Indians, were armed better than the Rangers. An Indian could let several arrows fly while one gun was being loaded. But an English sailor named Samuel Colt dreamed up a new design for a repeating pistol during the long voyage home to Boston from Calcutta. He patented the Colt six-shooter the year Texas secured its independence from Mexico.

It was a Texas Ranger who killed hero Sam Bass.

Outsiders frequently accused "The Hats" of straying beyond their range of constituted authority. Ranger Captain Frank A. Hamer was scrupulous about matters of legality, so when he made his offer to kill Bonnie and Clyde Parker, he had himself commissioned into the regular constabulary of the neighboring states where the outlaws intended to take sanctuary.

The Texas Ranger with the greatest range was the great song about this fearsome band of lawmen. John Lomax said it was "the first important ballad of the far West," and noted that it was a favorite of both sides in the Civil War. His son Alan collected the version printed in *The Folksongs of North America* from two girls in Hazard, Kentucky. Shoemaker discovered a variant in Pennsylvania. And on the farthest range of all, Professor Kenneth Goldstein found the Scots outback of Glasgow singing about the Texas Ranger.

THE TEXAS RANGER*

(From Mr. William Sunderland.)

Come, all you Texas rangers,
    Wherever you may be,
My name is nothing extra
    To you I will not tell.
I am a jolly ranger,
Although I wish you well.

Our captain he informed us,
    Perhaps he thought it right,
"Before you reach your station,
    My boys, we have to fight."

*From G. F. Will, "Four Cowboy Songs." JAF Volume 26, 1913, 185-188.

I saw the Indians coming,
   I heard them give the yell;
My heart it sank within me,
   My courage almost fell.

I saw the smoke ascending,
   It seemed to reach the sky;
My feelings at that moment were,
   "Now's my time to die."

We fought for nine long hours,
   Until the strife was o'er;
The sight of the dead and wounded
   I never saw before.

There was six as good rangers
   As ever travelled west
Lay buried with comrades,
   Peace be their rest!

Perhaps you have a kind old
     mother,
   Likewise a sister to like you,
Likewise a good old sweetheart
   To weep and mourn for you;

If this is your situation,
   Although you like to roam,
I'll advise you by experience
   You had better stay at home.

My old mother in tears
   To me did say,
"To you they are all strangers,
   With me you had better stay."

But I thought she was old and
     childish,
   The best she did not know;
My mind was bent on ranging,
   And with them I was bound to go.

THE INTERESTING THING ABOUT THE LEGEND of Paul Bunyan is not the man or his marvels, but the legend itself. How much of the primeval Trickster is there in Paul? So far as I know, no folklorist has suggested that his ultimate origin may be in that amorphous figure that moves between brilliance and stupidity, always with a superhuman power to do things, some of which are beneficial to ordinary human beings. It is not merely the incidents and the intellectuality that bring the aboriginal Trickster to mind in the Paul Bunyan stories so much as the indefinable something in his personality, his attitudes. But for one who is saturated in the Indian tales about Coyote, the resemblance is unmistakable — especially if one restores the obscene anecdotes about Paul.

And even more fascinating than this question is the process of denial and restoration that seems certain to go on for many years yet. In the selection of articles about Bunyan that follow, one should read not only for the information disclosed by the several scholars, but for their own emotional attitudes toward Paul and his legend. No one takes middle ground on Paul; one either destroys him or constructs him. One either searches the past for evidence that a real prototype existed, or one turns over boards and wet rocks hoping to find something, somewhere, in all this time overlooked by previous research, to establish the harder thesis that there was no traditional beginning for the gigantic lumberman.

Of the two wilful determinations, the one that wishes to believe seems least healthy. It is sobering to find in so many religiously faithless people a compulsion to believe in something less probable and less useful than God. The Abominable Snowman has more adherents among students of anthropology than the Holy Ghost. Authorities on the prehistory of Polynesia cannot really believe that once upon a time an archbishop in the British Isles actually counted back through the *begats* in Genesis and deduced that the world was created at nine in the morning of the twenty-third of October, 4004 B.C — yet they are quite content to date the arrival of the Maori Fleet by counting back genealogies, not written but unwritten, of precisely the same authenticity. The United States government has commissioned a team of astrophysicists, funded with more than half a million dollars, to study flying saucers — not people who believe in flying saucers but *flying saucers,* or to be perfectly fair about the commission, *Unidentified Flying Objects.* Several other teams of otherwise intelligent men are doing their human damndest to decipher what dolphins are trying to say to them.

What all these folk have in common with the religiously orthodox they hold in contempt is the determination to *believe.* Most of what is the subject of true belief, in Eric Hoffer's definition, is impalpable nonsense, but it is believed because it at least is something to believe in. The lost soul is not the believer in today's world; no, the really abandoned wretch is the man who is not committed to anything, not dedicated.

This is all by way of saying that the legend of Paul Bunyan has not been studied with the objectivity scientists and even folklorists impute to themselves. One cannot believe and be objective, for belief after all is the willing renunciation of reason.

PAUL BUNYAN IN 1910*

The Bunyan legends are unique in one respect. However old they may be as oral legends they are very late in written form. So far as we have been able to discover, writers first recorded Paul's activities only thirty-four years ago.

On June 24, 1910, in the Illustrated Supplementary Section of the Detroit *News Tribune* appeared an unsigned story called "The Round River Drive." Looking into the authorship of the tale, I was informed

* By W. W. Charters. JAF Volume 57, 1944, 188-189.

by Ford M. Pettit, Director of Reference Work on the staff of the Detroit *News*, that *The Deacon Seat Tales* in which the story appeared were written by James MacGillivray. Subsequent correspondence with Mr. MacGillivray at Oscoda, Michigan, confirmed Mr. Pettit's statement. Consequently, to Mr. MacGillivray belongs the distinction of being the first known writer to record any of the exploits of Paul and his hardy crew. However, the Bunyan stories appear in such out-of-the-way newspapers that later search may wrest this honor from him. Indeed, he and I would be glad to be referred to any printed tales that antedate his story.

The portion of the *News Tribune* item which told the story of "The Round River Drive" reads as follows:

She broke up early that spring. The river was runnin' high, and black from the color of the snow, of course, and all hands went on the drive. Bunyan was sure that we would hit either the "Sable" or Muskegon, and he cared not a dam which, fer logs was much the same allwheres.

We run that drive for four weeks makin' about a mile a day with the rear, when we struck a camp what had been a lumberin' big and had gone ahead with its drive, what must have been almost as large as Bunyan's from the signs on the banks. They'd been cuttin' on a hill forty too, which was peculiar, for we didn't know there could be two such places.

We drove along for another month and hits another hill forty, deserted like the last one, and Paul begins to swear, for he sees the price of logs fallin' with all this lumberin' on the one street.

Well, we sacked and bulled them logs for five weeks more, and blamed if we didn't strike another hill forty. Then Bunyan gets wild. "Boys," he says, "if we strike any more of them d—n camps, logs won't be worth 30 cents a thousand, and I won't be able to pay you off—perhaps some of you want to bunch her? Let's camp and talk it over," he says.

So we hits for the deserted shacks, and turnin' the pyramid corner, we was leadin' butts right into—our schoolma'am. And there at her feet was those two coons what had been blown up months ago, and at their feet was the hams! Then we knowed it was Round river, and we'd druv it three times.

Did we ever locate it again? Well, some!

Tom Mellin and I runs a line west, out of Graylin' some years afterwards when logs gets high, thinkin' to take them out with a dray-haul and we finds the old camp on section 37. But the stream had gone dry, and a fire had run through that country makin' an awful slashin' and those Round river logs was charcoal.

The next recorded tales did not appear until 1914. In that year two bits of Bunyanana have been located.

In the *American Lumberman*, Douglas Malloch conducted what would now be known as a column, entitled "The Lumberman Poet." On April 25, 1914, in this column, "The Round River Drive" appeared again. But on this occasion the story was told in verse. Since the verses were unsigned, it was assumed that they were written by Mr. Malloch.

But some Bunyan fans have attributed authorship to Eugene S. Shepard. Specifically, the Haney bibliography of Paul Bunyan cites a reference to the *Wisconsin State Journal* which gave byline credit for the verses to Mr. Shepard. Other scattered reprints attributed the authorship to Mr. Shepard and the *American Lumberman*. On the other hand, Charles E. Brown of the Wisconsin Folklore Society informs the writer that upon one occasion when the verses were read to an audience in which Mr. Malloch and Mr. Brown were present, Mr. Malloch told Mr. Brown that the verses were his. More recently in correspondence with Mr. MacGillivray the following paragraph appears in a letter dated May 26, 1942.

In our transposition of the prose story [which appeared in the *News Tribune*] to doggerel, Mr. Malloch made a rough draft of the verse while [we were] together in attendance at a Lakes States Forest Fire Convention at Lansing — I think in 1912. I have blue penciled [in the copy which he sent us] Mr. Malloch's part of the transposition. The other is mine. It was agreed between us that it would run in his *American Lumberman* as his.

It would thus appear that this best known of the Bunyan tales was the joint product of Mr. Malloch and Mr. MacGillivray, written in their spare time while attending a convention which may have had its boresome moments.

The second item to appear in the record as of 1914 is a booklet by W. B. Laughead entitled *Introducing Mr. Paul Bunyan of Westwood, California*. This was an advertising booklet issued by the Red River Lumber Company, of which Mr. Laughead was an officer. He is an ardent and veteran Bunyan fan. The booklet has become a permanent advertising medium for the company and has gone through many annual editions. Under date of June 5, 1941, Mr. Laughead writes: "We are mailing enclosed our first (1914) publication, a mailing card folder entitled 'Introducing Mr. Paul Bunyan.' We have been told that this is a collector's item."

These are the first three Bunyan items in print that have been unearthed to date. Since that time the records of Paul's exploits have been growing substantially. The first six sections of the serviceable Haney bibliography indicate a steady writer interest. A rough chronological analysis of the Haney items shows no entries prior to 1916 (although we have found three as indicated above). But in the subsequent years it appears that there are two items in the 1915-19 period; seven in 1920-24; nine in 1925-29; twenty-five in 1930-34; thirty in 1935-39; and nineteen from 1940 to the date of her article.

If any Bunyan collector can refer me to material published prior to the *News Tribune* story of June 24, 1910, I will be deeply appreciative.

PAUL BUNYAN IN 1910 (CONTINUED)*

Is the Paul Bunyan legend an old tradition in the American lumber camps which recent writers have collected and perhaps elaborated, or is it all essentially a literary concoction of the last thirty years stimulated by activities of the lumber companies? Though one can, of course, find old men who testify to hearing these tales in the woods fifty or sixty years ago, there is always the possibility and the suspicion that their memories play them false and that they have been influenced by reading or hearing the literary elaborations.

For any adequate judgment as to the condition of the legend at a particular time, some documentary evidence should be of considerable value. It is to furnish such evidence for the year 1910 that the present note is written.

At that time I was teaching in the Lincoln High School, Portland, Oregon, in close association with Edward O. Tabor, now a prominent attorney in Pittsburgh. It occurred to us that a good way to make a living during the lean summer months was to peddle the same horse doctor books with which Tabor had made a killing among Iowa farmers. But when we got to the part of eastern Oregon where we planned to work, we found enormous wheat fields and big woods, but few horses. This is how we came to be lumberjacks.

We spent the summer of 1910 working in the camp of the Palmer Lumber Company at Palmer Junction, Oregon, some fifty miles north of LaGrande. During all this time Tabor kept a careful diary, so that when we began to hear tales told, he made notes on them. Among other things we heard stories about Paul Bunyan told by a lumberjack named Duffy. Recently I asked Tabor whether he had read any of the books about Paul Bunyan, and it appeared that he had not, but had his entire impressions from the accounts heard thirty-five years ago. Fortunately, he has been able to find his old diary. For the rest, I let him speak through his diary and accompanying letter.

S.T.

From Edward O. Tabor's Notebook
Palmer Junction, Oregon, Summer, 1910:

Paul Bunyan digging Puget Sound—first logger in the West. His big blue ox—fed bales of hay—men could drown in its tracks—winter of the blue snow —windmills pump water 3 hours before breakfast for the crew—3 men to oil it—3 windmills run hot boxes twice a week.

Big camp—waiters on roller skates in the diningroom—potato peels carried out by cartloads and fed to the blue ox—prune seeds shoveled out of the kitchen window. A garden rake was the curry comb for the blue ox. You had to climb a Sycamore to get the hayseed out of his left ear. Paul's son and his 48″ cylinder

---

*By Stith Thompson and Edward O. Tabor. JAF Volume 69, 1946, 134-135.

threshing machine in Dakota and their eighty-five 3-horse teams to carry away the grain, looked like the tail end of the Ringling Brothers Circus — 3 men riding on horseback telling the farmers "next." Took two men to blow the whistle because there was so big a crowd for dinner.

Old man Bunyan is now running the Jerusalem Short Line hauling holy water from the Dead Sea to the River Jordan.

DEAR STITH:

The above sketchy notes are copied almost word for word from a Notebook which I have kept and which happens to have 3 pages given to our lumber camp experinces in Oregon in 1910. I wish I could remember the stories which I told your mother and your brother, Bill, about Paul Bunyan. At that time, we remembered the story distinctly and I can remember how your mother and brother enjoyed the tales fresh from the woods. The notes in my book recall some of the themes vividly, even now. I wish we had Duffy and Duffy's language and brogue to give the story the proper flavor. No university man could do that. Victrola recordings might. Duffy should be found, if he still lives, to preserve a body of great themes. . . .

I remember one theme not mentioned above, namely, that when Paul decided to either move camp or haul big timber (trees 300 feet long), he would hitch the blue ox's tugs, which were elastic, to the camp or timber and then would get Babe (the blue ox) to take three or four steps forward, each step being about 20 rods, and he would stand still, with his breast and yoke forward, his feet planted in the ground, and he would wait a second or two until the elasticity in the tugs pulled the camp or the timber up to him, and then he would repeat this performance until the camp was moved. Duffy had better language than I have. The Puget Sound theme was very dramatic as I remember it. Paul had cleaned up all the lumber in the Middle West and when he came to the Pacific coast he found the trees so big and the work to be done so large and the facilities so small, that he decided to dig Puget Sound in order to have room enough to float his logs. He hitched Babe to this giant scoop or shovel, and in a day or two, he dug out Puget Sound and had enough water for the logs and the mill.

Many of the lakes in Minnesota and in Washington were made by the hoof prints of Babe.

Our gang also made a great deal of the winter of the blue snow. I also seem to remember that he had Big Swede as a helper, but details slip me. . . .

Sincerely yours,

EDWARD O. TABOR

My memory agrees with this account except for one detail. I think I remember an opening of the story, "Back in the days before Old Man Puget dug the Sound."

S.T.

W. B. LAUGHEAD'S GREAT ADVERTISEMENT*

If an old-time lumberjack happened upon a present-day volume of Paul Bunyan tales, he'd find little to remind him of certain anecdotes

*By Max Gartenberg. JAF Volume 63, 1950, 444-449.

bandied about in the woods nearly a hundred years ago. From Paul's first appearance in print the stories began to take on those artificial details and embellishments which are a parcel of the literary art. Obscenity and too technical details were done away with; language was made more syntactical, and the conversational element, in most cases, was subdued. Almost at once casual places and characters received fixed names, and incidents and allusions of the most fragmentary character were expanded into plots pages long. What had formerly been occasional and changing in the hands of collectors became a more-or-less fixed and settled legend canon.

The oral legend of Paul Bunyan apparently originated in the Great Lakes States camps during the second half of the last century. It followed the migration of lumberjacks to the West Coast during the eighties and nineties, then rapidly disappeared, in both East and West, amid the hustle and bustle of booming cities. Cheap pulp literature, labor unions, domestication—later radio and the movies—all contributed to its demise. Of course, fortunately, a few old-timers remained, who were finding it harder and harder to assemble an audience as appreciative as the greenhorns of old; and from their time-gnarled memories were to be wrested the barest scraps of what had always probably been a loose-hanging cycle.

The first collection of such scraps—an unsigned story called "The Round River Drive"—appeared in the Illustrated Supplementary Section of the Detroit *News Tribune* for June 24, 1910. Written by James MacGillivray, "The Round River Drive" commences with preparations for that fabulous voyage and then drifts into a miscellaneous account of many still-famous adventures. In the course of his numerous digressions, the author relates the incidents of Bean Soup Lake, Paul's Griddle, the Buckskin Harness, Pyramid Forty, Double-Jawed Phalen, and others, before returning to his original narrative. This framework method already suggests other purely literary changes; but on the whole the work is composed in a natural, earthy prose which nicely approximates the speech of men in work gangs. Yet in spite of its great appeal—and though perhaps appreciated for the moment—"The Round River Drive" soon vanished from public notice with most other newspaper fiction. Nothing was again heard of Paul Bunyan until four years later, when an unknown poet of some talent set "The Round River Drive" to verse.

The verse redaction of "Drive" sticks close to the original prose, even to following the framework structure; but unlike the many doggeralizations of Bunyan tales which succeeded it, the stanzaed "Drive" actually sharpens its original's authentic flavor. Such lines as

> We put one hundred million feet
> On skids that winter. Hard to beat,

You say it was? It was some crew.
We took it off one forty, too.
A hundred million feet we skid—
That forty was a pyramid;
It runs up skyward to a peak—
To see the top would take a week.
The top of it, it seems to me,
Was far as twenty men could see.

show the work of a good metrician with a sharp if not subtle ear. The cadence of the poem is throughout iambic tetrameter, but it is evaded often and skillfully enough to prevent the whole from sliding into the dull regularity of many long four-measured poems.

"The Round River Drive" in verse first appeared in the *American Lumberman* magazine of April 25, 1914. Although its author is still unknown, many speculations have been woven about his identity. Earl Clifton Beck claims he was Douglas Malloch. Now the poem did appear in "The Lumberman Poet" column, of which Malloch was then the editor, but Malloch occasionally printed poems by other writers without acknowledgment. Moreover the "Drive" is so superior to the great mass of his verse as almost positively to exclude Malloch's authorship. Lake Shore Kearney, who reprinted it in his *Hodag and Other Tales of the Logging Camps*, attributes it to Eugene Shepard; and the version in the *Wisconsin State Journal* for February 24, 1929, gives Shepard and his wife, Karetta, as its joint authors. In 1937 it appeared for yet a fifth time in an anthology of *Poetry out of Wisconsin* as the work of William N. Allen.

Despite its merits, the verse "Drive" proliferated the Bunyan legend only slightly farther than its earlier prose counterpart. Subsequent Bunyan popularizers were to owe both a debt (though an unsuspected one) of considerable size; but in the meantime a more popular medium than a local newspaper or a lumber trade journal had to be secured. At a time when commercial publishers would not have given the tales of Paul Bunyan a second look, an imaginative lumberman dabbled with the idea of using them to advertise his wood.

How Archie D. Walker, then secretary of the Red River Lumber Company, first came to hear of Paul Bunyan is uncertain. The lumberman played no part in camp life; it is very probable that Walker had read "The Round River Drive" as it appeared in the *American Lumberman*, quickly recognizing its possibilities. The same year he employed his cousin, W. B. Laughead, a former lumberjack turned free-lance advertising man, to compose a handout pamphlet using the Bunyan material. This, the first of the now-celebrated Red River Lumber Company booklets, called *Introducing Mr. Paul Bunyan of Westwood, California,* came off the presses before the year was up.

W. B. Laughead, whose pamphlets have become the model for almost all of the later Bunyan collections, hailed from Xenia, Ohio, where he attended the public schools, quitting high school to work as a chore boy in the logging camps of northern Minnesota. Laughead remained there from 1900 until 1908; during those years he was assistant bull cook, timber cruiser, surveyor, and construction engineer, as well as chore boy. It was almost inevitable in the course of these jobs that he run into the Paul Bunyan stories. And many of these appear for the first time in his pamphlets, blended now and then with material from "The Round River Drive," one version of which he evidently knew.

The booklet was postcard size and contained about thirty unnumbered pages of Bunyan anecdotes and cartoons alternated with advertising, including photographs of lumber stocks and logging operations. This became the basic form for each of the pamphlets which followed. In various sections—the Introduction, for instance—some advertising was run into the stories. One tale, that of Big Joe cooking the beans on Mount Lassen, was suggested by the eruption of that volcano in June of 1914, and three photographs of the scene are somewhat irrelevantly included. The exigencies of advertising prevented Laughead from expanding the stories to any large extent. He forbore "jumping" pages when advertising intervened, and this led to a type of condensed narrative which permitted large amounts of material to be used.

The oral anecdotes of Paul Bunyan had probably identified none of the characters by name, except Paul himself. Although casual tags might be invented on the spot—as we use Joe Smith or Tom Jones today—secondary persons were as often singled out as "the other feller," "the cook," "the chore boy," or "the cruiser." The authors of the two "Round River Drives" follow both procedures. However unrelated the various stories were, the framework endued the whole with a kind of unity. But Laughead, sandwiching his tales between large chunks of advertising matter, could no longer weld them together in this way. It was Laughead who first hit upon the idea of giving the minor characters distinctive names, which are today inseparably associated with the legend itself. In so doing he created altogether new heroes of whose life each tale was another chapter. He describes his method:

To my best recollection the name "Babe" was invented as a funny name for such a big animal. About "Benny" for the little blue ox, I am not so sure, but I probably invented it. He is made up from scraps and it is possible I had heard him named.

Johnny Inkslinger was a natural. Camp clerks were called Ink Slingers, and to provide a character to save Paul's ink I added the "Johnny."

Names like "Shot Gunderson" and "Chris Crosshaul" were always floating around to make fun of the Scandinavians with, so I picked them up for a couple of foremen.

When lumbering was at its height in the Lake States many of the loggers came from Down East. It was fun to mimic the French-Canadians with story cliches like . . . "The two Joe Mufraws, one named Pete," and "The Habitant that wore out six pairs of shoepacs looking for a man to lick." That is the source of "Big Ole" and the bully who wanted to fight Paul Bunyan. For Ole there was also a recollection of a strong man who carried a heavy load, sinking knee-deep in solid rock. He could have had an origin in connection with Paul Bunyan. Some say it was Paul who sank into solid rock.

Sourdough Sam came from a reference to a cook whose sourdough barrel blew up and took off an arm and a leg. The Sourdough Lake incident was an elaboration inspired by a lake of that name in Minnesota. Sam's connection with the bees and mosquitoes was another adaptation. I had heard of double end mosquitoes in connection with Paul. Bringing bees overland on foot has been told of other frontier characters, but whether this preceded the Paul Bunyan myth or not I do not know.

These examples will indicate the process of my writing. The point is that they were derived from memories. At that time it was just another advertising job. It never occurred to me it was "Folk Lore" or anything that would interest a critic. I had made no research or attempt to document sources.

Intended solely to attract the notice of prospective buyers, the pamphlets were sent to sawmill men and lumber dealers, but in the stuffy halls of commerce such imaginative stuff could not long last. Largely because so many of these 1914 pamphlets were filed in wastebaskets that edition is today a collector's rarity.

Walker seems to have been the only lumberman to see the merit of these tales. In spite of this early discouragement, he had Laughead prepare a second edition, called *Tales about Paul Bunyan, Vol. II*, which appeared in 1916. The size of this booklet was now somewhat enlarged, and the cover wrought of sturdier paper. Without adding much new material, Laughead revised his text and improved his illustrations. Again the same patrons were wooed, and another rare edition was brought into being.

In 1922 — still not soured by defeat — Walker had Laughead draw up a much improved booklet. Now called *The Marvelous Exploits of Paul Bunyan*, its text and illustrations were printed on heavy slick paper, its pages numbered, and its cover illustration drawn in color. Despairing of the patronage of his fellow lumbermen, Walker decided to make the new pamphlet available to the public at large. Accordingly, free-lancer Laughead was appointed full-time advertising manager for the Red River Lumber Company; he drew up whole page advertisements describing the booklet, which were run repeatedly in the *Mississippi Valley Lumberman* and the *American Lumberman* magazines. Paul Bunyan's name was adopted by the company in its business dealings and letters. Subsequent to the enormous popularity of the material, Laughead's drawing of Paul Bunyan's head—with its moon face, double chins, and bristling catwhiskers—was copyrighted by the Red River Lumber as a trademark for its lumber and wood products.

Thus *The Marvelous Exploits of Paul Bunyan* appeared with considerable fanfare. Its popularity, however, exceeded all expectations. Within a few months after its publication the entire edition of ten thousand copies was exhausted, and a reprint of another five thousand copies could not satisfy the requests of children, teachers, folklorists, statesmen, librarians, soldiers, and sailors—persons of all interests and walks of life—which inundated the company's offices and are still perplexing its successors. "Jimmy Roosevelt wrote Archie Walker what a kick his father got out of the book. A commissar of Soviet Russia was interested in the propaganda angle and wanted a copy for translation." Only recently a woman wrote the Paul Bunyan Lumber Company, present owners of the Bunyan trademark, for a copy of the pamphlet, which she had received in Manchuria several years ago and was now worn out.

To meet the swelling demand a new edition was put out almost every year until 1944, when the final Thirtieth Anniversary Edition presaged the liquidation of Red River Lumber. In all, over one hundred thousand copies were given away. After the 1922 pamphlet few radical changes appeared. The title, *The Marvelous Exploits of Paul Bunyan,* was sometimes altered. The size of the booklet was latterly reduced, and Laughead, cognizant of the impression his work had made in the worlds of scholarship and letters, tampered with his introductions; but his texts and illustrations became fairly standard.

Even while the great advertisement continued to appear, newspapers from coast to coast printed regular columns of Paul Bunyan stories sent in by subscribers, and syndicates released boiler-plate tales of the now-famous lumberjack for use by country weeklies.

As early as 1916 appeared the first real critical examination of the legend by K. Bernice Stewart and Homer A. Watt, soon to be followed by others by Constance Rourke and Esther Shephard. From 1924 onward book collections began coming out, and even the reverend *Encyclopaedia Britannica* could no longer overlook Paul's humble but enormous stature, publishing a brief article on him in its 1929 edition. In due time poetry, plays, music—the medium of almost every art—explored the themes that had been made world-known by the great advertisement. And thus did a lumberman's advertising scheme become American folklore.

MORE LIGHT ON PAUL BUNYAN*

Paul Bunyan is one of our great folk heroes. He is probably as well known as any other folklore figure, and his stature and the tall tales about his mighty deeds have increased with the years. Staff members of the Forest Products History Foundation, as part of their research duties, have sought to gather the folklore of the forest products industry. One of the problems to which we have addressed ourselves has been the origin and development of the Paul Bunyan tales. Was Paul Bunyan a real folklore creation of the logging camps, or was he the creature of the imagination of writers? At the beginning of our search we had grave doubts about Paul's genuineness as a real folklore figure.

Although at least one investigator believes that the Bunyan stories may be about a century old, Paul's first appearance in print seems to have been on June 24, 1910. The Detroit *News Tribune* that day printed a story about "The Round River Drive." W. B. Laughead, who wrote the advertising matter for the Red River Lumber Company in which Paul was first widely publicized, stated that he heard the Bunyan tales around Bemidji, Minnesota, in 1900 and the next year in California, where they had been carried by Michigan loggers. The origin of the tales was unknown to Laughead. Edward O. Tabor in the summer of 1910 jotted down in his diary Bunyan stories told by a lumberjack named Duffy. A Minnesota investigator concluded that Paul was a spurious folklore creation, for none of the old lumberjacks in the Lake States to whom he had talked knew of Bunyan.

Paul Bunyan lore is still being created and not solely by writers. In the summer of 1947 the present writer visited Hermannsville, Michigan, searching for the records of old companies in the forest products industry. At the office of the Wisconsin Land and Lumber Company I asked if there were any old-timers whose memories might be tapped for recollections of former times. One employee had spent a lifetime in the industry, and when I asked him if he had ever heard any of the Bunyan yarns, he laughed and said: "I am Paul Bunyan." Noting my surprise, he explained that at that very moment he was engaged in writing labels with a Paul Bunyan twist for items to be exhibited in the company's logging museum at Blaney Park, Michigan.

One of the curious things about the Bunyan saga is that many old lumberjacks aver that they never heard Bunyan tales in the old-time camps and that the Bunyan stories are modern creations. Most of the old Minnesota lumberjacks whom we have interviewed belong in this

*By Rodney C. Loehr. JAF Volume 64, 1951, 405-407.

category. A few, however, say that they did hear the stories in the logging camps.

Since so many old lumberjacks felt that the Bunyan tales were not true folk creations, it seemed possible that Paul Bunyan might have been a writer's confection and might have made his way to the lumber camps by book, newspaper or word of mouth. It is not difficult to find lumberjacks who heard the Bunyan stories after they appeared in print. The problem has been to find lumberjacks who had heard Bunyan tales before their appearance in print, say before 1900. Another difficulty is that a considerable body of the Bunyan lore is unprintable for most mediums. Such lore may have existed long before printable stories were contrived.

We have found a few lumberjacks who say that they had heard Bunyan stories at a time that considerably antedates Paul's recognized appearance in print. Joseph Chartier of Merrill, Wisconsin, first started to work in the woods about 1871 and heard Bunyan tales around 1900. John Moberg, Lake George, Minnesota, heard his first Bunyan yarn in 1895. This story had to do with the logging of North Dakota during the winter of the "Blue Snow." Gabe Harmon of Missoula, Montana, listened to Bunyan tales in Virginia before he went to the West in 1901.

Our real find, however, was a man who thought that he had heard Bunyan stories from their creator. Wesley Straw, an old lumberjack of Darby, Montana, has worked all of his life in the woods. He was born in Potter County, Pennsylvania, in 1864 and started to work in the woods at the age of fourteen. For a time he was a lumberjack in the forests of Pennsylvania and West Virginia. Then, in 1903 he went to the Black Hills, where he built log chutes, and from there he moved to the Bitter Root Mountains in Montana. Straw says that he heard the Bunyan tales in Pennsylvania in 1880. These stories were told by a Bill James, a Pennsylvanian from the hard coal region who had struck out for the woods. James was a good storyteller and Straw thinks that he invented Paul Bunyan. All of the old loggers liked to listen to the stories which James had to tell about Bunyan, his partner Paul Sockalett, and the Blue Ox, which had only one eye located in the middle of its head.

In those days, Straw said, good storytellers and singers achieved a sort of local fame. Their presence at a camp was welcomed because of the entertainment they provided. Besides Bill James, he recalled Jack Grimes in West Virginia who had a favorite story about a constipated dog who through a mistake ate a piece of dynamite. Variants and switches on this theme were current in Army camps during the last war.

One old-timer says that "a lumberjack wasn't much, if he couldn't tell a few Paul Bunyan stories, and those stories could be heard anywhere where a bunch of lumberjacks was gathered." According to another old woodsman: "There was generally one or two good storytellers in a camp and any young fellow just starting sure got filled up on them. Some of the old-timers would put in a whole week thinking up a good one to spring on a kid on Sunday morning."

It seems likely that Paul Bunyan was a true folk creation and that his exploits were related in some camps long before he appeared in print. That Paul was not widely known before he achieved the printed page is not surprising. There were thousands of lumber camps scattered over the country. Some professional lumberjacks spent their lives in the camps and were highly mobile. Conceivably, they could have carried the Bunyan tales with them. Other woods workers were lumberjacks for a season or two and then turned to other vocations. Many camps were short-lived. The work in the woods was hard and the hours were long. Many lumberjacks were willing to go to bed after their supper was over. Only on Sunday did they have much free time. It is easy to see, then, why tales about Paul might not have been widely known. In addition, Paul had other heroes, real and imaginary, with whom to compete for the lumberjack's attention, and it was not until the writers elevated him that Paul Bunyan achieved his present high position.

Research into the Bunyan saga has to be pursued with caution. Lumberjacks have a keen sense of humor, which they are apt to exercise at the expense of the tenderfoot inquirer. They sometimes relate a series of Bunyan yarns to try the credulity of the listener and then confess that they never actually heard these stories in the camps. One may even have the experience of the young and earnest inquirer who walked up to an old jack and without preliminaries asked if he had ever heard of Paul Bunyan. The old lumberjack squinted for a moment, paused in his whittling, shifted his cud of chewing tobacco, and said: "Yes, I knew Paul and his wife. She had a double row of teats and used to give milk for our camp."

IX

Whippers and Witches
and Heavenly Helpers

FOLKLORE IS THE LAST REFUGE OF A RELIGION, and religion is the ultimate resting place of folklore. Since they both serve the same end, they both come to the same end. The principal purpose of religion is not, as some people imagine, the means of achieving freedom from fear of the unknown, or assuring life everlasting. If people really believed in the uncollectable insurance of their various mythologies, there would be more students enrolled in harp conservatories, as Mark Twain remarked. So far as the disclosures of historical anthropology serve our knowledge, the last cult on earth to believe wholly in the afterlife was the Druids, who would lend you money in this world to be repaid in the next.

This is not to ridicule religion any more than is fashionable. Religion would be much more respectable and respected if its

truth were told. Its function is to assure good behavior by sanc-
tifying the rules of a stable society, The trouble is that since
other parts of a culture are moving forward rapidly, moral stability becomes increasingly unreal when it is dependent on ancient rules. The earliest Decalogue was a list of prohibitions like
forbidding a cook to boil a kid in its mother's milk; the latest
Decalogue forbids the coveting of a neighbor's goods. Business
enterprise could live with the former, but if the latter Command-
ment were enforced, it would mean the end of civilization as anybody knows it. But what can a society do but uphold the old
rules when there are no new precepts? It is ironic and more than
a little sad to find the least respect for a religion and least belief
in it among people who of all members of their society are least
self-reliant, and therefore more dependent on the stabilizing
force that only religion has been able to offer.

On a less sublime level, it is the same for folklore. Folklore is
the detritus of an advancing culture, as superstition is any religious belief no longer held by the majority of a society. So both
tend to sift to the bottom and to the margins of a society, where
they are preserved — often with astounding ferocity — by people
who share least in the affluence of their culture. The faith of such
people passes understanding. It would move mountains, if mountains could be moved by faith. Yet all that faith and ferocity accomplish is to keep the irretrievably dead past standing unburied
to be ridiculed by people committed to the future.

In 1837 Captain Frederick Marryat, one of the most accomplished and sophisticated Englishmen of his day, came to America to see for himself whether the young nation was quite as bad
as his countrymen had assured him it was. Generally he found
the people to his liking, but every once in a while he would see
something that made him wonder not only about the United
States, but mankind as well. Like the time he looked in on a
nativistic cult in New York State.

I went out to see the shakers at Niskayuna. So much has already been
said about their tenets that I shall not repeat them, farther than to observe that all their goods are in common, and that, although the sexes
mix together, they *profess* the vows of celibacy and chastity. . . .

They commenced their dancing, by advancing in rows, just about as
far as profane people do in L'été when they dance quadrilles, and then
retreated the same distance, all keeping regular time, and turning back

to back after every third advance. The movement was rather quick, and they danced to their own singing, of the following beautiful composition:

> *Law, law, de lawdel law,*
> *Law, law de law,*
> *Law, law, de lawdel law,*
> *Lawdel, lawdel, law*

Keeping time also with the hands as well as feet, the former raised up to the chest, and hanging down like the forepaws of a dancing bear. After a quarter of an hour they sat down again, and the women made use of their large towel pocket-handkerchiefs to wipe off the perspiration. Another hymn was sung, and then the same person addressed the spectators, requesting them not to laugh and inquiring if any of them felt a wish to be saved — adding, "Not one of you, I don't think." He looked round at all of us with the most ineffable contempt, and then sat down, and they sang another hymn, the burden of which was, "Our souls are saved, and we are free, from vice and all iniquity," which was a very comfortable delusion, at all events.

In 1925, as everybody knows, a young biology teacher in Dayton, Tennessee, had himself arrested to determine whether his state really believed its absurd anti-evolution law. A permissive judge allowed several famous but irrelevant witnesses to debate the Bible. During the preparations for the sideshow, H. L. Mencken, then a reporter for the *Baltimore Sun*, ventured into the mountains near the town to see a Holy Roller revival. His remarks are less respectful of the religious ceremony than were Marryat's, and even funnier:

… an Episcopalian down here in the Coca Cola belt is regarded as an atheist. … Even a Methodist, by Rhea County standards, is one a bit debauched by pride of intellect. It is the four Methodists on the jury who are expected to hold out for giving Scopes Christian burial after he is hanged.

… once one steps off the state roads the howl of holiness is heard in the woods, and the yokels carry on an almost continuous orgy. …

I describe the thing as a strict behaviorist. The lady's [an enormous mountain woman whom Mencken in a previous passage likened to a female aurochs] subjective sensations I leave to infidel pathologists. Whatever they were they were obviously contagious, for soon another damsel joined her, and then another and then a fourth. The last one had an extraordinarily bad attack. She began with mild enough jerks of the head, but in a moment she was bounding all over the place, exactly like a chicken with its head cut off. Every time her head came up a stream of yells and barking would issue out of it. Once she collided with a dark, undersized brother, hitherto silent and stolid. Contact with her set him off as if he had been kicked by a mule. He leaped into the air, threw back his head, and began to gargle as if with a mouthful of BB shot. Then he loosed one tremendous stentorian sentence in the tongues and collapsed.

One does not detect sufficient difference in the narratives of the two writers to argue forcibly that there has been a significant advance in the religious sophistication of American folk society in the intervening century. On the contrary, there is some evidence that the two cultures, folk and sophisticated, are drifting further apart. Not long ago several literate clergymen in the heart of Kentucky's hill country discovered in the sixteenth chapter of Mark, verse 18, a prophecy that "they" shall take up serpents, heal the sick by laying on of hands, and perform other wonders. That was the beginning of the serpent cults in this area, and already several fiercely divisive issues have sprung up among them; all, it seems, are fighting for the same ecological niche, and the biological Law of Competitive Exclusion is being borne out in that the competition is more bitter among these denominations than between them and more orthodox sects like the Baptists. The East Pineville Church of Christ should win, if we apply the information deduced by anthropological studies of similar situations, since its pastor has herded all his group's psychic energy into the contention, by prohibiting all dancing, smoking, drinking, immodest dress, and sinning.

Down in Dayton, Tennessee, meanwhile, enlightenment has come at last. Where once William Jennings Bryan argued for a literal interpretation of the Bible and died, so the folklore goes, of a broken heart when Darrow exposed him for a fool (Darrow denies that cause of death; "Hell," he said, "he died of a busted gut") — where Bryan immolated himself in the cause of ignorance, there is a university: the William Jennings Bryan University.

The old gods are not dead. They linger on at the edge of the clearing, peering around the barn at night, hoping some love of the old ways will turn apostasy away; some act of sincere penitence, perhaps, will restore honor to their ancient servitors, and bring themselves once again to receive the homage and worship of mankind.

St. Anthony of Padua appears in religious art holding the Christ Child. This is so because a miracle was granted to him in a vision, when the Christ Child, evidently ignoring the laws of anachronisms, actually came to earth and rested in his arms. This happened, Anthony's hagiographers tell us, because he was a gentle saint.

He was born in the year of our Lord 1195. In 1210, when he was fifteen years old, he was received into the Augustinian order. Five years later he left this fraternity to join the Franciscans, for whom he undertook long and very successful journeys as a preacher.

There was at that time the beginning of a movement toward liberalism in Church affairs. One of its leaders was Elias, the head of the Order of St. Francis. Anthony opposed both the philosophy and his superior, an insubordination that ordinarily would not have been tolerated; but Anthony was beyond rebuke or suppression as the greatest preacher of his day. He began to preach for the past, for a return to the strenuous Christianity of a better time. Led by his exhortations, fraternities of penitential enthusiasts formed in the wake of his visitations. These people found the way to go back to a holier age by marching, singing, and scourging themselves with whips. Blood was the substance to wash away the sins of the world.

St. Anthony himself died in 1231, and in the following year he was canonized. His followers grew; twenty-five years after his death they had swarmed over northern Italy and beyond — down to Rome, up through the Rhine Valley. Church authorities were at first tolerant of the marchers; severe penance for sinners seemed like a good idea, especially when the trouble of administering it was assumed by the flagellants themselves. But civil authorities had a different, more immediate view of the matter, for their constituents were not unanimously pleased to have hordes of poor people parading through their town, begging and otherwise requiring food, making a nuisance of themselves, camping in the town square or nearby fields. How dangerously unstable a situation all this led to can be seen by its reconstruction in the Swedish motion picture, *The Seventh Seal.*

Permissiveness toward any kind of demonstration, even demonstrations advocating pure virtue, encourages probing of other limits of tolerance, and before long the Church noticed in the flagellants a willingness to question the authority of Rome. The Church has never in its history been enthusiastic about enthusiasts, and when enthusiasm deteriorated into rebelliousness, both were put down vigorously.

But when the Black Plague struck in the middle of the fourteenth century, the troubles of the world (there were severe earthquakes, too) were taken to be a promise of the unleashing of the full wrath of God, a wrath that had to be turned aside by propitiation. Obviously, God was not satisfied by the way the world was being run. By now the reader will realize as the churchmen did, that the flagellant cults were a nativistic endeavor, a despair cult like the Ghost Dance. It had its prophets (shamans in defiance against the authority of the Church), its apostles, its communicants, and even its tangible message from God. An angel had been to earth to see the prophet and had given him a letter ordering those who would be saved to signify their chosen status by marching and whipping themselves. So the flagellant cults sprang up again, even more vigorously for the repression. A delegation crossed *sur le pont d'Avignon* and presented themselves and their grievances to the Pope. But Clement VI was no bleeding-heart liberal, and he wasn't having any of that, thank you. He declared all flagellant cults heretical, and to show what he meant by that exactly, he had a few of the brethren ignited at the stake. Ideas can be killed by bullets and bombs and burning, but not by tokenism, by hitting selected targets and instituting a holding pattern for the rest. Condemning a few bemedaled fellows at Nuremberg did not convince millions of Germans that their Nazism was immoral or even inexpedient, as some people deceive themselves into believing. The Church found this out after a while, and there were more burnings and nearly universal suppression, until the movement died.

Died, that is, in the general population. But among the folk, who retain, as we have seen, old ideas, the flagellants disappeared underground—an easy thing to do in an age when laws are not enforced. The disease had been cured in the large body of the population, but there was infection latent in the men who came with the Conquistadores to the New World, and there, in the absence of its natural enemies, the mania of flagellation spread like the rabbit in Australia. The Third Order of St. Francis established his roots in what was to be the American Southwest and infected even responsible people with its ideas about penance. The *Historia de la Nueva Mejico* of Gaspar de Villagra, published in 1610, describes how the *conquistador* Oñate and his soldiers observed Holy Week by stripping themselves to the waist and whipping themselves "until streams of red blood flowed" down their backs.

Some people would believe that the Penitentes of the Southwest derived from the Aztec blood rituals. No doubt the bloody sacrifices that were both a popular entertainment and a propitiation of the fierce Aztec deities made reception of the ritual of St. Francis easier on these shores, but the movement of the penitential brothers here is almost wholly an importation of the nativistic endeavor begun by the prophetic St. Francis. The marching, the singing, the attire and lack of it, the whipping, the crucifixion of a man representing Christ—all are the same. The only notable change is that some New Mexican flagellants use whips of cholla cactus instead of scourges with bits of glass embedded in the thongs.

Psychologists unacquainted with the universality of certain religious ideas and their motivation have tried to account for this mania by supposing that somehow masochists concentrated in limited areas of the Southwest. They are wrong. The flagellants are fairly normal people, but they are members of a folk society where belief and commitment are more powerful than reason and individuality. Masochists, like geniuses, are a biological constant. If more of either appear in any place at any time, there are cultural reasons for their incidence.

In the case of the Penitentes, the operative factor is that the universal urge in man to expend psychic energy has been limited in expression. In folk societies religion is often the only means of expression, and so any extreme religious concept can become an obsession. Happiness, the psychologists ought to know, is being possessed by an obsession. If other outlets for psychic energy are denied, absent, or suppressed, a religious expression can become far stronger than the urge to protect one's body or life. Martyrs are people whose obsession is satisfied by an ecstatic culmination. The flagellants do not often go to the extreme of immolation, but get sufficiently close to drain off the psychic tension until the next festival of whipping. Flagellation can be as satisfying as sex or war — and it is no coincidence that women present at public flagellation show themselves very eager to get the blood of the brethren on their dresses.

CACTUS WHIPS
AND
WOODEN CROSSES*

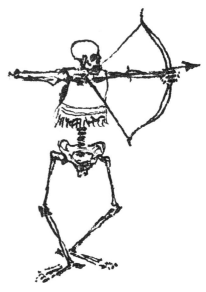

When Holy Week occurs this year in the isolated mountain valleys of northeastern New Mexico, cactus whips will scourge bleeding backs, and men with cracking sinews will sag beneath the weight of the heavy wooden crosses they drag upon their shoulders. During this Easter season, like other Easter seasons for some three hundred years, the blood of the flagellant Penitente Brotherhood will redden the New Mexico sand, involuntary moans will pierce the usually quiet nights, and beautiful *señoritas* will shiver with a strange pleasure when drops of blood fleck their Sunday dresses during the "earthquake" ceremony.

Centuries ago hardy Spanish colonists settled the rich but tiny and isolated valleys north of Santa Fe, New Mexico, pushing up the Rio Grande Valley into what they called the *rio arriba* ("up-river") where that river cuts through the *Sangre de Cristo* ("Blood of Christ") Mountains. There, for decades, New Spain existed on the fringes of civilization; then Spain fell upon evil times, and this frontier was left to shift largely for itself, economically, politically, and religiously. For the capitol at Santa Fe, contact with the outside world was sporadic at best; for the isolated mountain villages, cross-cultural contact was virtually nonexistent. Thus life in the mountain hideaways went on, generation after generation, much as it had in the beginning. Threshing with animals, belief in *brujos* and *brujas* ("witches"), fear of the *mal ojo* ("evil eye"), and brutal chastisement of the body in penance for the sins it had committed all continued more or less unchanged.

Punishment of the body as a means to grace is an old idea in the his-

*By Juan Hernandez. JAF Volume 76, 1963, 216-224.

tory of religion. The ancient Egyptians sometimes flogged themselves in honor of Isis; Spartans were whipped before the altar of Artemis Orthia; Roman women suffered ritual scourging during the Lupercalia. Toward the end of the eleventh century Cardinal Damian advocated self-flagellation as a penance and acquired a sizable following. St. Anthony of Padua, in the thirteenth century, founded the first Christian fraternity for regular and public self-whipping as a religious ceremony. The movement spread from Italy through Austria, Hungary, Bavaria, Poland, and Germany. As late as the sixteenth century, despite objections of the Church, in France and Spain rich and poor walked with leather whips through the streets, whipping themselves until they drew blood from their tortured bodies, singing at the same time penitential hymns and entreating the mercy of God. Penitent processions in Mexico and in the Philippine Islands continued into the nineteenth century, and various other forms of self-inflicted penitential physical suffering are to be found today in Mexico and Central America.

About four hundred years ago there was founded in Spain the lay order of Los Hermanos Penitentes ("The Penitent Brothers"). It was not a flagellant society, but a fraternity of men of good morals who met for religious study. This order was brought to Mexico by the Franciscan friars and officially called by them the Lay Third Order of the Franciscans. From Mexico it was brought to what is now New Mexico and southern Colorado by these friars and by some of the followers of the later *conquistadores* who had previously been members. At some time during this century the mild form of Los Hermanos Penitentes changed, and it is recorded that Juan de Oñate and his men flagellated themselves in penance in 1594. Thus flagellation was part of the sixteenth century way of life brought to New Mexico, just as were community religious "miracle" plays, and neither has completely disappeared.

To understand such cultural survivals in the middle of the twentieth century, one must understand the land, its people, and their history. The *rio arriba*, the present stronghold of the Penitentes, extends on the east from Raton south through the Mora and Las Vegas area, across through the Santa Fe region, up on the west through Cuba and Dulce (bounded by the Jicarilla Apache Reservation), and on north across into the area of southern Colorado around the counties of Archuleta, Conejo, Costilla, Las Amimas, Alamosa, and Saguache. Penitente influence also is to be found in part of the *rio bajo* ("down river") country south of Santa Fe, as far down as Guadalupe, Torrance, and Bernalillo counties. It is interesting to note that in seven of the thirty-one counties in New Mexico, Spanish-speaking people make up 80 per cent or more of the population.

Much of this area, especially the *rio arriba*, is high mountain country, fragmented into tiny valleys through which flow snow-fed streams.

This water is diverted by hand dug *acequias* ("irrigation ditches") or by flumes hand-hollowed from huge pine logs. The tiny farms are self-sufficient. Houses are made of *adobe*, the clay being sun-dried on the spot and used as material for building houses, churches, barns, stores, and walls. Except for the valleys, the land is upland, semi-arid plain, or sparse juniper and pine forest, useful only for grazing.

The early colonists were mostly males, who married women of the indigenous Pueblo Indian population. The resulting generations spoke Spanish, called themselves Spanish, but developed a culture which took on a flavor all its own. It was a simple folk culture, depending marginally on the written word and possessing many illiterate older adults. Much transmission of folk knowledge is by word of mouth, handed down from generation to generation. Here sixteenth-century Spanish dances are both known and danced on Saturday nights; sixteenth-century-style ballads are still sung; here corrupted forms of miracle plays and pageants are a matter of village heritage, some of them recognizable variations of those in use in sixteenth-century Spain. Some plays and ballads are nonreligious, however, describing the exploits of folk heroes whose Robin-Hood-like good deeds are exceeded only by their success with the not-so-languishing *señoritas*. Here, in villages accessible only by wagon or Jeep, "miracles" still occur, and the existence of witches is either accepted or is a matter for serious disputation. In recent years there has been court testimony about men turning into toads, being killed unwittingly, and then turning back, in death, to their human form. There is no well-developed werewolf belief, but the notion is accepted that a *brujo* of more than average talent can change his shape.

Here infants and young children still suffer from *mal ojo*, cast upon the child purposely by *brujas* who wish to do them harm, or by completely innocent persons who praised or coveted the infants too much. Fortunately, *mal ojo* may be cured either by an *arbolarro*, good *bruja*, or *currandera*, all of whom possess powers to cure ills of both natural and supernatural origin. Here, if a young man plays fast and loose with a girl, she or her mother may pay a *bruja* to put him under a spell; a variety of evil things may befall him, until he recognizes the source of his *mal suerte* ("bad luck") and uses the same methods to have the spell removed, or else marries the girl. Folk medical lore here also warns against *mal aire*—vaguely conceived evil forces which inhabit the air and in some unknown way enter a person and bring on or accentuate illness. Although they never heard the word "psychosomatic," these people fully believe that emotion—fright, rage, sorrow, desire, and so on—bring on actual illness. A *susto* ("serious fright") is believed to cause a temporary "soul loss," which in turn may cause illness for which medicine is of little use. It is common that "hot" illnesses are treated by "cold" remedies and "cold" illnesses by "hot" remedies, but what is "hot" and "cold" varies from village to village. It seems interesting that there is no hint of the supernatural about venereal diseases, their cause or cure, and these people are far too realistic to believe such ills are "caught from a toilet." Despite a full awareness of the germ aspect of disease, the natives still may place ultimate blame for the appearance of the germs upon supernatural or social factors, thus applying bacterial and magical theories to the same disease.

This is the land and the culture in which the flagellant brotherhood of Penitentes grew to strength. Priests and friars were never numerous; no bishop visited the area for one hundred years after 1760 and the remaining Franciscan friars were expelled in 1828 by the Mexican revolutionary government. Thus two hundred years ago the isolated villages began to depend upon themselves and their Penitentes for many religious rites. Control passed quickly from church officials to local *hermanos mayores*, and rites took strange forms unauthorized by the original rules of the order; more and more it became a primitive worship of pain and death. A hundred years later, when priests again arrived, the local brotherhoods did not care to relinquish their power, and in the "cold war" which followed, the priests were able to drive the order only somewhat underground. Open ceremonies became secret rites, and the order became a secret one; yet this was a peculiar form of secrecy, for at one time more native Spanish-American adult males were Penitentes than were not. The Anglos who entered the territory in increasing numbers ridiculed these practices with the result that rites were more often held at night, far back in the mountains, and intruders were threatened. Rumors are still current of persons who "disappeared" because of interference with Penitente rites. Hence this flagellant brotherhood is known only locally. Encyclopedias make either no mention of it or, at best, a brief statement; one major encyclopedia, for example, in devoting one sentence to the group makes two errors of fact: that members were converted Indians, and that the order died out before 1900! This lack of knowledge is less surprising when one learns that a generation or two ago a member who seriously violated secrecy reputedly was punished by being buried alive! Until recent years *compañeros* at flagellant processions carried rifles. Now they throw rocks through the car windshields of onlookers.

The center of Penitente activities is the *morada*, the special meeting place of the brotherhood. Each village normally has one *morada;* some have several. In one valley where the author once lived, there were two small villages, each of which had two *moradas*. The *morada* is generally unprepossessing; it varies in size with the financial condition and numbers of the local unit and varies in location with the desire for secrecy of the group. Usually it is of *adobe*, with one large room which serves as a chapel and one or two small rooms in the rear in which secret sessions are held, and where the whips, chains, and other paraphernalia are stored. There are one or two small, high windows for the chapel, none for the secret rooms. In the chapel, which nonmembers may enter for certain semipublic acts of devotion, there are benches and an altar with a few *santos* ("saints"). Sometimes there is a carved wooden figure representing death. It may be an unclothed skeleton or a skeleton clothed in a woman's black dress; in either case it may or may not be seated in a two-wheeled cart, *la carreta de la muerte*. The skeleton holds a drawn bow with an arrow, signifying the imminence of death. Folklore contains stories of more than one scoffer to whose heart the arrow unaccountably sped. It is this preoccupation with death which has caused the brotherhood to be called a cult of death. Outside the *morada* stands a large wooden cross, and others are stacked behind the building—gruesome reminders of past and future crucifixions.

The ritual for the initiation of neophytes, usually in their middle or late teens, varies with local units. The prospective *hermano* ("brother") is brought to the door of the *morada*; he asks ritual religious questions and receives ritual answers from the assembled brothers. Examples are, "Who gives us light?" "Jesus." "Who fills the house with joy?" "Mary." "Who keeps the faith?" "Joseph." He takes an oath of allegiance, loyalty, and secrecy, and various secrets of the society are revealed to him. Then the new member asks the forgiveness of God and the assembled brethren for his sins, performs acts of humiliation and penance, may wash the feet of the members, and is given the first blood penance, three to nine ritual incisions in the back in the form of a cross administered by the *Sangrador* ("Bloodletter"). The member then may ask for various ritual penances by lashing: five lashes for the five wounds of Christ, seven lashes for the seven last words of Christ, and forty lashes for the forty days in the wilderness. So vicious are the lashes that few initiates remain conscious throughout the full course. After the lashing is over (and henceforth the brother normally is lashed only by himself), he is cared for by one of the officers of the order, the *Enfermero*. Reportedly, the ritual cuts cause the blood to flow more freely and thus prevent complications which might otherwise arise; supposedly, the penitential nature of the wounds prevents infection.

Women are not admitted to the brotherhood, but do walk as "followers" behind the processions in some villages. There are reports that an occasional woman will engage in some form of "active" penance, although not whipping. The author was told of a woman who had "sinned" with a number of men and, to do penance for these sins had walked barefoot on cactus. As related to him, she was unable to walk well the rest of the short time she lived, but she had died before the author moved into her village. Women do sometimes sing *alabados* ("chants") and the wives of the officers prepare food during Holy Week.

The highlight of the Penitente year is Holy Week, when they enact much of the Passion of Christ. Already on each Friday in Lent they have recited the Stations of the Cross in some church or *morada*, which may be witnessed by anyone. At night, ceremonies take place secretly within the *morada*, then about midnight a procession moves from the *morada* to the church or chapel and back again, usually with a few brothers flagellating themselves in a relatively mild manner. During these and other ceremonies the brothers sing ancient *alabados* to the music of the homemade *pito* ("reed flute") and sometimes the *metraca* (a hand-carved noisemaker of the ratchet type similar to those used by groups to celebrate the New Year).

Throughout the holy period the *morada* is the center and source of all activities. Members often do not return to their homes during this period, preferring to sleep and to take their food in the *morada*. The meals are prepared in the homes of the officers of the local society, each man having contributed according to his means: a sheep, corn, beans, flour, vegetables, or other foodstuffs. Beer and liquor, usually so popular, temporarily are eschewed.

The Holy Week ceremonies begin on Wednesday or Thursday, with religious meetings during the day and a procession with the *carretta de la muerte*. This cart of death is drawn by a man or men by their necks or other parts of their bodies so as to make this penitential task extremely difficult. Sometimes a man pulls the cart by what seems a good, broad leather belt around his chest — but there is cactus under the belt! Tradition says that during this procession the effigy of death may loose her arrow at the unbelieving scoffer. The *carretas* seen by the author ranged from two to three feet in height and from two to four feet in length, all with solid wooden wheels. At this and other processions the hand-carved *santos* of the local area are often carried. In this particular religious procession, the priest is conspicuous by his absence. The *Cristo* ("Christ") has been chosen, by lot or election, within the *morada*. No extreme honor is attached to enacting *Cristo*, but the person is usually below middle age, a devout Penitente, and is not chosen twice.

Within one or two hundred yards of the *morada* there is a hill known as *Calvario* ("Calvary"). Late Holy Thursday night a formal procession of true flagellation occurs. At the head of the procession usually comes a statue of Christ, or some *santos*. Next comes the chosen *Cristo* dragging his cross on his right shoulder. He is aided by an *acompañador* ("accompanying brother") who represents Simon of Cyrene. Often others, representing the two thieves, also carry crosses, but the number depends on the size of the local lodge. All the members are present, the *pitero* playing his flute, and the *rezador* praying or reading from his handwritten copybook. All chant *alabados,* more or less in unison, which urge penance and plead for salvation and mercy. Those actually engaged in flagellation march in the center of the procession, surrounded by *acompañadores* or *compañeros* who carry lanterns, help those who fall, lend both moral and physical support to the ceremony, and throw rocks at nonmembers who have failed to remain at a respectful distance. In general the officers of a local chapter are called the "Brothers of Light." This is usually translated *Hermanos de la Luz,* which term is sometimes used when speaking of the whole cult. The Brothers of Light usually are those who have flagellated themselves in earlier years. The common members are called Brothers of Darkness, possibly because during flagellation they are supposed to wear hoods. When one ceases his flagellation and in the next procession acts as an *acompañador,* he is said to have "returned to light." These references to "light" and "darkness," so reminiscent of the ancient influence of Zoroastrianism on Judaism, have long since lost any such esoteric meaning for the Penitentes.

Those actually engaged in flagellation who wear black hoods over their heads do so partly to keep their identity secret, partly to prevent pride. Their backs are bare, they may wear a crown of thorns, and their trousers may be the traditional white *pantalones* of the *peon;* their feet are bare. The whips used are of various types; often they are of the type of yucca cactus locally called *amole* or Spanish dagger. These whips are about three feet long, four inches wide, and an inch thick, with the fibers pounded out to resemble a frayed rope—if one can imagine a rope with ravelings which cut like sandpaper with each slanting blow. Other whips have leather thongs and leather or wooden handles. Rarely are the leather thongs plain; at the least they contain knots, at the worst they hold bits of glass, lead balls, or the barbs taken from barbed wire. When the Penitentes chant of "giving their blood," this is no idly symbolic term.

Usually one or more of the Penitentes, instead of scourging himself, will walk in the processions with cactus bound tightly to his bare back and chest, dragging heavy chains from raw ankles. Various thorns and cactus can be used, for the stark, brutal flora of the area offer adequate variety for anyone's satisfaction. Those Penitentes actively flagellating themselves usually take a few steps, swing the *diciplina* ("whip") over one shoulder, take a few more steps, and swing it over the other shoulder, pausing with each blow. Before a hundred yards is passed, the whip has little fresh skin to touch, blood spatters at every stroke, and may so stain the trousers that the legs, too, appear to bleed. It is no wonder a Penitente flagellant march sometimes is called the "Procession of

Blood." In older days unbleached trousers were worn; today they are likely to be faded blue jeans. Often a white handkerchief is tied around the forehead of all the members as a sort of recognition sign. The wounds, although exceedingly painful, are not deep and the muscle structure is not damaged. After a few months, remarkably little scarring remains. Although cactus may be stuck to any portion of the body, flagellation is confined solely to the back and shoulders.

During the night a *velorio* ("vigil") usually is kept by nonmembers of the society at the local church. This *velorio* is visited sometime during the night by a procession from the *morada*. *Alabados* are sung by the persons keeping the vigil. These *alabados*, like many of the rituals, are in a Spanish pronunciation no longer in normal use, with many ancient words and forms of speech preserved nowhere else. Typically one or two good singers carry the solo parts with the rest of the men singing the chorus. Women do not participate fully in the singing of *alabados*, and in general they are sung chiefly by members of the brotherhood.

On Good Friday further ceremonies and processions occur. As in the previous processions, the line of march varies from village to village, but sooner or later processions, complete with banners, *santos*, flagellation, and men dragging crosses, will visit the cemetery and the chapel or church and then return to the *morada*. The chief Good Friday procession, usually in the afternoon, is the march to Calvary. Before this final act of penance is undertaken, a rather lengthy service is held in the *morada* chapel, with chants, prayers, and hymns. After night has fallen comes the final and most barbaric of all the processions. This is the enactment of the crucifixion, with the thorn-crowned *Cristo* again staggering under his cross to *Calvario* and with brutal scourging of already lacerated backs. When *Calvario* is reached, the cross is placed in a previously prepared hole with the *Cristo* upon it. In the old days a hammer drove iron nails through his hands and feet; more recently the *Cristo* is tied with thongs. In either case, at this point all those in the procession as well as the families and friends kneel and pray, say rosaries and chant. Often a brief prayer is given by a Penitente. Usually the *Cristo* has fainted before even this brief prayer is over; the cross with the man still on it is taken down and borne quickly and triumphantly back to the *morada*. The *alabados* chanted on the return procession are triumphant, and there is no whipping. In the *morada* the erstwhile Christ is cared for. In the old days the *Cristo's* side was slashed, and occasionally he died. It is said that in such a case the man was immediately buried, and his shoes placed outside the door of his house to signify his passing. There are constantly recurring rumors of the recent re-use of nails, side slashing, and deaths, but the extreme secrecy of the order makes this impossible for a nonmember to trace to a specific village in a specific year.

Late Friday the populace gathers at the Penitente chapel (occasionally in a church) for the symbolic re-enactment of *las tinieblas* ("the earthquakes"), commemorating the traditional three hours of darkness and disturbance of natural forces which occurred when Christ died. Inside the chapel part of the *morada*, on the altar, are thirteen candles. These represent Christ and the apostles and are the only light. Hymns are sung, prayers are said, and the candles are extinguished two by two. Each extinguishment symbolizes the departure of a disciple. Finally only one candle (Christ) is left, and it is carried into the secret room in the rear leaving the chapel, after the last psalm, in total darkness. The *rezador* recites the Apostles' Creed and then the earthquake is re-enacted by the clanking of chains, beating on pieces of tin or improvised drums, the racket of the *metracas*, the cries of women, and the slap of the whips of the self-flagellating Penitentes who now virtually surround the congregation. When quiet is restored, someone asks for a prayer for a loved one in purgatory, and the *tinieblas* and lashing are repeated, on a minor scale, for each prayer that is asked. Finally the prayers are over, the lighted candle is returned to the chapel, the Penitentes return to the rear rooms or to the *morada*, all the candles are lighted, and triumphant hymns are sung. It is at this point that each pretty *señorita*, and many a young *señora*, surreptitiously looks at her Easter dress for signs of blood. That one or more of the Penitentes (who after all are men) has gone close enough to a woman during the darkness to splatter her with a little of his blood is sure proof of her feminine desirability!

Other than the Holy Week ceremonies, the activities of the Penitentes only occasionally call for active physical penance. Flagellation may occur on the birthday of the saint of the local village or on the birthday of St. Francis himself (occasionally called "Big Frank" by those Anglos in the area who look upon the Penitentes as barbaric). Penance by crawling to a shrine on the knees is relatively well-known in the area, as it still is throughout Mexico. During the year Los Hermanos Penitentes behave as do members of any other religious fraternal benefit society, assisting each other in time of trouble. This is particularly true in time of death. In normal non-Penitente deaths there is an all-night *velorio* (wake or vigil) with a paid chanter of prayers reading from his copybook. The wake is attended by relatives and friends, both male and female. Food is always served, and sometimes beer or liquor makes its appearance. Many hymns are sung during the night. In the morning those keeping vigil, and others follow the deceased to the church for the regular service and then a procession to the nearby cemetery. If the deceased is a Penitente, the brotherhood turns out in force for his *velorio*. The corpse is carried briefly to the *morada* and then returned to the house. Along with the hymns, Penitente *alabados* are sung, and often one of the members will do the prayer reading instead of the paid chanter. Reportedly there may be flagellation if the deceased was a particularly well-liked and successful *hermano mayor.* A small financial gift is sometimes made the family. Reportedly, high in the mountains, homemade caskets are sometimes used, and if the deceased is a member of the brotherhood, it is they who prepare and provide the rude pine box in which he rests and the wooden cross which marks his grave.

Like some other fraternal organizations, the Penitentes frequently have been involved in politics. Since Spanish-Americans take their politics very seriously and very emotionally, it is not surprising that units from different villages fail to agree politically. There is no over-all organization of the local groups in the brotherhood and no formal cooperation, although there is a well-developed sympathy and "we-feeling." Nevertheless, political battles have caused enmity between some villages and even have caused the split of a *morada* into two *moradas*, in more than one case. Not many years ago political activity, often corrupt, was so important in some local units that it was erroneously stated that the Penitentes were little more than a political organization.

Two major local art forms owe much of their development to the Penitentes: *alabados* and the wood carvings of *santos, carretas de la muerte*, and the like. Scholars in several universities in the area have been most interested in the cultural survivals to be found among the group which is host to the Penitentes. The best of these studies shows that there yet is preserved a considerable number of the old *alabados* sung in the area. Although some of these ancient hymns have been memorized by a number of persons, they are preserved in their normal state in small copybooks in the possession of officers or members of the local Penitente units. After the copy has received hard usage, it must be recopied in another little book. At times this was done only after some pages were practically illegible. Thus over the years quite observable variations have come to appear in hymns which certainly had a common origin. Few of these hymns clearly originated in Mexico; none have Indian origin. They all outdate any Anglo or French influence in the area. The only possible conclusion is that these *alabados* are of Spanish, of local, or of mixed Spanish and local origin. The tunes are so simple as to be virtually untraceable.

These factors explain why other Penitente rituals and activities also differ from one village to another; sometimes this divergence has become significant and easily observable. After all, each local unit is an autonomous group; its practices vary from year to year as well as varying from practices of other villages. There is no hierarchy which can demand of each *hermano mayor* that his lodge be conducted in some particular way. On the contrary, the author has plenty of evidence that activities, ritual, and ceremony do differ significantly in the same village during the tenure of different sets of officers.

The question may yet remain for some readers, "Why do they do these things?" The answers must be given and accepted, not in terms of modern American culture but in terms of the related subcultural values and beliefs of the flagellants themselves. First, these people live in a harsh world, close to violence, and are violent to each other: assault and battery, arson, feuds, and murder are significantly more common there than in the nation as a whole. Medical aid is scarce, and suffering is more common. Second, they believe in a God who is merciful, but who also, through a very real Purgatory and Hell, can be merciless unless propitiated. Propitiation may be by prayer or "active" penance, with "active" penance the more efficacious. Granted the sincerity and depth of these beliefs, a few brief hours of pain (probably deserved) are a small price to pay for a year of ease of mind. "A little suffering in this life is better than much suffering in the life to come." To the Penitente the whip and the pain bring him closer to God—and more than this no man can ask. The symbolism of cross-bearing is the clearest of all: "Christ was crucified; why should we not do it for Him?" To the Penitente the symbolic sharing of suffering with Jesus brings him closer to God. Thus the pain and suffering of the flagellant serve a very real psychological purpose and meet what is for him an important felt need. Those natives who either are being assimilated out of the violence of the subculture, who are less deeply religious or who are religious but feel no need for active penance, do not practice or approve of flagellation.

Throughout the valleys of the *Sangre de Cristo* Range, change is on the march. Children are attending school, learning English, and are both bilingual and bicultural. Here and there the tractor is replacing the horse and iron plow, as the horse replaced the oxen and the wooden plow. Many a countryman buys his *chiles* in the store, already ground, rather than growing them himself and hanging them to dry as romantic and aromatic pendants from the rafters of his adobe home. Villages which once could be reached only by wagon are now visited weekly by pickup trucks; the carvers of the wooden *santos* and *carretas de la muerte* have begun to discover the tourist, and practice their art for solely secular reasons. The road to the *morada* may be graded and ditched—at least one is graveled—and nearly every village has a gasoline pump. Penitentes died on Bataan and as paratroopers in Korea. Yet this area still remains a voluntary cultural island, a unique mixture of the past and present, of the young man who can fix a balky carburetor but who worries because his baby with the colic may be suffering from the *mal ojo*. Children listen wide-eyed while grandmother tells (in Spanish) of the witches she has known.

This Easter, like a hundred Easters past, there will be clandestine meetings; for the *paisanos*, work will come to a standstill; crosses will be inspected and strengthened, and then, on the holiest nights, there again will be heard the swish of cactus whips, wet with the blood of penitent sinners, the tuneless *pito* and *metraca* will silence the coyotes, and the strains of the simple and deeply religious *alabados* rise in the night air as the *Cristo* again staggers under his cross on the way to Calvary.

We have already met the people of the New Mexico village of Hot Springs, now Montezuma. We have met the brothers Lorenz, and we have found them and their neighbors to be ordinary people, restricted in their understanding and their outlook by their membership in a particularly backward folk society. Certainly there is no mass mental or emotional abnormality evident in their behavior as we have seen it. They do not behave as we do, but they are not much different from us as biological organisms. Integrated into our culture, they would disappear as unusual people in a generation or so.

But observe them in Hot Springs under the obsession of an ancient Latin nativistic endeavor. We are told the Lorenz brothers are nearly the only males who do not engage in self-flagellation, and we can believe that if we choose. If they are exceptions, then their behavior is aberrant and must be explained. It is they who are the loose bolts in the smooth folk machinery of Hot Springs.

I have been told that today the Penitentes have disappeared in Montezuma, and one can believe that, too, if one wishes. But one does not have to, and one would be a gullible folklorist if one believed everything his informants tell him. The Penitential movement is still very strong in the rural Southwest, when there are outside observers to see it and to report it — and neither of these is expedient. There are polygynous households of Mormons in Denver, but their presence is not officially noticed by those who would, if it were generally known, have to do something about it. Let bleeding flagellants and polygynous Mormons lie, and there is less trouble in a troubled world.

PENITENTES IN A NEW MEXICAN VILLAGE*

There were two Catholic societies in Hot Springs to which most of the natives belonged. Everyone, men and women, belonged to the Association de Santa Maria de Guadalupe. This association had meetings twice yearly on Hermit's Peak, and people came from great distances to attend, our friends said. The first meeting of the year was usually held on May first, or the nearest fine day; the second and more important meeting was always on September first. Everyone went up then with food and clothing; there was a picnic, and some families had built little huts where they could stay overnight. Huge bonfires were built that could be seen for miles around "so everyone know we praying for the holy man." Though the fires were so big we were told that they would not ignite the pine needles. People came up at this time to be cured, and trails, fences, and crosses were repaired, everyone contributing if money was needed. The meetings were not secret, and we were invited to attend. All the male members of this society had large rosaries with metal medals, which they kept at home, and which were supposed to be returned on the owner's death.

The Holy Man around whom all this centers was a hermit by the name of Juan Maria de Castellano. He lived on the mountain and died before any of our friends were born, though we were told that there were some old men living who had seen him. We were shown, with great veneration, a photograph of him, This seemed to be a photograph of another photo, or of a painting. It showed a tall bearded man with a staff and cape. Juan himself gave this to Fernán's grandfather, José. We were told many stories about him, for he was "a saint, not the same as other men."

The second society, also more than local in membership, was that of the Penitentes, a group of Catholic flagellants. What we learned of them was of course fragmentary, since even nonmembers were cautious of discussing them. Only men belonged, and members were bound to secrecy. We were told that the Lorenz brothers and their uncle Fidel and Mr. Jones were the only male members of the community who did not belong to the Penitentes. Her sons probably avoided the sect (if all of them did) because of Mrs. Lorenz's violent antagonism to the flagellant practices.

The Penitentes had strong political and social power, not only in Hot Springs but in Las Vegas, and we were told that any native who wished to advance in politics had to become a member. Antonio told us that the priest disapproved of the organization and refused to lend the

*From Helen Zunser, "A New Mexican Village." JAF Volume 48, 1935, 115-178.

church cross for the processions. However, he allowed the members to come to church.

Fernán, since all his friends belonged, was more in sympathy with the Penitentes than his brother was. He told them that Romancita wouldn't let him join but told her that he didn't want to go. She shuddered when they were mentioned and spoke with horror of two little boys who had joined.

At Lent, and especially on Ash Wednesday and Good Friday, the members beat themselves "terrible." During Holy Week they went in procession to Hermit's Peak. They did not allow photographs to be taken because they "don't want to be laughed at." In procession they were said to wear only loin cloths; at night, to go naked except for a strip of black cloth around their faces. After Holy Week they look "poor" and their cheeks are sunken. Long after Holy Week, our friend Giatano would not go swimming with us because his back was scarred.

The self-whipping is done with large flat whips of the yucca (Spanish bayonet), which is pounded into threads, then woven into a light web. Glass is used to cut three small slits on each side of the back before the flagellation in order that there be bleeding, instead of bruising. The day after there are said to be no ill effects.

The *mirada* or meeting house, contained many old images, though many had been stolen or exchanged for new ones, and was always kept locked. In Hot Springs the *mirada* is directly behind the town in a thin wood, with a cross near it large enough to support a man. At the services, which are held at night all during the year, no lights are used except for one candle. The dead are called on to appear. Chains rattle, bells ring, and cold hands are felt. No one speaks, but there is a complicated set of signals. The leader has a board with a nicked wheel, which he rattles for silence, or as a signal for marching. He is instantly obeyed. A peculiar whistle announces the approach of a stranger, and everyone falls upon his face. The shrill pipe whistle that is used is called "Mary's crying."

A funeral ceremony of one of the members was described, in which "about fifty" moved around the coffin in two circles, one moving left, the other right, all night long.

Near the local *mirada* was a small heap of stones with a little cross set on it. Such crosses are come upon rather often, along the road or on a narrow trail. We were told that they mark a spot where a coffin has been set down to rest.

Everything said about the Penitentes was told in great earnestness and in secret. During Holy Week the processions passed going up to Hermit's Peak, and we were asked not to look, although it was daylight and they were on the main road. We saw three groups of six or seven at different times on their way to or from Hermit's Peak. Their wailing and singing, high pitched and eerie, could be heard from afar. When we came out of the house, the singing stopped, except for one voice, when on Good Friday a group crossed our private field. They were too far for us to see anything except that they were fully dressed and carried a cross. Once also, when we were picnicking, we looked down and far beneath saw a white-clad procession winding among the rocks.

No religion can exist without a myth to give it warrant and credence. The fact or assumed fact of the experiences of the founding prophet become distorted by his followers, and as Marx could say before his death, "I am no Marxist," so St. Anthony of Padua could have said, had he remained longer on this earth, "I am no flagellant."

Myth grows through accretions, and the more believers, the more wonders to believe in. The early Christian Church was inundated with experiences of enthusiasts who saw what they wanted to see. Some of these things were incorporated into the official canon of belief, when they were compatible with what had already been accepted. But as time went along, the notions became wilder until they crossed the fatal line into heresy. The layman is not aware of how quickly improbabilities grew. If the Gospels are read in the order of their composition — Mark, Luke, and Matthew especially — it can be seen readily that the Christian mythology becomes steadily more miraculous and more difficult to accept in the nature of things. Later writers were expunged along with their writings at the various Church councils that kept the myth within visual distance of possibility.

The story that follows is a little thing, a mere mustard seed, but it is the stuff of myth. It helps to establish a dogma: that Penitentes who do not fulfill their obligations on earth are doomed to remain on the earth.

THE GHOST OF A PENITENTE*

A certain evening during Holy Week the Penitentes entered the church in Taos for the purpose of flogging themselves. After flogging themselves in the usual manner, they left the church. As they departed, however, they heard the floggings of a Penitente who seemed to have re-

*From Aurelio M. Espinosa, "New-Mexican Spanish Folk-Lore."
JAF Volume 23, 1910, 395-418.

mained in the church. The elder brother (*hermano mayor*) counted his Penitentes, and no one was missing. To the astonishment of the other Penitentes, the one in the church continued his flagellation, and they decided to return. No one dared to re-enter the church, however; and while they disputed in silence and made various conjectures as to what the presence of an unknown Penitente might mean, the floggings became harder and harder. At last one of the Penitentes volunteered to enter alone; but, as he opened the door, he discovered that the one who was scourging himself mercilessly was high above in the choir, and it was necessary to obtain a lighted candle before venturing to ascend to the choir in the darkness. He procured a lighted candle and attempted to ascend. But, lo! he could not, for every time he reached the top of the stairs, the Penitente whom he plainly saw there, flogging himself, would approach and put out his candle. After trying for several times, the brave Penitente gave up the attempt, and all decided to leave the unknown and mysterious stranger alone in the church. As they departed, they saw the mysterious Penitente leave the church and turn in an opposite direction. They again consulted one another, and decided to follow him. They did so; and, since the stranger walked slowly, scourging himself continuously and brutally, they were soon at a short distance from him. The majority of the flagellants followed slowly behind; while the brave one, who had previously attempted to ascend to the choir, advanced to the side of the mysterious stranger and walked slowly by him. He did not cease scourging himself, though his body was visibly becoming very weak, and blood was flowing freely from his mutilated back. Thus the whole procession continued in the silence of the night, the stranger leading the Penitentes through abrupt paths and up a steep and high mountain. At last, when all were nearly dead with fatigue, the mysterious Penitente suddenly disappeared, leaving his good companion and the other Penitentes in the greatest consternation. The Penitentes later explained that this was doubtless the soul of a dead Penitente who had not done his duty in life—a false Penitente—and God had sent him back to earth to scourge himself properly, before allowing him to enter heaven.

Demons are the gods of displaced religions. The missionaries of the southwestern Pacific islands, themselves marginal to their own culture, know very little about the objective study of religion, and would not accept this etiology of demons even if they knew about it. So when on their own hook they furnish their Melanesian catechists with pidgin words like "devil" for the native word for god (*masalai*), they once again prove the universality of the fundamental concepts and processes of religion.

As demons are displaced gods, witches are displaced servitors of those gods. With us witches are a superstition, since the commonality no longer believes in them, but where they are believed in, they are believed in strenuously. Margaret Murray made the point, in her classic study *The Witch-Cult in Western Europe*, that even through the Jacobean period those who did *not* believe in witches were more apt to be mentally unstable than whose who did. Witches get more attention in the King James Bible than the original texts warrant because its scholarly translators had to please King James, who was out of his head with fear of witches. Shakespeare and Bacon (the first pragmatic scientist) and Raleigh and Browne, like other intellectuals, had a healthy respect for witches, but the king's respect was unhealthy. He saw witches under the bed (where, as succubi, they were most likely to be anyhow). Even as late as the waning years of the eighteenth century, John Wilkes broke up one of the ultra-sophisticated "Hell Fire" clubs when in the middle of a blasphemous black mass he threw a painted monkey into the communicants from back of the altar. The assembled atheists were frightened witless by the appearance of the devil they had pretended to invoke.

Our easy assumption that belief in the aboriginal totemic religions of northern Europe ended with Augustine's mission is absurd. Pope Gregory the First (rightfully called "The Great") himself understood the tenacity of the old religion when he directed his missionaries,

Let the shrines of idols by no means be destroyed but let the idols which are in them be destroyed. Let water be consecrated and sprinkled in these temples; let altars be erected . . . so that the people, not seeing their temples destroyed, may displace error and recognize and adore the true God. . . . And because they were wont to sacrifice oxen to devils, some celebration should be given in exchange for this . . . they should celebrate a religious feast and worship God by their feasting, so that still keeping outward pleasures, they may more readily receive spiritual joys.

And that is why today, one thousand four hundred years after Gregory, we celebrate the feast of the Germanic fertility goddess Eostre at Easter, retaining her fertility symbols of rabbits and eggs; Walpurgis Nacht on May Day; Halloween on All Souls

Day; and most curious of all, Yule (the birth of the new sun) on Christmas. There is scarcely one Christmas tradition, from virgin birth to mistletoe, that is not pagan in origin.

Priests of the new religion do their blessedest to discredit their predecessors by maligning their character. That is why the ancient word for "light" became "Lucifer," the name of the devil. And that is why the witches in the following selections are wicked. But the old priests and priestesses loved their gods as the new priests loved their God. Their rites were not dark and terrifying, but light and joyous. One of the witches' ceremonies managed to make it into the new religion without slanderous distortion—the dance around the Maypole; and what is more joyous and innocent than that?

WITCHES IN THE OZARKS*

The old belief in witchcraft is rapidly dying out even in the Ozarks, and very few of the younger people have the slightest interest in the subject nowadays. Many of the old folks, however, still believe that certain women can call up the Devil by repeating the Lord's Prayer backward, and obtain supernatural powers by selling their souls to Satan. Isabel Spradley tells me of an old woman near Van Buren, Arkansas, who "put a spell" on her neighbor's tomato plants simply by drawing a circle in the dust, marking a cross in the center of the circle, and spitting in the center of the cross!

*From Vance Randolph, "Ozark Superstitions." JAF Volume 46, 1933, 1-21.

I have been told of another Ozark witch who killed several of her enemies by means of a "hair ball"—just a little bunch of black hair mixed with beeswax and rolled into a hard pellet. The old woman tossed this thing at the persons whom she wished to eliminate, and they fell dead a few hours later. It is said that the fatal hair ball is always found somewhere in the body of a person killed in this manner. In one case, according to my informant, the little ball of combings was taken from the dead girl's mouth.

Some of the old-timers used to drive three nails into the outside of a door, in the form of a triangle, to keep witches away from the house. One man told me that the three nails represented the Father, the Son, and the Holy Ghost, and were particularly efficacious in protecting an expectant mother from the powers of evil. Burning coffee in a sick-room is said to fumigate the place, and also to prevent witches from injuring the patient. If one of the hens lays a very small egg, the housewife often throws it upon the roof, remarking humorously that since it isn't big enough to cook, she may as well feed it to the witches. Bewitched clothing is treated by washing it in milk and hanging it out-doors overnight in freezing weather—this is supposed to take the curse off it somehow. Another way to discourage witches is to take a buck-eye and face the rising sun as you bore a hole in it with a sharp pointed "flint rock." Churns are sometimes bewitched so that the butter won't come, but this can be remedied by placing a new horseshoe or a silver coin in the bottom of the churn.

The mistletoe is held in some sort of superstitious veneration and is said to be used by witches in casting spells and the like, but I am unable to learn anything very definite about this. A bunch of dried mistletoe is sometimes hung up in a smokehouse to keep the meat from spoiling. Trees that rub together in the wind and make a loud noise are regarded with suspicion, and it is said that the bark from such trees is used in conjuring. The redbud or Judas tree is bewitched, at least in the spring, and it is not well to spend much time near a blooming redbud after sunset. The great pileated woodpecker, which the natives call a woodhen, is supposed to have some sort of supernatural powers, and various portions of its body are highly prized by witches.

If a group of persons are seated about a fire, and the sparks which pop out seem to be directed toward one particular individual, it is said that this person is somehow connected with the powers of evil. Another tale is, however, that such a person is merely concealing some weighty secret. Some old people cherish a belief, said to have been borrowed from the Osages, that by burning the heart of a murdered man his relatives may make certain that the murderer will be punished for his crime. There are whispers of such rites being carried out in the back hills even today, but the rumors cannot be verified, and it is not prudent for an amicable outsider to investigate these matters too closely.

In some parts of the American Southwest Catholic priests are required by their parishioners to do more for the old gods than celebrate Christmas and Holy Week. They are called upon in extreme circumstances to exorcise witches and to undo the harm caused by witches. I recall a meeting of the American Folklore Society in New Mexico where a local folklorist read a paper on local witches known to him. He had a large map, and as he spoke, he put into the map a pin locating the residence of each of the numerous daughters of Satan. I have often wondered what made him choose the pin as an identification method; there seemed to be more to the choice than logic.

THE WITCHES OF NEW MEXICO*

A correspondent of the St. Louis *Globe-Democrat*, writing from San Mateo, May, 1888, gives an account of the witch superstitions current in that territory (containing 175,000 inhabitants, 25,000 of these Americans) among the Mexican population. The witches, he observes, are generally women, but sometimes men — generally old, and rarely very young.

Our witchology is full, detailed, and graphic. Every *paisano* in New Mexico can tell you their strange habits, their marvelous powers, and their baleful deeds. They never injure the dumb animals, but woe to the human being who incurs their displeasure! Few, indeed, are bold enough to brave their wrath. If a witch ask for food, wood, clothing, or anything else, none dare say her nay. Nor dare anyone eat what a witch proffers; for, if he do, some animal, alive and gnawing, will form in his stomach. By day the witches wear their familiar human form; but at night, dressed in strange animal shapes, they fly abroad to hold witch meetings in the mountains, or to wreak their evil wills. In a dark night you may see them flying through the sky like so many balls of fire, and there are comparatively few Mexicans in the territory who have not seen this weird sight! For these nocturnal sallies the witches wear their own bodies, but take the legs and eyes of a coyote or other animal, leaving their own at home. Juan Perea, a male witch, who died here in San Mateo some months ago, met with a strange misfortune in this wise; he had gone off with the eyes of a cat, and during his absence a dog knocked over the table and ate up Juan's own eyes; so the unfortunate witch had to wear cat's eyes all the rest of his life.

Before they can fly, witches are obliged to cry out, "Sin Dios, sin Santa Maria! (Without God and without the Holy Virgin!)" whereupon they mount

*From "Witchcraft in New Mexico." JAF Volume 1, 1888, 167-168.

up into the air without difficulty. If you are on good terms with a witch you may persuade her to carry you on her back from here to New York in a second. She blindfolds you and enjoins strict silence. If you utter a word you find yourself alone in some vast wilderness, and if you cry, "God, save me!" you fall from a fearful height to the ground—but are luckily never killed by the fall. There are several courageous people in the territory who have made journeys thus upon the backs of witches. At least they are ready to swear so, and they find ten thousand believers to one sceptic. One striking peculiarity about New Mexican witches is that anyone named Juan or Juana (John or Jane) can catch them, and that no one else can, except a priest with holy water. To catch a witch, Juan draws a nine-foot circle on the ground, turns his shirt inside out, and cries, "Veuga, bruja! (Come, witch!)" whereupon the witch has to fall inside the circle, and Juan has her completely in his power. This ability to catch witches, however, is seldom exercised, for, let Juan once catch a witch, and all the other witches in the country join hands and whip him to death.

And now, having briefly outlined the nature of witches here, let me give you some veracious anecdotes of their exploits, religiously believed throughout this section. Lorenzo Labadie, a man of prominence in New Mexico, once unknowingly hired a witch as nurse for his baby. He lived in Las Vegas. Some months afterward there was a ball at Puerta de Luna, a couple of hundred miles south, and friends of the family were astonished to see the nurse and baby there. "Where is Senor Labadie and his family?" they asked. The nurse replied that they were at a house a few miles distant, but too tired to come to the ball. The friends went there next day and found the Labadies had not been there. Suspecting the nurse to be a witch, they wrote to Don Lorenzo, who only knew that the nurse and baby were in his house when he went to bed, and there also when he woke up. It being plain, therefore, to the most casual observer, that the woman was a witch, he promptly discharged her.

The correspondent gives an account of two other cases of supposed enchantment. In the first of these a bride found a strange cat in her room, which disappeared before it could be shot and was replaced by an owl, which flew against the girl's cheek, cut it, and disappeared as mysteriously as the cat. The sore could not be cured until the witch, with whom the bride had lately had a quarrel, was appeased with presents. In the second case, one of the most respectable inhabitants of the town offended a well-known witch named Marcellina, a thin, withered woman of perhaps fifty years of age. Marcellina retaliated, as the victim affirms, by turning him into a woman, a state in which he remained for several months and recovered only by bribing the witch to effect the retransformation. This woman Marcellina was, last year, according to the correspondent, beaten to death with clubs by two men whom she had bewitched, and the murder went unpunished.

———————————————

The real tragedy in the eternal contentions between religions is not the defeat of the losing gods but what happens to the human beings who are caught between the old ways and the new. One does not make omelettes without breaking eggs, and one does not establish a new religion without killing innocent people who grew up serving the cause of what they had been told was righteousness. In the islands of the Pacific Ocean some missionaries fought for their respective denominations against other Christian intruders by arming their converts and sending them off to kill or to try to kill the forces of the opposing missionary. Cotton Mather, the most eminent of the early Puritan intellectuals, ran into cases of what we know now were Huntington's choreics. The orthodox view of such people was that the convulsions to which they were subject, the lack of muscular control, the rolling on the floor, the frothing at the mouth, the screaming, and the demonic grimaces were clear and irrefutable signs of possession by devils. There was only one cure: hanging. Mather saw these people somewhat differently; they were not simply possessed by demons, but were in full realization of what they were doing: blasphemously making farce of Christ's agonies on the cross. The cure was the same. In the Salem witchcraft mania also, there was poor Bridget Bishop, damned by God to beauty. When she enhanced her beauty with pretty clothes, she appeared in the dreams of the good Puritan husbands as a succubus. Of this, Cotton Mather said, "there was little occasion to prove the witchcraft, this being evident and notorious to all beholders." Bridget was hanged on the tenth of June, 1692, on Gallows Hill.

The most poignant tragedy in the *Journal's* witchcraft articles is this story of a Yaqui woman, reported in 1899 by V. Granville, writer for a Los Angeles paper.

A YAQUI WIDOW BECOMES A WITCH*

That witchcraft and idol worship are not yet dead among the Yaquis I soon discovered while wandering among the people of the small villages along the river. At an Indian hut I was shown a "*bruja*" or witch doll, by an unusually intelligent Yaqui woman, the mother of seven children, whose husband had been put to death, she averred, on the accusation of having the "evil eye." The doll was ten inches long, made of black cloth and stuffed with wool. It was stuck full of the sharp thorns of the maguey plant, and it was believed that the enemies of the family suffered excruciating pain so long as the thorns remained in the doll. The story that the mother told me was pathetic. She said, in excellent Spanish: "My husband was a good man, a miner at the placer diggings on the Rio Aros. He was away from home most of the time and came to see us only two or three times a year. I lived at the village with the little ones, so that they could go to the padre to learn to read.

*From V. Granville, "Yaqui Witchcraft." JAF Volume 13, 1900, 64-65.

It cost almost all my husband earned at the mines to buy us food and clothes and pay the padre. But there were those in the village who were jealous of me and the little ones because we had more than they, and the reason was that we drank no tequila, and they, our enemies, spent all their money for drink. One day when my husband came to see us and brought money, old Pedro and some of the other men came and asked him to join them at the *cantina*, where other miners were drinking and spending the money that should have gone to the wives and little ones. My Diego refused to go, and the men went out and one of them fell down on the ground and declared that he was hurt in his head, and that my Diego and I and all the little ones had the 'evil eye'; that we are all as the people that they used to burn as witches. And that night, when Diego went to the corral after dark to look after the burros and cow, some men seized him and dragged him to the river, where they tied rocks to him and threw him into the river to drown. And when I and the little ones tried to save him, the men beat us and drove us back to the house. After that they made us leave our house in the village and come here, half a mile away. And then it was that I made the *bruja* to protect us, and the people are now afraid of us, and each one in the village gives us so much of his corn and *frijoles* not to name the *bruja* for him; for when it is named for anyone and the thorns stuck in, the person suffers great pain and soon dies. They killed my Diego, and they must support his wife and little ones, so I scare them all the time with the witch doll."

When the promised return of a Culture Hero or a high god has been too long delayed, people become understandably impatient. If a precise date has been unwisely predicted by the nativistic prophet, and the world does not cooperate by coming to an end, faith is shaken. William Miller, an unlettered Massachusetts farmer, gained basketsful of followers by predicting the end of the world in 1843. The year 1843 came and went and the world rolled on, heedless of its responsibility. The Millerites still sat in laundry baskets waiting to be hauled up to heaven, but as Miller revised the date each time it went by unobserved, their impatience grew. Reading the Millerite hymns of this period, one is amused by the petulance of their tone. "You were supposed to be here this year, Jesus; why have you not come for us?" Eventually the frailty of human flesh became too much for the strength of the spirit, and the Millerites got out of their baskets, went west, and formed various Adventists groups (such as the

Evangelical Adventists, the Advent Christians, the Life and Advent Union, the Age-to-Come Adventists, and the Seventh-Day Adventists), all canny enough to keep the date of the millennium vague.

Another reaction when no calendrical time has been announced is for the forces of tradition to bring the god to earth in unofficial visits or to provide surrogates either to make special visitations or to remain on earth until the god's return. This is the theme of the next four selections illustrating the beliefs of the supernatural West.

Among the Spanish-Indian folk groups of Mexico and the southwestern United States, enormous liberties have been taken with the Christian myth. Aztec and Maya legends, tales, and myths combine in religious abandon with their Christian counterparts, producing a result that is instructive to the anthropologist if not to the orthodox. Not much edification was given to the Yaqui when this story of San Pedro and Jesucristo was invented:

One time San Pedro and Jesucristo were walking along. Jesucristo sent San Pedro up to a near-by house to get a cooked chicken. On the way back Pedro ate one leg of the chicken.

When Jesucristo saw what San Pedro had brought back, he asked, "Why has this chicken but one leg?"

"It never had another leg," answered Pedro. "All of the chickens around this part of the country have but one leg, Sir."

The two proceeded and came to a big tree under which were sleeping many chickens. All of the chickens had one leg tucked up out of sight under their feathers.

Pedro pointed to them and said, "You see! All of the chickens have but one leg apiece."

Jesucristo took a rock and threw it at one of the chickens. It woke up and stood on both feet.

"Oh," said Pedro, "a miracle!" He then took up a rock and threw it at the rest of the chickens. "You see," he said, "I can perform miracles, too"*

Most of these syncretistic stories are not so egregiously disrespectful. Many are in fact small morality tales — *ejemplos* — whose purpose is to teach dogma and thus fulfill the second function of myth: to lay down explicitly a pattern of correct behavior.

*Ruth W. Giddings, *Yaqui Myths and Legends*. Tucson, Anthropological Papers of the University of Arizona, No. 2, 1959, p. 46.

JESUCRISTO AND THE RICH MAN*

Once there was a very rich man, like a rich Mexican. Jesus Christ came to his house dressed in rags and covered with sores, asking for the crumbs of bread. They told the rich man, "There is a poor man at the door."

"Let him come in." But, when he saw the sores so ugly, "To the door with him!"

Jesus Christ went further to a poor man's house; he knocked at the door.

"Pase, señor." The poor man and his wife were there. "Pase, señor; pass over this side; sit on the bedding."

"But I am covered with sores, I do not like to sit on your white sheet."

"Oh, sir, what does that matter?" said the woman; "I can wash the sheet."

They had no food in the house. The poor man said to his wife, whispering, "Go to the plaza and try to borrow a little flour." She came back with a little flour that she had found and made *tortillas*. The man and his wife sat one on each side of the poor man and fed him.

Then Jesus Christ held up his hands, and there fell from the roof maize and wheat and beans and chile and onions and all sorts of food. The house was full. And from the rich man he took away all that he had.

In the twenty-eighth chapter of the Third Book of Nephi in the copy of *The Book of Mormon* which I pinched from a Mormon motel, I find the word of the Lord to three Nephite disciples:

And he said unto them: Behold, I know your thoughts, and ye have desired the thing which John, my beloved, who was with me in my ministry, before that I was lifted up by the Jews, desired of me.

Therefore, more blessed are ye, for ye shall never taste of death; but ye shall live to behold all the doings of the Father unto the children of men, even until all things shall be fulfilled according to the will of the Father, when I shall come in my glory with the powers of heaven.

And ye shall never endure the pains of death; but when I shall come in my glory ye shall be changed in the twinkling of an eye from mortality to immortality; and then shall ye be blessed in the kingdom of my Father.

And again, ye shall not have pain while ye shall dwell in the flesh,

*From Barbara Freire Marreco, "New Mexican Spanish Folk Lore."
 JAF Volume 29, 1916, 536-546.

neither sorrow save it be for the sins of the world; and all this will I do because of the thing which ye have desired of me, for ye have desired that ye might bring the souls of men unto me, while the world shall stand.

With all due respect for the story of the two gold tablets, it seems fairly clear that Joseph Smith (or Moroni) got the idea of the heavenly tarriers from the twenty-first chapter of the Gospel according to St. John, in which Christ elects John the Beloved to remain on earth to fulfill the divine offices:

Then went this saying abroad among the brethren, that that disciple should not die; yet Jesus said not unto him, He shall not die; but, If I will that he tarry till I come, what is that to thee?

The motif has been attractive to other peoples than the Mormons. The Jews have a beautiful legend believed by some Talmudists to go back to the time of Isaiah. The world, says this legend, rests upon thirty-six Just Men, chosen as the Jews themselves were chosen, to take upon themselves the sorrows of the world. These "Lamed-Vov" are ordinary men, not selected for any personal qualities, but it is their existence that enables the world to continue. They suffer, for they are frozen with the sorrows of mankind. In his poignant book *The Last of the Just,* André Schwarz-Bart repeats from a Hasidic story the revelation that "when an unknown Just rises to Heaven, he is so frozen that God must warm him for a thousand years between his fingers before his soul can open itself to Paradise. And it is known that some remain forever inconsolable at human woe, so that God Himself cannot warm them. So from time to time the Creator, blessed be His Name, sets forward the clock of the Last Judgment by one minute."

And there is the persistent story of the Wandering Jew, which first appeared in the literature of the Western world in the thirteenth century. In this legend Ahasuerus (or Cartophilus) pushes Christ aside from his doorway, where the Lord had stopped to rest on the way to Calvary. "Move on," ordered Ahasuerus; but Christ replied, "I will stand here and rest, but thou shalt go on until the last day." The tale has been told by several authors in several ways; Eugene Sue made the Wandering Jew as old as his years; George Sylvester Viereck (the former Nazi spy) gave the Jew the joy of the world by keeping him at a virile young manhood through the centuries.

Austin E. Fife, who collected the tales from which I have chosen two to illustrate the legend of the Three Nephites among the Mormons, believes that the Wandering Jew legend reached the Mormons and was absorbed by the Nephite legend, along with the legend of John the Beloved. He cites documentary evidence that the belief in the intercession of the Three Nephites was well established in Utah in 1851. Whatever its origin, the legend of the Three Nephites has enriched not just the folklore of the Church of Jesus Christ of Latter-Day Saints, but all our story.

TWO TALES OF THE THREE NEPHITES*

Five years prior to this incident, two Mormon elders had been accused of criminally assaulting a young woman on the Island of Vancouver. For some reason they were proved guilty of the charge and sentenced according to the law of the island. (The church, as well as the missionaries who were involved, believed that the act was purposely committed by enemies of Mormonism who arranged the evidence in such a way that it was possible to convict the Mormon elders.)

The church immediately closed the mission and refrained from sending additional elders into that field. Later, when the church officials believed that the people had partially forgotten the incident, they sent my father and John J. Oldroyd to open the mission. They found the natives of the island as hostile toward the Mormons as ever. Everywhere they were looked down upon as potential criminals. People shied away from them.

One evening they decided to hold a street meeting. They knew feeling was running high and that they would probably be molested, but they decided to go ahead regardless. After obtaining a permit from the city officials, who again reminded them of the intolerance of the people, they commenced their meeting. They had little more than started when down the street marched a large group of men and boys carrying several large pots of melted tar and several old feather ticks. The leader walked directly to my father and asked him if he was a Mormon. Much to the satisfaction of the mob, my father answered him in the affirmative.

Some of the members of the mob began to tear open the feather ticks,

*From Austin E. Fife, "The Legend of the Three Nephites among the Mormons."
JAF Volume 53, 1940, 1-49.

while others stirred the still warm tar. Just as the mob leader and two or three of the mobsters began to tear the clothes from my father's body, a white-haired gentleman (no one saw him arrive at the scene) grasped the leader by the wrists and said in a loud commanding voice, "I have heard these boys preach back in the Old Country, and they are all right. Now let them alone."

At this the mob leader showed signs of wanting to fight. (The mob leader was a huge, muscular type of man.) Immediately, the newcomer grasped him at the nape of the neck with one hand and by the belt with the other and shook him so soundly, taking him completely off his feet, that when he had finished the mobster could not stand without assistance. Members of his mob picked him up, gathered up their feathers and tar, and departed much faster than they had appeared.

My father and his companion thanked the white-haired man for what he had done and asked him to stay and attend the remainder of the meeting. He accepted their invitation and stood directly in front of them throughout the services. In the meantime, a large crowd had assembled partly to hear what the elders had to say and partly to get a glimpse of the man who had humbled the mobsters. Eventually the crowd got so large that automobile traffic was completely blocked on the corner where the meeting was being held.

After my father and Mr. Oldroyd had both spoken and it was time to close the meeting, the white-haired gentleman was still present. All during this time he had stood in identically the same place, scarcely moving. Mr. Oldroyd closed the meeting with prayer, as was the custom, and then looked at the spot where the man had been standing. It was vacant. (This was before anyone in the crowd had moved at all.) No one had seen him go, not even the people who had been standing at his side.

Quite a commotion followed. Members of the crowd were personally questioned as to whether they had seen the man leave or not; no one had even so much as seen him move from the spot.

It seems that someone in the crowd would have seen him leave if he had left in the usual way — by walking. Remembering that the crowd was large and the people were pushed closely together, also that he had been pointed out and looked at by everyone, it seems strange that no one saw him leave. He would have had to push his way through the crowd in order to depart from the scene, yet he disappeared instantaneously. Many said that they saw him standing in front of the platform during the offering of prayer.

As I understand it, the Nephites are supposed to be able to appear and disappear at will; on this was based the conclusion that he might have been one of those three.

At the time of the following incident, we, John D. Mayer and family, were living at Barnes' Hotel, Mississippi City, Mississippi. My father was owner and proprietor of the hotel. When two years of age, I became very ill with acute meningitis from taking cold with the measles. My body was so badly drawn that the back of my head and my feet were touching. My family had called in five of the leading physicians of New Orleans, Louisiana; all pronounced the case hopeless.

One afternoon my father was standing on the lawn in front of the hotel talking with some of the boarders when a well-dressed man with skin so fair it was almost transparent appeared before him and asked if he had any work he could do. My father, paying little attention to him, answered no—that he had all of the workmen that he needed. Then the stranger gave his name as Osburn and said, "I only want a room and board for work. I am traveling without money." And when asked what kind of work he could do, he answered, "Anything." So arrangements were made that he work for his room and board. Then he said, "I understand that you have a very sick child," and in the course of conversation asked to see me. He seemed so concerned that my father had all confidence in him in the sickroom. He met my mother and expressed his regret as to my severe illness.

That was all he said about my condition at the time, but he kept in very close contact. He set to work about the place, supervised the building of a beautiful little cottage, did some wonderful carving and found work in some of the buildings in the city, but he would never accept money. He said that he had no need of money. He mentioned to my sister and others that he said things to the dead just the same as the living. The servants and many of the boarders were much concerned over his being there, and called him a spiritualist, and were afraid to be near him.

One eve, after Mr. Osburn had been at our home several days, the doctor called the family together and told them that I would not live through the night. After the doctor had hurried away, Mr. Osburn came and stood at the door of my room. On being invited in, he went to my mother and said, "Don't grieve. Your baby is not going to die. I have communed with the other world and she cannot go. She has a work here that no one else can do. She will pass the crisis tonight, and you will all see an improvement in the morning."

Mr. Osburn remained at our home for several weeks during my convalescence, and one day while my father was in New Orleans, Louisiana, he came to my uncle who was making his home with us at the time and told him that he had an important appointment and would have to leave immediately. My uncle asked him to wait with us until my father's return, but he said, "I can leave easier while he is away. He holds me." As he spoke, he vanished.

All during my girlhood I had heard members of the family mention the visit of this strange man, but I had not heard the story until some time after we had met some of the Mormon elders and the family had been converted. My father and aunt and uncle who were living with us had been baptized into the Church in England when my father was just a boy, but had lost all trace of the church. They at once renewed their covenants, but the rest of us did not have the courage to be baptized. We drifted along for years, and when I finally asked my mother to come and be baptized with me, she told me this story and stated that this was the answer to the stranger's statement that I was spared for a work that no one else could do.

The first poltergeist story in American literature was told by the great Puritan divine, Increase Mather, father of the great booby Cotton Mather, and son of Richard Mather, who in producing Increase, succeeded in part in his determination to heed literally the injunction "increase and multiply." In *An Essay for the Recording of Illustrious Providences,* Increase reports with humorless credulity the disquieting events that occurred in the *Daemon*-infested home of one William Morse in the memorable year 1679.

On December 8, in the Morning, there were five great Stones and Bricks by an invisible hand thrown in at the west end of the house while the Mans Wife was making the Bed, the Bedstead was lifted up from the floor, and the Bedstaff flung out of the window, and a Cat hurled at her; a long staff danced up and down in the Chimney; a burnt Brick, and a piece of a weatherboard were thrown in at the Window: the Man at his going to Bed put out his Lamp, but in the Morning found that the Saveall of it was taken away, and yet it was unaccountably brought into its former place.

The diabolical molestations persisted for several months, and then suddenly stopped. What is most remarkable about the report that follows of the Texas poltergeist (aside from the important people connected with it—a president of the Humble Oil Company, a vice-president and director of Standard Oil of New Jersey, and a president of Standard Oil of New Jersey) is that Mather's story is in many respects exactly like that of the Woodson haunting, even to the appearance of a small Negro boy. For some reason the writers of this article did not mention the Puritan poltergeist for possible diffusion.

Until Unidentified Flying Objects and their little green pilots caught the febrile imagination of the American public, the surest way to get one's name in the paper, as well as to attract visits from important personages in the various foundations for psychical research, was to report poltergeists. Of course a little more sophistication in terminology is required nowadays to bring real scientists into the investigation. One does not go for the poltergeist immediately; what one does is to describe the events and make tentative suggestions about the possibility of *psychokinesics*. Duke University will send representatives on the strength of that word.

What is behind all these phenomena? Well, there are more things on earth than are dreamt of in our philosophy, aren't there? And who can know the whole of what possibilities exist in the universe? And that.

There is hope for the cynic. He can usually stop the mysticists for a moment or two by quoting Thomas Paine: "Is it more probable that nature should go out of her course, or that a man should tell a lie?"

TRACKING DOWN A TEXAS POLTERGEIST*

Late in the autumn of 1948, a historian was rapidly going through some executive papers of Humble Oil & Refining Company when he encountered a letter which presented a strange contrast to the reports of experiments with methanol gas with which some humorously inclined clerk had filed it. The historian was also a folklorist, so, instead of passing rapidly over the document, he read it with particular attention. The pertinent parts follow:

Jan [illegible] '26

Mineral Wells
Manager Humble Oil Co. Cisco

Dear Sir

I know you will think I am batty but I hope I am not. I understand from Mr. R T. Woodson who is figuring with you to lease the old B Y. Woodson farm 6 miles south of Cisco. B Y Woodson was my wifes Grandfather. . . . Now this is a Spooky Story but Its a fact In the Early day in the Setling up of that Teritory B Y Woodson bought that place from yet an earlier Setler with the one Room log-house which Still remaines in part & after living there some years

*From Kenneth W. Porter and O. G. Lawson, "Texas Poltergeist, 1881."
JAF Volume 54, 1951, 371-382.

thare got to be some Strange things going on thare would be Knocking on the wall outside & finally whatever it was would get up Stairs while the family was all in the Room & throw Rocks Eggs Butcher Knives & all Kinds of things from up Stairs & they would rush up Stairs & make a Search & not a thing to be found & hundreds of People went thare & witnessed that performance & the mistery was never Solved & Every one believed that there was Some Kind of Treasure under the house & all at once all of that monkeying quit. If you will go & have a look around just whare the house stands you will find a Tea Pot dome with lots of black Oil & gas rocks on it & thare may be oil there. I forgot to say that the first Strange thing that happened thare was late one night my wifes father & another man was in the Room Setting by the fire & all of a Suddent a small cole black little Negro Boy Stood before them & Said nor done nothing for a fiew minutes & then Vanished. Say I'll be(t) an oil well you wont go down there & spend a night in that house all alone. Now if you Will put down a well at the South West Corner of the log Shack you are bound to get a big oil well as thats whare the Spook always started to perform I go down thare every Fall to gather Pecans ... Let me hear how you like this Spook Story. . . . yours Truly

A C. TRAWEEK

714 E. HUBBARD ST

The historian, with the folklorist now in the ascendancy, asked Professor Mody Boatright if he knew anyone in Cisco who might be interested in following up this story, and Professor Boatright suggested an oil man, Mr. O. G. Lawson, who had assisted in gathering material for his Gib Morgan book. Mr. Lawson enthusiastically welcomed the opportunity, and for nearly two years, in the intervals of his work as oil-field gauger, hampered by snow, sleet, rain, mud, bad roads, and illness, he relentlessly followed up every clue until he had traced the spook to its lair and learned as much about it as is now likely ever to be known.

Mr. Lawson's efforts for the first three of four months were not productive. He was acquainted with the locale, which is what is usually called the "German Settlement," but inquiry of several elderly men in the community, including one who went in for reminiscences extending back as far as the Cisco cyclone of April 28, 1893, revealed no knowledge of the "spook story."

Emil J. Wende, born in 1886 within two-and-a-half miles of the Woodson log cabin, was the first child born in the "German Settlement," and had, as a boy, picked cotton on the Woodson farm, but had never heard the story. Mr. Lawson was inclined to think from this negative evidence that "there was nothing to it." But early in April, 1949, Mr. Wende took Mr. Lawson to call on Lafayette Walters, an elderly man who owned a section north of the Woodson quarter and had formerly farmed the latter; there Mr. Lawson finally hit pay dirt, a vein which, rich in itself, also led him to the mother lode.

Mr. Walters' daughter May had been well acquainted with the Woodson family and had heard the story, both from old Mrs. Woodson and from one of her sons. She had heard of the Negro boy and that he would appear in the fireplace. Another story was that Mrs. Woodson was sitting in front of the fireplace, wishing she had some tobacco, when she felt something fall into her lap; it was a piece of her dead daughter's dress. One of the Woodsons had told her that when he was a boy and he and another boy would be sleeping in the attic, they would hear a noise which would seem to come into the attic from one end and pass out at the other, a sound like a big bird flying and snapping its beak, and they would always cover their heads.

Late in August, Mr. Lawson accompanied the Walterses to Mineral Wells to call on Mr. R. T. Woodson, who, they had informed him, was living in the house as a boy of twelve at the time of the "spook story" and is the last surviving witness. He made half a dozen visits in all in the course of a year, taking notes, reading them back to Mr. Woodson and getting further suggestions, and gathering up loose ends. He also took pictures of the site of the log house, now heavily grown-up in trees, with only the stone chimney standing.

The account of the strange occurrences in the Woodson household, based upon Mr. Lawson's notes of Mr. Woodson's recollections, is not only a fascinatingly inexplicable "spook story," but is also a valuable portrayal of life in North Central Texas in what was still essentially the frontier period.

The old Woodson place is five miles south and half a mile west of Cisco, Eastland County, North Central Texas, and about two hundred and fifty feet from the Leon River. The river "heads" a few miles west, and its bed near the Woodson farm is usually dry except immediately after rains. The part of the Leon valley in which the Woodson home was located is surrounded by low-lying hills. The farm, which is still reasonably fertile, has been in the family for over seventy years and is still owned by R. T. Woodson.

The Woodsons were originally from Fayetteville, Lincoln County, southern Tennessee, but had lived for a short time in Coryell County, Texas. B. G. Woodson, with his wife, five sons, and a daughter, settled on the banks of the Leon in 1877. He had two teams and two wagons, and in exchange for one team and wagon he bought the rights of an earlier settler to a quarter section of land; by this bargain he took over the payments on the land, which amounted to one dollar an acre with forty years to pay out in. Although not among the very first settlers in Eastland County by a score of years, the Woodsons were among the earliest in the Cisco neighborhood; two years after their arrival, "there were not more than half a dozen families in the locality."

The country was full of wild game, particularly deer and wild turkeys. R. T. Woodson often saw as many as a dozen deer in a herd. His greatest boyhood pleasure was going hunting at night with dogs in the company of his brothers. The panthers had mostly left the country, but he remembers two or three being killed. Hogs were marked in the spring and then allowed to run wild and feed themselves through the summer; it was a neighborhood sport to round them up in the fall. Some were razorbacks with large and long tusks with which, by striking sidewise and upward, they could cut a dog to pieces.

The Woodson farm was very fertile, and the industrious Woodsons made the most of its fertility. The original settler had cleared away the timber, mostly post oak, from about ten of the 160 acres, and every year they would clear a little more until finally the whole quarter section was under cultivation. The Woodsons, as if in reward for their industry, were favored by good fortune during the first four or five years of their settlement. Rainfall was plentiful, corn ears were large, and crops abundant. Their principal "money crop," however, was the wild pecans which grew along the banks of the Leon in unusual size and numbers, and which they would haul into Cisco by the wagonload and sell to buyers from the North. One unusual piece of good fortune was the arrival of a stray milk cow, which the elder Woodson fed and milked and, after advertising for thirty days, "bid in" at public sale for about three dollars.

The previous settler had built a very small and crude house which Mr. Woodson soon replaced with a larger one. It was built of logs with their outer and inner surfaces hewed flat with an adz and with boards nailed on the outside over the cracks. It consisted of three rooms—a main room, fourteen by fourteen feet, an upstairs room of the same size, and a lean-to kitchen, fourteen by ten feet to the east of the principal room. On the north side of the main room stood a stone fireplace and chimney, eighteen feet high and five feet wide. On the west of the main room was a roofed-over porch, six feet deep and the same length as the main room. A door led from the main room into the kitchen and another opened on the porch. A rather narrow and steep stairway rose to the upper story from near the door into the kitchen. The downstairs room had one window, looking to the south. The upper room had no door and only one window, immediately above the window in the main room; no steps or ladder led to the upper story from outside the house. The kitchen was equipped with two stick-and-mud chimneys, one for a fireplace and one for a stove. The house was raised eighteen inches or two feet from the ground and the dogs slept under it.

There was a barn about 75 yards west of the house and a cellar about 15 yards southeast.

The Woodsons were recognized as a substantial family for that time and place in more than numbers. Their house, though small for so large a family, was unusually well constructed, with lumber floors instead of the more common packed dirt. Its large stone fireplace was a distinctive feature. A particularly prized possession was a large family Bible which had cost thirty-five dollars — an evidence both of their prosperity and of their religious interests — and which R. T. Woodson still owns. Mrs. Woodson, who died in 1908 at the age of about seventy-eight, is remembered by old inhabitants as "perfectly truthful and very religious," a "Christian woman if there ever was one," who "lived her religion in her daily life." R. G. Woodson, the father, who died of a broken hip in 1911 at the age of 92, was not superstitiously inclined or easily frightened, but was rather of "a skeptical turn of mind." The sons were all lifelong total abstainers from tobacco in any form.

It was in this industrious, substantial, Godfearing, non-smoking frontier family that the extraordinary manifestations of the spring of 1881 took place. They began on a windy Sunday night in March, 1881, and continued four weeks and a day. The family were sitting around the fire, after dark, when knocks sounded on one of the boards covering a crack in the house, apparently on the porch. The father, thinking it was a neighbor who had come for a visit, went to the door, but no one was there. The knocks continued and he decided that they were caused by a harness hanging on the front porch being banged against the wall by the wind. He laid the harness down on the porch floor, but the knocking persisted.

Thereafter knocking on the boards occurred nearly every night and was usually preceded by the sound of a cat mewing three times outside the house. Probably no one in this frontier community was reminded of one of the lines of the First Witch in *Macbeth:* "Thrice the brinded cat hath mew'd." Or *did* someone have that line in mind? The noises would usually end at midnight with a sound like a large bird, such as a turkey, flying straight up into the air. Soon other manifestations began to take place, and more and more happened in the daytime.

R. T. Woodson, who was then twelve years old, slept with two of his brothers, Bose and John, aged thirteen and ten, on a mattress laid on the floor of the upstairs room. Their older brother Columbus, twenty-eight years old, also slept in the attic on a separate mattress. A fifth brother, Sylvester, was away working. Their sixteen- or seventeen-year-old sister *presumably* slept downstairs in the same room as the elder Woodsons. Often at night, before the knocking commenced, some sort of small animal would run up the stairway and hide behind a large trunk which stood near the head of the younger boys' mattress, growling and "popping his teeth," while the boys cowered closer together in the dark and pulled the covers farther up over their heads.

The family at first was frightened and worried about these happenings, and lost so much sleep that it interfered with their work the next day; but after a couple of weeks they began to take them more as a matter of course and paid less and less attention to them. The neighbors, however, became interested and would come in to listen; as the word of these strange happenings spread, people even came from as far as Fort Worth, a hundred miles away, but no one, it is said, had any explanation for the noises.

Probably, however, this means that no satisfactory explanation was presented as to how the noises were produced, for there is little doubt that A. C. Traweek was right in saying that many did believe the noises had something to do with buried treasure; stories of treasure trove, usually so many "jack loads" of gold from Spanish days, were common in the neighborhood. In fact, about the time of the knockings, three Anglo-Americans and a Mexican came into the community with a chart and asked permission of the owner of the land just north of the Woodson place to dig in the cliffs along the Leon for money supposedly buried by two South Texas cattlemen who were attacked by Indians on their way back from Kansas. The owner gave permission, on condition that he should receive a share, but one day when he returned from dinner the prospectors had left hurriedly and the farmer could see where a box had been dug up. The landowner, a very poor and ignorant man, came over to the Woodson cabin to tell about it wringing his hands and crying real tears. The Woodson boys went over, and sure enough, they could see a hole about eighteen inches or two feet square and a flat rock which looked as if it might have been put over the box of treasure. This was not the only party of treasure seekers known to have been operating in the country round about.

The Woodsons and their neighbors finally became so accustomed to the knocking that they began to joke with it—"pranking," Mr. Woodson calls it. They would ask the ghost to "make a noise like a broom," and immediately they would hear a harsh sound exactly as if someone were sweeping with a coarse broom, or they would ask it to "go like a drunk man," and it would plainly make a shuffling noise exactly like a drunken man walking and dragging his feet. They would also ask it questions which could be answered with one knock for "yes" and two for "no." When a neighbor named Ira Townsend was visiting, someone asked: "Did Ira Townsend ever steal a sheep?" A single emphatic knock answered in the affirmative. Ira Townsend jumped out of his chair, shouting "That's a lie! I never stole a sheep in my life!" But, after calming down, he recollected, and admitted, that as a Confederate soldier he did once steal a sheep for food!

As the noises continued, manifestations of a visual nature began. Rocks were thrown from upstairs, striking the living room floor close to the door leading into the kitchen. They would come down one every half minute or minute; this would keep up for an hour or so, then the rocks would stop for two or three hours and then begin again. Sometimes the rock-throwing would stop for a longer period. The rocks would usually be thrown during the day and sometimes nearly half a bushel would be lying on the floor. Each stone usually had a letter on it, sometimes more than one; they tried many times to put the lettered stones together to form a message, but never succeeded. Butcher knives, table knives, forks, salt cellars, and bottles would also be thrown down the stairs, but usually at night. The table implements were the family's property, the rocks were sometimes recognized as being from around the house. The bottles were usually reduced to fine pieces, as though thrown with great force, but sometimes enough would be left that they could be recognized as from around the house.

Once, while helping to grub roots in the field, young Woodson had a great deal of trouble digging up one bush, with a very crooked S-shaped root. He left the "grub" lying in the field, but one evening, just after dark, it was thrown down the stairway. Mr. Woodson did not, apparently, attach any particular significance to the shape of the root, despite the fact that it formed the initial letter of the name of the real hero of *Paradise Lost*, "The Accuser of the Brethren."

The missile-throwing was not confined to the stairway. Frequently, of an evening, when the family were out at the barn, milking, rocks would be thrown through the trees. But despite the number of objects thrown, inside the house and out, no one was ever struck, nor was anything ever thrown when anyone was looking in the direction from which the missile came.

A hen was sitting on eggs in one corner of the living room, and eggs would disappear from beneath her and be squeezed down into the room from upstairs. Mr. Woodson can well remember the eggs dripping down through the cracks in the ceiling. The hen, however, never seemed to be disturbed. These egg-squeezing manifestations always occurred in the daytime.

The older brother Sylvester, who was away working, had left some of his clothes in the large trunk upstairs. One day one of his shirts was found lying on the stairway with a glove on either side and his hat in the middle. They put the clothing back and it was not again disturbed.

One spectral manifestation of a benevolent nature is recorded. Mrs. Woodson was occasionally troubled by indigestion, and some of the neighbors had advised her to chew a little tobacco when an attack came on. One day she was sitting before the fire, wishing she had some tobacco—presumably her husband, as well as her sons, was an abstainer from the weed—when she felt something fall into her lap. It was a piece of tobacco! It will be remembered that another version of this story makes the object which fell into Mrs. Woodson's lap a piece of her dead daughter's dress—perhaps a warning that she should think of higher matters than tobacco.

The father was determined, if possible, to trace these manifestations to their origin. The boys had thrown rocks up on the roof, as boys will, and he got up on top of the house and swept them off; perhaps he thought of the stone-thrower as possessing wings with which it could swoop down on the roof and wished to eliminate such a readily available supply of ammunition. Or perhaps he thought that an active boy might be able to climb from the upstairs window onto the roof! Although the elder Woodson was a peaceable man, with no known enemies, he had had some slight differences with a neighbor, so he slipped out of the house one night, went south a half mile or so, and returned by cautiously walking up the dry bed of the Leon, but saw nothing. He resorted to drastic means in an attempt to deal with the three mews which frequently prefaced the other nocturnal noises. They had five or six cats around the house, so he ruthlessly killed them all, but the mewing continued as before.

The front door was held shut by the pioneer device of a wooden pin inserted at an angle in a hole bored in the door jamb. One evening the pin was thrown to the floor. The father then had all the members of the family get in the center of the room and join hands, but still the pin would be taken from the hole and thrown on the floor. This happened five times, but never when anyone was looking at the pin.

Perhaps the most startling manifestation, but one quite different from the others, occurred rather late one evening when the older brother, Columbus, and Charlie Rucks, who had built the stone fireplace and two years later married the Woodson daughter, decided to sit up, to see if they could see or hear anything which might help to solve the mystery. They were sitting by the small fire, talking in low tones, when a naked little Negro boy, apparently about three years old, stood before them in the rather dim light, but plainly visible. The child uttered no sound, but stood before them for a few minutes, then vanished into thin air in an instant, as he had appeared. The woman narrator, Miss May Walters, it will be remembered, had the child appropriately appear *in* the fireplace. A century or so earlier the child's identity would have been no mystery to most people. The Devil was commonly known as the Black Man, so a black child would have been assumed to be one of his imps. Columbus Woodson died the following winter, unmarried, but no one, apparently, suggested that this appearance was a death warning.

One wonders, too, whether or not the year in which these strange happenings took place reminded anyone of the concluding couplet in "Mother Shipton's Prophecy": "And this world to an end shall come/ In eighteen hundred and eighty one." If so, Mr. Woodson does not remember it.

Four weeks and a day after the windy Sunday when the first knocking was heard, the manifestations ceased as abruptly as they had begun. Just after breakfast a rock was thrown down the stairway – and that was the end. One wonders what the Woodson family's feelings were at the cessation of those exciting and inexplicable sights and sounds which had focused on them the attention of the whole neighborhood. Perhaps relief was mingled with a vague sense of loss.

To Mr. Woodson those ghostly happenings of seventy years ago were so fantastic, so unreasonable, so unbelievable, that even now it almost hurts him to think of them, and he almost hates to talk of them, because he does not see how anyone could believe them. During forty-five years in Mineral Wells, where the story was not known, he told it only once, to his next-door neighbor, who he does not think believed him. Mr. Woodson would not believe such a story himself if anyone else told it, yet he insists that it is all true, that he remembers those incredible occurrences in detail as if they had happened yesterday.

He hopes, though now eighty-two years old, that their meaning will yet be revealed to him. Perhaps, he more than half believes, buried treasure actually was at the bottom of it all. He remembers that, after the log house had rotted down, he was back at the old home and saw a hole under the chimney, as if someone had been digging. If he were physically able, he would go back himself and spend at least a week digging. After the discovery of oil at Ranger, in 1917, many of the local stories about buried treasure were transferred to petroleum, so oil is another possibility. That was the belief of his nephew, the letter-writer A. C. Traweek. Yet, although two dry holes, a well with a slight showing of oil, and even a twenty-barrel well, have been drilled within a radius of a mile and a half, the Woodson quarter-section itself, with its "Tea Pot Dome with lots of black Oil & gas rocks" and with its ghostly background, although leased more than once, still remains untested, a challenge to some daring wildcatter.

The graveyard has always been more important to the folk than to their more urbane fellowmen. It is hard to think of a sophisticated medieval story without the *mise en scene* of the manor, or of peasants outside the graveyard. For action, live and dead, it's the boneyard every time for the folk.

Remember Thurber's Birge family?

Old Nate Birge sat on the rusted wreck of an ancient sewing machine in front of Hell Fire, which was what his shack was known as among the neighbors and to the police. He was chewing on a splinter of wood and watching the moon come up lazily out of the old cemetery in which nine of his daughters were lying, only two of whom were dead.

Cemeteries are the proper theaters for folk medicine as well. Since most of the ailments to which the human flesh is heir are psychogenetic, they can be cured by the same process that caused them. The people who read this book go for their therapy to physicians and psychiatrists; the people who made the material of this book go to the graveyard. A dead cat, swung over the left shoulder at midnight and thrown with all the faith one can put into one's arms, is every bit as efficacious as a forty-dollar session with the Shrink.

A MIRACLE IN THE GRAVEYARD*

In a certain part of the country, there used to be several sheep thieves. Every night some person in the neighborhood would miss some sheep.

One night three boys started out in search of some lost sheep. They came to the graveyard in the neighborhood, and here the road divided into three directions. They came to the conclusion that one boy should take each of the roads, and when they found their sheep they should all meet in the graveyard. The one getting back first was to wait for the others. One boy found his sheep and got back early.

A certain boy in the neighborhood passed by the graveyard and saw this boy sitting on a tombstone and thought he was a ghost. He ran home to tell his crippled father about what he had seen. His father wouldn't believe him until his son carried him to the graveyard to see the ghost. The boy put his father on his back and carried him to the graveyard. His father hadn't walked for ten years.

When they came to the grave where this boy sat with his sheep, the son said to his father, "Now do you see him?"

His father said, "No, I don't. You will have to carry me closer."

He took him close enough for the boy on the tombstone to see them, and thinking that it was one of his friends coming with a sheep, he asked, "Is he fat?"

This frightened the boy so much that he dropped his father and ran home as fast as he could. But after all his father beat him home, though he hadn't walked a step in ten years.

*From Charles Neely, "The Lame Man Recovers His Legs."
JAF Volume 47, 1934, 263-264.

X

Having Fun

SOME YEARS AGO, when I still had time for pleasure, I used to go of a Sunday to a clearing in southern Delaware, the northernmost part of the Deep South, and from one in the afternoon until midnight listen to a succession of hillbilly and country bands. Each band had its half hour, followed by an intermission of the same length, during which time all us country folk would wander about the park, pitching pennies, losing dimes on the wheel of fortune, buying hot dogs, watching the Indian snake oil pitchmen. On one of those Sunday afternoons I saw an Amish boy, over from southeastern Pennsylvania, incongruously standing in his large-brimmed black hat and black, buttonless, austere suit, pitching pennies. The Amish, I knew, forbade all pleasures except serving God by hard work; they rode, when they had to ride, in antique horse-drawn buggies and fought the government on sending their children to schools where they would be exposed to the wickedness of the outside world. Yet here was one of them, a member of the faith, judging by his clothes and his pathetic, adolescent beard, pitching pennies into small-mouthed jars for prizes he couldn't possibly have taken back to Huff's Church. After watching his feeble attempts at vice for a while, I made his casual acquaintance, talking about nothing until I felt close enough to remark, "You shouldn't be here, should you?" He turned to me with all the sadness of the world in his eyes and said simply, "We are human, too."

One is suffused with love for human beings, the only creature on the earth that has to consider his own inevitable end and the hardships of the road in getting there, when one is permitted to see the poor human being through the chinks in the armor he wears against the world — whether it be the Amish in black suit, hat, and beard, or the fat man in the dark glasses and the Hawaiian shirt. We are all human beings, God help us, and that is both bad enough and good enough to say for any of God's creatures.

In the cities of this fantastic civilization, we have innumerable toys to amuse ourselves with, while waiting to cross that lonesome valley. Most of them are metatactic toys, things once useful but now good only to play with — trolley cars, organized sports, collecting of antiques or anything else from the past, campers, boats, five-foot shelves of Harvard classics, gardening, hunting, fishing, barbecues on the patio, a thousand things we can do; and if we do not choose to do, we can watch someone else doing — in the ball park, in the movies, on that greatest wonder of the world, television. But what about the folk, hidden away from all these things by the mountains, the prairies, their religions, their traditional ways of life that have no room for the present? Vance Randolph, the folk historian of the Ozarks, tells it like it is for his people:

The people who live in the Ozark Mountain region of Missouri and Arkansas are singularly isolated from the outside world, and know almost nothing of the civilization which has grown up about them. They live by growing a little fruit, raising a few lean hogs, cutting railroad ties, and distilling execrable corn whiskey, and have made very little progress since their ancestors wandered west from the southern Appalachians more than a century ago. They still sing old English and Scottish ballads, use many quaint words and phrases which are no longer a part of the ordinary American vulgate, and cling to a great many superstitious beliefs which have been rejected and forgotten in more enlightened sections of the country.*

The folk are deprived in play as much as they are deprived in work and its products. For them there is no metataxis; if they have a spinning wheel in the parlor, it is there to spin yarn, not to hold an electric bulb and a lampshade. Some of our children this Christmas will get robot horses worth a thousand dollars on which they can ride smooth-shod over the status of the neighbors' children for a day or two. Back in the hills or on the edge of the desert, a boy might hope for a stick with a horse's-head handle. The father of the boy with the robot horse may get an electronic organ so that he won't have to waste his time at that addictive boob-tube. Back among the folk, both boy and dad might have to make their own toys.

It is a delight when one looks through the chinks in the armor against the world and sees a glimpse of the brightly human amid all the darkly human that is the most of life. Take the Church of Jesus Christ of Latter-Day Saints, for example. Almost immediately after Joseph Smith's revelations established the Church in 1830, the Saints' neighbors harried them out of the East. On their first move, the Mormons went willingly enough, since one of their tenets was that the world center of the Church was to be in Jackson County, Missouri. But in Missouri they met with fierce opposition, partly for their religious beliefs, partly for their abolitionist sympathies. They were forced out of Jackson County. The largest group of deportees went to Kirtland County, Ohio, but this colony failed after its bank failed, and that hiving place vanished. Meanwhile, those Mormons who stayed in various parts of Missouri found themselves in open warfare with the Gentiles, and the Gentile governor drove them out of the state, in midwinter. They re-established their colony in Nauvoo, Illinois, some twenty thousand of them, a number that drew both political parties to seek their support. But the Mormons wished a plague on both their houses and ran their leader and prophet, Joseph Smith, for President. This, and the revelation he had about polygyny, caused his arrest and lynching. Then the final exodus, in a prairie winter, pushing handcarts because they were too poor for wagons, to the desert state of what was to become Utah, where, they declared, they would make their stand.

*Vance Randolph, "Folk-Beliefs in the Ozark Mountains." JAF Volume 40, 1927, 78.

The Manifest Destiny of the expanding nation could not permit an autonomous religious state like the Mormons' Deseret, and it was inevitable that the colony be absorbed. There was much violence, death, and consequent hatred on both sides. The legacy is visible today; the Mormons strike us as a sour, intolerant, hateful, clannish, and thoroughly humorless cult of quasi-Christian misfits.

But get to know the Mormons — and somebody will begin telling you tales of J. Golden Kimball. With Brother Golden, the chink of the Mormons opens. J. Golden Kimball was the son of Heber Kimball, one of the original twelve apostles and Brigham Young's first counsellor. He was six feet and three inches in height, thin as a toothpick, wiry and tough, but with a strange, quite incongruously thin, high, querulous voice. Because of his parentage, and because heredity determines much of the hierarchy in the Mormon Church, J. Golden was destined for a high position in the clergy. But his trouble was the life of a cowboy he had followed until his elevation. It must be remembered in hearing J. Golden Kimball stories (and they must be heard; no print can convey the shattering dichotomy between his position and his vocabulary) that as president of the Committee of Seventy, he was immediately under the twelve apostles and president of a body that produced bishops and other important functionaries. He was in fact equivalent to an important Italian cardinal in the Roman Catholic Church.

One day, not long before his death at the age of eighty-five, he stepped off the curb at the corner of South Temple and Main, intending to cross the street. He moved feebly, for old age did not meet him kindly. Suddenly a carful of young louts blasted by him, just barely ticking his black coat. J. Golden raised his cane, shook it with anger and feebleness, and shouted after them, "You son of a *bitch!* Have you no respect for the priesthood?"

Once he was musing during a June sermon on marriage. As so often happened in his sermons, he deviated from his text.

This is the month of June, and that's the mating time. Now, I suppose some of you young folks will be getting hitched up. Well, I just want to warn you not to expect too damned much of each other, and then maybe you won't be disappointed. Now, when I got married, I thought

I was marrying an angel. And there have been many times since when I wished to hell I had.

I've often wondered what would happen if the perfect man married the perfect woman. I'll bet he'd shoot her inside of a week if she didn't poison him first.

Young people and old ones, too, get married for all manner of reasons. Some select a girl because she has pretty eyes. Some because she has pretty hair. Some men marry a woman because she can cook. I knew a man who chose a girl because she could sing. He married her. And the next morning when he saw her without any paint and powder on, he saw part of her hair on the dresser, and her false teeth in a glass, he looked at her and he said, *"Sing, for hell's sake, sing!"*

J. Golden's outrageous stories and flamboyant vocabulary finally drove the Church to proclaim a manifesto on swearing, which was a personal rebuke and a great shame to him. He died not long after the manifesto, in 1938. It was decided to hold his funeral in the Great Tabernacle, despite the objections of many of the apostles, who said it was needless, that the Tabernacle could not come close to being filled even by the funeral of one of themselves. But when J. Golden died, it was filled, and huge crowds surrounded the building. It was the biggest funeral since the death of Brigham Young himself.

See J. Golden Kimball, see the Mormons in this chink in their armor, and see the humor of the folk.

For the last hundred years those who loved the play party most dearly have been pronouncing its death, yet it still persists, dying here, perhaps, to be resuscitated there, and coming to life here again. Probably it will never entirely die so long as there are folk societies holding a storm-knife against the inhumanity of forced isolation. However much man dislikes man, man nevertheless needs man. This ambivalence is the cause of his being a gregarious cannibal, but in spite of his inheritance as a naked ape, he caresses more than he kills, he joys more than he saddens.

It was the need for the companionship of his fellows that made the American folk societies orient themselves around their impassioned religion. That female aurochs of Mencken's backwoods Holy Roller religion was rejoicing in the sheer gladness of good fellowship as much as worshipping her God. The secular equivalent of the camp meeting was the play party. It had fairly obvious acquaintance with the devil's work among peoples who condemned dancing, the fiddle, and frivolous songs. But it had no fiddle—that instrument of Satan incarnate—or other musical instruments, and the gyrating was not dancing in the strict sense (one is reminded of the Negro ring shout, which is absolutely differentiated from dancing in that it does not require the crossing of the legs), so it was tolerated by even the most dour of the rural Puritans. Its spontaneity also turns away the devil. Vance Randolph tells us that in the Ozarks "the news is simply 'norated around' that there is to be a frolic over at so-and-so's place, and anybody is welcome who cares to attend." For miles they come, where any journey is a travail. Sometimes there is food, sometimes not; usually there is a jug of liquor outside in the dark and opportunities for what the hillman, according to Randolph, "elegantly describes as 'tom-cattin.'" And occasionally, he continues, "a party breaks up at dawn in a drunken riot."

It is this very informality that will insure the continuance of the play party, even when the name has disappeared. The meeting is spontaneous, the party is simple, no musicians or trained singers are either needed or welcomed, no dance hall is necessary; all that is required is young folks who are lonely, who want to take pleasure in the company of one another, and who know the common stock of lyric songs and simple dancing games.

THE
PLAY PARTY
IN IDAHO*

The play party is a survival of our grandfathers' days, which today is found only in those isolated districts that are more or less separated, very often by reason of their physical geography, from their more thickly settled neighbors. Like the Celts in early England, the play party has been pushed back, foot by foot, across the entire country, until today it has taken its final stand in certain mountain fastnesses where its enemy, sophistication, cannot further pursue it. The play party came to America from England with the middle classes and slowly marched with our pioneers to all the far corners of our country. Herbert Quick, in his book *Vandemarck's Folly*, tells of it in Iowa two generations ago; Dr. George Morey Miller in his book called *The Dramatic Element in the Popular Ballad*, tells of its presence in the state of Washington some twenty-nine years ago; Leah Jackson Wolford in her book *The Play Party in Indiana* describes the play party most fully as she and her parents have known it in that state, and the *Journal of American Folklore* has published numerous studies relating to various characteristics pertaining to this form of amusement as it has appeared in different communities.

Today in Northern Idaho those conditions exist which are most conducive to the survival of the play party, and here it is now a flourishing fashion in rural districts. The country is largely mountainous, and travel is cut to a minimum by the deep canyons, the dangerous grades, and the mountain streams. During the long summer evenings when the roads are good, the country people may drive to town to attend the movies, or ride to a neighbor's home to sit on the porch and visit for an hour or two; but there will be no social gatherings of any kind in these months which will include more than a very small portion of the entire group. Here and there in the district a family will drive into town on Sunday mornings to attend church services, but this is the exception

*From Leona Nessly Ball, "The Play Party in Idaho." JAF Volume 44, 1931, 1-26.

and not the rule. In the part of Idaho that I know best, there are no Ladies' Aids, no Young People's Societies, no Women's Clubs, nor Men's Smokers. Isolation is the rule in these mountain communities.

The fall months bring with them, however, one form of social gathering which is distinctly popular with the entire group in the isolated districts. This is the public sale. Each year a farmer here or there will have reached that time of life and that state of affluence when he can sell his belongings and go to California; others who have attained neither age nor affluence will be selling out to go to Canada and start life anew, and still others will be selling out in order to live nearer relatives, or to try truck farming, or to move to town. Each of these people in turn will have a sale and serve a free lunch at noon; and to each of these sales the neighbors will come, generally with all the family, and spend the entire day. The farmer's goods will be sold of course (the valuable things going for mere songs and the worthless articles bringing the average up handsomely, as is always the case), but this buying and selling will, after all, be but a minor aspect of the affair. The really important phase will be the social contact which this gathering provides.

The movies and visits of summer, then, and the public sales of the fall afford the opportunities for sociability that gregarious man requires, but what entertainment will be provided for the winter months? Always with the rains and the snows of winter comes the play party, the most important social function of the year. To one who has lived all of his past years in the city, the play party affords a great awakening. It was about nine years ago that I attended the first play party I had ever seen and caught my first glimpse of the social environment of pioneer days. Here I learned for the first time all the words of many songs, fragments of which I had heard from my parents for years, and here it was that I first saw these songs in their natural habitat. Here it was that I first heard "Skip to My Lou" through all its eighteen verses; here it was that I learned that "Old John Brown Had a Little Indian" belonged to a dance step, and not to the knee-trotting game with which it was connected in my early childhood; and here it was that I heard "We've Got a Pig in the Parlor" fade gently out into "Swing Your Left Hand Lady Round and We'll All Promenade." Since that time I have attended many of these parties, but they have never grown an old story. Often after I have thought I knew every one of the repertoire numbers, the crowd will form a ring, seemingly without a word of agreement, and spontaneously swing into a play party song which I have never heard them sing before.

I have never heard the play party referred to as such by any of those who participate in it. If the play party is given in a private home, which is very rare indeed, then it is merely called a "party." If it is given in the schoolhouse, it follows a school program and the entire festivities of the evening are grouped together under the cognomen "school entertainment."

The first play party of the year will come on that Friday evening which is nearest to Hallowe'en. The teacher will start the machinery by assigning "pieces" for each of the pupils to speak, and as the children practice their verses, the word floats over the countryside that on the appointed evening the Mountain Prospect School will give an entertainment. The country schools that I know average about twelve pupils each, and these youngsters are the "moccasin telegraph" by which the coming play party is announced. That is, it is announced merely by connotation. The pieces will be rehearsed to any who will listen; the one-act play which will follow the pieces, will be grandly enlarged upon to anyone who cares to hear. The play will be liberally sprinkled with the well-known neighborhood jests, and these selections of humor will become familiar to everyone, far and near, long before the program is given. But the play party itself seems never to come out into open conversation. Of the ballads Professor G. L. Kittredge has said: "As civilization advanced, they were banished from polite society, but they lived on among the humble, among the shepherds and plowboys and 'the spinsters and knitters in the sun,' until even these became too sophisticated to care for them, and they were heard no more." The play party has now, too, been driven from polite society, and it lives on only in those mountain nooks where sophistication has not intruded.

Perhaps it is the impending arrival of this enemy that keeps the play party in such retirement as it maintains. Perhaps it is merely shy in daylight. Whatever the reason, it remains closely hidden and secure until the proper setting for it has been prepared. Then the play party comes into its own. For three or four hours it will emerge from its seclusion, and pretend the world is young again, and that folk have gathered to do it honor. It will be alive and boisterous; it will revel in shouting and singing and stamping, and it will reach a peak of mad merriment and then suddenly come to an end. The next day it will be again completely disguised under the all-inclusive name "school entertainment."

With the announcement that such an entertainment will be given, as I have said, all the wheels in the social machinery of the district will start into motion. Young and old will turn at once to thoughts of raiment, and the former will unite in demanding new outfits for the season's opening affair. The latter will content themselves with airing and pressing their best apparel, and they will go about familiar tasks humming or whistling certain well-known play party airs. The young lady of the family will hunt out her freckle cream and spend hours in beautifying her hands, while the young man will pump and carry and heat the tubs of water for the baths without one word of complaint. The children will stumble blindly about, mumbling studiously at their pieces, endeavoring by this means to escape the greatest possible number of chores. The phone will be ringing more or less continuously, and each mother in the district will stand for hours with receiver to ear, attempting to solve the problem of what refreshments she will take to the party. An ingenious mother in this district will train her smallest child to hold the receiver for her while she sits beneath the phone calmly paring potatoes, yet never missing a word of the discussion—even rising at times to interpolate a suggestion here and there where it will do the most good—as many an honest family can testify. There is never any conception of privacy about the rural lines. As many as twenty women may be engaged in a discussion at one time, each offering beneficial advice, and with these facilities the arrangements are soon made. Certain families will provide the sandwiches for all, as many as six kinds being decided upon; others will bring cakes for the crowd—light cakes and dark cakes, loaf cakes and layer cakes; others will bring the salads, which will consist, if the roads to town are in bad condition, or any relish from sweet pickles to chow-chow; and still others will provide the coffee, sugar, and cream. The cook wagon outfit nearest the school will be asked to supply all the dishes and the mammoth coffee pots and dish pans. Mother will thrust a folded dish towel into her coat pocket and will probably have to sacrifice it for a dishrag which no one else thought to bring.

At last the evening arrives, and everyone far and near goes to the brilliantly lighted country schoolhouse. There are absolutely no restrictions as to eligibility. Anyone in the Mountain Prospect district may attend, or anyone from any other district, or anyone from no district at all. Young people from town will drive out, city high school students will attend, and perhaps strangers who have come from a distance, and everyone will be made welcome. The wealthiest family in the district will rub elbows with the poorest, and the latter will have just as good a time as the former. The schoolhouse will be too crowded, of course; it always is. But games are possible despite the crowding, and no one seems to mind in the least. Even the children, who have to pay for the crowding by having to sit quietly in the piled-up seats against a far wall after the play party begins, will take it good-naturedly and watch the crowd contentedly until they fall asleep.

At the commencement of the party, however, the seats are found standing correctly in their orderly rows, and only the initiate will realize that they are not permanent fixtures. There is nothing whatever in this very proper schoolhouse to remind one of a dance hall. It is far more like a theater, for across the upper end, cutting off a space perhaps six feet deep by eighteen feet wide, will be strung a gayly colored calico curtain. From behind the curtain will come worried exclamations, giggles, chords from a concealed organ, all interspersed with constant admonitions to "Shhhhh!" from the sorely beset teacher. In the upper corner of the room will be several long tables heavily laden with market baskets of all shapes and sizes, all alike heaped high and rounded over with spotless cloths, mingled with two-quart fruit jars full of all kinds of salads, sweating cream cans, and leaning tower effects worked out in plates. The atmosphere will be weighted down with suppressed excitement and an odor of ground coffee.

As for the program itself, it will be the usual school exercise of "speakin' pieces," and these will vary from the four-line selection lisped blushingly by the smallest of first graders, to the "Address of Logan," declaimed loudly and feelingly by the high-collared young gentleman in the eighth grade. The sympathies of most of the audience are with the former, whereas my own are always with the latter; he has so many things to contend with. His boots are absolutely sure to squeak horribly with every appalling step he has to take; his collar will either threaten to choke him to death or will give up the endeavor with a loud pop and a flying button, and who shall say which is worse? His friends will always torment him with a taunting "Hey, Bills!" and his younger brothers and sisters will inevitably call out something which will disgrace him for years to come. And finally, it is always on this trying occasion that his voice will do its first terrifying breaking. It may have been a perfectly trustworthy organ for fifteen years, and come to be regarded with the utmost confidence, but inevitably it wrecks its possessor on some occasion like the play party. It could have broken at a hundred other times just as well and caused him no distress whatever, but with fiendish ingenuity it must happen in the middle of "Logan." As a result the unfortunate possessor of the break will have one or two fights outside in the autumn darkness before the evening is over, and perhaps half a dozen more within the next two weeks of school, before he regains any portion of his lost prestige. Yes, my sympathies are decidedly with the eighth grader.

There will be single recitations, and there will be dialogues; there will be solos and quartettes and choruses before the curtain is haltingly drawn together amid the applause of the audience. Then it will almost immediately be swished open again on the play. The plays of the cities always face two possibilities: they may be successes or they may be failures. This is never true in our rural communities, for here the play is always an amazing success. The act as it left the author's hands bears ro relation whatever to the act given in this country schoolhouse. The teacher, always a Normal graduate, or a university junior-to-be next fall, will supply the one-act play which her pupils will act in such a way that the author himself would never recognize it. This is because in rehearsing there will be added here and there the many jests on the best known members of the community; and so, little by little, the drama is

created by the school until in the end the play emerges, not as an individual composition, but as a communal development. The twenty-
five dollars paid for the privilege of giving the play would seem entirely
wasted. Nearly always the act will be a society play which the teacher
saw given in her university. To be just right it should have a London
setting, but one from New York or Boston will do in case of necessity.
This is because the incongruity at once sets the audience off into gales
of laughter, and within the first ten minutes the spell is completely
woven. There must be a lord, or a world-famed genius, as one of the
leads in the production and a beautiful heiress is always an essential.
This is a trying part, for many of the dramas have a heroine who
smokes, and even cubebs are a trial to the novice. The organ and a few
borrowed easy chairs will indicate anything from the duke's castle to
the House of Lords. Both setting and cast enhance the delight of hearing a member of Parliament, for instance, tell at Lady Cardigan's ball
the tale of Simmy Ransome's cow that is named Dr. Mary Walker on
account of her unfortunate fondness for trousers, she having consumed
as many as three pairs in one forenoon. It is always a mystery how the
play ever reaches an ending, so often does it have to stand and wait
wooden-faced (at which these children soon become adept) for the
laughter to die down; but come to an end it always does, and that rarely
later than nine-thirty. At its conclusion the teacher announces that
"this ends our little program, and we thank you one and all for your
kind attention." To all appearances the evening has come to an end.

But the teacher no sooner backs, bowing, through the curtains, than
the audience rises as a single individual, and for a few moments bed-
lam reigns. The women and children retreat to the safety of the cloak-
room. The men grab the rows of seats, and, row by row, they are carried to the most out-of-the-way wall and stacked as high as can be
reached. The organ will be rolled out into the entry, and the tables
arranged so as to take up the smallest possible amount of room. Within
a bare five minutes the last protesting youngster is captured and wig-
glingly thrust into his particular niche in the layers of the desks, and
the ring at once forms. Perhaps the first game will be "Two Young
Couples Skating Went." If the crowd is very large there may be four
or even six couples swinging at once in the center, each individual apparently bearing a charmed life, for I have never known of an accident.
The lines are sung with a swing that only folk melodies have, and a
more joyous game than those of the play party has never been known.
There is so much repetition that any newcomer can at once learn the
words and the tune.

Forty years ago, as today, the play parties were a flourishing institution in Northern Idaho and differed but little from the games of today.
The play parties then were of necessity held in homes and not in school-

houses: they were all night affairs, and not merely three-hour parties. There were sound reasons why this should be so. The crowds were pulled over greater distances than today, and horses, not motors, furnished the power to climb the steep Palouse Hills; the horses, then, needed rest, and the drivers recreation. The greater difficulties in the way of social gatherings at that time made it advisable to get the very utmost of pleasure out of each hard-earned evening. Moreover, chore time came at six or seven in the morning regardless of the fact that bedtime might have come but a few hours earlier. For these reasons, then, it was customary to prolong the play party from chore time to chore time, so that when the stock was attended to, the family might retire for the greater part of the winter's day.

For another difference, the play party of the eighties had no cook wagon from which dishes might be borrowed, and no hostess ever had enough to go around. It was too risky to borrow, for the chances were that most of the dishes would be broken on the rough ride to or from the party. On this account the couples shared a plate and had it refilled more frequently if necessary. This worked very nicely, but the shared cup of coffee presented difficulties. As often as not one member wished her coffee with no sugar and lots of cream, while the other wished his with lots of sugar and no cream. This seems to have been a constant annoyance, and even today Father loves to rehearse how many times he had to drink his coffee at a play party as Mother seasoned it, regardless of his preferences. Often, in telling of past grievances, he will take an extra cup of coffee at the play party of today just to assert his independence. Truly this was a serious flaw in the party of the past.

Another difference between the play party of yesterday and that of today is found in the fact that those pioneers did not consider clothes the important factor that they have become today. Those who had fine things wore them, but those who had not did not stay home to weep. Instead, they attended the party in mother-hubbard and overalls, and thought little of it. The first play party memory of one woman I know centers around the clever way in which she saved her ten-year old self from a violent death in a mad play party game, by hanging desperately to the overall buttons around the waist of the young giant who was her partner.

The last difference between the play party of forty years ago and that of today is found in the fact that games which were most popular then are missing from the play party of today, and have become definitely children's games to be played on the school grounds at recess. Among these old games which are now missing from the grown-up parties are "Water Merino Tansy," "Little Sally Rosser," "Farmer in the Dell," "Thus the Farmer Sows His Seed," "Polly Put the Kettle On," "Here

We Go Round the Mulberry Bush," and "London Bridge." Still other
old play party games survive today only as songs, and these largely
fragmentary. Among these are "Pop Goes The Weasel," "Billy Boy,"
"Old Dan Tucker," "Dem Golden Slippers," and "Goodbye Liza Jane."
Forty years ago these were all popular at play parties.

The play party grows in merriment as the evening passes, and a little
before twelve it will probably reach its height, but about this time it
becomes aware that it is unable to compete with a worthy opponent
that has entered the room. This enemy makes itself known by the clat-
ter of dishes and the discovery that the elder women are systematically
arranging a long series of high-heaped plates in that order which long
experience has proved is most satisfactory for the coming onslaught.
An all-pervasive odor of boiling coffee makes itself manifest, and slowly
the young people discover that their elders and their youngers have all
left the play party to join the side of the opposing forces. The love affairs of the district are always disclosed by the fact that it takes those
participating in them about three games to realize that all the rest of
the crowd is otherwise engaged. When parents see a son or daughter
taking part in this small ring so blissfully unconscious of the impending
feast, they realize at once that all is over but the charivari. Dad begins
immediately to figure whether he will have to give up Meg and Dolly,
his best milkers, or whether he will be able to square his debt to Son by
turning over old Pet and the young stock; and Mother at once begins to
figure on new tablecloths and linens, realizing with a pang that now she
has finally accumulated enough extra bedding to secure her freedom
from this kind of sewing, she must part with it all, along with the grandmother silver spoons and the prized Aunt Myra plates. The young
people dance on blithely unaware of the furor they are causing in pa-
rental bosoms.

As the odor of coffee and salads grows, however, even these couples
manifest an accumulating uneasiness, and eventually the play party
ends, a little sullenly and resentfully, perhaps, but still it ends. The
young people agree that they will eat, yes (pretending to the last that
they are forced to it by others), but that they fully intend to resume the
games immediately supper is over. Why, the evening has only begun!
The idea of quitting this early! It really is unheard of! Do you think that
any of the parents there agree that it is ridiculous to stop so early and
relate the hours of the play parties that they knew back in the eighties,
and nineties, and the nineteen hundreds? No, indeed. They look quietly
on the storm, with perhaps a smile of amusement over the follies of
youngsters in general, and forget entirely that things were once better
arranged. And so little by little, between protests as it were, the young
couples manage to edge slowly but craftily into advantageous places

about the laden tables, and while they are thus engaged, the fathers of the district will cannily begin restoring the seats and replacing the organ against the needs of the coming Monday morning. And so the play party dies, albeit unwillingly, and each member of the crowd will in time find himself supplied with a well-stocked plate and a cup of coffee —a tin cup of coffee, which means that the coffee is no hotter than the cup which he must juggle safely through the milling crowd to the refuge of his small son's seat, into which he must carefully fold himself. This feat would be totally impossible of achievement to any but the steel-nerved farmer, who can manage it repeatedly with surprising agility.

The crowd attacks the supper with a contented sigh, and for a time there is little of conversation. The school children edge craftily about between bites, busily engaged in storing a supply of cake and sandwiches into certain well-known desks, in anticipation of the hunger of Monday morning recess, and the young people endeavor to persuade the teacher to give another "school entertainment" at the earliest possible date. After the plates have been refilled a time or two, conversation will be resumed and will become more or less general. The shortcomings of all will be rehearsed, and the play's jokes retold with sundry additions and improvements. The young couples who made the ring for the final games will come in for much good-natured bantering, and when this begins to pall, all the horse trades of the past years will be retold with the keenest enjoyment.

The mothers will now begin to pick up, by which they mean the process of collecting all the jars, and bowls, and cake plates, and leftover sections of cake, and restoring them to their proper baskets. The basket, when it is repacked, is given to Dad to carry out to the car, Mother never failing to remark at this stage, that she knows perfectly well if she doesn't send Robert along to watch him like a hawk every single minute, he will be absolutely sure to put the basket in the wrong car; or set it on the running board and later manage to drive neatly right out from under it, or put it on the ground and let every car there run over it most likely—like a man always will. With this cynicism she will pick her baby out from among a dozen or more without an instant's hesitation and proceed to bundle it well for the ride home, the while assisting the school children on with their coats and giving Mrs. Johnson the recipe for her cake.

It is at this stage that the amount of confusion makes it seem impossible to believe that the schoolhouse will ever achieve order again; coats, hats, vanity cases, dishes, crumbs, and fragments will be everywhere. Several women will be madly doing dishes and piling them in orderly stacks for the return to the cookhouse. Children will salvage the extra supplies and attend to their concealment under the name of "clearing up." The young people show their desire to be helpful by taking themselves out to the various cars to await the redistribution that is always necessary just before starting for home. For the most part the crowd has come in family groups, and it will return in the same arrangement; the only exceptions are the couples who are definitely known to be engaged and the young people from town. The fathers will promise to help the children find and don all their outer garments, but will inevitably desert the task to gather around the doorstep and smoke, while discussing prospective crops and prices. The road and telephone-line work, which must be done before the snows set in, will be planned in detail, and the farmers who "trade work" will take this opportunity for arranging definite schedules, as will those who own machinery in partnership.

Within the schoolhouse the mothers will gradually bring order out of chaos. The wraps will be carefully sorted and distributed. The last dish will be dried and placed in its proper stack, and the wet dishtowels will be wrapped in paper and returned to coat pockets. The various costumes that appeared in the play will be packed away, and the last crumb brushed up. The room, little by little, is cleared and emptied, and one by one the lamps go out. There is always a last flurry around the cars, which are artistically arranged about the hitching racks, the biggest of Cadillacs chummily nudging the most disreputable of Fords. Then with a good deal of calling last words back and forth, the premises are definitely deserted. The play party has come to an end.

The songs of the play party do not impress the outsider with their complexity or musical sophistication. Such critics looking from the outside into their own culture might condemn the Beatles sound for simplicity of lyrics like "I Want to Hold Your Hand," or in ignorance of the psychedelic scene, criticize "Mr. Tambourine Man" because one cannot reasonably ask a tambourine player to "play a song for me," since tambourines do not carry melodies.

Play party songs are transcriptionally simple and their lyrics simpler, but there is much more in them than meets the ear. The simplest song might be a direction for a movement, as "Weevily Wheat" in the following collection calls for a weaving movement in the accompanying dance. The first song, "Bounce Around," is another name for the play party in some parts of the West. B. A. Botkin, the authority on the play party, points out that in the song "Old Brass Wagon" the movements are based on

... the longways dance, in which the leader and his partner "lead through" or go up and down between the facing rows of boys and girls, swinging first each other, then the next girl and boy in line, each other again, and so on until all have been swung and every couple has had its turn.

The nonsense phrases likewise are communications of directions:

Thus "Old Brass Wagon," beginning with "Lead her up and down the old brass wagon," follows the successive swinging of players by the lead couple with "One wheel off and the axle dragging," "Two wheels off the old brass wagon," etc., while *Jutang* rings the changes on the word "Jutang," in a rigmarole of dance directions: "Round up four in Jutang, Jutang, Ju," "Do-si-do in Jutang, Jutang, Ju," "Change and swing in Jutang, Jutang, Ju," etc.

SONGS OF THE
PLAY PARTY*

Some thirty years ago, in most country places, the Missouri play party was at the height of popularity as a serious form of amusement — serious not in the sense of lacking in fun and jollity, but in the sense that it was held not as a revival of old customs or in defiance of better taste, but because it yielded more genuine pleasure and recreation than any other form of amusement known to those who took part in it. In the neighborhood where I was born and reared, the play party was the common form of amusement at the gatherings of young people of the best class. As a little girl, I was permitted to sit up and look on when the parties were held at my father's or my grandfather's home.

These play parties were really dances. The players did not dance, however, to the music of instruments, but kept time with various steps to their own singing. But they were not called "dances": they were called simply "parties." The better class of people in the country did

*From Mrs. L. D. Ames, "The Missouri Play Party." JAF Volume 24, 1911, 295-318.

not believe in dancing. Regular dances, where the music was furnished by a "fiddler," were held, for the most part, only in the homes of the rough element. They were generally accompanied by card-playing, and frequently by drunkenness and fighting. The better class ranked dancing, in the moral scale, along with gambling and fishing on Sunday. It was not good form and was tabued on grounds of respectability.

At that time, also, the country church was alive and flourishing. Many, perhaps most, of the people who attended the parties, were church members. The church rules forbade dancing, and there was no thought of evading the letter of the law. Therefore, if the boy or girl danced a single quadrille to the music of a violin, he had "broke over," as the common expression was, and knew that at the next protracted meeting he was a fit subject for reconversion and that the preacher's pointed words were aimed straight at him; while, on the other hand, he might dance to the time of his own singing from seven in the evening to three o'clock the next morning, and suffer therefrom no qualms of conscience. It was not dancing: it was only playing.

The invitations to these parties were by word of mouth, delivered by one or more young men on horseback, who were said to "get up" the party. All of the eligible young people within a radius of from three to five miles were invited. The preparations made by the hostess consisted in removing the carpets and furniture from the rooms to be used by the players. Chairs and benches were placed around the sides of the rooms. It was not customary to serve refreshments. When they were served, they consisted of pies and cakes, and perhaps apples or cider. The young people came to the party on horseback, in carts, buggies, spring wagons, and "big" (farm) wagons, or if there happened to be snow on the ground, in sleighs and on sleds.

The playing would begin as soon as four or five couples had arrived, and would continue, with only short intermissions for breathing spells, until the party broke up. This might be anywhere from midnight to three o'clock in the morning. Sometimes the playing went on in two or three rooms at one time. The playing consisted in keeping step to the singing, and at the same time going through various movements: as swinging partners by one hand or both; advancing, retreating, and bowing; dancing in circles of four or eight; promenading singly or in pairs, sometimes hand in hand, sometimes with crossed hands; weaving back and forth between two rows of people going in opposite directions, and clasping right and left hands alternately with those they met. Sometimes the words of the song sung by the players indicated the various movements. At other times the players were supposed to know the manner of playing. They never "called off" the changes, as was done in the regular dances; and the method of playing depended somewhat upon the whim of individual leaders.

The words of the songs they sang were a very crude lot of rhymes—crude in sense and in form. The tunes were frequently familiar airs borrowed to suit their needs.

The playing was generally started by a song that went like this:

BOUNCE AROUND

We come here to bounce around,
We come here to bounce around,
We come here to bounce around,
    Tra, la, la, la!
    Ladies, do-si-do,
    Gents, you know,
    Swing to the right
    And then to the left,
    And all promenade.

Just us four to bounce around,
Just us four to bounce around,
Just us four to bounce around,
    Tra, la, la, la!

These words and the movements accompanying them were repeated till the players felt the need of a change. The parties took their name later from this song. In a few years this kind of party was dying out in most places. In our neighborhood it gave way to a much milder sort of party, known as a "social." To distinguish the play party from the "social," it was called a "bounce-around."

Other dance songs used are given below.

JIM ALONG JO

Cat's in the cream jar,
    Run, girls, run!
Fire in the mountains,
    Fun, boys, fun!

Chorus

Hey, Jim along, Jim along, Josie!
Hey, Jim along, Jim along, Jo!

First to the courthouse,
    Then to the jail,
Hang my hat on a
    Rusty nail.

SHOOT THE BUFFALO

Oh, we'll shoot the Buffalo,
Yes, we'll shoot the Buffalo,
And we'll rally round the cane-brake
    And shoot the Buffalo.

Oh, the girls will knit and spin,
And the boys will sit and grin,
And we'll rally round the cane-brake
    And shoot the Buffalo.

Oh, the hawky shot the buzzard,
And the buzzard shot the crow,
And we'll rally round the cane-brake
    And shoot the Buffalo.

Oh, the Buffalo will die,
For we shot him in the eye,
And we'll rally round the cane-brake
    And shoot the Buffalo.

Oh, the Buffalo is dead,
For we shot him in the head,
And we'll rally round the cane-brake
    And shoot the Buffalo.

If there were not stanzas enough to make the play sufficiently long, the same stanzas were sung again and again. When one set of players exhausted themselves, they yielded the floor to others who had been resting and talking.

WEEVILY WHEAT

Come, honey, my love, come trip with me
    In the morning early,
Heart and hand, we'll take our stand;
    'Tis true I love you dearly.

Chorus

Oh, I won't have none of your weevily wheat,
    And I won't have none of your barley,
But I must have some of the best of wheat
    To bake a cake for Charley.

For Charley he's a nice young man,
    Charley he's a dandy;
Charley loves to kiss the girls
    Because it comes so handy.

It's over the river to see the gay widow,
    It's over the river to Charley,
It's over the river to feed my sheep
    And measure up the barley.

If you love me like I love you,
    We have no time to tarry,
We'll keep the old folks fixing round
    For you and I to marry.

In the above song all the stanzas after the first were sung to the tune of the chorus.

SKIP-TO-MY-LOU

Lost your partner,
    What'll you do?
Lost your partner,
    What'll you do?
Lost your partner,
    What'll you do?
Skip-to-my-Lou, my darling.

To this the boy answered, as he took some other fellow's partner and swung her around,

I'll get another one,
    Better one, too,
I'll get another one,
    Better one, too,
I'll get another one,
    Better one, too,
Skip-to-my-Lou, my darling.

The young man who was robbed of a partner then had to secure a new one in the same way. Sometimes the attempt to secure a partner failed, the boy who was with the girl swinging her around himself. The refusal was accepted, and the disappointed young man tried again while they sang,

> Can't get a red bird,
>   A blue bird will do,
> Can't get a red bird,
>   A blue bird will do,
> Can't get a red bird,
>   A blue bird will do,
> Skip-to-my-Lou, my darling.

Sometimes the young man whose partner had been taken turned immediately and took her back, while they sang,

> Gone again,
>   Skip-to-my-Lou,
> Gone again,
>   Skip-to-my-Lou,
> Gone again,
>   Skip-to-my-Lou,
> Skip-to-my-Lou, my darling.

> Common as corn-bread,
>   Commoner, too,
> Common as corn-bread,
>   Commoner, too,
> Common as corn-bread,
>   Commoner, too,
> Skip-to-my-Lou, my darling.

> Chicken in the dough-tray,
>   Shoo, shoo, shoo!
> Chicken in the dough-tray,
>   Shoo, shoo, shoo!
> Chicken in the dough-tray,
>   Shoo, shoo, shoo!
> Skip-to-my-Lou, my darling.

CAPTAIN JINKS

> I'm Captain Jinks of the horse marines,
> I feed my horse on corn and beans,
> And court young ladies in their teens,
>   For that's the style of the army.
> We'll all go round and circle left.

We'll circle left, we'll circle left,
We'll all go round and circle left,
   For that's the style of the army;
The ladies right and form a ring,
And when they form you give'm a swing,
And when you swing you give'm a call,
   And take your lady and promenade all.

OLD DAN TUCKER

Old Dan Tucker, he got drunk,
He fell in the fire, and he kicked up a chunk;
The red-hot coals got in his shoe,
And whew-wee! how the ashes flew!

Chorus

Get out of the way for old Dan Tucker,
He's too late to get his supper!
Get out of the way for old Dan Tucker,
He's too late to get his supper.

Old Dan Tucker was a fine old man,
He washed his face in the frying pan,
He combed his head with a wagon wheel,
And he died with the toothache in his heel.

Daniel Tucker, he's a Quaker,
He drinks buttermilk by the acre,
Supper's over, dishes washed,
Nothing left but a little bit of squash.

Old Dan Tucker was a fine old man,
He used to ride the Derby ram,
He sent him a-whizzin' down the hill,
And if he hasn't got up, he's a-lyin' there still.

Sometimes during a resting spell the players would choose partners
by means of a game called "Clap-in, Clap-out." In this game the young
men retired to another room, leaving the girls alone. Some girl would
then name a boy as her choice for a partner. He was then called into the
room to guess who had chosen him. He indicated his guess by sitting
down by the girl. If he guessed the right one, the girls kept silent, and
another boy was called in to try his luck. If the first boy made a mistake, all the girls clapped their hands. He thereupon had to withdraw

and try it again later on. This was kept up till all in the company had
partners.

The devices for choosing partners served a useful and practical purpose. There were always bashful girls and boys who would miss their
share of the fun and have no partners unless they were led out and
helped along by these partner-choosing games.

Other games played in resting spells or by those who found the
dancing too strenuous were "Simon Says Wigwag"; "Brother, I'm
Bobbed"; "See, Laugh, and Say Nothing."

Occasionally a small group of boys and girls would get into a corner
as the playing went on, and play what were known as real "kissing-
games." Here are the words to one:

> King William was King James's son,
> And the royal race he run.
> He wore a star upon his breast,
> Pointing to the east and west.
> Go choose your east, go choose your west,
> Go choose the one that you love best.
> If she's not here to take your part,
> Choose another with all your heart.
> Down on the carpet you must kneel,
> Sure as the grass grows in the field.
> Salute your bride and kiss her sweet,
> Now rise upon your feet.

Following are part of the words of another:

> Possum pie
> Made of rye,
>   Possum was the meat,
> Rough enough and tough enough,
>   More than we all could eat.

This was played as a counting-out game. This thing, however, was rare.
Kissing games were frowned upon by most of the young people and all
of the elders; and those girls who took part in them forfeited, to some
extent, the respect of the rest.

These parties were not rough and boisterous gatherings, as might
be supposed by some on account of the character of the poetry and
music which sustained them. To be sure, they were noisy and merry,
rollicking and jolly, but they were participated in by young people
who were proud of good blood and good behavior; and they were conducted in a spirit of decency and order. There were well-established

metes and bounds of conduct, beyond which one could not go with impunity. The character of the amusement indicated merely a lack of social experience in those taking part.

These play parties as I have described them were the chief form of social activity of my uncles and aunts, of my parents, and of my grandparents before them, all of whom grew up in Missouri, either in this county (Boone) or in the adjoining county of Audrain. Here are the words of one of the songs that comes down from my grandmother's day:

> Come, all ye young people that's wending your way,
> And sow your wild oats in your youthful day,
> For the daylight is past, and the night's coming on,
> So choose you a partner and be marching along, marching along.

Before I was old enough to attend these parties, this style of party had gone entirely out of fashion in our neighborhood. Many of our set went away to school and saw enough of the ways of the world to make us look contemptuously down upon the noisy and undignified parties held by that unsophisticated set of young people of a few years before. We still did not dance, but were ridiculously sober and sedate and correct at "socials," as our parties were called.

These old-fashioned play parties, however, are not by any means entirely out of date. In many rural neighborhoods, remotely situated, they have never ceased to be the chief form of amusement at social gatherings of young people.

Good talk even beats good singing. Aside from the animal pleasures (like wallowing in a tub of grapes or luxuriating in the Pacific sun), nothing in man's composition compares for intellectual and emotional satisfaction like good talk. Gab is not only a gift, it is a developed craft as well. A man (or a woman) has a born talent for talk, but he must train himself at the craft of it before he can go beyond to make it an art. And since language, as Max Müller said a century ago, "is our Rubicon, and no animal dare cross it," it is particularly satisfying to those of us who see ourselves "as men at least, but little lower than the gods and angels."

Good talk is the only uniquely human enjoyment. The animal vices and pleasures leave us long before we are prepared to leave them, but talk goes on to the grave. Consider the vast superiority in human satisfaction of the Drama Quartet reading *Don Juan in Hell* over even so magnificent a spectacle as *My Fair Lady.*

Folktales are the medium for good talk among the folk. Their materials are often lost beyond their memories, as in the case of all the following stories. It would be pretentious and tedious to trace the evolutionary path of the stories recounted by Vance Randolph; all are very old, ours before this land was ours. That is, the motifs and plots are old and un-American; but as one learns to appreciate literature, one finds that the plot is not the thing. A plot is a framework to hold the language, nothing more.

Take as an example the legend (or perhaps the fact) concerning a speech made in the Arkansas State Legislature by a member when some unspeakable creature proposed that the name of the state be changed, following the Civil War. In books emanating from New York, where they have the plot but not the language, it runs like this:

MR. SPEAKER, YOU BLUE-BELLIED RASCAL! I have for the last thirty minutes been trying to get your attention, and each time I have caught your eye, you have wormed, twisted, and squirmed like a dog with a flea in his hide, damn you!

Gentlemen, you may tear down the honored pictures from the halls of the United States Senate, desecrate the grave of George Washington, haul down the Stars and Stripes, curse the Goddess of Liberty, and knock down the tomb of U. S. Grant, but your crime would in no wise compare in enormity with what you propose to do when you would change the name of Arkansas! Change the name of Arkansas—hell-fire, no!

Compare the lily of the valley to the gorgeous sunrise; the discordant croak of the bull-frog to the melodious tones of a nightingale; the classic strains of Mozart to the bray of a Mexican mule: the puny arm of a Peruvian prince to the muscles of a Roman gladiator—but never change the name of Arkansas. Hell, no!

But this is the way the folk tell it back in Arkansas:

MISTUH SPEAKER, GOD DAMN YOUR SOUL! For more than thirty minutes I have been trying to get your attention, but every time I caught your eye you've squirmed like a damned dog with a flea in his ass.

I guess you know who I am, Suh. My name is Cassius M. Johnson, from Jackson County, Arkansas, where a man can't stick his ass out the window and shit, without it gettin' riddled with bullets.

Why, Suh, I was fo'teen years old before I had my first pair of pants, and they was of buckskin. But at the age of seventeen, Mistuh Speaker, *I had a jock on me the size of a roastin' ear—and it was the pride of Jackson County!* And *you* propose to change the name of Arkansas? *Never*, by God, Suh, *never!*

I'm out of order? How can I be out of order when I can piss clear across the Mississippi River?

Where was Andrew Jackson when the Battle of New Orleans was fit? He was right thar, Suh, *up to his ass in blood!* And *you* change the name of Arkansas? Never, while I can defend her!

You may shit on the grave of George Washington. Piss on the monument of Thomas Jefferson. You may desecrate the sacred remains of the immortal General Robert E. Lee. You may rape the Goddess of Liberty and wipe your ass on the Stars and Stripes, and your crime— your crime, Suh—will no more compare to this hellish design than the glarrrree of a lightning bug's ass to the noonday sun. And you propose to change the name of Arkansas? Never, by God, Suh, never!

You may compare the lily of the valley to the glorious sunflower. Or the sun-kissed peaks of the highest mountains to the smokin' turd of a dung hill. Or the classic strains of Mozart to the *fart* of a Mexican burro. You may compare the puny penis of a Peruvian prince to the *ponderous ballocks of the Roman gladiators!* But change the name of Arkansas? *Never, by God, suh, never!*

That's better, but print gives only the reading of it. The rhythm, the melody, the anger cannot be imagined by anyone who has not heard an Arkansawyer recite that state's classic oration.

If you have the imagination to make a stick with a horse's-head handle superior for its purpose than an electronic robot, apply it to these few tales, this barest sampling of what the folk entertain themselves with in the evenings of good talk in front of the fire.

FOLKTALES FROM ARKANSAS*

JACK AND THE SACK

One time a fellow named Jack done something pretty bad. Some say he killed the Mayor or raped the Mayor's wife, or maybe he just stole the Mayor's saddle mare. Anyhow, it was against the law. The posse caught him in the big timber south of Doomsbury. They tied him up in a

*From Vance Randolph, "Folktales from Arkansas." JAF Volume 45, 1952, 159-166.

big sack, and two soldiers was told off to drownd him in the river.

The soldiers stuck a long pole through the top of the sack, so they could carry it on their shoulders. Pretty soon they come to a tavern. It was a terrible hot day, and dry, so the soldiers just left the sack a-setting by the road and went in to drink some beer. Jack hollered out that he wanted some beer, too, but they did not pay no attention.

Poor Jack couldn't see nothing, but he could hear all right. So whenever anybody come along the road he begun to holler: "I won't do it! I won't do it!" Pretty soon a farm boy stopped, and he wanted to know what it is that Jack won't do. Jack says: "These goddam soldiers are taking me to marry the rich man's daughter. But I won't do it! I want to marry Polly Brown!"

The farm boy thought about it awhile, and then he says it wouldn't be no use to marry Polly Brown, because she just works in the tavern and she hasn't got no money. "My gosh," says he, "I wish somebody would give *me* a chance to marry the rich man's daughter!" But Jack says, "There's things in this world that money won't buy, and Polly Brown suits me right down to the ground." And he says, "If you want to marry the rich man's daughter, just untie the rope and let me out of here. Then I will tie you up in my place, and them damn fools will never know the difference."

So the farm boy untied the rope and let Jack out. And then the farm boy got in the sack, and Jack tied the rope just like it was before. Pretty soon the soldiers come out of the tavern. They put the pole on their shoulders and went on down the road. When they got to the ferry the farm boy knowed something was wrong. He begun to kick and holler, but the soldiers did not pay no mind. They just throwed him in the river and went on back home.

About a week after that the two soldiers seen Jack in the tavern, and one of them says: "That boy is a dead ringer for the outlaw we drownded." The other soldier looked at Jack pretty careful. "Well," he says, "the people in Garland County is all kinfolks, and they breed around regardless just like rabbits. Pretty near every man you see is somebody else's cousin, and lots of 'em brother and sister even, so they all look like peas in a pod," says he.

The other fellow thought about this awhile and seen how sensible it was, so he wagged his head like a oldfield schoolmaster. Then the soldiers just went on a-drinking their beer and never paid no more attention.

THE PIG IN THE CRADLE

One time there was a fellow stole a pig from his neighbor. The neighbor seen he was a pig short and suspicioned what become of it, so him and the sheriff went to the fellow's house in the night, There wasn't no light, but the sheriff hammered on the door till you could hear the pictures falling down off the wall inside. Finally the fellow opened the door and he says: "For God's sake, don't make so much noise, as we got a mighty sick baby here."

The sheriff says, "We have come to get the pig you stole from this man." But the fellow says, "I never stole no pig, and I ain't got no pig, and don't talk to me about pigs while our baby is dying of the small-pox." Soon as he heard "smallpox," the neighbor run off down the road for fear he would catch it. But the sheriff says: "Smallpox don't scare me none, because I have had the smallpox, and it's my job to search this here premises." So he looked all over the place, but he didn't find no pig.

After while the sheriff give up, and then he come back to the house and says: "Let me look at that baby, and I will soon tell you if it's got smallpox or not." But the fellow had the baby in the cradle, and he says, "You can hunt pigs all you want, but pulling quilts off'n my sick baby is something else again, because the night air will kill it sure. The sheriff is paid to fight road agents," says he, "and not go around a-murdering people's children."

While they was a-cussing, the baby begun to wiggle under the covers, and pretty soon it hollered, "Oink, oink!" like that. So the sheriff jumped quick and pulled off the quilts, and there was a pig laying in the cradle. It wasn't no baby at all. But when the sheriff turned round to arrest the fellow that stole the pig, he was plumb gone. He had done slipped out the door and run off in the dark, and it wasn't no use to look for him. So then the sheriff carried the pig back where it was stole from, and that's the end of the story.

THE TOAD-FROG

One time there was a pretty girl walking down the street, and she heard somebody say: "Hi, Toots!" But when she looked around there was nobody in sight, just a little old toad-frog setting on the sidewalk.

So then the pretty girl started to walk on down the street, and she heard somebody say: "Hello, Beautiful!" But when she looked around there was nobody in sight, just this little old toad-frog.

So then the pretty girl started to walk on down the street, and she heard somebody say: "You got anything on tonight, Baby?" But when she looked around there was nobody in sight, just this little old toad-frog setting on the sidewalk.

The pretty girl looked down at the little old toad-frog. "I know it ain't you a-talking," she says.

"It's me, all right," says the toad-frog. "I'm a handsome young man, by rights. But I'm turned into a toad-frog now because an old witch put a spell on me."

The pretty girl studied awhile, and then she says: "Ain't there anything you can do to break the spell?"

The toad-frog says there is only one way, and that is for a pretty girl to let him sleep on her pillow all night. The pretty girl thought it was the least she could do to help this poor fellow out. So she took the little old toad-frog home and put him on her pillow when she went to bed.

Next morning the pretty girl's father come to wake her up, and he seen a handsome young man in the bed with her. She told her father about the little old toad-frog, and the witch that put a spell on him, and how it all happened. But the old man didn't believe the story, any more than you do.

THE MAGIC COWHIDE

One time there was a boy named Jack, and his folks died and left a good farm. But when they come to divide up, it was his two older brothers that heired the farm, and Jack didn't get nothing but an old cow. Pretty soon the cow died, so Jack didn't have nothing, and then his brothers says he better go to town and get a job somewheres. Jack skinned the cow and started out to sell the hide, or else maybe he could trade it for something. Every house he come to he would ask the people, but they all says they don't want no stinking old cowhide.

When it come night Jack laid down on the ground, and he put the cowhide over him. Pretty soon he woke up and the sun was shining. There was a lot of crows on top of him, a-pecking away at the cowhide. Jack grabbed one of the crows and made a little cage for it out of willow switches. He thought maybe he could split the crow's tongue and learn it how to talk.

Pretty soon he heard somebody a-coming, so Jack hid in the brush and held the crow's bill shut. It was two robbers, and they was talking how they had buried a lot of gold under the fireplace in Sim Lawton's cabin, while Sim was out a-working so he didn't know nothing about it.

After the robbers was gone, Jack walked on till he come to a house, and the man says his name is Sim Lawton. "Well," says Jack, "me and the crow was talking about you last night." Sim he just laughed. "The crow says there's gold buried on your place," says Jack, "and I'll show you where it is, only you must give me half." Sim laughed louder than ever. "Take half and welcome," he says, "but you two birds have got to do the digging, because I won't turn my hand to no such foolishness." So then Jack prized up the hearthstone, and sure enough there was a big sack of gold pieces.

They split the gold even, but Sim says he will give half of his share for the crow, and Jack let him have it. Sim figured he would travel around with the crow and find out where folks has hid their money. So Jack walked on down the road with three-quarters of the robbers' gold wrapped up in his cowhide.

Jack stayed at the hotel all night, and the next day here come Sim, and he is pretty mad. "This fool crow won't talk," says he. "It just goes, 'Quark, quark,' and so I want my money back." But Jack just laughed in his face. "The bird talks all right," he says, "but a man can't understand crow language till he sleeps three nights under the magic cowhide."

Sim wanted to borrow the cowhide for a few days, but Jack wouldn't hear of it. So finally Sim handed over the rest of the robbers' gold, and Jack give him the stinking old cowhide. Jack had all the gold now, and he went to Little Rock. Sim Lawton took several trips down there to look for him, but Jack was plumb gone. Some say he went pardners with them Hot Springs gamblers and got rich, but the folks never did find out for sure.

A book should leave its reader with an image to remember, a mnemonic to carry him back to the book often for a savoring of its delectation. And of all the images folklore bears to my mind, only one is more striking than the thought of Ozark hill folk running naked through the mountains, and that is the sight of the Mormon ladies in this J. Golden Kimball story:

J. Golden Kimball was often dispatched as a trouble-shooter in the small and struggling communities in the desert above the present Lake Mead. Once the word drifted back to Salt Lake City that one of these desert villages was becoming known for the frivolousness and vanity of its women. On request of the Church and the husbands of the extravagant ladies, Brother Golden made the hot journey to the south. He had the ladies congregate in the church and spoke to them thus: "I hear you ladies are committing the sin of vanity. I know your good husbands are working hard out in the fields all the day with the crops, with the horses, with the cows, with the pigs, trying to make a living for you. And you ladies are squandering that money on fripperies and vanity and clothes and silly fashions. I declare I believe you ladies are so giddy that you'd wear a feather sticking out of your ass—if it was in style!"

NAKED IN THE OZARKS*

The Ozark hill folk are not particularly moral people, but they are inclined to be prudish. Commonplace urban behavior shocks them sometimes, and they are scandalized by tourists in modern bathing suits. Elderly mountaineers feel that exposure of the naked body, especially

*From Vance Randolph, "Nakedness in Ozark Folk Belief."
 JAF Volume 56, 1953, 333-339.

the female body, is vulgar and degrading. "Decent women wear dresses," said one of my neighbors, "and them that don't ought to stay in the whorehouses." It is said that many Ozarkers have never seen their wives naked, although they live together for years and raise large families. Mixed bathing in the nude is practiced only by very low-class squatters, or newcomers from the mining camp. Respectable hill folk are against it. This prejudice supplies a contrasting background for the nakedness involved in Ozark magic and folk religion.

In the spring of 1920, when I lived in southwest Missouri, a fisherman from Joplin was walking through the woods just at dawn. He saw a man and a woman in a little field. "They was both stark naked," he said, "chasing each other up and down like rabbits." The clearing he indicated was near my home, and I knew the couple who lived there. They were quiet, hard-working folk. The man came from a good backwoods family, and the woman attended the village church. Such people might "cut up" a little at some drunken party, but I couldn't imagine them running naked out of doors at four o'clock in the morning. I did not believe the fisherman's tale. Several days later I mentioned it to a friend who had lived in the neighborhood all his life. "Yes, I've heard of such doings," he said with a grin. "It's supposed to make the corn grow tall." When I asked where people ever got such a notion, he said that doubtless the pioneers brought it from Tennessee, or Kentucky, or Virginia. "It's just a kind of a joke," he added, "because nobody really believes in them things nowadays. But I'll bet that young fellow's grandpappy thought it was just as true as God's own gospel."

Since that time I have become intimately acquainted with the people who live in the Ozark country, and interviewed hundreds of old-timers. There is no doubt in my mind that many early settlers believed that newly cleared fields were benefited by some kind of nude skylarking. Many of them thought that certain crops grew better if the persons who sowed the seed were naked. This sort of thing is not widely practiced today, and most of my neighbors say that they never even heard of it. But I know that such tilling and planting rites were carried out in isolated places less than thirty years ago.

There are several tales about a "wild clan" in southwest Missouri who produced phenomenal turnips by reason of some secret magic. A very old woman said that before sunrise on July 25, four grown girls and one boy did the planting. "They all stripped off naked," she told me. "The boy started in the middle of the patch with them four big gals a-prancin' round him. It seems like the boy throwed all the seed, and the gals kept a-hollering 'Pecker deep! Pecker deep!' And when they got done, the whole bunch would roll in the dust like some kind of wild animals. There ain't no sense to it," the old woman added, "but them folks always raised the best turnips on the creek."

Once in McDonald County, Missouri, a giggling farm girl led me to the top of a high ridge. "I'll show you something funny," she promised. Down in the holler was a clearing with a tiny cabin. After a while we saw a man and two nude women romping and tumbling on the ground, in a freshly plowed garden patch. "Them people belong to the New Ground church, and that's their religion," the girl told me. "They've got beds in the house, but they think it's better to waller in the dirt." She said nothing about crops or planting. But the earth in that particular spot was prepared for seeding, and later in the season I saw turnips growing there.

An old gentleman in Aurora, Missouri, told me that the early settlers had a ritual for sowing flax. Just before sunup the farmer and his wife appeared in the field, both naked. The woman walked ahead of the man, and the man did the sowing. They chanted or sang a rhyme with the line, "Up to my ass, an' higher too!" Every few steps the man threw some of the seed against the woman's buttocks. Up and down the field they went, singing and scattering seed, until the planting was done. "Then," as my informant put it, "they just laid down on the ground and had a good time." It was considered essential that no outsider should see the sowing or hear the song, because if that were to happen the crop would be a failure.

A farmer near the Missouri-Oklahoma line was telling about the superstitions of some "peckerwood folks" who lived there in the early 1890's. "Soon as they got their bread planted, that fellow would take his wife out to the patch at midnight. He'd make her take off every stitch of clothes and run around the crop three times. And then he would throw her right down in the dirt and have at it till she squealed like a pig!" This procedure was said to protect the corn against damage from frost, drought, crows, and cutworms. One of the girls in this family had married a Cherokee, and my informant regarded the practice as part of an Indian ceremony. But several old Cherokees whom I interviewed said that they never heard of any such foolishness.

Most farmers believe that cucumbers should be planted "when the sign's in the arms," which means that the moon is in Gemini. But many old-timers think that the main thing is to get the seed covered before daylight on May 1, by a naked man in the prime of life. It is believed that the quality of a cucumber depends upon the virility of the planter. Cucumbers grown by women, children, or old men never amount to much. There are several vulgar jokes and stories about this. To say that a girl "ought to be raising cucumbers" means that she needs a vigorous young husband.

A man named Meece, who lived near Reeds Spring, Missouri, in the 1930's, used to go naked into the field sometimes. Many persons have seen him plowing, with his overalls hanging on a fence. But I'm not sure that this eccentricity had any connection with fertility rites. Mr. Meece held peculiar notions about hygiene and therapeutics. It may be that he was merely taking a sunbath, rather than attempting to "spook" the crop.

It is said that watermelons are best planted in the dark, preferably just before dawn. An old gentleman in Barry County, Missouri, told me that this was because the pioneers preferred to be naked when they did the job. "A man don't want folks to come along the road and see him cavorting around without his britches," said he. "So the old-timers used to go out before sunup, and get it over with. It don't take long to plant a few hills of watermelons, and then you can come back to the house and put your clothes on."

Ginseng or sangroot is supposed to strengthen the sexual powers of aging men. Some say that for best results, the root should be pulled from the earth by a nude woman. Many persons are familiar with this theory, but I have never known a sangdigger to admit that he practiced it. I interviewed Cass Little, of Anderson, Missouri, who had a vast experience in gathering roots and herbs. "Yes, I've heard of that naked woman business," he told me. "Maybe some of them old fellows did take a girl along to pull up the roots. But there ain't nothing to it."

In many parts of the Ozark country there are tales of a woman "shaking her apron at the moon." It means that she wants a new dress. Some people say that if a young girl slips out of the house at night, stark naked, and waves her apron high above her head, it is a sign that she will get new clothes very shortly. She is supposed to repeat a magic rhyme while shaking the apron, but I have not been able to obtain the words. The fact of "apron-shaking" is known to many hill folk, however, and one often hears humorous allusions to it.

May Stafford Hilburn, of Jefferson City, Missouri, tells of an old woman who "kept the witches away by running three times around the cabin, just at dusk-dark, shaking a white rag above her head as she ran." I heard the same tale in McDonald County, Missouri, except that in my version the woman was naked, and she waved an apron instead of a rag. I remarked that perhaps the housewife herself "talked the Devil's language," but my informant didn't think so. "You got to fight fire with fire," he said solemnly.

Old residents tell of a backwoods conjure to protect a house from cyclones. The essential thing is for a naked adult to run toward the approaching storm with an open knife. The edge of the knife is supposed to "split the wind" so that it passes by on either side. Otto Ernest Rayburn recalls a reputed witch who tried to scatter storm clouds by swinging an axe while she yelled, "I'll cut ye hyar, I'll split ye thar. There is no mention of nakedness in Rayburn's account, however.

Many of the fireside tales about witchcraft refer to nude women. According to one legend, a girl who wants to become a witch must strip in the graveyard at midnight, and hang her clothes on an infidel's tombstone. Then she gives her body to a nude stranger, supposed to be the Devil's representative. This performance is witnessed by at least two naked initiates and is repeated on three consecutive nights. An understandable reticence falls upon people who have dabbled in such matters. There are many tales of witches dancing naked in the fields, but they differ little from stories current in other parts of the country.

At Pineville, Missouri, I heard a woman tell of young girls who "went prancin' around plumb bare" at midnight on May 1, in some forbidden ritual to identify their future husbands.

It is said that a girl who urinates on her nightgown, hangs it before the fireplace to dry, and then goes to bed naked in a room by herself, is sure to see her future husband before morning. The story is that his image appears as soon as the nightdress is dry enough to be turned. There are many jokes about this practice, most of them a bit ribald.

Many hill folk drive nails into peach trees. Some say that iron makes barren trees fruitful, or keeps the peaches from falling off before they are ripe, but others are evasive or noncommittal. "Them's family matters," one old man growled when I asked why a certain peach tree was thickly studded with big old-fashioned nails. My wife, who was acquainted with the clan, made some discreet inquiries. She learned that the nails were put there at night, by the farmer's buxom daughters. Also that each girl pulled off her nightgown before she drove a nail into the tree. But they wouldn't talk about the performance, except to say that it was a "charm." We never did find out what it was supposed to accomplish.

Some people believe that it's dangerous for women to undress near a redbud or Judas tree (*Cercis canadensis*), especially in the spring. I remember two girls who wanted to change into their bathing suits, and walked a long way to avoid some redbud trees. "Do they poison you?" I asked. "No, just bring bad luck," one of the girls answered. These were not illiterate farmer's daughters. They came from a town of some twenty thousand population, and both of them had attended a college.

Country women are advised never to expose their bodies near a blooming redhaw (*Cretaegus*), since this tree is associated with rapes and unfortunate pregnancies and disastrous abortions. I have heard similar tales about the lady's slipper (*Cypripedium*), which grows in the deep woods. A young girl who finds a stinkhorn fungus (*Phallus impudicus*) regards it as a good omen. Old women say that back in the 1870's adolescent girls would strip off their clothes and dance around this plant. If a virgin touched the stinkhorn to her vulva, it was a sure sign that she'd get the man she wanted.

Most Ozark children wear heavy underclothes in the winter and are not permitted to shed them until May 1. In some families, when a youngster puts off his flannels for the season, the parents make him run three times around the yard, stark naked. This is a prophylactic measure, to prevent the child from catching cold. A schoolmarm in Greene County, Missouri, told me that her mother made her do this every spring, under cover of darkness, until she was seventeen years old.

Nudity sometimes plays a part in the treatment of disease, especially where it is believed that the illness may be caused by some supernatural spell. If a small boy has a fit, the parents are advised to strip him instantly and make him walk home stark naked. This is done sometimes even in very cold weather, when the ground is covered with snow. Some hill folk say that if a child is bewitched, he should take off his clothes and stand around nude, while the garments are boiled in a kettle out of doors. A girl who thinks that her dress has a spell on it is supposed to go out naked at midnight, rinse the dress in milk and hang it on a tree, after which she "sleeps raw" the remainder of the night.

To relieve neuralgia or neuritis, especially if the pain is in the back or legs, one has only to walk around the room three times every morning, without a stitch on but the left shoe and stocking. Some of the older generation take this quite seriously. A federal judge told me that his wife, nearly seventy, had done it every morning for years. "I told Lucy she was too old to go traipsing around like that," said he, "but she thinks it's good for her sciatica."

Some people believe that certain medicines are most effective if the patient is nude. A woman near West Plains, Missouri, made her twelve-year-old daughter undress three times a day, and then administered a dose of eggshell tea. Eggshell tea is made by boiling toasted or charred eggshells in water. I never knew what was wrong with the girl, or whether the eggshell tea cured her. But I set down the story here, for the record.

A possum hunter in Howell County, Missouri, told me that early one morning he saw two girls stark naked, cooking something in a soap kettle out of doors. Years later, when he became intimately acquainted with one of them, he mentioned the incident and asked what they were doing. The woman laughed, saying that she and her sister had experimented with a "mistletoe conjure." I have myself seen women boiling kettles of mistletoe, but the women were fully clothed. I was told that they were making "love medicine," but was unable to get any details of the procedure.

I believe that the nakedness associated with planting, charms, witchcraft, and medicine was always more or less secret. Many persons who have lived in the Ozarks for years know nothing of it. A member of the village Chamber of Commerce told me that "such yarns are made up by newspaper reporters." But this man's neighbors declared that his own parents had gone naked into the fields to plant turnips as recently as 1912.

There is much less secrecy about the nude frolics of the New Ground Christians, generally known as Holy Rollers. Even the civic boosters in the towns know that men and women sometimes undress at religious meetings. Amos Harlin tells of a fellow in Howell County, Missouri, who got excited at revivals and tore off his clothes. "At the last possible moment, with stark nakedness only one button away," somebody threw him out into the darkness. I have
seen, at Holy Roller meetings, women lying on the floor with their dresses pulled up over their heads. Backwoods girls don't go much for lingerie in the summertime, and some of them wear no underclothing at all.

The Reverend Jim Sharp, an evangelist from Jasper County, Missouri, went preaching down to Oklahoma City in 1905. He and his wife Melissa, followed by several disciples, attracted quite a crowd because they were barefoot. Suddenly one of the worshippers shouted, "Take off your clothes! We shall walk naked in the streets!" So they all stripped and started down the avenue, shouting and singing hymns. Many people rushed away in alarm, but "one big fat woman kept alookin' back," as Sharp remembered when I interviewed him at Joplin in 1935. Finally the police came and led them off to jail. "We was still naked," said Sharp, "and with them policemen marching beside us, it looked like the city had ordered a nude parade and sent the police for a escort!" Sharp later called himself "Father Adam," and it may have been this adventure that gave him the idea, since nudists were known as Adamites in those days. Jim Sharp was born and raised near the Missouri-Arkansas border, and knew all about the backwoods practice of "praising God in the raw." He was familiar with some of the planting rituals, too, but suspected that they were allied to witchcraft or devil-worship.

Holy Rollers sometimes gather at camp meetings near the highways, where comparatively large groups dance naked in the moonlight. In 1915, near Galena, Missouri, a flock of these people used to do the "holy dance" in broad daylight, and were seen by many citizens. A villager concealed himself near the stompin'-ground and made several photographs. Frank Fox, photographer at Galena, showed me one of these pictures. Three bearded, naked men stared straight at the camera, with perhaps twenty nude women in the background. The fellow who made the photograph said he saw "men and women acting like minks" on the ground, but the figures in the picture were all standing. A lady at Crane, Missouri, told me that the leader was a preacher named Youngblood. Later on, when the children of some good local families joined the "holy dance" gang, the respectable villagers chased Youngblood out of the county. When I lived at Galena in the 1930's, the congregation said they had "done give up" dancing naked. But even then it was common gossip that such ceremonies were still carried out in private homes, only three or four miles from the village.

In 1917, near Walnut Shade, Missouri, the New Ground folk worshipped in two log cabins, about three hundred yards apart. They would preach and shout in one cabin for a while, then all march naked and singing to the other building. Some local people saw as many as fifty nude men and women at one time, and there was little attempt at concealment. A photographer named Rutledge made several pictures, and copies are still to be found in the vicinity. I saw several of the Rutledge photographs at Forsyth, Missouri, in the 1930's. It is said that a county official made prints and sold them to the tourists, until somebody told him it was against the law. Lew Beardon, a lawyer at Branson, Missouri, gave me one of these photographs in 1940. It shows nine men and seven women, all nude. One of the women is leading a naked child, apparently about six years old. The men and women in this picture were all residents of the county, and I knew several of them personally.

At several other places on White River, bands of fanatics used to march about naked, especially in the spring, as recently as 1922. Some of them held Easter services, where they danced nude around big fires in the woods. I was told that George E. Hall, a professional photographer from Taneyville, Missouri, made pictures showing a naked preacher standing on a stump, while naked men and women rolled on the ground before him. A fellow who ran the drugstore at Reeds Spring displayed a large photograph of local people dancing nude on a hillside. A physician named Shumate, also of Reeds Spring, had several of these pictures. "The men was mostly old, with beards," I was told, "but the women was all ages from twelve to sixty. And every one of em' naked as a jaybird's ass in whistlin' time!"

The respectable townspeople regarded the vagaries of the "buck-brush parsons" as a joke, until one of the Stockstill boys came marching into the town of Forsyth. He was about thirty years old, and his given name was Austin, but everybody called him Oss. He was stark naked, carried a Bible under his arm, and kept yelling, "I'm lookin' for twelve apostles!" I asked a villager how this demonstration was received. "Well," said he, "most of the business men stayed in the back of their stores, but the womenfolks all run out to look." A local officer hesitated. "If the damn fool was drunk, I'd know what to do," said he. "But Oss ain't drunk, he's just got religion. There ain't no law against religion." Later on W. E. Freeland, editor of our weekly newspaper, expressed a similar opinion: "A man started to parade around the square here in Forsyth, clad only in his religious beliefs and with a Bible in his hand. He was arrested as an indecent man. Well, he might have pleaded he was only a religious devotee." After Stockstill marched around for a while, the sheriff locked him in the pokey. "I don't want no bond," said he. "Jesus didn't post no bond. I'll stay in jail, just like He done." They turned him loose after a week or so, but the authorities made it clear that there must be no more foolishness on the streets. The New Grounders held their nude parades in the woods thereafter, but Oss Stockstill's exploit is still remembered on Bear Creek.

Such incidents are seldom mentioned nowadays, but things happen in the hills which are not reported by the newspapers at the county seat. Twenty-six years ago I thought that these colorful folkways were disappearing very rapidly, and predicted that most of our Ozark superstitions would soon be forgotten. I wouldn't make such a statement today. The old planting rituals are apparently unknown to the younger generation, and the same is true of many household conjures which involve nudity. But backwoods Christians still tear off their clothes at Holy Roller meeting, orgies no less fantastic than those of the early 1900's. The ceremonies associated with witchcraft are secret, but nature worship is not dead, and I believe that men and women still dance naked in certain secluded groves. A great body of folk belief dies slowly, and some vestige of the ancient landmarks may be with us for a long time to come.

Index

449

452

453

The body text for *Folklore of the Great West* is Times
Roman, and the chapter heads are Trump Medieval Bold,
both set in Linofilm by Applied Typographic Systems,
Palo Alto, California. The book was printed and bound by
Peninsula Lithograph Company, Menlo Park, California. The
paper is Capstan Vellum, cream white, and the cloth is
Sailcloth from Holliston Mills, Norwood, Massachusetts.

Illustrations by Glen Rounds.

Design by John Beyer.